Negotiating Outside the Law

Negotiating Outside the Law
Why Camp David Failed

Raymond G. Helmick, S.J.

Pluto Press
London • Ann Arbor, MI

First published 2004 by Pluto Press
345 Archway Road, London N6 5AA
and 839 Greene Street, Ann Arbor, MI 48106

www.plutobooks.com

Copyright © Raymond G. Helmick 2004

The right of Raymond G. Helmick to be identified as the author of this work has been asserted by him in accordance with the Copyright, Designs and Patents Act 1988.

British Library Cataloguing in Publication Data
A catalogue record for this book is available from the British Library

ISBN 0 7453 2219 0 hardback

Library of Congress Cataloging-in-Publication Data
Helmick, Raymond G.
  Negotiating outside the law: why Camp David failed / Raymond G. Helmick.
    p. cm.
  Includes bibliographical references and index.
  ISBN 0-7453-2219-0
  1. Arab-Israeli conflict--1993---Peace. I. Title.

DS119.76.H455 2004
956.9405'4--dc22
                              2004010077

10 9 8 7 6 5 4 3 2 1

Designed and produced for Pluto Press by
Curran Publishing Services, Norwich
Printed and bound in Canada by Transcontinental Printing

Contents

Foreword by the Reverend Jesse L. Jackson, Sr. — vii

Introduction — 1

Part I Building Relationships

1. The path to the US/PLO dialogue, 1985–88 — 11
2. The Madrid stage and Oslo, 1990–93 — 37
3. Disappointments and postponements, 1993–95 — 51

Part II The Failed Negotiations

4. Sad millennium: the disintegration of Ehud Barak, May 1999 to July, 2000 — 81
5. Camp David — 128
6. Negotiations continue, August 1–September 28, 2000 — 172
7. Through the blood of the *intifada* to the Taba negotiations, September 29, 2000–February 8, 2001 — 202

Part III Aftermath

8. The web of civility dissolves: early February to September 11, 2001 — 251
9. America goes to war: September 11, 2001 to the indefinite future — 275
10. So what really happened at Camp David and Taba? — 289

Notes — 303
Index — 335

Foreword

Our quest in the Middle East remains what it has always been—to replace violence with nonviolence; to promote reconciliation and reconstruction over continued destruction and death; to choose coexistence over co-annihilation; to give future generations of Israelis and Palestinians a chance to live as neighbors with shared hopes, and a shared peace.

For too long, Israel and its neighbors have been caught in a downward spiral of destruction. One side is driven by fear of violence, and the other side is driven by despair. Fear and despair together end up recycling violence. We need to lift up a third way, to lift people beyond fear and violence, all the way to hope.

As part of that third force, my friend, Father Raymond Helmick, S. J., has authored this book, *Negotiating Outside the Law*. My brother Helmick makes the case that the whole negotiating process so far has failed because it has been based on predominance of military force, and has not been based on international law, and legal principles.

This is a book worth taking seriously, because Reverend Helmick is a serious peacemaker. He traveled with me to the Middle East in the summer of 2002, as part of a religious, peace-seeking delegation, guests of the Middle East Conference of Churches. Prior to that, in the spring of 1999, Reverend Helmick was part of the peace-seeking team that went with me to Yugoslavia, and ended up successfully negotiating for the release of three US soldiers from captivity.

Those three soldiers, Steven Gonzales, Andrew Ramirez, and Christopher Stone, had been captured while on patrol. I decided to try to negotiate their freedom, and put together Christian, Jewish, and Muslim faith leaders to go with me to Yugoslavia to try to win their freedom.

In early May of 1999, we succeeded. Father Helmick was the priest on our successful negotiating team. Bringing those young men home alive was a moment of great personal satisfaction for us, and an important demonstration of the power of nonviolent persuasion. Even Slobodan Milosevic could be appealed to; even Milosevic could respond to the power of faith and freedom.

Father Helmick helped make those negotiations work. Now he is making the case that applying the principles of international law will help resolve the crisis between Israel and Palestine. He has earned the right for his book to be taken seriously. He has earned the right for his ideas to be treated with respect. Perhaps Father Helmick has found a key to unlock the door to nonviolent progress in this volatile region of the world; that would be a source of great joy to all of us!

The Middle East crisis has resisted solution for far too long now. I will never forget going to Israel a quarter of a century ago, in 1979, and meeting with Teddy Kolick and members of the Knesset. I remember going to Lebanon to meet with Chairman Arafat, and then to Syria to meet with President Assad. After that, on that same trip, I went to Egypt to meet with President Sadat, who later gave his life in the cause of peace, to make an appeal for peaceful coexistence.

At that time, the United States had a "no-talk" policy with the Palestinians. I took a lot of public abuse for meeting with Chairman Arafat. Even today some hostility lingers, though now most observers have followed our lead towards a "two-state solution," and the United States has made public commitments to a Palestinian state.

In my campaigns for President during the 1980s, I forced the Middle East question onto the public policy agenda, pointing out that Israeli security and Palestinian justice are two sides of the same coin. In 1988, my campaign suggested an alternative policy in the Middle East, to move the process that began with President Carter at Camp David along to the next progressive step. I suggested that such a policy be built on several principles:

- The right of Israel to exist with security.
- The right of the Palestinian people to self-determination, including an independent status.
- The right of Lebanon to sovereignty and freedom from imposed partition.
- Normalized ties between the United States and all Middle East nations, based upon mutual respect for the sovereignty and independence of all countries.
- Demilitarization of the region and increased humanitarian aid that could enhance the stability and prosperity of all nations.
- An end to the U.S. military build-up in the Persian Gulf. (If only this platform plank had been given the proper respect...)

These principles were controversial at the time, but we kept marching down the road to peace, insisting year after year that making new friends did not require us to abandon an old friend. Now much of the world has come around to our point of view. Now the points I made back in 1979, and throughout the 1980s, do not seem so radical; they seem rational, and reasonable, and overdue.

The road was a long and rocky one to travel, but we have made it this far. Some day, we will make it all the way home. Some day, the hope that was unleashed at Camp David, not once but twice, will become reality. Some day, swords will be beaten into plowshares, and lions will lie down with lambs.

And when we get there, Father Helmick will know that he held a lantern to light the way; lit a candle rather than curse the darkness; and played a role in guiding an anxious world to Middle East peace and nonviolence. This book is part of his legacy. Read it, learn from it, and then, as he has done in his life, turn analysis into action.

Because the lands in question are home to three of our great religions, and the time has come to move away from kill or be killed. An eye for an eye and a tooth for a tooth leave us all blind and maimed. It's time to live and let live. It's time to take a different way.

The violence in the Middle East has us all living behind checkpoints now. We must pull down these walls and build bridges instead; we must stop the violence and proceed with reconciliation and reconstruction; we must pursue peace and shared existence. War is not an option. Through nonviolence and rebuilding and law, we can move from pain and fear and despair to joy and hope and growth.

That is our quest. That has always been our quest. This book is another big step down that road to peace in the Middle East. I commend Reverend Helmick for writing it, and I recommend it to you. Keep Hope Alive!

Reverend Jesse L. Jackson, Sr.
June, 2004

Introduction

This book, dealing principally with the period of intense negotiation at Camp David and Taba in 2000 and 2001, comes out of close contact, which I have maintained since 1985, with the Israel, Palestine, and United States leadership. Meetings I had then with Yasser Arafat, urging Palestinian acceptance of the preconditions that had been set for dialogue with the others, were followed quickly by the Israeli government of Prime Minister Shimon Peres and the US administration of Ronald Reagan.

All three leaderships have struggled through the last half-century and more with the Middle Eastern conflict, and I have been writing and often conversing with them in a concerted effort to help toward a peaceful resolution of their tangled and often violent relations. That may be a curious enough position for an American Jesuit priest, but one that was familiar enough to me, as I had been doing the same in Northern Ireland, in Lebanon, and many other places for many years before that. The period of the Camp David and Taba negotiations saw some of the closest of these contacts, and I had a clear sense that they had the attention of the parties. Some public accounting of that activity is now due.

I had drawn several serious conclusions about the choices made by Israel, Palestine, and the United States, particularly when it came to the degree of respect they paid to one another, a precondition for their making any real progress toward peace, and the underlying suppositions of their dealings with one another. I found that, in what we have called the "peace process," scant attention was given to the pertinent international law that should govern the case. This neglect of law introduced an element of chaos into the proceedings, often producing an atmosphere of illegitimacy and diktat.

In the pages that follow, I will first try to show how my own relation to the several parties grew over the years that led to this intensive period of negotiation (Part I). I will then spell out my own perception of what happened during the period of Camp David 2000 and Taba (Part II), and will finally look at the dire aftermath of what was seen as the failure of those negotiations: the violence on the part of both Israelis and Palestinians, the effect on their situation of the drama that engulfed the United

2 Negotiating Outside the Law

States, with 9/11 and the invasions of Afghanistan and Iraq, and the war of interpretation that was waged by the participants over what had actually happened at Camp David and Taba (Part III).

Conditions in the Middle East look discouragingly bleak as I write. My own experience over this time leaves me still anticipating that the conflict can and will be resolved, and that these two peoples have every capacity to live in peace and genuine harmony with one another. That is difficult to hold amid the violence we hear of day by day, but I hope readers will find in this account signs of the readiness both sides in the conflict have consistently shown each time there was real opportunity to advance toward peace, and understand the resources for peace they continue to maintain.

EARLY CONTACTS

In the 1970s, Palestinians, for me, meant Said Hammami, the elegant and self-effacing diplomat whom Arafat had sent to London to make reconciling contact with British Jews. One of the first he sought out was Richard Hauser, Austrian Holocaust survivor and social activist, accustomed to intervening for the resolution of bloody conflicts, with whom I then worked in the Centre for Human Rights and Responsibilities. Richard had married Hephzibah Menuhin, Yehudi's sister, and Hephzibah treated her concert career, playing piano brilliantly to Yehudi's violin, as her entertainment. She saw her real life's work in the social activism she shared with Richard and myself.

When Said had first asked Richard what he thought of Palestinians, his answer was that they were the last victims of Hitler, affected at secondhand by the catastrophe that had overwhelmed European Jewry. Richard and Said had groped, in those early days, for mutual understanding in a world marked by the October War of 1973, which made Richard desperate for the safety of Israel. It produced no rift between them. Their mutual regard, their complicity in seeking the peace lasted until, on January 4, 1978, shortly after Egypt's President Anwar Sadat had made his historic visit to Israel, Said was gunned down in his Mayfair basement office by the emissaries of Abu Nidal, who could not bear that Palestinians should seek any goal but destruction for Israel.

My ties to the Middle East continued through many meetings, any time he came to London, with Simha Flapan, whom Martin Buber had chosen as editor of *New Outlook*, one of the earliest Israeli journals totally dedicated to seeking the peace. Simha, a devoted Zionist, was at work, when I first knew him, on a study of Zionist relations with Palestinians up to 1947,[1] which he intended as the first of three volumes. But his research on the period of the 1948 war was leading toward his major book, *The Birth of Israel: Myths and Realities*,[2] in which he would record his shock at major inconsistencies he found in the received version of Israel's birth.

Not until 1979 did I first visit the contested region. Like any visitor, Christian, Jewish, or Muslim, I found myself overwhelmed at being in places so intimately connected with the origins of my faith, and found that the experience of being there a first time would recur each time I brought with me others for whom it was a first experience. I had become so imbued, however, with the sagas of contemporary Jews and Palestinians that it was their story that most gripped me. I have become accustomed since to telling Christian pilgrimage groups that, when they went there, they should see the Holy Land as more than a "Jesus Theme Park," and recognize that the holiness of the place has its real embodiment in the tortured lives of the Jews, Christians, and Muslims who live there.

The persons I met were extraordinary: Galia Golan, later so important to the Peace Now movement, and Naomi Chazan, who would be a peace-minded Meretz Party Knesset member and Speaker of the House, both just getting into their political and scholarly careers; Leah Tzemel, the courageous Israeli lawyer who dared to defend accused Palestinians in court; Mayor Teddy Kollek; Professor Israel Charny, with whom I would eventually share in arranging a 1982 conference on "The Holocaust and Genocide." By good fortune, a first tour group I brought to Jerusalem was put up at the Jerusalem Palace Hotel where I met and became friends with the proprietor, Rashid Nashashibi, head of one of Jerusalem's ranking Palestinian families. When I asked who was seriously documenting Palestinian experience, Rashid introduced me to Faisal Husseini, who was already building such a collection at Orient House.

My own business in London, which connected me with Richard Hauser, had been about Northern Ireland, where I spent a great deal of my time, helping to build a network of community associations and mediating among militant groups. As an American Jesuit priest, an ecumenical type doing doctoral studies at the Protestant Union Theological Seminary in New York, heavily committed to civil rights and, during the Vietnam period, to the anti-war cause, it had been natural for me to get involved with Northern Ireland. Working with Richard had brought me into similar contact with many other conflicts, from Cyprus to East Timor, to the travails of Iraqi Kurds, to ZANU and ZAPU striving to make Zimbabwe out of Rhodesia, to the South African ANC, and many others. After returning to the United States in 1981, I became heavily involved, as mediator among conflicting groups, in Lebanon, which I visited extensively in 1982 and 1983. That gave me further encounters with the Palestinians' grim reality.

STATES OF MIND

It had been my observation over a long time that we Americans, perhaps Europeans as well, started after the Second World War with tremendous support and sympathy for the Jews and for the enterprise of building the State of Israel, despite or even because of the stench of anti-Semitism that had been everywhere in our society. Germans were not the only ones ashamed of their behavior during the Holocaust. We tended to accept the version that Israel was "the land without people for the people without land," and hardly noticed the Palestinians. We even believed that "there are no Palestinians," or that "there is already a Palestinian state, and it is Jordan."[3]

But Americans tended to discover Palestinians at some point. Many had first recognized their existence at the time of the invasion of Lebanon in 1982, when Arafat began appearing on American television screens, to say "We are not rats, to be exterminated." Some had discovered Palestinians at the time of the first *intifada*, late in 1987, recognizing that these people had accepted Israel and were not protesting its existence, but protesting only occupation, resisting it with stones against bullets. When that discovery came, it aroused powerful anger at the indignities inflicted on Palestinians. The Americans most impressed with it were likely to revert all the way back to the anti-Semitism long buried within them.

I had discovered Palestinians myself in 1967, and it came directly from my concern for Israel. I realized that Israel, in taking all the territory, had done something that would permanently endanger Israeli society itself if it were not reversed. Coming to concern for Palestinians this way, and seeing others take this as reason simply to turn against the Israeli state and society, I could see clearly the wrong of that reaction. A third-party observer turned partisan about other people's conflicts can only be excess baggage. The quarrel belongs to someone else, and that partisanship can only add needless obstacles in the way of resolving it. I would understand this better as I became involved with other conflict situations, but right from 1967 I knew I could be partisan only of the peace and must cultivate, respectfully, both of these peoples.

THE INTERRELIGIOUS COMMITTEE

In 1985 I received Ronald Young's invitation to join a small group of American Jews and Christians on a tour of the Middle East. Ronald, not a Quaker himself but, like myself, an anti-war activist from Vietnam days, had just finished a three-year posting as the American Friends' Service Committee's representative in the Middle East. Hearing his invitation, I asked who were his Muslims, and he first answered that you couldn't do that. We discussed that often during our Christian–Jewish trip and set ourselves to find those American Muslims who could join with us in what eventually became, after another two years' work, the US Interreligious Committee for Peace in the Middle East.[4]

Ronald Young, traveling about the region with his wife Carol and first son Jonah from his base in Amman, had got to know a tremendous number of people, Israeli, Palestinian, Egyptian, Syrian, Lebanese, Jordanian, and become a welcome figure to all. We ten Jews and Christians on that first trip were unable to get visas into Syria, but visited extensively Jordan, Israel and the West Bank, and Egypt.

Among the most illuminating moments of that trip was a meeting, at the Knesset in Jerusalem, with Simha Dinitz, familiar from his long tenure as Israeli Ambassador to the United States. Though a Labor member, he took so hard a line about Israeli–Palestinian relations that I found myself asking, after he had left the room, whether we had really been listening to Ariel Sharon. He taught me the three unconditional interests of the Israeli society: that it be Jewish, democratic, and safe. I have never lost, since then, my grasp of those essentials.

In Egypt we met Tahseen Bashir, veteran diplomat who, as Ambassador to Canada and to the United Nations, had taken the most important steps toward reopening diplomatic relations between Egypt and the United States. He was a critical adviser to Presidents Sadat and Mubarak. Nabil Sha'ath, trusted adviser to Yasser Arafat, gave us invaluable insight into constructive thinking that was going on in the PLO, adding to what we had learned in Jordan from Abu Jihad (Khalil al-Wazir), the closest military adviser to Arafat, later to be the main architect of the 1987 *intifada*, and Hani al-Hassan, who had negotiated—through intermediaries of course, since no US official then was permitted to speak with an official of the PLO—with the US Special Ambassador Philip Habib the 1981 unilateral ceasefire of the PLO, and later the withdrawal of PLO forces from Beirut in September 1982. The most telling of our Cairo meetings was with the scholarly Sa'ad ed-Din Ibrahim, Director of the Center for the Study of Democracy in the Arab World, who gave me such valuable lessons on the democratic aspirations of Arab peoples that I have never passed through Cairo since then without seeking him out.

ARAFAT

On our last night in Egypt we got word that we would meet Yasser Arafat in Amman, my first meeting with him, the night following. Ronald Young and I, sharing a room in Cairo, sat up long into the night planning our strategy. We anticipated that Arafat, dealing with ten of us together, would inevitably so dominate the conversation that it would be hard to get very specific questions in.

Arafat at the time was conducting what appeared to be quite a serious peace initiative toward the Israelis in conjunction with King Hussein of Jordan. We had been briefed at the State Department before leaving the United States, and had stopped at US embassies in each country we visited. In each place we were told that the peace initiative was not really Arafat's priority, but ranked in importance, for him, behind re-asserting his leadership in the PLO after his evacuation of Beirut, and re-establishing his military position in Lebanon. We needed to ask him in detail about these priorities.

There had also been two gunboat raids, Palestinian guerrillas coming down the Israeli coast from Lebanon, both stopped at sea by Israeli naval forces, the first with the death of all Palestinians on board, the second with the capture of their crew. Such enterprises were clearly inconsistent with the peace initiative. Dividing our tasks between us, we agreed that Ronald would ask about the gunboats, I about the priorities.

In fact I managed to keep Arafat on the definition of his priorities for some three-quarters of an hour in the course of a five-hour meeting that stretched through the night into the dawn. Ronald never did manage to question him about the resort to violence during the peace initiative. I came out of that meeting in a kind of fury that we had talked all that time with Arafat without asking about the gunboats. I resolved to take this up in a letter to Arafat himself, but by the time I got to write it the hijacking at sea of the cruise ship *Achille Lauro*, with the murder of the aged Leon Klinghofer, the elderly American Jew who was cast overboard in his wheelchair, had eclipsed the gunboat question in importance.

My letter took up the way all parties, from the United States to Israel to Europe, from King Hussein to the Pope, insisted that Arafat, as condition for the peace, must renounce all use of force. I realized that if he renounced the Palestinians' right to resist occupation Arafat would simply cease to be his people's leader. I argued instead the actual futility of Palestinian guerrilla raids, which as pinpricks could only afford a rationale for heavy Israeli retaliation, and suggested a moratorium on all use of force: a moratorium to last not for some stated period after which the Palestinians would feel obliged to come out shooting again, but for an indefinite length, the duration of the peace initiative which they expected to result in the termination of all violent relations between the two peoples.

This interested Arafat enough so that he responded, not in writing, but through emissaries who visited me in Boston, particularly Afif Safieh,[5] then on a fellowship at Harvard University, inviting me to visit him in Tunis. Knowing that I worked closely with Bernard Cardinal Law, then Archbishop of Boston, the emissaries asked that I bring him with me on the visit. I was driving, at the time, an eleven-year-old Ford, in which several of them had ridden. My response was that I could visit Tunis with the impunity of an eleven-year-old Ford, but that the Cardinal was more like a 747: they break easily. They asked then that I bring a letter of introduction from him.

HELP FROM FRIENDS

Cardinal Law, very helpful throughout, asked Archbishop Pio Laghi, at the time the first Pro-Nuncio of the Holy See to the United States, up to Boston. We discussed the prospect at length. An excellent Israeli Consul-General in Boston, Michael Shiloh, had been to the Cardinal, asking that he intervene with the Vatican, asking the Pope to establish full diplomatic relations with Israel. I had drawn up, and discussed with Michael, a long advisory paper, to say that relations between the Holy See and Israel were in fact cordial and supportive, but that full diplomatic relations at that juncture were not advisable. I thought at this point that, with both Israelis and Palestinians asking our Catholic assistance, we should not allow this to be merely a local Boston enterprise, but that it should be a full offer of diplomatic good offices by the Holy See for the benefit of both peoples.

Archbishop Laghi wished I had made such a proposal some 15 years earlier, when the Holy See might have taken it up with enthusiasm. But by that time (early 1986) the Vatican was acting like most other governments, responding in its diplomacy only to what had just come up, without long-range plans.[6] Vatican officials would respond positively, he predicted, to the abstract idea of such good offices, but would retreat in panic once anything became concrete.

Very kindly, Archbishop Laghi stood from that time, figuratively, at my elbow to steer me through that particular jungle. With regard to my visit to Arafat, though, he recommended that I go with no letters of recommendation from anyone, speaking for no one but myself, since the initiative was mine. But I should let it be known that we had had these conversations (he saw to it that I had a similar full conversation with Cardinal O'Connor in New York and I took it on myself to contact Cardinal Bernardin in Chicago); that I would be reporting back to them, to the

US State Department and White House, and to the Secretariat of State of the Holy See; that they were all aware of the visit and expecting these reports, and might in fact act on them. That was so attractive a license, with no strings attached, that I have operated to it ever since.

Part I
Building Relationships

1
The path to the US/PLO dialogue, 1985–88

It has always been my experience that, when you write a really serious letter to someone in authority, you get a serious response. The letter I sent to Chairman Arafat late in November of 1985 confirmed this.

FIRST MEETING WITH ARAFAT

When I had met Arafat for the first time, the previous June, I found he conformed to none of the negative stereotypes by which we had all seen him portrayed in a constant barrage of media attack. He was instead a highly intelligent and cultivated man, anxious for serious contact with the American public, especially with Jews, serious about the peace initiative he had launched that year jointly with King Hussein of Jordan, who had always treated Arafat with suspicion and tended to keep distant from him in his own efforts at resolving the conflict. It had cost Arafat great effort to come to an understanding with the king, and in fact it would not endure beyond the next February, when the king angrily broke with him. But they were still cooperating closely when we met Arafat the night of June 22, 1985.

Arafat had led the discussion for most of our long meeting, narrating the many occasions he had tried to initiate negotiations, from his 1974 UN appearance with gun and olive branch to his support for the King Fahd proposal that eventually became the Fez plan,[1] to his unilateral ceasefire declaration in 1981, and the proposals for negotiation at the time of the Israeli invasion of Lebanon in 1982. His discouragement showed in his concluding each of these tales with "but they would not listen." Even when he spoke of current peace efforts, not yet concluded, this closing "but they would not listen" expressed his expectation of an unfavorable outcome, though it did not exclude the hope that this time the effort might succeed.

In briefings we had received on our way, officials at the State Department and in the various US embassies along our route had always questioned whether his peace initiative with King Hussein was truly Arafat's priority. First priority for him, they felt, was the unity of the PLO under his leadership, challenged as it was in Syria and in places the Syrians controlled, such as Tripoli in the north of Lebanon, and after that the re-establishment of his military position in Lebanon. It was left to me to press Arafat on these topics, and I was impressed by his response.

I had come away from that meeting dissatisfied that we had not raised the issue of two gunboat attacks on the Israeli coast, both unsuccessful, which in my opinion gravely compromised his peace initiative. I wrote to Arafat on November 26, after the hijacking of the Italian cruise ship *Achille Lauro* had raised the stakes of continuing Palestinian terrorism much higher. And in consequence of that letter I went to Tunis for what developed into three days of conversations with Arafat, March 4–6, 1986.

MEETINGS IN TUNIS, MARCH 4–6, 1986

Just before I traveled to Tunis, on February 19, King Hussein had broken off his joint effort with Arafat, feeling that the PLO had not met conditions important to him. US requirements had their place in this failure. The United States objected to the linking of commitments the Palestinians were prepared to make with statements of their grievances against the Israelis. Their suggestion had been a two-paragraph statement, in which the first paragraph would be recognition and acceptance of Resolutions 242 and 338 without conditions attached, and the second would state the position of the PLO on the rights of Palestinians, mentioning other Security Council resolutions. King Hussein felt none of three successive Palestinian drafts he was shown met this US demand and he consequently broke ranks with Arafat and the PLO. But the most lasting effect of this breach with King Hussein was its detrimental effect on the readiness Palestinians had been professing to go into a confederation with Jordan rather than insist on an altogether separate state.

Language was a question for our meeting, since I have no Arabic. I knew Arafat's English, very competent but clearly not his own language, from our earlier meeting. I asked that an interpreter be present, not to translate everything but only to mediate if there were a technical word that we had to be sure we understood the same way. The interpreter was Sami Musallam, a Lutheran Christian from Jerusalem and Arafat's English-language secretary. I asked if I might take notes, to which Arafat agreed, and he also took notes himself, while Sami took down, in Arabic, a full transcript of the conversation. We met as guests of the PLO's then ambassador to Tunis. Present also were three members of the PLO Executive Council: Faruk Kaddumi, who functioned as a sort of Foreign Minister; Hani al-Hassan, who had done the actual negotiating, with Philip Habib, of the 1981 ceasefire and the 1982 PLO evacuation from Beirut; and Abdel Rahin Ahmed, who represented the Iraqi interest in the PLO.

My letter had proposed a moratorium on all use of force by the PLO for the duration of the peace initiative, and argued that such an action would also witness to the authority of the PLO with the Palestinian people, both the residents of the occupied territories and the diaspora. By the time of our meetings, though, with all the support I had from church and state organizations in the United States, I no longer felt restricted to the content of that letter, but took up the entire matter of the three preconditions that the United States and Israel demanded from the PLO before there could be any dialogue: recognition of the right of the state of Israel to exist; acceptance of UN Security Resolutions 242 and 338;[2] and renunciation of terrorism. My letter, on the moratorium, related only to the terrorism issue. We discussed all three.

Taking up the moratorium first, Arafat made clear that a formal statement on this had to go through the formal decision-making bodies of the PLO. It had been referred to them and had much discussion, but no response was yet ready. He referred, however, to his Cairo Declaration of 1985, in which he had reiterated earlier denunciations and rejection of terrorism, and renunciation of any use of armed force outside the actual area of the occupied territories. There was so much lack of clarity in this area that we spent some time agreeing on a definition of terrorism, as distinguished from any legitimate use of force. My own definition made an analogy with war crimes. We hear people speaking now of "state terrorism," but in ordinary usage the word "terrorism" is reserved for the actions of non-state, unofficial parties. If they are not representative of a people, they have no legitimacy for the use of force, and all their armed actions will be terrorist. The same must be said if, as a truly representative body, they fail the tests of necessity or proportionality. It is central to my definition, however, that if a resistance movement is truly representative, those actions it undertakes which, if they were done by the official armed forces of a recognized state, would deserve to be punished as war crimes, should be classified as terrorist. Arafat pronounced himself quite ready to renounce any such actions.

A more general renunciation of violence in resistance to occupation, though, as moratorium or something more permanent, should not be seen as an obligation, though it could be volunteered freely as a way of proposing the peace. This was much in line with my own thinking, that such a renunciation should not imply that there was no right of resistance.

My own role in this, familiar to me from working in other conflict situations, was one of interpretation. I had followed the actions of the PLO over a long time. The literature was near infinite, but especially helpful to me had been the analysis of Alain Gresh.[3] I looked at Palestinian experience during the whole of Arafat's chairmanship of the PLO and expressed it in analytic language that was my own. The test would be whether my hearers agreed that my analysis actually described their experience.

The PLO, as I saw it, had first proposed, in the late 1960s and up to 1974, a solution it called the "Democratic State," a unitary state in the whole territory west of the River Jordan, in which Jews and Arabs would have equal rights as citizens, and Jews, Christians, and Muslims equal religious liberty. The proposition formed part of the baggage Arafat had brought with him from Fatah when it was first admitted into the PLO.

This proposition had had to be digested and eventually accepted throughout the PLO's complex structure, all its constituent bodies and the Palestine National Congress, as well as through two distinct bodies of Palestinian public opinion: the resident population in the occupied territories and the exiled population outside. People had to ascertain which Jews they were talking about in this policy that amounted to the acceptance of the Jews. Some wanted to speak only of "anti-Zionist" Jews, of whom a few can be found in Israel. Some wanted to restrict it to Jews whose families had been in Palestine before the Balfour Declaration[4] or before 1947.[5] Eventually Palestinians recognized that they were talking of all the Jews and accepted all in their Democratic State proposal. Chairman Arafat himself expressed this in the course of our discussion in these terms: "We offered a civilized solution, the Democratic State, but it was rejected, by the Israelis and by the Americans."

The proposal failed, then, as a means of communication between Palestinians and Israelis, yet it remained of great importance for the Palestinians themselves. It meant that acceptance of the Jews, as a people like themselves and of equal rights, had become firmly embedded in Palestinian consciousness.

I interjected at once that I rejected it too, for the same reasons as did Israel and the United States. The proposal meant the dissolution of the separate Jewish State of Israel in favor of a new entity. The Jewish (and US) choice was for the State of Israel as a Jewish state. Hence they rejected the Democratic State out of hand. I could understand this in terms of the traumatic experience of Jewish history, because of which Jews felt they could no longer live under the sovereignty of another people.

By 1974 the PLO itself had become aware of this as an internal contradiction in its own Democratic State proposal. In essence, it had meant the acceptance of the Jews as a people having rights equal to those of Arabs. It was predicated on the inalienable right of self-determination for all peoples, as asserted in the preamble to the Charter of the UN and enshrined in international law. If the Jews decisively rejected the proposal of the Democratic State, as they clearly did, then that was their choice and by right of self-determination they were entitled to it. The Palestinians might not see this as a wise or welcome choice, but they accepted it as the choice the Israelis have freely made and persist in. The PLO would not seek to undermine that choice or that state.

It took some time for the PLO to decipher this problem. It had to work a new policy through the whole cumbersome process in all the constituent bodies of the PLO and its PNC assembly, through the very disparate bodies of public opinion among the occupied resident population and the diaspora, but from 1974 the PLO began to speak of establishing a Palestinian state or entity on any Palestinian territory from which Israel would withdraw its occupation. There was much timidity at first about using the word "state," as that immediately implied acceptance of the Israeli state. Hence the inclusion of the alternative term "entity." Eventually it became clear that the PLO was talking of the whole Palestinian territory occupied in 1967 as a result of the June war, as it did not accept (nor did Security Council Resolution 242) any right to the acquisition of territory by force or conquest. By the time, in 1981, when the PLO declared, in Lebanon, its unilateral ceasefire, Palestinians had accepted a two-state solution, a Palestinian state living alongside Israel in peace. They rejected occupation. They did not reject Israel.

The legal basis for this Jewish entitlement to the state of Israel rested on the right of self-determination, identical to the grounds on which Palestinians claimed their own state.

The conversation now took quite a dramatic turn. Arafat asked Sami Musallam, the interpreter, for an exact Arabic translation of the formula I had used: recognition of Israel on the same basis as that upon which Palestinian claims rested, the right of each people to self-determination. With the group of executive committee members, he then had an animated exchange in Arabic for several minutes. Did the formula accurately express their experience? Arafat asked that I reformulate it, had Sami translate again, and further Arabic discussion took place. Then Arafat asked that I expand on the theme, spell it out in more detail. That too was translated and discussed for some time in Arabic, until first Arafat, then each of the executive members in turn—Kaddumi, Hassan, and Rahin Ahmed—said, "That is exactly our experience."

In principle, this meant that there was no obstacle to PLO acceptance of the three preconditions: right of Israel to exist, Resolutions 242 and 338, and the renunciation of terrorism. At a more practical level there was an obstacle. The Palestinians needed to know, before they made a declaration endorsing the preconditions, what response they would get. Arafat spoke, as he often had, of this recognition as his "last card." In this and subsequent conversations I often played into that image and said that, if he played that card, he would have a whole new hand. But that was figurative language only.

In substance, Arafat needed to know what response he would get from the US and Israeli governments if he did formally accept the three preconditions. He expected that there would be no acknowledgement at all, that his statement would simply be dismissed as of no consequence. He described what he regarded as "a game of strip tease." The United States and Israel kept asking him to take one thing after another off. When he did, they would only ask that he strip himself of something more.

In this, we were no longer dealing merely in symbols. My own task, for the next two and a half years, would consequently be to traffic between Palestinians, Israelis, and US officials to determine, and communicate privately among them, what responses they might expect from any actions they took toward one another.

THE *ACHILLE LAURO*

There were a few more events of my visit, further meetings with Arafat on the two following days, in which I took care to confirm what had been said in the first meeting. But before I had left Boston I had a telephone call from William Wilson, US ambassador to the Holy See. He had heard of my intention to visit Arafat. The Italian judge who was investigating the *Achille Lauro* hijacking had told him he would like to interview Arafat about Abul Abbas, the instigator of the hijack, and asked for his help. Wilson asked if I would put the question. I told him I had an agenda for this meeting and did not want to risk it, but that I would ask this if I had the chance. The opportunity came in my last session with Arafat, on March 6. His response was that he would gladly see the judge, that the interview should be informal and not an interrogation, that his relations with Italy were good and that the Italian State should request it.

I wrote my reports, for my Catholic hierarchy friends, the White House and State Department, and the Vatican Secretariat of State, and went along to discuss them at the State Department and the National Security Council. Cardinals Law and O'Connor, with the nuncio, Archbishop Laghi, presented the report themselves to Vice President George H. W. Bush, but were unable to present it at the White House, where instead it was put in the hands of Chief of Staff Donald Regan. I brought it to my Israeli friend, Consul General Michael Shiloh, and went through it in detail. He was just returning from his Boston assignment to the foreign ministry in Jerusalem, and agreed to seek appointments for me with Prime Minister Shimon Peres, Foreign Minister Yitzhak Shamir, and Defense Minister Yitzhak Rabin when I would be in Jerusalem in the summer. This was the time of the "rotation," in which the posts of prime minister and foreign minister were to be held in turn by Peres and Shamir, each for two years.[6]

MEETINGS IN ISRAEL, JUNE 1986

Just before I left for Jerusalem that summer of 1986, I had the opportunity, through the friendship of Cardinal Law, to spend a Fourth of July outing at the Bush summer home in Kennebunkport, Maine, and before dinner to discuss all these topics at some length with the Vice President and his house guest, James Baker III, at that time secretary of the Treasury. When I arrived in Jerusalem on July 10, I found that, despite Michael Shiloh's efforts, Foreign Minister Shamir had taken the trouble to prevent my seeing himself, Prime Minister Peres, or Defense Minister Rabin. Instead, Mrs. Yael Vered, counselor on religious affairs at the Foreign Ministry, would see me.

Mrs. Vered was quite absolute that ministers of government had no time for seeing me, that there was already effective peace with the Arabs despite the lack of formal agreements, no trouble with the Palestinians, and that the only proper person for Israel to deal with over Palestinian questions was King Hussein of Jordan. No Yasser Arafat, please. With her assistant Mr. Zvi Ne'eman afterwards I was able to reach agreement that Palestinians had a real desire and readiness to reach peace with the Israelis, but he found it simply perverse of me to believe that Arafat or the PLO could be any part of this. He hoped Israel might find an alternative voice to speak for the Palestinians, and in fact this had been Israeli policy for many years. I found that he was speaking from a briefing book the size of a telephone directory that had been prepared in the office to refute everything Arafat or the Palestinians had told me. I would have no opportunity, though I did ask, to get a look at that book.

As of that moment, my visit to Israel seemed a waste of time, but for help I received from Hanna Siniora, editor of *Al Fajr* newspaper, a Christian Palestinian, who told me of communications the Palestinians were having with the US embassy in Tel Aviv and introduced me to Uri Savir, then as ever the right-hand man to Prime Minister Shimon Peres. I had introductions to several Knesset members as well, and found a meeting with Aharon Harel, Labor Party MK,[7] particularly encouraging.

Harel spoke of readiness in the Labor Party to meet the PLO on terms of:

- Mutual recognition. If the PLO would recognize the State of Israel and Resolution 242, then reciprocal recognition would be guaranteed. A statement would be issued within the hour, he said, recognizing:
  (a) The national rights of the Palestinians. He spoke of a speech Peres had given in April to the Labor Party Plenum, in which he spoke of recognizing the Palestinians *as a nation*.
  (b) The PLO as legitimate spokesman.
- Cessation of terrorism (by which he meant all force) as of that time. Harel thought the formula I had earlier suggested, of a moratorium, would be the appropriate one.
- It was important to have a reconciliation between Arafat and King Hussein first. The lack of it terribly constrained Labor's chances to move. In any negotiation it was important to have both Hussein and Arafat. Hussein, said Harel, could choose between only two choices, to act with Arafat or with Syria, but in fact it would not work without Arafat. It would be ideal to have all three: Hussein, Arafat, and the Syrians. Labor would welcome that.

That conversation left me all the more anxious to see Prime Minister Peres, and MK Harel volunteered to call Peres himself to set the appointment. The prime minister, however, was on his way to visit Morocco. I had appointments to see King Hussein in Amman and go on to Syria, where Melkite Patriarch Maximos Hakim had promised to introduce me to government figures.[8] Since meeting Peres had the highest priority, I waited in Jerusalem, letting the Jordanian and Syrian appointments pass.

Meanwhile I met MK Elazar Granot, the general secretary of the Mapam party.[9] He had had a disappointing experience with the PLO himself over the past year, winning Peres' approval for his offering what he thought attractive terms for a Palestinian peace at the meeting of the Socialist International in Vienna, but he was still waiting for a Palestinian reply. He agreed with my interpretation of the Palestinian experience over the years, as I had presented it in Tunis. He felt that Peres' two-year term as prime minister had been wasted, and that there was no hope with Shamir, who would take over as prime minister by rotation in October. Like Harel, Granot feared that Israel faced a war with Syria if a settlement were not found soon. Both saw that it would be more terrible than any previous one, since everything was now targeted by missiles, but Granot recognized that it would be most terrible for Palestinians.

Prime Minister Peres had returned by now from Morocco, but after reporting on his meetings there to colleagues, he had the visit of US Vice President Bush to deal with.[10]

A third meeting was with MK Mordechai Virshubski of the Shinui party. When Shamir took over, he felt, his first action would be to press the growth of Israeli settlements in the Palestinian territories, though he would be limited by lack of cash. This would increase the drift toward war. Virshubski, Granot, and Harel had been among five MKs who met a group of five Palestinians (including Dr. Walid Khalidi[11]) in Boston two years earlier, and had emphasized the need to use Peres' term well.

On July 27 I met Uri Savir at the prime minister's office. He had already read with care all my reports of the March meetings with Arafat, and told me that Aharon Harel had given Peres a full and cordial account of my meeting with him.

Savir said that the Israeli government had two alternative ways of reacting to everything regarding Arafat and the PLO. One was that it was necessary to contact and come to an understanding with him. The other was that Arafat and the PLO were hopeless cases, and that Israel had to wait for them to go away and be replaced with some other leadership. He understood my belief that contact was needed, and said this had been attempted in all good will by many others before, sometimes by people of higher rank. If the other hypothesis was correct, that Arafat and his organization were hopeless cases, then my effort was not a real service but was keeping them alive when they should be fading from the scene.

I responded that I had listened carefully every time I heard Israelis tell me that they believed there was some other address to turn to than the PLO. I had never heard any reason for their belief that there was another address other than that they didn't like the address they were given, and had concluded that this was self-deception. Savir said he would report our conversation back to Peres and let me know whether there would be a meeting. It was not, he said, a matter of time. Peres understood the importance of the matter, and would have time if he thought a meeting appropriate. But he might not want it.

Savir's answer came through Hanna Siniora, who had continued to pursue the matter. The message was that if I came back to Jerusalem with something concrete from other Arab parties, particularly from King Hussein, Peres would be glad to meet me, but that as of then he did not want to encourage what I was doing. The phrasing, I felt, needed careful interpretation. I took it not to mean that Peres would be unhappy to see me succeed, but rather that he could not (as a matter of internal Israeli politics) take any direct part in this himself. This I could understand.

Siniora asked that I come by his office the following day before going on to Rome. By this time I had waited too long to go directly on to Jordan, as planned. My departure was on the night of July 31, and I had to get to Rome if I were not to find people in the Vatican Secretariat of State gone on their vacations. Hanna gave me messages that both Israelis and US officials in Vice President Bush's delegation had asked that I should pass on when I met Arafat.

What I had been told by Aharon Harel, and had been so anxious to hear confirmed by Peres, had been reported very fully to Peres, I was told, and had met no objection, but it could not be attributed directly to him as a proposition.

Uri Savir had passed on to Siniora a proposal for a meeting preparatory to the proposed reopening of the Geneva International Conference,[12] an event that had been in the air throughout all these dealings. This was to be understood as a sounding, not an offer. The proposal was for a meeting of US, Russian, Israeli, Palestinian, and Jordanian officials. The United States and Russia would share the chairmanship. The meeting was meant to discuss and narrow differences on such matters as 242, the territories, and self-determination. There would be no preconditions (that is to say, the PLO would not be required to accept 242 and come to a cessation of violence as preconditions in this format), and the pre-conference was intended to lead on to the full international conference.

The US proposal had been passed on to Siniora, he told me, in a group of people from the US State Department who had been at the Bush meeting with Palestinians. Richard Murphy was one of the group, but Mr. Wat Cluverius, of the embassy in Tel Aviv, did the talking. The proposal was similar to what I had been told, for the Israelis, by Aharon Harel. If Arafat, using a two-paragraph formula that had been suggested by the United States in Amman in February, or in whatever way he could, would recognize 242/338 without condition, he was guaranteed a reciprocal statement from the United States within one hour. US officials agreed to sit down in advance with Palestinians from the occupied territories acceptable to the PLO to discuss the language of that reciprocal statement of recognition. It would be in terms favorable to self-determination in the context of confederation with the Hashemite Kingdom of Jordan as proposed in the February 11, 1985, accord. They would also discuss in advance the form for presenting these two statements. Their insistence on having the PLO statement one hour in advance of theirs arose from the long history of distrust, as they feared the PLO might renege on its statement if the two were intended to be simultaneous.

TO ROME, BAGHDAD, AMMAN, AND TUNIS

With that I traveled on to Rome. I had already discovered that, among my Jesuit colleagues, the Superior General of the order, Fr. Peter Hans Kolvenbach, with his long experience in Lebanon, was the best informed about the Middle East of any I knew. His support was also invaluable to me. Hence I made it a point, throughout this long summer of traveling to various countries, to check in with him regularly. I also needed to report all that I had heard to the diplomatic office of the Holy See, and quickly before it shut down, as always, for the month of August.

What I then experienced confirmed what Archbishop Pio Laghi, the Holy See's nuncio to the United States, had predicted, that while the Vatican would welcome, in the abstract, the idea of offering its good offices to mediate between the parties, panic would break out as soon as the proposition became concrete. Officials feared that, if they offered their office as conduit between Israelis and Palestinians, the Israelis would answer: we will not lift our finger to remove that Palestinian message from your basket unless you first establish full diplomatic relations with us. With that, one of the fundamental strategies of my effort disappeared. I would have to look elsewhere.

MEETING WITH KING HUSSEIN

I had promised to meet Arafat again in Tunis after my time in Israel. Just before I left Jerusalem I had received a phone call from the PLO saying I should go to Baghdad rather than Tunis for that meeting, and had told then of my need to go to Rome first. But it took so many days to arrange a visa for Iraq that, by the time I arrived, Arafat had already left. My next meeting with him would be postponed by a month in which much more would happen. At that I went directly on to Jordan, hoping to pick up on an already arranged meeting with King Hussein that I had missed by staying so long in Jerusalem. This I did, but first I had to wait out the end of Ramadan, staying two weeks with my Jesuit colleagues in Amman.

The king, when I met him, could not have been more gracious and responsive. Archbishop Laghi was an old acquaintance of his, having been the apostolic delegate to Jerusalem during the critical period around the 1967 war.[13] The most interesting part, for King Hussein, of my original proposal, that the Holy See make available its good offices, was no longer in prospect. We discussed my meetings with Arafat and with the various Israeli officials. I was mindful of Uri Savir's promise that I would see Peres if I brought back meaningful proposals from King Hussein, but there was nothing of substance there, and by now it had become more important that I get back to Arafat.

I had to wait longer in Rome before going to Tunis for that meeting, since Arafat was at a conference of the Non-Aligned Movement in Harare, where his speech, on September 5, came very close to affirming the three pre-conditions for dialogue with the United States and Israel. He did this, though, in the context of a lengthy denunciation of Israeli behavior toward the Palestinians which, doubtless, made it less appetizing to the Israelis. I was back in Tunis for a meeting with Arafat on September 9. While waiting in Amman I had drawn up a full report of the things I had heard in Jerusalem, and the Palestinian Catholic Monsignor Ibrahim Ayyad had kindly written, in an elegant hand, an Arabic translation.

SEPTEMBER 9 MEETING WITH ARAFAT

On this occasion I met with Arafat alone. He wanted first to impress upon me how unsatisfactory to Palestinians Resolution 242 was by itself. It made no reference to them other than asserting (in its section 2b) the necessity "for achieving a just settlement of the refugee problem." Palestinians could live with that, but found it further tainted by the subsequent agreement of October 3, 1977, between US Secretary of State Cyrus Vance and Israeli Defense Minister Moshe Dayan, which interpreted the reference to "the refugee problem" in 242 as meaning all refugees, both Arab and Jewish, of the entire Middle East region. This agreement of Vance and Dayan had come just after the October 1, 1977, meeting of Vance and Soviet Foreign Minister Gromyko, from which had come a joint statement convening the Geneva Conference under US/USSR joint chairmanship. Dayan described his October 3 meeting with Vance as his "six-hour battle"[14] (a parallel to the six-day war of 1967), and it was followed on October 4 by a Carter address to the UN General Assembly which, in Arafat's understanding, withdrew from a US/USSR joint statement of October 1 about reconvening the Geneva Conference, effectively canceling that long-awaited event.

The substance of the Vance–Dayan agreement of October 3, 1977, was to establish an equivalence of the Arab refugees, not even described as Palestinian, and the Jewish emigrants to Israel from all Arab countries, an "exchange of populations," so that the specific Palestinian refugee problem, as a separate concern, was simply wiped off the books.

It should not be imagined, Arafat believed, that this was the actual intention of the Security Council when it passed Resolution 242 on November 22, 1967. But this Vance–Dayan interpretation was now the official policy of the United States and Israel. What was to prevent, then, even if Arafat and the PLO got to an actual international conference on the basis of 242/338 alone, that the United States and Israel would say: "Why are you here? Since you have accepted 242, which we interpret so, everything is already settled, and the status quo is now established as the final solution."

Nonetheless, Arafat had determined that 242 and 338 were now integral to "international legality," and as such he had formally and definitively accepted them, by name, over the opposition of Iran, Libya, and dissident Palestinian factions, in his address to the Harare Conference on September 5.

That he had done so was disputed, and I represented to him, at this point, that other Palestinians, even members of his staff with whom I had spoken while awaiting him in Tunis, had argued to me that the September 5 address was not an unconditional acceptance of 242/338. They had referred to a statement by Faruk Kaddumi in Harare denying that the recognition was unconditioned. They were mistaken, said Arafat. The Arabic full text of his address, which is authoritative, would show that he attached no condition to his acceptance of 242 and 338.

He had, in his Harare address, spoken of other items, such as his call for the international conference and his recognition of other resolutions of the UN and the Security Council, but those items were distinct and not conditional on one another.

We were, at this point, deep into the technicalities of the argument over the preconditions. It was not, Arafat held, a condition imposed on him if he was asked to recognize all the solemn resolutions of the UN as constituting international legality on this question, since they are such as a fact of international law. But to demand that he affirm these two resolutions and not others is a pre-condition. Nevertheless, he did so without qualification of his acceptance, and without conditioning it on any other factor, because in themselves they are a part of this international legality.

I pointed out to him, as reason for the special emphasis on 242, that it has special symbolic importance for the Israelis. For them, it constitutes the international community's acceptance of their legitimacy as a state. He accepted this, and said that it was not the intention of the PLO to take away from the Israelis their state, and this was an element in his acceptance of 242 and 338. Nevertheless, he said, the Israelis were mistaken in seeing only in 242 the international community's acceptance of their legitimacy as a state. The true basis was Resolution 181 of the General Assembly on November 29, 1947, by which the UN had provided for the establishment of the State of Israel and also of an Arab State of Palestine, a resolution of which only one part had been fulfilled.

I had come looking for an Arafat response to what I had been told of statements from Israel and the United States (Harel's for the Israelis, and what Hanna Siniora had reported to me of his meeting with US officials, including Wat Cluverius). I had sent my account of all that to Cardinal Law in Boston. He had checked it out with the State Department and been told, and recounted to me on the phone, that what Wat Cluverius had told Hanna had been overstated. Consequently I could give Arafat only partial assurance on that.

There was another reason for hesitation. Arafat told me, in confidence, that in making his Harare statement he had relied on an agreement made during a recent visit to Romania to see President Ceaucescu. Ceaucescu had previously conferred with the Israeli government and had their promise of reciprocal action if Arafat would make a public statement containing five points:

1. Acceptance of an international conference, with the five permanent members of the Security Council and all the parties to the Arab–Israeli conflict (so designated, with explicit mention of Israel, and not designated as "the Middle Eastern conflict" or some other phrase that failed to mention Israel by name), to negotiate a comprehensive settlement.
2. Acceptance of a preparatory conference along the lines proposed by French President Mitterrand and Soviet First Secretary Gorbachev.
3. Acceptance of open dialogue and discussion between all the parties to the Arab–Israeli conflict.
4. Acceptance of Resolution 242 and 338 by name.
5. Acceptance of international guarantees for all parties.

Arafat had chosen to use his address at the Harare conference for this purpose. He stressed the seriousness of the commitment this choice of Harare represented. It was an important forum, and his address, against the express opposition of the Iranians, Syrians, and Libyans, had come directly after the speech of President Khadafy.

He did not tell me the content of the Israeli promises to President Ceaucescu of reciprocal action if he fulfilled his agreement with Ceaucescu. We discussed at length the initial Israeli responses to his address, which were skeptical. He intended, he said, on that same afternoon, after we had concluded our meeting, to contact President Ceaucescu and inquire about the fulfillment of the Israeli commitment. He stressed, also, the confidentiality of this information about his agreement with Ceaucescu, as it had not yet been given even to his closest lieutenants in the PLO, but he agreed that I should report it in full to the Holy See and to the US government as quickly as possible. I did in fact report it at once to Mr Peter Murphy, Chargé d'Affaires at the US embassy to the Vatican during the vacancy of an ambassador, and to Msgr. Jean-Louis Tauran in the Vatican's Secretariat of State, following that up with a full written account to Archbishop Laghi in Washington that was copied to the US Department of State.

Since the Ceaucescu initiative and the Harare address needed time to play themselves out, Arafat felt he needed an additional ten days before he could take up, separately, the matters that had been communicated to me by Israel and the United States. Since he was not yet in a position to give me a formal answer on whether, in the light of the offers of reciprocal statements from Israel and the United States, he would make the type of statement I was seeking, I agreed to return to Tunis to see him again after that time.

Before leaving, I wrote down for him, on a sheet of paper, the three elements such a statement would properly contain. First there were the two paragraphs of the proposed statement that had been requested by the US delegation at the Amman talks early in the year, and presented to him by King Hussein:

- A recognition and acceptance of Resolutions 242 and 338, without conditions attached.
- A paragraph that would state the position of the PLO on the rights of Palestinians.
- A renunciation of the use of force, in any event for the duration of the peace effort.

I reminded him of what King Hussein had said when, in my meeting with him, I had referred to the US proposal, as had been my habit since I discussed it at the State Department late in March, as "the two-paragraph formula." King Hussein interjected at once: "Remember, there are three items," referring to the requirement that there be a statement on the use of force.

That third item, cessation of force, remained very much a problem. Arafat reaffirmed his absolute stand against terrorism, as he had affirmed in his Cairo Declaration the previous year, and his limitation, as in that declaration, of any acts of armed resistance to military occupation to the actual occupied territories. He expanded at great length on his rejection of two recent acts of terrorism: a hijacking in Karachi (he was glad the hijackers had been caught) and the attack on a synagogue in Istanbul (a "horrible crime," an "outrage," "totally contrary to everything the PLO stands for").[15] He saw both of these acts, and other terrorist attacks since his Cairo Declaration, as fundamentally sabotage against the peace effort he and the PLO had been mounting over all this time. But to go beyond the Cairo Declaration's terms to a general cessation of violence, even in the form of the moratorium I had suggested for the duration of the peace effort, was something he could do only if authorized by the full leadership of the PLO.

I reminded him of our conversations in March, when I had strongly urged the moratorium, and he had argued that he had too few "pressure tools" or "cards" with which to go into negotiation. He could not afford to play them carelessly. My response was that he might be hoarding his cards for a situation that would never arise, making them useless. He had played the one card, his acceptance of 242/338, in his Harare address. The other card, the matter of armed resistance, remained in his hand.

I suggested an invitation to the Israelis for a mutual cessation of violence for the duration of the peace effort. We discussed the many clear advantages to this and he promised to consult the rest of the leadership on it before our next meeting. But even when I handed him the sheet of paper on which I had written the three items that would be looked for in a statement from him (the two paragraphs plus the statement on the use of force) he pointedly told me that the last item was not yet even under discussion. He told me, as he had in our March meetings, that no such condition had been imposed on the Algerians, the Vietnamese, and others at the time they entered into discussions with their adversaries, so that this was the imposition of novel conditions on the Palestinians. I pointed out the difference in their situations: those others had, at the time of the negotiations, real military prospects of gain from the continuation of military operations, whereas the PLO had none.

As we ended out meeting, I mentioned to Arafat that an effort he had made ever since becoming chairman in 1969, to develop a political negotiation approach to the Arab–Israeli conflict, had now reached a critical stage. I commended to him the example of two holy men, both soldiers like himself, who in their time had been, like him, the hope of the Arabs and of the Islamic people: Nur-ed-Din before Damascus and Salah-ed-Din before Aleppo.[16] Arafat understood the reference at once, and supplied the explanation: "They showed how to treat an enemy as not an enemy, and so won from him the peace."

REPORTING TO WASHINGTON

Returned to the United States, and reporting back to the State Department in Washington, I found a disappointing result. Officials I saw there were panicked by the very fact that I had named two of their own officers in my report of the meeting Hanna Siniora had with me. They denied that they had offered a reciprocal statement if the PLO would formally and unconditionally recognize Resolutions 242 and 338. But their reason for this denial was that they would have violated a US statute, forbidding even indirect communication between US officials and the PLO, had they made such a promise to Siniora. Hence it had to be denied. All the same, they said that Arafat, by making a statement unconditionally accepting 242/338, was in a position to compel a reciprocal recognition by the United States. My report, even though carefully kept private to very few eyes, had worried them. It may be that, by writing my report at all, I had provoked this negative reaction and spoiled an opportunity.

I understood something very basic from this. The mid-level officials in the bureaucracy with whom I had been dealing at the State Department and National Security Council were necessarily frightened of having their names connected with any such report. It was all their careers were worth, and it crippled them drastically in trying to deal with the conflict. My conclusion was that I could no longer deal with them and must find an alternative route to communicate with the US government.

My recourse, from this point on, was always to send copies of everything I wrote to William Wilson, now no longer ambassador to the Holy See.[17] As a close personal friend and adviser to President Reagan, Wilson would consistently meet Reagan at the plane each time the president made his frequent visits to his mountain ranch in California, which in fact Wilson had obtained for him. They would spend much of the vacation on horseback together. In that way, all this material got to the highest level of government where there were not the constraints that afflicted the middle-level bureaucracy.

MEETING IN KUWAIT

My return to Arafat was later than I had meant it to be. Instead of the two weeks I had planned, it came only a month later, in Kuwait, where I met Arafat on October 8, perilously close to the October 14 "rotation" in Israeli government by which Shimon Peres would yield the post of prime minister to Yitzhak Shamir. This time there were again others present: Hani al-Hassan, principal negotiator for the PLO during the 1982 discussion leading to their withdrawal from Beirut and leading architect of the

February 11, 1985 accord with King Hussein, who had been present for two of the three sessions of my March meetings with Arafat, and Abu Tariq, the former PLO diplomatic representative to Libya, who had recently been expelled from that country by Khadafy. We talked after a late dinner for the whole of Arafat's delegation at a Kuwaiti government guesthouse.

Even before our private meeting started, when we met before dinner, I told Arafat that I returned with less than when I had last seen him in Tunis.

The vague formula I had received from the State Department, that Arafat was in a position, by his own action, to compel a favorable US response, had far less appeal than the earlier formulas reported by Aharon Harel and Hanna Siniora. It was consistent with what had been a constantly reiterated US position for many years; that if he unconditionally recognized 242/338 then the United States would talk to him.

That was the theme for the bulk of our discussion. I argued that it was worthwhile for Arafat to issue a clear, simple statement that would, first, recognize Resolutions 242 and 338 as a part of international legality, and second, state as the PLO's position that all other UN and Security Council resolutions on the question of Palestine and the Middle East are equally a part of international legality.

In his September 5 address at Harare, Arafat had already explicitly recognized Resolutions 242 and 338 as a part of international legality. He had spoken in the same speech of the other resolutions as equally a part of international legality and called for an international conference to resolve comprehensively the Arab–Israeli conflict. These had been among the points he had agreed with President Ceaucescu during his August visit to Bucharest, all of which he had stated in his Harare address. The explicit naming of the State of Israel as party to the conflict had been an essential part of the agreement.

The Western media had generally interpreted the Harare address as making the recognition of 242/338 conditional on the international conference. Arafat himself, when I had seen him on September 9, insisted that this was a misinterpretation, and that the recognition of 242/338 was unconditional, appealing to the Arabic text of his statement. Both US and Israeli official responses read his recognition of 242/338 as conditional. When I had asked in Washington how US officials assessed the Harare address, I was told it showed that Arafat had not the authority in the PLO to make a statement that would meet their terms.

As I asked for a simpler statement (effectively the "two-paragraph" statement that the United States had been calling for since the previous February in Amman) to counter the claim by Western media and the Israeli and US governments that he had made his recognition of 242/338 conditional on the conference, Arafat wanted to know why it should not be. He did indeed want an international conference at which the whole conflict could be resolved politically by negotiation.

This was a warning sign that I needed to argue against making the international conference a condition. My response was in two parts. First, I accepted that the Harare statement did not in fact, as I read it and as Arafat himself said was its real meaning, condition the recognition of 242/338 on the international conference. Second, I argued, if the recognition were conditioned on the conference, this would be a new condition, a novelty. I had often enough heard Arafat himself speak of his sense that Israel and the United States set conditions for the PLO and, when those conditions were met, set new ones, what he called the "strip tease." I had often told him that I thought he was mistaken if he thought that was the case in the matter of making his recognition of 242/338 the condition for US officials to talk with him. Whether or not the US position was wise, I believed it had been consistent for more than ten years. The price had not changed. But if he were now to set a novel condition, the international conference, for his recognition of 242/238, this would be the strip tease in reverse.

We were in a serious argument now. Arafat had good reason to be suspicious. He was being asked to act on vague promises of a US response to his actions, when much more explicit commitments, as he understood them in the case of his agreement with President Ceaucescu, had not been honored by Israel. My own expectation, as I said repeatedly, was that a truly appropriate US response would be made to such a statement as I was proposing, but I understood Arafat's need to weigh it with great care.

I asked what could be lost by making this simpler and clearer statement, even if the United States and Israel made no response. Nothing new would in fact have been said, as all parts of the statement I was proposing were already in the Harare address, even if not recognized, or if recognized not acknowledged, by Israel and the United States. Clarity was to his advantage. Yet Arafat replied that he could ill afford to be seen by his Palestinian following as constantly pursuing the United States and Israel with more and more concessions and getting nothing in return.

A striking element in this meeting was the very active participation of the two counselors, Hani al-Hassan and Abu Tariq. Each had much to say, assessing both Arafat's and my arguments, neither of them one-sidedly endorsing or rejecting my proposal but helping Arafat to deliberate on it. When I had seen him on September 9, Arafat had insisted on an entirely private meeting between the two of us, because even his closest lieutenants were not aware of all we discussed. Arafat himself had told Hani al-Hassan of what had been covered in our September 9 conversation at the start of this meeting. Abu Tariq evidently knew of it already. So the presence of these two meant that Arafat was now able to carry on the deliberation among his counselors, and was thus freer to act among the rest of the leadership of the PLO than he had been in September.

Arafat was unwilling to be rushed to hasty action by the prospect of the rotation in the Israeli government, by which Shamir would replace Peres as prime minister on October 14, just a few days away. He believed Peres would retain sufficient power as foreign minister, and that even after the rotation a failure by Shamir to follow through on peace possibilities that Peres and Labor recognized would bring down the government and bring about elections on the issue of peace. The Chairman told me, as he had before, that he preferred negotiating with Likud rather than Labor, on the basis that Likud's harsh language could be believed more than the more moderate but ultimately deniable statements by Labor. He would sooner contend with the wolf than the fox.

And at the last stage of our discussion, in the small hours, now, of the morning on October 9, Arafat said he would make the statement I was proposing, the simple, clear affirmation, without conditions, a) that the PLO accepted Resolutions 242 and 338 as a part of international legality, and b) that the PLO also recognizes all the other UN and Security Council resolutions as equally part of international legality, if His Holiness the Pope would ascertain what the US response to this statement would be and could assure him that it was satisfactory.

Arafat was appealing now to the original suggestion I had made early in the year, that the Holy See use its good offices to help the parties to this conflict come to an understanding, a proposal already much weakened by the panicky negative response I had received from the Vatican's Secretariat of State during the summer. I made my report to the Holy See by way of a full memo to Cardinal Law on October 11, asking that he communicate that request to the Pope, and handed it on further to Bishop Jorge Mejia, Secretary of the Pontifical Commission for Justice and Peace, whom I met in Boston on November 3. What action was taken on it I have never been told.

TWO YEARS' HOLDING ACTION

It would be more than two years before this activity culminated in the establishment of an official US/PLO dialogue. My own role merged with other players over this time. On Arafat's recommendation, my communication with him now went through his nephew, Dr. Nasser al-Kidwa, of the Palestinian Observer Mission at the UN.

Ambassador William Wilson was my actual confidant and friend at court through all this period, reflecting on developments as they occurred and representing it all to the US President Ronald Reagan, on those frequent visits to the ranch in California. We witnessed, from our distance, and discussed the Moshe Amirav conversations with Palestinians in Jerusalem,[18] and many other developments.

What most contributed to freeing up Arafat and the PLO to make the clear and unmistakable statements affirming Resolutions 242 and 338, the legitimacy of the State of Israel, and the full renunciation of terrorism, in short all the three pre-conditions, was the *intifada*, the uprising among the resident Palestinian population in the West Bank and Gaza, that began early in December of 1987. Its significance lay in the way it energized and empowered this population, which had lived under military occupation, as of then, for over 20 years.

Until then, these had been people to whom things happened, who had no control over the circumstances of their lives. They had always been distrusted by the PLO leadership and by the exile Palestinian population living in diaspora, for fear that they would make a deal with the Israelis that abandoned their diaspora compatriots to their exile, and because they were so easily subject to Israeli compulsion. Successive Israeli governments, in their reluctance to deal with the PLO, had tried to invent leaderships that could pretend to speak for the Palestinians while actually serving Israeli interests instead. Now the occupied population spoke clearly for itself. From this point on, every action of Israeli government, every action related to Israel by other governments, including the United States, was a response to what these Palestinians were doing. Even though the response was wholly negative and extremely painful, the Palestinians had seized the initiative. They controlled the agenda, and the experience was exhilarating.

Their *intifada* had two characteristics that made it possible for the Israeli peace camp to embrace and support it. First, it was at least relatively non-violent. There were no guns or bombs, only stones, thrown mainly by children, who stood their ground courageously before massed gunfire and the instruction of Defense Minister Rabin to his forces to "break their bones." In a world that had treated them only with indifference, this won them international sympathy. The Israeli army had the power easily to defeat any military threat that all the Arab nations together could bring against them, but before this assault of the powerless they were helpless.

The second characteristic was that their protest was not against the State of Israel, but against occupation only. This amounted to a public endorsement, not only by a remote PLO leadership outside but by the clear assent of the resident population, of the legitimacy of the State of Israel, and a demand that a Palestinian State be allowed to live alongside it in peace. This is what enabled the Israeli peace forces to embrace the *intifada*. The uprising itself was a plea for peace and mutual recognition. It confirmed for me the interpretation I had made during my March 1986 visit to Arafat in Tunis, that the PLO, under Arafat's leadership, had already reached full acceptance of the State of Israel, and had won the assent to this of the Palestinian population.

The role of the PLO in this remains open to dispute. Many believed that the uprising was spontaneous, sparked only by the rather obscure incident in which several Palestinians in Gaza were run down by an Israeli van early in December. I have heard the late Faisal Husseini narrate how he and Sari Nusseibeh had prepared for such an uprising over the previous year, with the encouragement of Abu Jihad, Arafat's principal military aide who, once it was in motion, coordinated the activities of the *intifada* through instructions from abroad.[19] It demonstrated, for Arafat and the PLO, the superior value of a campaign of non-violence over any military stance they could take, making it possible for them strategically to renounce the use of military force as the instrument of their struggle.

In the atmosphere of this success, the PLO held its Palestine National Congress in Algiers in September 1988.[20] Formal recognition of the State of Israel and the declaration of the independence of a Palestinian state were on the program. I wrote to Arafat at great length on August 17, urging that recognition of Israel and arguing that the declaration on Palestine specify the Armistice Line border of 1949, the "Green Line" that had been the border between 1949 and 1967, as the boundary of the Palestinian state, not the border laid down in the 1947 UN Partition Resolution, which they would never get, nor declaration of a Palestinian state on the whole territory between the Jordan and the sea, as some were asking. The 1967 line was in fact what they chose.

I also took up with Arafat the one resolution of the General Assembly that constituted the greatest obstacle to any acceptance of the whole range of UN resolutions as having the force of international legality. This was the "Zionism is racism" resolution.[21] It affronted the Israelis so drastically that it simply had to be withdrawn, by action of the General Assembly, and the Palestinian observer delegation should be directly instrumental in its repeal. To say that Zionism is racism was to delegitimize the entire enterprise of the Israeli state and society. It was the equivalent of the way

Israel and the United States tended to identify all Palestinians not only with the PLO but also explicitly with terrorism. I always wanted to see both these ways in which the two peoples delegitimized one another withdrawn simultaneously.

Much correspondence passed between Ambassador William Wilson and myself over this period, and he described his horseback conversations with President Reagan on the subject. Wilson was striving to form his own judgments on the situation through all this. After the PNC meeting, he put me in contact with a friend he had met, from the opposite end of the US political spectrum from himself, through their joint membership on the California Board of Regents. This was Stanley Sheinbaum, the liberal Democratic publisher of *New Perspectives Quarterly*. Stanley was just organizing a group of American Jews who were to meet a PLO delegation in Stockholm and try to work out the means of bridging the impasse between the PLO and the United States.[22] I saw to it that Stanley had all the materials of my own reports and correspondence, and flew to New York to meet him, between flights, in an airport cafeteria, for a lengthy strategy discussion.

By now the US presidential election was upon us. Ronald Reagan had had his two terms and could not succeed himself again. Traditionally, in this political season, nothing can be accomplished that involves risk for any candidate. Reagan was anxious to pass on the palm to his Vice President, George H. W. Bush, as his successor. We decided that we three, Wilson, Sheinbaum, and I, would approach President Reagan after the election, when he would be "lame duck." He would then be beyond being hurt politically himself. We would ask him to make clear at last to Arafat what US response would be made to a clear acceptance of the three preconditions by the PLO.

The election was, as always, on the first Tuesday in November. George Bush won easily. Reagan went out to his ranch for the Thanksgiving holiday. As a preliminary to the meeting we three hoped to have with him later in Washington, Wilson and Sheinbaum went together to see Chief of Staff Ken Duberstein and National Security Adviser Colin Powell in California to let them know what we were about. Their reception was cordial. The officials agreed that their visitors' purpose was commendable, but still held that it was too politically dangerous for Reagan, even as lame duck, to touch this matter at all. If we tried to approach the president with this, Wilson and Sheinbaum were told, these officials, as his advisers, would stop us.

Arafat, by now, had announced his intention of addressing the UN General Assembly with his acceptance of all three pre-conditions. The US

State Department refused to give him a visa to come to New York for the purpose. The General Assembly voted, in consequence, to travel *en masse* from New York to Geneva to hear him.

I had learned by now, through my own experience with the middle-level bureaucrats of the State Department and NSC, that it was impossible to make the breakthrough between the PLO and the United States through the work of US officials. The Wilson–Scheinbaum conversation with Powell and Duberstein had just demonstrated that it was equally impossible for US non-officials to get through. We turned now to a foreign official, the Swedish Foreign Minister, who had shown strong interest in the Stockholm meetings Stanley Sheinbaum had set up with the PLO. It was, in a way, a revival of my original idea of seeking the good offices of the Holy See as mediator, but appealing to the Swedes instead.

When Arafat addressed the General Assembly, US Secretary of State George Schulz made the instant appraisal, practically de rigueur after any major Palestinian statement, that he hadn't said it right, and the statement had no value. The Israelis responded, as usual, that there was nothing new in Arafat's statement. A press conference was called for the following day, and seen as a last chance for the Palestinians to make their point.

President Reagan intervened himself at this point, telephoning Secretary of State Schulz to say that, whatever Arafat said in the morning, he would, this time, say it right.[23] Overnight, Assistant Secretary of State Richard Murphy spoke by telephone to the Swedish Foreign Minister, stating the exact terms that would be deemed acceptable in an Arafat statement in the morning. The Swedish Foreign Minister in turn phoned through to Bassam Abu Sharif in Geneva, reciting the text, which Bassam copied down for use in the morning while Arafat bridled at receiving practical dictation of his language. The State Department, when it received the press conference statement, ruled it satisfactory, and the way was thus cleared for the establishment of an official US/PLO dialogue, to begin in the New Year. President Reagan had done a service to the incoming President George Bush, getting that decision out of the way so that Bush would not have to make it himself.

What conclusions can be drawn from this intricate chain of events? My own interest is in what it showed of the mentality of the main participants, of their capacity and inclination to make the peace.

The US process was mired throughout in fears of the political consequences to particular office-holders or officials if they were found to be involved in anything that worked to the advantage of Palestinians. There was strong commitment to the good and safety of Israel, but more than that there was anxiety that any action toward lessening the antagonism between Israelis and Palestinians would be interpreted as hostile to Israel, with dire consequence to the career of anyone involved. The then Secretary of State Henry Kissinger made this commitment, in a memorandum of understanding with Israel in 1975, as part of the Sinai II agreement separating Israeli and Egyptian forces in the Sinai peninsula, that no US official would have any contact whatever with any official of the PLO.[24] This was later amplified by escalating Congressional actions heavily lobbied, even policed by opponents of relations with the Palestinians.[25] It had been understood somewhat more leniently in 1981, when Ambassador Philip Habib had negotiated, indirectly, through the mediation of Lebanese Army officers, the PLO's unilateral ceasefire against Israel, and again in 1982, when he negotiated the withdrawal of PLO forces from Beirut. But in the circumstances I saw in 1986, State Department personnel went into total panic over the imputation that things they had said to Hanna Siniora amounted to indirect communication to the PLO, and it paralyzed them.

Arafat showed something I found quite unusual in a leader with ultimate responsibility for a people, all but a head of state. He had learned new things while in that position. His initial Democratic State proposal, with its equality of Jews and Arabs, of Jews, Christians, and Muslims, itself something about which he had to have reflected seriously even before he and his Fatah organization were accepted into the PLO, had proven inadequate. He thought it through further, recognized where its inadequacies lay, and developed, by painful incremental steps, the alternative proposal of the two states living together in peace. Most leaders in such positions as himself have already had all their ideas and possess no such flexibility or capacity to learn.

Beyond that, he had skillfully led his people, in all the complexity of their organizations and the differences between the resident and the exile populations, to accept first the one and then the other proposal as something that truly commanded their assent. He had won from them recognition of the Israelis' right to their state as a parallel to their own demand for a Palestinian state. These accomplishments are rarely acknowledged. They deserve high respect, from Israelis as well as Palestinians.

Now that, in our current time, the question has been raised acutely again whether Arafat is genuinely a "partner for peace" or instead an obstruction that has to be pushed aside, it is simply inconceivable to me that he should be working for the destruction of his own greatest and most hard-won accomplishments.

The Israelis I met were also dedicated to achieving peace with the Palestinians. The great obstacle for them was ambivalence. They could not decide whether to deal with Arafat and the PLO or not. This was best expressed to me by Uri Savir, on behalf of Prime Minister Peres, who did not know whether dealing with Arafat was the most necessary thing for Israel or a hopeless task to be avoided. Numerous attempts had been made to find an alternative address for the Palestinians, and mostly it meant trying to find quislings, who would try to speak for the Palestinians without representing them in fact. The Israelis made their greatest mistake of this sort after the beginning of the *intifada*, when they threw their weight on the side of the Islamist clergy, and actually supported Hamas, even financially, as rival to the PLO in the early years of the *intifada*. They have had reason to regret that since.[26]

2
The Madrid stage and Oslo, 1990–93

My own activity came to a pause of more than a year at this point. I took it that the establishment of an official US/PLO dialogue meant that I should step back and not interfere. I told Arafat and the Israeli and US officials I dealt with that I would back out of these contacts, so as not to get in the way. I did not find myself drawn back in until mid-1990.

THE INTERRELIGIOUS COMMITTEE

Much of what I did during this interval period centered on the US Interreligious Committee for Peace in the Middle East, the group that had sprung from our visit, as Jews and Christians together, to the Middle East in 1985.[1] Since we had announced ourselves as a committee of American Jews, Christians, and Muslims at a press conference in Washington in June, 1987, the Committee had grown from the initial ten of us to several hundred from many parts of the United States. We understood that our task had to do primarily with US policy toward the Middle East, and at our annual convocations we made a point of visiting congressional offices, where the appearance of Jews, Christians, and Muslims approaching political leaders together with a common view always created surprise.

It was not easy to hold such a group together. While each had understood that Israelis and Palestinians, and other Arabs as well, had a common interest in promoting the peace, our American Muslims joined out of solicitude for Palestine, our American Jews with a primary concern for Israel.

BREAKDOWN OF THE US/PLO DIALOGUE

The dialogue with the United States had gravely disappointed the PLO. Israel had not agreed to join in it, despite the meeting of the three famous pre-conditions. The government of Prime Minister Yitzhak Shamir stayed with the traditional Israeli contention that there had to be some Palestinian negotiating partner other than the PLO. It had been Israeli policy, for as long as there was a PLO, to classify it as a purely terrorist organization with which it would have no dealings, to denigrate Arafat himself and refuse to accept the word of Palestinians that this was their authentic representative. The Israeli alternative was to invent Palestinian representatives who would act to Israeli bidding, and who for that reason were in no way genuine representatives of the Palestinians themselves.

US participation in the dialogue had been restricted to one official only, Mr. Robert Pelletreau, then US Ambassador to Tunisia, later ambassador to Egypt and still later a ranking State Department officer on the Middle East. Pelletreau could speak only to Yasser Abed Rabbo, an Arafat adviser who has since become a major Palestinian peace negotiator. The agenda of their discussions was narrowly limited, mostly to a conveying by the United States of Israeli demands on the PLO. Any matter of interest to the PLO could be handled only indirectly, through contacts between the Egyptian government and the US embassy in Cairo. Increasingly, Arafat tended to place his hopes on Arab support, and in particular the siren calls of Iraq's Saddam Hussein, who at this time was still the darling boy of anti-Iranian US policy.

Late in May of 1990, Abul Abbas, organizer of the 1985 hijacking of the cruise ship *Achille Lauro* and still, as head of the Palestine Liberation Army (a constituent body of the PLO), a member of the PLO's Executive Committee, mounted a feckless gunboat attack on the beaches near Tel Aviv. All his gunmen were killed or captured. The United States put Arafat on notice that he must expel Abul Abbas from the PLO and condemn the raid or see the US/PLO dialogue suspended. Saddam Hussein was patron to Abul Abbas, and would not countenance Arafat's doing this. That was the context of my June 6, 1990 letter to Arafat, urging that he accept the US demand and dissociate himself from Saddam Hussein.

That was more easily said than done. We were on the eve of the Iraqi invasion of Kuwait, on August 2, 1990, which would turn Saddam Hussein, in the view of the United States, from golden boy of US diplomacy to enemy of all things good and sacred. Yet even before the invasion the PLO's dialogue with the United States was suspended. Arafat had acquired the reputation of Saddam Hussein's ally.

THE GULF WAR OF 1990–91

From the time of the initial invasion of Kuwait I had a great deal of correspondence with both Arafat and the George H. W. Bush White House. I did not believe a war was the right way to settle the issue of the Iraqi invasion, and had what seemed strong encouragement from the White House to think it might be averted. Arafat, as I saw it, rather than taking the side of Saddam Hussein, tried to produce a mediated solution, relying on diplomatic intervention by the Soviet Union. Only a superpower, it seemed, could effectively intervene with Saddam Hussein, and the United States showed little interest in fostering the "Arab solution" that the Middle Eastern countries favored. But the Soviet Union could not make that intervention without an Arab interlocutor. Arafat attempted, along with King Hussein of Jordan, to be that Arab interlocutor. Such was my perception of a situation most people saw simply as a Palestinian and Jordanian alliance with Iraq. Both would incur severe punishment at the hands of the United States and its European and Arab allies.

Arafat's own intervention with Saddam[2] came to a head just before Christmas. As the armies massed against Iraq in the Saudi desert, Hussein had held all Westerners, American or European, as hostages in Baghdad, describing them as "guests."[3] Arafat pleaded with Saddam Hussein, in such a vehement scene of argument as Hussein would tolerate from no one at all, to release his hostage "guests."[4] Shortly before Christmas Saddam Hussein did exactly that. But the price was the murder, in retaliation, of one of Arafat's oldest companions, his Intelligence Chief Abu Iyad (Salah Khalaf).

A young Palestinian, Hamza Abu Zaid, had shown up at Abu Iyad's doorstep in Tunis, claiming to have defected from the murder squad of Abu Nidal, which for years had hunted down and killed any PLO representative who worked for a peaceful settlement of the conflict with Israel and had a price on Arafat's own head. The PLO had accepted him into the bodyguard unit of Fatah's security chief, Hayil Abd al-Hamid (known as Abu al-Hol), Abu Iyad's close associate. Hamza used that position to murder both Abu Iyad and Abu al-Hol on January 15, just as the UN Coalition deadline was running out on Saddam Hussein and the attack on Iraq about to begin.[5]

Considerably later, in a letter of July 16, 1991, I wrote to Arafat that:

> I happen to realize that it was largely because of your insistence to President Hussein that he freed the thousands of hostages—"guests"—that he had been holding, releasing them just before Christmas. It seems clear to me, too, that President Hussein was the one who ordered the murder of your faithful colleague, Abu Iyad, and that the motive was to intimidate yourself.

Arafat, apparently somewhat scandalized to have the murder attributed so directly to Saddam Hussein, responded:[6] "...an unjust campaign was unfolded against us which also intended ... to increase confusion such as happened concerning the martyrdom of Brother Abu Iyad who was assassinated by one Israeli Mosad (*sic*) agent."

Attributing the assassination to a Mossad agent was intelligible and even consistent if I took into account my own conviction that Abu Nidal himself, in his calculated sabotage of any Palestinian move toward acceptance of Israel, had become an agent of Mossad, which was using him to discredit Palestinian peace approaches and prevent any possible emergence of a Palestinian state alongside Israel.[7]

In that same letter of July 16, 1991, I even recommended to Arafat that he arrange an election for leadership of the PLO that he might expect to lose; an issue that Arafat reflected on seriously both on its own terms and in terms of his relation with me. The outcome of the Gulf War had left both Arafat and King Hussein weakened in their international standing and deprived of any financial support from the wealthy Arab nations of the Gulf. A new wave of Palestinian exiles, this time expelled from Kuwait as sympathizers with Saddam Hussein and his invasion, had descended on Jordan. King Hussein had renounced Jordanian responsibility for the West Bank, leaving to the now indigent PLO the task of paying the salaries of teachers and civil servants. Arafat's efforts seemed to have failed, and he himself to have become a dead weight on the Palestinian cause.

An actual election would not have been an easy task for the Palestinians. I thought it possible to take a census of Palestinians in exile to form a voters' list. For the resident population in the occupied territories, no election could be free under occupation control, but it seemed it might be possible under international supervision, which could conceivably be available if the PLO were to demand it. The Israelis, we were sure, would not allow Jerusalem Palestinians to vote, so for them, the elected assembly would have to appoint representatives.

By the time of my suggestion, however, midsummer 1990, US Secretary of State James Baker III had already begun herding all the recalcitrant parties to the Middle Eastern conflict towards the Madrid Conference which would finally open on October 30, something that White House chief of staff John Sununu had told me to expect in phone conversations even before the conclusion of the Gulf War. The PLO would, on the face of it, be excluded from the conference by Israeli demand. Baker, however, made his arrangements with Faisal Husseini, the leading Palestinian resident leader in Jerusalem, and saw to it that the PLO approved all members of the ostensibly non-PLO Palestinian delegation.

CONTACTS WITH SHAMIR

My contacts, for some time, had been more with Palestinians than with Israelis. A Boston rabbi friend, however, Roland Gittelsohn, encouraged me during 1990 to open a correspondence with Prime Minister Yitzhak Shamir. I had been in indirect contact, through his assistant Uri Savir, with Shimon Peres during his time as prime minister, but had not previously attempted to contact Shamir. The occasion came after an incident on October 8, when Palestinians on the platform of the Al-Aqsa Mosque in Jerusalem, Noble Sanctuary to the Muslims and Temple Mount to the Jews, threw stones down on the heads of Jewish worshippers praying at the Western Wall.[8] The Israelis responded by dispatching soldiers to the platform. In an ensuing skirmish, the soldiers fired and killed several Palestinian civilians.

I wrote to Shamir on October 13, 1990. I had seen contradictory accounts of who was to blame, both sides pointing fingers at each other, and told Shamir that my concern was not with that, but rather with the poisoned relations between the two peoples, both so ready to believe the worst of each other, to the grave endangerment of both sides. Assuming he accepted that the two peoples would always have to live side by side, I saw that as no way to live, with such hatreds polluting their life of the spirit and such traps lurking at every step.

Recognizing that the safety of Israel was his first concern, I argued that the country's safety could not be based on military defense alone. If anyone were to tell him that Israel should relax its military stance and rely instead only on winning the friendship of its neighbors, he would know enough to throw him out of his office. He should be equally ready to rebuff anyone who argued that Israel could rely only on making itself a fortress in defiance of its neighbors. The military superiority Israel had, with its small population, over anything that all the Arabs together could bring against them was a transitory situation, which could not last for any length of time of real significance in the life of a people. Without seeking reconciliation with the neighbors Israel's state and society could not long survive. With that friendship, Israel's military needs would look much different. I recognized how Shamir himself had dedicated his life to the building and safety of Israel. I did not expect he would want, as his legacy, to see its destruction.

I told him how I had learned, years before, from Simha Dinitz,[9] the three essential interests of Israeli society: that it be Jewish, democratic, and safe. I had ever since believed that there was a fourth equally essential interest for Israel: that it should have an open border. This was a perspective that I had already been pressing on Arafat for some years by then. I felt that it had not rooted itself in Israeli minds simply because Israeli thinkers and the Israeli public had never really envisioned what it would mean to have the land partitioned between themselves and the Palestinians.

Jews, especially religious Jews, love to call the West Bank territories Judea and Samaria. There, rather than in Tel Aviv or on the coastal plains, lay the ancient biblical kingdoms of Israel and Judea, the sacred locations of Jerusalem, Hebron, and Shechem. I have always found it important for Palestinians to recognize the importance for Jews that some of them be able to live in these places, and for Jews to recognize that these are the Palestinian territories that they cannot have for their own. I have urged that Palestinians accept the presence of some Jews among them, as in fact they did before the present conflict began.

Hebron stands as a test case for Palestinian welcome to such Jewish residents. The trouble is that the wrong Jews are there. The settlers who forced their way, against even Israeli law, into Hebron soon after the 1967 war, and the thousands who have followed them since to the neighboring settlement of Kiryat Arba, came to force the Palestinians out. The Israeli government has as much responsibility to remove these violent extremists from the area as the Palestinians have to curb their own variety of terrorism; more, in fact, since Israel is required as the occupying power to protect the civilian population it controls, under the Fourth Geneva Convention.[10] That some Jews should be able to live, and worship if they are so inclined, in Hebron and elsewhere in the West Bank, while not in any way required by law, is a condition for the peace. But this can only happen by Palestinian agreement. Israelis cannot legally take it as their own.[11]

I had long advocated, and now repeated to Shamir (as a solution) that some number of Jews (agreed by the Palestinians) be permitted to live in these Palestinian places. There should be no return to the situation of 1948–67, when Jews were unable to go to or live on that land. I suggested they should have a choice of citizenship, Israeli or Palestinian—one or other and not a dual citizenship. If they chose Israeli citizenship, as seems more likely, they should be free to vote in Israeli elections, but should live under Palestinian law and protection.

This arrangement needed to be reciprocal. Equal numbers of Palestinians should be free to return to their ancestral homes in Haifa or Jaffa or elsewhere in Israel, and on the same conditions: a choice of one or other citizenship, not both, but to live under Israeli law. The likelihood is that they would choose Israeli citizenship, since it carries advantages, as the Israeli Arabs understand.

Numbers, I wrote, should be agreed, on the principle that neither side threatens the demography of the other's territory. The probability is that no more than 100,000 Jewish settlers would agree to remain in the Palestinian territories under such conditions. Those who did would be the ones ready to live at peace with Palestinians.

The border, in these circumstances, could be made open. Each people would have a state with internationally recognized borders, with its own law and all the institutions of a society, yet each person, able to move freely across the whole territory, would have access to the whole.

Given the urgency for Israel of making serious peace proposals, I argued to Shamir that the wartime period constituted an ideal opportunity. People had taken it for granted that Israel had gained license to do anything it pleased about Palestinians once Iraq invaded Kuwait, but actually the war gave Israel the opportunity to initiate serious efforts for peace while the pressure was off. Soviet, British, and US governmental voices were already telling us that they would take up this question at the conclusion of the Iraqi war, and Israel would then deal from a weaker hand.

For this, however, Shamir would have to break through the greatest single obstacle to any peace initiative, which was Israel's refusal to deal with the PLO or its chairman, Yasser Arafat. I recounted to him my own experience of Arafat as the one who had prepared his people for peace with Israel, and the respect I had gained for him. All the time that Israeli governments, both Labor and Likud, had claimed they would find nicer Palestinians to deal with had been illusion. Nothing could be clearer than that this is the leadership that the Palestinians insist on, and that the search for others was a search for quislings. No one who did not genuinely represent the Palestinians could make peace with Israel.

This letter opened up a new channel of communication. Shamir had Justus Weiner, director of the Department of American Law and External Relations in the Justice Ministry, who was active in the ministry's Human Rights Department, respond on his behalf. He enclosed the Zamir Commission report on the investigation of the Temple Mount incident, and invited me to discuss the subject when I was in Jerusalem.

The invitation was warm enough so that John Sununu, then White House chief of staff,[12] took up the cause and advocated that my meeting should be with Shamir himself and not with Weiner only. It was arranged that this should occur early in March of 1991. Feeling that, as a Christian and a Jesuit, I should not approach Shamir alone without some serious Jewish company, I asked Rabbi Roland Gittlesohn, who had first suggested my writing to Shamir, to come with me. His health had failed so much by that time that he could not do it, so I turned instead to another old friend, Dr. Richard (Red) Schwarz, a law professor at

Syracuse University who, over several years, had organized one of the most significant American Jewish–Arab dialogues in the United States.

After much telephoning from the White House, our intended departure day, when it arrived, coincided with the heaviest of the bombing campaign over Iraq. Airlines were canceling flights over the whole region. After a full morning spent seeking passage on one line after another I found the trip had become impossible at that time and notified Red Schwarz, John Sununu, and Justus Weiner that it would have to be postponed.

We had every intention of making the trip to see Shamir as soon as the war situation had settled more, but the Baker shuttle diplomacy, beginning promptly after the war, occupied the stage fully. It seemed much better to continue writing letters than to intrude personally at this stage. I conferred with chief of staff Sununu on this, and he agreed. In a subsequent letter to Shamir I developed further on the stake Israel had in negotiating a solid peace, on the open border theme, and on the necessity of recognizing the leadership the Palestinians so clearly regarded as their own. Shamir's responses continued to come through Justus Weiner, and from this point on I began receiving a constant stream of papers arguing every point of Israeli policy.

THE MADRID CONFERENCE

Secretary of State James Baker had truly corralled the various parties (after the upheavals of the Gulf War had so recast all their situations and interests) into readiness to take part in what would become, late in October, the Madrid Conference.[13] Yitzhak Shamir paid it sufficient respect to show up for the opening session at the Royal Palace in Madrid. After that, in the opinion of most of the observers I talked with, he treated it as a holding action, seeing to it that the conference would not produce results he would not want to live with. Madrid would not serve as the meeting place for subsequent sessions. After much hauling and shoving over whether the location would be within an Israeli or an Arab orbit, the parties agreed to meet in Washington on the State Department's premises.

The arrangements Shamir demanded, as the price of Israeli participation, were staggering in their complexity.[14] To begin with, he would not accept the comprehensive negotiation all the Arabs wanted, with Israelis confronting a united delegation of all the Arab countries with which they had been at war since 1948. Shamir would agree only to bilateral negotiations, Israel dealing with one Arab country at a time. That meant separate negotiating sessions with Syria, Jordan, and Lebanon, and separate Israeli negotiating teams to deal with each of them. Coordination, for

Israel, of this complex system fell to Michael Shiloh, my old friend from when he was consul general in Boston in the mid-1980s, now number two in the Washington embassy.

The negotiations were made more labyrinthine still by Shamir's insistence that there be no independent Palestinian delegation. Instead, some Palestinians could be members of the Jordanian delegation. None could come from the Jerusalem municipality, none from the diaspora. None could come as a professed member or representative of the PLO.

Such rules, of course, were made to be defied. On arrival in Washington, the Palestinians refused to enter the room designated, at the State Department, for the Jordanian delegation's meetings with one of the Israelis' separate negotiating teams. Instead they sat many days in the corridor outside until the Israelis finally agreed to meet them in a room of their own, not as another delegation but as a distinct part of the Jordanian delegation.

Secretary of State Baker had obtained written agreement, during the preparations for the conference, that the PLO should have a recognized headquarters in Jerusalem—Orient House—under the leadership of Faisal Husseini. The Palestinians in turn made Faisal head of their delegation, despite his being from Jerusalem. They then made a distinction between a negotiating team and a consultative team within the Palestinian delegation. The negotiators—among them Saeb Erekat, who defiantly wore his PLO scarf to all the meetings—came from the West Bank and Gaza but not from Jerusalem. The consultative team included Hanan Ashrawi, already well known from her many television appearances over the years, who became spokesperson for the delegation. They came from Jerusalem or from the diaspora. The Jordanians, who had given Jordanian citizenship to all Palestinian refugees within their country, made Professor Walid Khalidi, the most distinguished Palestinian refugee academic in the United States, head of their delegation. Faisal Husseini, officially head of the Palestinian delegation but not allowed into the room with the Israelis because of his Jerusalem address, stayed home and led the deliberations of his delegation over the phone from Jerusalem, while the distinguished and elderly peace activist, Dr. Haidar Abdel Shafi of Gaza, one of the founders of the PLO, led the negotiating team. Secretary Baker arranged, meanwhile, that the US embassy in Egypt would grant a visa, for each session, to Nabil Sha'ath, Arafat's trusted confidant, to come to Washington and constitute a liaison between the Palestinian team and PLO headquarters in Tunis.

Because of the unwieldiness of this system, a distinct set of multilateral negotiations, which involved all the Middle Eastern countries, together with other countries sponsoring the entire Madrid Conference, dealt with a number of broader questions, ranging from allocation of regional water resources to refugees. The multilateral negotiation on refugees, for instance, when it first met in Moscow in 1991, elected Canada to chair their activities. Canadian embassies and the Canadian foreign ministry, as a result, have become the best resources for finding what is happening about Palestinian refugees.

Despite these problems, some euphoria attended this opening of real negotiation. As happens consistently when the Israeli public sees some real hope for peace, they turned to those they thought could best accomplish what they hoped for. By the latter part of 1992 the Labor Party won an Israeli general election, bringing Yitzhak Rabin to the office of prime minister with a commitment to make the peace. My own first contact with him, in a rather abrasive letter of January 27, 1993, came when he lost his temper over Hamas provocations and had more than 400 of their activists arrested and dumped over the Lebanese border. This tactic, altogether prohibited in international law, had worked for previous governments, though never for so large a number of deportees. Lebanon refused to receive them, and for many months they were perched in a miserable camp in the no man's land at the Israeli–Lebanese border, entertaining the international press to their great propaganda advantage.

Rabin's election had so pleased me that I expected to have written a far friendlier first letter to him. Instead I had taken him to task for a blunder and for an action of weakness in the face of his right wing. Before concluding I told him how sorry I was for the censorious tone. He would have on record, I said, the many letters I had been writing both to Shamir and to Arafat. Shamir had not responded in person, but always had someone respond for him in terms that took cognizance of the concerns I raised. I had always admired the fact that he was that open to strenuous criticism, and felt that he, like Mr Arafat too when he received my letters, must have had to sit down and pour himself a good stiff drink before embarking on one of them.

This letter received, very promptly, a friendly response written, on Rabin's behalf, on February 14 by his personal bureau chief, Eitan Haber, who picked up each of the themes of my letter in turn. The contact previously made with Shamir had held, and would lead to regular correspondence thereafter.

CONTACTS WITH PRESIDENT CLINTON

The new US President, Bill Clinton, began his term telling everyone that he would give his attention almost entirely to domestic policy: "It's the economy, stupid!" We heard rumors that his assistants found it hard, in his first two years, to hold his attention on foreign policy issues.[15] Nevertheless, he intervened, as the first foreign policy task of his administration, in the matter of these Palestinian deportees and sent his Secretary of State Warren Christopher to the Middle East to try to remedy the matter. Consequently I wrote to him, on February 22, 1993, congratulating him on this, giving an account of my dealings with Arafat and Shamir, enclosing a copy of the letter I had sent Rabin and giving him a full 13 pages of analysis of the situation. As I had always done in writing to President Bush, I enclosed that with a covering letter to the new White House chief of staff, Thomas "Mac" McLarty. Just as with the previous chief of staff John Sununu, I had an immediate response from McLarty assuring me that the letters had been seen. This would become a pattern for future correspondence.

There were two other matters taken up in that letter to Clinton. Early in December, 1992, before the deportation crisis a delegation of us from Ronald Young's US Interreligious Committee for Peace in the Middle East had made one of our regular visits to the Middle Eastern countries. We had been visiting together, as a Jewish–Christian–Muslim group, all the several national delegations to the Madrid Conference during their meetings in Washington. We had become regular visitors to Dan Kurtzer,[16] one of the several officials held over from the Bush administration into Clinton's, at the State Department. We had raised with him the question of resuming US dialogue with the PLO. We knew that the new Rabin government in Israel would find it hard, a political embarrassment, to initiate dialogue itself with the PLO. Resumption of the US/PLO dialogue would make it easier. Kurtzer had answered delphically that the PLO knew quite well what it had to do to restore its dialogue with the United States. That, of course, as a way of not giving such information to the PLO, had rung all sorts of bells with me, and I went along quickly to New York to report it to PLO-UN observer Nasser al-Kidwa and ask if it were that clear to the PLO how they could restore the dialogue. As expected, he found it rather a puzzle.

In Jerusalem we met Yossi Beilin, deputy to Foreign Minister Shimon Peres and clearly the strongest peace advocate in the new government. One of our Muslim members, Dr. Mian Ashraf of Boston,[17] asked why Israel did not now have direct contact with the PLO, given the strong sentiment for it in the Meretz Party and even among many Labor MKs. Beilin answered that the ground rules of the negotiations had not been set up by the Rabin government but by its predecessor; that all the Arabs, including the Palestinians, had agreed to them; that the system was in fact working, so please do not ask the Rabin government to change it. But Beilin did not stop there. He went on to say that the negotiations, an absolute necessity for Israel, required for their success an active mediating role from the United States. Without that, they would fail and the result would be another war. We had noted the letter that the Israeli ambassador to the UN, Gad Yaacobi, had published in the *New York Times* November 27, 1992, just before we left on our trip, pleading for that strong US mediator role, in very much the same terms of a threat of failure and even war if it did not happen. We took Beilin's statement as a serious signal, asking that the United States set the precedent, and I conveyed it in that letter to Clinton.

There was yet another matter. While we were in Egypt, we had been received at the Arab League headquarters by their secretary general, Dr. Ahmed Abdel-Meguid, the first time that a partially Jewish delegation had been welcomed there. Rabbi Joseph Ehrenkranz of our delegation had, some years earlier, invited Abdel-Meguid, then Egyptian ambassador to the UN, to address his Connecticut synagogue. Joe Ehrenkranz asked whether the Arab League, as a confidence-building gesture, would lift its boycott of Israel. Abdel-Meguid told us that Egyptian President Hosni Mubarak had already offered, following a suggestion from the United States, a lifting of the boycott in exchange for an end to Israel's settlement policy in the West Bank and Gaza. This had happened when Shamir was still prime minister, and the Egyptians had received not even the courtesy of a reply.

I picked up Joe's request, speaking to Abdel-Meguid as we were leaving the building, and suggested that, as the new Rabin government began to make at least partial steps to end the settlement policy, the Arab League take comparable partial steps to end the boycott, specifically that a first step could be to terminate the inclusion of non-Israeli Jewish firms in the boycott, or the inclusion of non-Jewish firms that did business with Israel. I promised Abdel-Meguid a full letter spelling out this proposal and sent it to him on January 27. I sent a copy, as well, to Robert Pelletreau, whom we had met in Cairo, now as US ambassador to Egypt.[18]

My letter to Abdel-Meguid drew a detailed and cordial response, of February 15, 1993, not conceding the partial steps I had asked, but setting the terms on which it would become interesting. My letter and Abdel-Meguid's response, too, were included in what had become a very bulky package of correspondence for Clinton.

TO THE WHITE HOUSE LAWN

My dealings with the Middle East problem, through this period, were substantially in the context of the Interreligious Committee. None of us knew anything of the clandestine meetings in Oslo, the back channel between Israel and representatives of the PLO.

It had been initiated first by Terje Roed-Larsen, then director general of a Norwegian think tank, FAFO, the Norwegian Institute for Applied Social Research, which was studying conditions in the Israeli-occupied territories. Larsen spoke to Yossi Beilin of the possibilities of a secret back channel during a fairly obscure academic conference in Tel Aviv in April 1992, several months before the election that brought Yitzhak Rabin and the Labor Party to victory and Beilin to the post of deputy foreign minister under Shimon Peres.

Beilin interested two Israeli academics in the project, Yair Hirschfeld of Haifa University and Ron Pundak of Tel Aviv University. After an initial period in which only the academics met, they and Shimon Peres' political assistant Uri Savir were meeting, on comfortable out-of-the-way country estates in Norway, with Abu Ala and other ranking Palestinians, aided by Norwegian diplomat Jan Egeland and the gifted Norwegian foreign minister, Johan Jorgen Holst, whose wife, Marianne Heiberg, had written the FAFO report that was the initial kernel of this process.

Yossi Beilin brought the result of their meetings to Shimon Peres, who then won Prime Minister Rabin's approval for it, astounding us all with the August 1993 announcement that a formal agreement was in the immediate offing. This was the Declaration of Principles on which, it was promised, a five-year program of negotiations would be based.[19]

Several of us of the Interreligious Committee attended the signing on the White House lawn, a new dawn, as it seemed, in the long saga of bloody conflict between Israel and the Palestinians. That the signing should happen on his lawn was a free present for President Clinton, who had had no involvement in the process. Sam Shapiro, a good friend of mine from Boston who sat beside me at the ceremony, pointed out how there were at least 300 cameras from the Israeli Right trained on Rabin, ready to report, to his damnation, if he should make any physical gesture of acceptance toward Arafat. We had all been instructed to sit in absolute silence in our seats, but when President Clinton drew the clearly reluctant Rabin to the famous handshake with Arafat, the entire assembly leaped to its feet with such a roar as you would hear at a vital goal in a football stadium.

Israelis and Palestinians alike caviled at the Oslo Declaration of Principles. It specified astonishingly little of what a settlement of the conflict would be. Almost everything was tentative. It did lift the taboo on many topics, such as Jerusalem, refugees, and the real prospect of a Palestinian state, yet without determining any outcomes. But as their real accomplishment these two peoples, Israelis and Palestinians, recognized for the first time, solemnly and publicly, what they had been unable to recognize for all the years since 1948, one another's legitimacy as peoples with definable rights. That, it seemed, was something that could never be withdrawn.

The Madrid Conference had proven unsuccessful, other than as the route that led to Oslo. The Israelis had had to learn that no one other than the PLO could deliver the peace they sought in the Washington sessions. The actual form of the Israeli recognition of the Palestinians in the Oslo protocol was to acknowledge that they were a people led, by choice and legitimately, by the PLO.

3
Disappointments and postponements, 1993–95

The euphoria that greeted the Oslo development would give way gradually to deep disillusionment as delays, preemptive efforts to prejudice the outcome of the talks, and violent episodes disrupted the heady expectations generated by the Rabin–Arafat handshake on the White House lawn. Among those most alienated were the Palestinians who had made up the delegations to the Madrid Conference. They bitterly resented the fact that they had been left uninformed of this entire back channel negotiation. Henceforth they regarded themselves as outsiders.

EARLY RESPONSES TO OSLO

I wrote to President Arafat quickly, on September 20, 1993, congratulating him on the Oslo accomplishment and analyzing where opposition could arise now to frustrate it.

I saw this opposition as being of two kinds. First came the rejectionists, conspicuous and threatening violence. It did not matter much whether they gave a religious rationale like Hamas and Islamic Jihad or a secular one, as did several of the long entrenched terrorist movements. The Oslo development had reduced their appeal to the public dramatically, but they would surely regain their popularity if Palestinians, particularly in the desperate poverty of Gaza, did not experience concrete and visible economic development. Their objection was symmetrical to that of the Israeli rejectionists, likewise a mix of religious zealots and secular extremists like Ariel Sharon,[1] Rafael Eitan,[2] Rehavam Ze'evi,[3] and their parties, who understood well how they could always profit from Palestinian terrorism as a way to keep Israeli anxieties alive, and knew how to play it up. And yet, with the promises of financial assistance from the countries that had sponsored the agreement, I thought much of Gaza could be put to work promptly in construction, building houses and schools and restoring the basic services that had been ruined during the *intifada*. That, I wrote, would considerably reduce the threat of new terrorism.

The second potential source of opposition, already visible during the Madrid negotiations of the previous two years, came from within the PLO and was more serious, though its meaning was less obvious. The negotiating team had been unhappy, Abdel Shafi believing for some time that the Washington negotiations were going nowhere and should be cut off. Team members such as Saeb Erekat, Faisal Husseini, and Hanan Ashrawi threatened to resign because they felt they had not been informed or consulted, but simply bypassed by the Oslo negotiators. I understood Arafat's need for secrecy on this back channel, as too many people—Israelis, Palestinians, US officials—were prepared and able to stifle any sign of real progress, had they known of it.

But behind this experience was a more widespread popular distress. The Western media were claiming already that the style of government and negotiation in the PLO were too centralized and non-participatory, though I noted, in my letter, that people held to Arafat's leadership, valuing it even when their complaints were loudest. They wanted their distress addressed, but by Arafat himself.

Democracy had high priority in the aspirations of Palestinians, but Arafat's experience of all his years leading a resistance movement from exile had not prepared him for the role of administrator of an open society. He tended to rely mainly on those who had returned with him from exile, leaving small room for popular expression or for those in the resident population who actually had most to offer for the development of an open Palestinian society: the skilled intellectual class and the activist young generation who had been the backbone of the *intifada*.

The *intifada* by now had come to an end, effectively since the beginning of the Madrid Conference in 1991. The Israelis, dreading the *intifada* and knowing its power, even wanted an official declaration at this point that it was over. The invigorating experience that Palestinians had had, of being the protagonists, setting the agenda, I wrote to Arafat, was now a thing of the past. Since then they had again become people to whom things happened through the actions of others rather than themselves. Ever since the beginning of the Rabin government, for all the renewed hope that had grown with his victory, people felt that everything was actually getting worse. More of their children were being killed, more arrested and abused, more houses destroyed. Opportunities had vanished with the closing of the territories and their separation from Jerusalem itself. The number of Israeli settlements and the confiscation of land had actually increased despite apparent promises. Palestinians found themselves with no way of responding except the Hamas and rejectionist way, by violence. People felt impotent now after their experience of the *intifada*. Arafat took the whole burden of negotiating their future on himself and that left his people with no part in what was happening to them.

Thus began, in this September 20 letter, what became the central theme of my writings to Arafat over the Oslo years: that he needed the mobilized strength of his people if he or they were to succeed in making the peace. If they were not to be disappointed and disillusioned in the wake of Oslo, people must again have the experience of being real participants, deciders of what should happen and not simply people to whom things are done.

In the areas that came under Palestinian autonomy—Jericho, Gaza, and other West Bank territories as they would be brought within the Palestinian system—the active experience would be that of building the institutions of a society. That need involve no abrasiveness toward Israeli society, and in fact would be one of the things that reassured Israelis that the Palestinians were people they could live with.

Part of what the autonomy regime would have to do—absolutely necessary if the Israeli public were not to feel it had been deceived, and be tempted to renounce the agreement—was to show Palestinian readiness and ability to build a society compatible with and able to cooperate with Israeli society, to show that they were not enemies. The danger that Palestinians would need to guard against, I wrote to Arafat, was that they should leave Israelis altogether in charge, believing that they could only accept what the Israelis gave them. That impression would destroy their sense of being masters of their own lives, exercising self-determination. It ought never be allowed to happen.

The great virtues of the *intifada* had been, first, its non-violence, and second, it clearly being a protest against occupation, and not against Israel. Where it had been weak was when it had used even limited violence—the stones that were an alternative to guns or knives. Palestinians judged, at the time it began, that the stones, as an outlet, were a necessary form of expression. It was their understanding that the stone meant the restriction of violence, not its propagation. The *intifada* was weakened, further, whenever it let itself be misunderstood as an expression of hatred for Israelis, rejection of them and their state, because then it lost the moral ascendancy that was its central strength, the reason Israel could not defeat it. There was no excuse, I wrote, or need for any level of violence now, after the accomplishment of Oslo, and every care should be taken, both by the exclusion of violence and the close guard against anything that could smell of a rejection of Israel and its society, not to lose or risk that moral ascendancy.

About a year before the *intifada* an extraordinary Palestinian–American student of Gandhi's non-violence strategy, Moubarac Awad, had returned to Jerusalem to train people in these techniques. Awad represented what had become a fully developed professional discipline, having studied in Gene Sharp's school of Gandhian practice at Harvard University.[4] The Israelis had feared his work so much that they deported him even before the *intifada* had begun, and it was never clear to me how far Awad's teaching had influenced the *intifada* itself. It was my sense that Arafat had never been comfortable with Awad as a person. Yet I strongly recommended that he have someone, whether Moubarac Awad or another, though certainly a Palestinian, on his immediate staff to plan and organize such expressions of non-violent insistence on self-determination. This should not be just someone who had read a few things about it but someone professionally trained.

This was one of my letters that received the most positive response in a personal letter from Arafat himself. Dated November 24, 1993, the letter was full of warm terms of "great appreciation" for a "valuable letter," and said he "read with great interest [my] views and pieces of advice." Arafat went on to speak of the need for Israeli implementation of agreements and the need for the international community, especially the United States, to provide the assistance needed to make the agreement succeed.

LETTER TO RABIN

Meanwhile I wrote, on November 13, to Prime Minister Rabin. Congratulating him on the Oslo agreement, I told him he had joined a very select company of Israelis. There were only two other members of his club: Chaim Weizmann and David Ben-Gurion. His action, in reaching this accord, equaled in courage and in long-reaching consequence the accomplishments of those founding fathers of the State of Israel. I was convinced that he had secured the lasting future of the nation they first built. It was evident, even in watching the interaction between himself and Arafat there on the lawn, including the famous handshake, with how much difficulty and anguish he had come to that moment. He had overcome all that for the good of Israel. It was a crowning event in the search for peace that would always live in history.

That much said, I took up what I saw as the greatest single danger to Israel's prospect of peace, the "ticking bomb," as I called it, that could, more readily than any other, blow up the whole effort, namely the situation of the Israeli troops in southern Lebanon, the occupied area Israel described as its "security zone." Many of my friends had disagreed with my assessment of this, and their opinions were the reason it had taken me two months to write to Rabin after Oslo.

Rabin, I wrote, must have seen the dangers that lurked in Lebanon during his misadventure of the previous year, when he had tried to exile the more than 400 troublesome Palestinians there. I regarded that occupation of southern Lebanon as the readiest weapon for those who would oppose the peace. I believed Rabin could deprive them of it by withdrawing his troops.

Any agreement on southern Lebanon, I wrote, would really be made with Syria, whatever formal deference were paid to the Lebanese government. It was on this account that my friends tended to disagree with my assessment. They thought the Syrians would not agree to any easing of that situation but would hold it as a threat over Israel. I had hopes that the threat might be removed. I had not believed, for some years, that the Israeli occupation of this "security zone" was truly a defense of Israel, or a source of security for Galilee, but saw it rather as a liability for Israel.

Israel had thought of it first as security against Palestinian guerrilla attack from the bases they called "Fatahland." The PLO had now no interest in mounting attacks from there, and the Syrians, as the effective power in Lebanon, had every reason to restrain any attacks from there by the Palestinian rejectionist factions.

Hezbollah, the radical Shi'ite party and militia which was the real power in the area, had doubtless strong sympathy links with the Palestinian Hamas/Islamic Jihad opposition to everything about Israel. It had even come into existence, as rival to the more progressive Amal movement,[5] because of Israeli behavior in Lebanon since the 1982 invasion. Hezbollah, however, had never claimed a rationale or justification for raids across the border into Israel. Occasions when they had fired their Katyusha rockets into northern Galilee, as in the previous summer, had always been reprisal for attacks on their villages by the Israeli occupiers. Those attacks themselves had also been reprisal, for Hezbollah attacks on Israel's occupying troops in Lebanon.

The Syrians, since asserting their full control of Lebanon in 1990, had suppressed all the private militias that had been the cancer of the Lebanese state during the years of civil war, preventing government's effective control over the districts they ruled. The one exception was Hezbollah. Neither Syria nor anyone in Lebanon, government or representatives of the factions, could argue for the disarming of Hezbollah so long as Hezbollah could present itself basically as defenders of the independence and territorial integrity of Lebanon (Arab land) against foreign (Israeli) occupation. While Israelis saw attacks on their troops as terrorism, the Lebanese or Syrian public saw it as justified resistance to an illegal occupation.[6]

This argument for Israeli withdrawal from southern Lebanon was to become a regular theme of my correspondence with Rabin over the next two years. I would write several times to Syrian President Hafez al-Assad as well. I understood the Syrian reluctance to agree on any partial steps short of a comprehensive peace settlement with Israel, but believed it could still be in Syria's interest to restrain, by agreement, attacks by Hezbollah or the Palestinian rejectionists across the Lebanese–Israeli border if Israel would remove its occupation.

With the prospects of peace initiated by Oslo, there was now a much more concrete reason for rejectionist forces to try to subvert such hopes. That applied equally to the secular rejectionists based in Damascus or Baghdad and to the resident Hamas/Islamic Jihad who had such easy access to Lebanon's Hezbollah. I could see no easier place for them to stage wrecking actions to destroy the peace. And so long as Syria and its Lebanese surrogates were inhibited from disarming and checking Hezbollah by the very fact of continued Israeli occupation, there was no feasible way for Syria itself to police the secular Palestinian rejectionists, to expel their leadership from Damascus, or to prevent their plots against Israel from Lebanese soil. Israeli forces, far from controlling dangers from southern Lebanon, had become hostages there to radical rejectionist forces and their hold on Syrian policy.

Israel, to have peace with Syria, would eventually have to return the captured Golan Heights. I had much sympathy for the view imputed to Rabin, most likely correctly, by US government spokespeople, that it would overburden Israeli public opinion to ask people at that juncture, before they had seen it proven in their own terms that the agreement with the PLO could be trusted, to accept the return of the Golan to Syria, in return for whatever terms the Syrians might offer. At the same time, it seemed to me most dangerous that Israel should be telling the Syrians, just as they were so aggrieved with the PLO for having made an agreement with Israel without consulting them, to sit about in the waiting room until the Israelis got around to paying some heed to them. Sooner or later, that was bound to make Syria an active opponent of the agreement.

This letter drew an even more welcoming response from Rabin's bureau chief, Eitan Haber,[7] than my earlier one about the 400 exiles. Haber assured me that my thoughts about dealing with Syria over the occupation of Lebanon had been noted.

The Oslo agreement had provided that two limited territories, Gaza and Jericho, should come under a degree of Palestinian jurisdiction right away. The Jericho enclave had such tight limits that Arafat, when he made his return to Palestine after all the years of exile, chose Gaza as his place of residence and administrative center. Soon the evidence of security agreements between the Israeli army and new Palestinian police forces could be seen in joint patrols of Israelis and Palestinians, their vehicles riding together in convoy, to maintain order in the Palestinian territories.

TERRORIST ASSAULT AT HEBRON

Both Rabin and Arafat had recognized, at the time of the White House lawn signing, that rejectionist elements of both sides would mount terrorist attacks to overturn the efforts at negotiation. They had both sworn that such tactics would not deter them. The Palestinians, wanting to avoid anything like civil war, had aimed at dealing with the political arm of Hamas, hoping to isolate it from the military wing. Hamas, not wanting to be seen as enemy to the PLO or spoiler of the popular peace process, cooperated to the extent of abstaining from new violent attacks.

Cataclysm came instead from the Israeli side in the form of the first massive resort to terrorism against the Oslo opening. Physician Baruch Goldstein, of the Kiryat Arba settlement outside Hebron, donned his military vestments on the morning of February 25, 1994, took up his ouzi, entered the Hebron Tomb of Abraham and the Patriarchs, known to Arabs as the Ibrahimi Mosque, opened fire and murdered 29 people at their prayers, wounding some 75 more, before being overcome and killed himself.[8] The response of the Israeli Army was mainly to suppress Palestinian protest at the carnage, and in that process they killed some 19 more Palestinians in the streets.

There was no demolition of Baruch Goldstein's home as there would have been for a Palestinian killer. Instead his gun was sent to his widow as a memento, and the Qiryat Arba residents were allowed to set up a large and conspicuous monument to commemorate him and his monstrous deeds as heroic.

Both communities, Jewish and Arab, were shocked by this wanton slaughter, but it was Arafat who, in his angry response, broke the pledge both leaders had made, that they would not be deterred from the work of negotiation by terrorist attack. For six weeks he suspended negotiations with the Israelis, setting a precedent that Israeli opponents of the negotiations would later follow with glee.

I wrote to Arafat again on March 7, beginning with compliments for his having contained much of the rage among Palestinians over the Hebron massacre, and quoting to him what Robert Pelletreau had said to our Interreligious Committee group, when we had met him in Cairo on yet another trip around the Middle East. Steps to the implementation of the Oslo Declaration of Principles that were supposed to have begun on December 13 had already been delayed, to the disgust of the Palestinians.

Pelletreau spoke of how delay would cause erosion of confidence, but that when the implementation actually got under way it would gain strength again. Setbacks like the Hebron killings ought not be allowed to cause more delay. It was up to both Arafat and Rabin to control their own fanatics, extremists, and simple criminals. Both Palestinian and Israeli authorities now had so much need for one another that neither must undermine the other's credibility with their own public.

On the very day I was writing, March 7, the newspapers had reported that seven of the 15 members of the Israeli cabinet had called for removing the entire Jewish settlement of some 400 from Hebron. I had long advocated the acceptance of some Jewish residents in the Palestinian territories, with Hebron as test case, and that comparable numbers of Palestinians should be allowed to return, reciprocally, to Green-Line Israel. I argued now that rather than expelling all the Jews from Hebron, Rabin should set and enforce rigorous standards of behavior, not only for them but also for the much larger number in the neighboring Kiryat Arba settlement, standards by which the violent elements among them could be forced out, leaving it possible for those Jews who were willing to live there at peace with their neighbors to remain.

By the end of the letter I returned to the theme I had already raised with Arafat before, of how necessary it was that the resident Palestinian population in these territories have a real participatory role in what happened to them, such as they had experienced earlier during the *intifada*. This was becoming more and more acute as Arafat, thrust now into the unfamiliar role of administering a civil authority (hardly yet a government), showed himself little adapted for it.

My respect for Arafat has always remained strong, based on what I had seen him do, leading his people toward liberation from their occupation while also preparing them to live at peace in a state that would coexist with Israel. As an accomplishment, that had vast importance. He had dedicated his life and all his great leadership skill to it, risking dangers from rejectionists who regarded that as a traitorous exercise and were ready to murder anyone who proposed it.

The black and white issues that had been his experience during all that time in exile, though, had not prepared him to deal with all the shades of gray that go with administering civil authority. The population over which he had only unsatisfactory shards of authority, the Palestinian "street," as we liked to call it, felt left out of the action.

Two groups had an immediate claim to position in the new administration. First were the young people, with their record of real heroism, who had been the *intifada*. They now felt left aside. Then, since Palestinians had always prized education as the one thing, short of their life, that could not be taken away from them, they had many skilled and competent experts in all the things that their deprived people needed most. These educated specialists also found themselves shut out of the planning and decision-making process, which was left to those who had worked with Arafat in his exile.

I had been many years teaching now, in a university setting, and had learned to recognize and treasure the gifts and commitment of the young people who surrounded me all the time. Writing to Arafat, on this and other occasions, I found myself urging always his attention to these young people around him. His whole population would be deprived and dispirited if they did not have the access to control of their own lives that they had experienced in the *intifada*. I wrote this consistently to Rabin as well, that he recognize and accept Arafat's and the Palestinians' need for such active participatory involvement. For Arafat even to count as a serious negotiating partner for Rabin and Israel in making the peace, he had to have some power. I saw no other available source of it than in the mobilized support of his people.

I wrote to Rabin also that same day, March 7, enclosing a copy of my long letter to Arafat, repeating my suggestion that, rather than removing all the Hebron settlers as much of his own cabinet had suggested, he should set rigorous standards of peaceful behavior for Jews in Hebron, in Kiryat Arba, and anywhere in the occupied territories. Solicitous as Israel was for the safety of its own citizens, his government had primary responsibility for the safety of Palestinians as well, and had to protect them against the rampages of the most intransigent of the settlers. Rabin, this time, responded in a personal letter,[9] recognizing particularly the need to forge on with negotiations despite such violent interruptions as the Hebron massacre, and for Israeli government to restore stability to Hebron, calm its residents, and agree to "the stationing of a temporary international presence in Hebron." Government, he said, "has banned two Jewish extremist groups advocating terror and violence. Through these steps, my Government and I want to make it clear: No form of terrorism and extremism retains legal standing in Israel."

As 1994 passed into 1995, these themes deepened in my writings to both Arafat and Rabin. From Palestinian intellectuals in the United States I heard the same complaints as from the population in the West Bank and Gaza, a growing dissatisfaction with what the Palestinian Authority could accomplish. Progress was slow in a frequently obstructed political process. Continued expansion of Israeli settlements presented an increasingly dangerous spectacle. Palestinians suffered continuing violations of their human rights and dignity at the hands of occupying forces: checkpoints, destruction of their homes, confiscations of their lands, searches, and humiliations. Economic improvement in their standard of living, in areas administered by the Palestinian Authority, failed to materialize.[10]

As these disappointments grew, both the religious rejectionism of Hamas and Islamic Jihad and the more secular appeal of the older and more secular rejectionist groups grew with it. This period still remained relatively free of overt terrorist action, but Israel kept urging Arafat, all the same, to curb Hamas and the other groups, to jail them all, and American opinion echoed this appeal. The same groups in Israel or the United States who complained about each Palestinian violation of human rights kept demanding altogether arbitrary suppression of any expression of opposition to Israeli decisions by Palestinian opposition groups. Even the expression of Palestinian impatience was regarded as terrorism or "incitement."

Arafat had small patience with dissent or criticism of the Palestinian Authority's performance. He held all things so tightly in his own control that any such criticism was essentially criticism of him. Several times he imprisoned critics, and all of us who had any voice with him had to object. Each time he would retreat from such arbitrary action, in some embarrassment. He could not control Palestinian behavior by police power alone. To lead, he had to be the liberator of Palestine, able to show accomplishment that, so far, was lacking. I remained convinced that he needed a mobilized public that understood such accomplishments as its own. Effectively the Palestinians needed a new *intifada*, but it could succeed only if it were rigorously non-violent; not even stones.

On April 5, 1995, I found myself writing to Arafat:

> A power disparity is at work here. The Oslo process does indeed leave all the essentials to be negotiated. The Israelis, supposing (as I do) that they signed in good faith, have all the same a near monopoly of power, and the temptation is always at hand for them to decide by power moves things that they have agreed formally to negotiate. There is no lack of experience, among them, in "creating facts," operating by *fait accompli* that is backed by the power of their occupying army. There is no genuine negotiation when the power disparity is so absolute. That means that it is not in the Israeli interest any more than it is in your Palestinian interest that it should be so. What the Israelis can be denied, by this power disparity, is peace, which can only be attained by a genuine negotiation.
>
> You have as yet no comparable power, such as would make you a serious negotiator. You have not sufficient support from the Arab

states, especially from the wealthier of them. You have, in your peace negotiation, no support that can be taken seriously from the Western powers, Europe, or the United States. The only available source of genuine power for your Palestinian cause will be in the mobilization of your people. And that mobilization is what I am asking for. It has not yet happened.

NEW AGREEMENT: OSLO 2

Significant progress in the Oslo process finally came in September 1995, with the signing in Washington of the interim agreement known as Oslo 2, a 400-page document that provided in great detail for the withdrawal of Israeli troops from further parts of the Palestinian territory beyond the original Gaza/Jericho enclaves.[11] The agreement described the West Bank in terms of three areas, plotting out the course by which more and more territory would be put in Palestinian hands. Area A, from its beginning, would embrace the principal Palestinian cities of the West Bank—Jenin, Tulqarem, Nablus, Qalqilya, Ramallah, and Bethlehem. Here the Palestinian National Council, as the Palestinian Authority was referred to in the agreement, would have full control, over administration and security. Hebron was treated as a special case because of the 450 Israeli settlers who had ensconced themselves in a number of tiny spots among the 130,000 Palestinian inhabitants. Israeli forces would remain in a large part of the city for their protection, but otherwise the Palestinian police would have overall responsibility for security. Only 2.7 percent of the actual territory of the West Bank was included in the Area A, but roughly a third of the Palestinian population (558,000 out of 1,561,000) lived there. The territory described as Area B, another 25.1 percent of the West Bank comprising a great number of Palestinian towns and villages, though for the time being without their attached lands, would have Palestinian administration but the Israeli army would continue to exercise security control. The bulk of the territory (72.2 percent), Area C, containing Israeli settlements with all their attached or claimed lands and all vacant land, remained entirely under Israeli control, but more territory was to be transferred to Palestinian control at six-month intervals.[12]

The agreement mandated the election, 22 days after the withdrawal of Israeli troops from Area A, of an 82-member Palestinian Council. All women prisoners, and all male prisoners who were sick, elderly, or young would be released at once, more on the eve of the election, and further releases would be discussed later. The Palestinians were to revoke, within two years, any articles of the Palestine National Covenant[13] that called for the destruction of Israel. Israel pledged to increase the Palestinian share of West Bank water and to join in a search for new natural resources. As certain sacred sites now came under Palestinian control, the agreement guaranteed access for Jews to Rachel's tomb in Bethlehem, the tomb of Joseph in Nablus, and the tomb of Abraham and the patriarchs in Hebron.

MURDER OF RABIN AND CAMPAIGN FOR HIS REPLACEMENT

Rabin's assassination on November 4, 1995, stunned us all with the realization of how determined the Israeli right wing was to foil the Oslo process and how much of what had been accomplished had depended on Rabin alone. A shocked Shimon Peres stepped immediately into the prime minister's office. Those of us committed to the Oslo process reassured ourselves that he would continue to advance it. I wrote to him at once, with a covering letter to Uri Savir, through whom I had dealt with the then Prime Minister Peres back in 1986. I took this as an interim letter, before it would become clear what Peres could accomplish in the aftermath of Rabin's death. I reviewed, of course, what I had kept writing to Rabin about Palestinian frustration and the need to disengage from Lebanon, but Peres' first business would be to get himself elected prime minister in his own right.

Peres and Rabin had long been rivals within the Labor Party. Had he called a snap election, Peres would doubtless have won overwhelmingly, but that would have been because of voters' anger about the assassination. Peres wanted no Rabin sympathy vote, and postponed the election, intending to wait until the expiration of the term in November 1996. He appeared, at the time of his accession, unassailable, and Binyamin Netanyahu, the Likud candidate whom many blamed for the constant inflammatory oratorical barrage he had waged against Rabin, accusing him of treason in following the Oslo process and appearing to incite violence against him, seemed an unlikely opponent to Peres. But between November and the election, which would actually come in May, things went badly wrong for Peres and Labor.

A new voting method would be used for the first time in this election. Instead of the winning party choosing a prime minister from among its elected members as in a normal cabinet system, the prime minister would be elected separately from the rest of the Knesset, in a vote between just two candidates, one from Labor and one from Likud. Israeli elections had led to increasingly fragmented Knessets, the ranks of the major parties shrinking each time in the face of a multitude of single-issue parties.[14] The intent of the new system was to consolidate the vote around the two major parties, but in fact it would have just the opposite effect. Having made their ideological choice between two tendencies in their vote for prime minister, voters would then feel free to split their choice even more radically among the minor parties, fragmenting the result still further.

THE DEATH OF YAHYA AYYASH

The head of Shin Bet, the Israeli internal security force, disgraced by having let Prime Minister Rabin be murdered on his watch, knew he had to resign. Wishing to depart on a note of triumph rather than failure, he found it in the killing of Yahya Ayyash, the "engineer" of Hamas, designer of their most sophisticated bombs. An explosive device was placed in a cell phone to blow Ayyash's head off when he answered a call. A helicopter overhead was able to detonate it after confirmation that the voice on the phone was that of Ayyash.[15]

The effect was to stir up a hornets' nest. Since the outburst of revenge attacks that had followed the Goldstein murders in Hebron, Ayyash was reputed among Palestinians to have restrained Hamas from suicide bombs and other attacks on Israeli civilians, at the request of the Palestinian Authority. He had had primary responsibility for a lull in Hamas bombings that had lasted since the previous August. A rash of attempted suicide bombings had indeed followed the assassination in Malta late in October of the Islamic Jihad leader, Fatih Shikaki, but Hamas had had no part in that.[16]

Hamas waited deliberately until after the Palestinian Legislative election.[17] On February 24, 1996, it launched two suicide bombings. The first, on the crowded number 18 bus in the heart of Jerusalem, in the rush hour at 6.42 in the morning, killed 27 people, including the bomber, and wounded 77.[18] Less than an hour later, a man dressed as an Israeli soldier joined a group of young soldiers waiting to hitch rides back to their bases in Ashkelon, and detonated an explosive, killing himself and one of the soldiers.[19]

Peres responded at once by promising "war on Hamas," but it was too late. The Israeli newspaper *Yediot Aharanot* reported "a sharp drop in Mr Peres' standing in opinion polls against...Netanyahu...." The paper found that if the election had been held on Sunday, after the bombings, 48 percent of its respondents would have voted for Peres and 46 percent for Netanyahu, whereas before the bombings, according to various polls, Peres would have held a 10 to 15 point lead.[20]

Hamas spokesman Sayid Abu Musamih said:

The armed wing of Hamas had staged the latest attacks independently of the group's political leadership, which has been holding talks with the Palestinian Authority on curbing violence and becoming a political movement. The only way to control the activities of the armed wing is through talks between it and the Palestinian Authority.[21]

So much repeats itself in the Middle East. The problem already took the shape we see more recently in the times of the Al-Aqsa *intifada*: does one deal with Palestinian outrage by repression or by negotiation?

Arafat, in these circumstances, had his police hunt down Hamas suspects in the bombings, and by the night of the bombing had arrested 120 in the Gaza Strip and the West Bank. He had declared early in the day: "This is not a military operation. This is a terrorist operation. I condemn it completely. It is not against only civilians, but against the whole peace process."[22] Yet he told foreign diplomats that he did not intend to attack leaders or institutions of Hamas not linked to the armed wing, but was making extensive efforts to strike a deal with the political forces of the movement. Peres announced this day that elections, rather than wait until November, would be held on May 29.[23]

By March 1 new bumper stickers were seen in Jerusalem. Instead of the "Goodbye, friend," that had echoed President Clinton's tribute to Rabin at his funeral, the new stickers said "Goodbye, friends," meaning those killed in the bus attack.[24] Ori Nor, the Palestinian affairs correspondent for the Israeli newspaper *Ha'aretz*, wrote an op-ed column in the *New York Times* (March 1) entitled "Don't Corner Arafat," in which he argued: "In a nervous nation, Mr Peres' get-tough approach has enormous emotional appeal. But more damage than good may come from packing Mr Arafat into this dangerous corner or from stalling the peace process."

The political leaders of Hamas, Nor wrote, had pressured the military to hold its fire in order to negotiate its way into the new Palestinian political arrangement. With Hamas asking, on February 29, for a week's cease-fire with Israel, Nor concluded: "Israel must not sacrifice the peace process in its effort to fight the militants."

But on Sunday March 3, a Hamas bomber blew up another bus (of the same popular number 18 line) on a narrow stretch of the Jaffa Road in Jerusalem, again at 6.25, in the morning rush hour. The death toll this time was 19. Peres announced that he would seal or destroy the houses of the suicide bombers, and demanded that the Palestinian Authority or Arafat outlaw and disarm the military wings of Hamas and Islamic Jihad.[25] The Hamas militants split. A dissident group called "Cells of the Martyr" had unleashed all these bombs, while the Izzidin al-Qassem Brigade had offered the eight-day respite.

That Tuesday, March 4, brought yet another devastating bomb. This time the bomber tried to enter the Dizengoff Center, the largest shopping mall in Tel Aviv, was not admitted, but blew himself up in the crowded street outside, killing 14, among them many children dressed in Halloween-like costumes for the Jewish feast of Purim.[26] The death toll by now for these few days was 61, and would rise to 63 as two more of the wounded succumbed in the following days. Peres' favorable opinion figures withered under the assault.

THE KANA'A DISASTER

April brought a new catastrophe of an altogether different sort as Israel clashed violently with the Hezbollah guerrillas in the "security zone" of southern Lebanon.

The affair developed as similar episodes had before. Hezbollah guerrillas ambushed Israeli soldiers in the areas of occupation. The Israeli Army responded by raiding nearby villages from which they thought the attacks might have originated. When they saw their own civilians being killed, children among them, Hezbollah fired Katyusha rockets into northern Galilee, where Israeli villagers had to take to their bomb shelters for safety. The pattern was familiar and often repeated.

But this time, as had happened once before in 1993, Israel mounted a massive retaliatory attack beginning on April 11, first sending Apache helicopters against a Hezbollah headquarters on the ground floor of a high-rise building in Beirut, their warplanes simultaneously bombing a guerrilla depot near Ba'albek in the Beka'a Valley, just 700 yards from a Syrian base. Helicopters pursued cars used by Hezbollah leaders.[27] A *New York Times* editorial on April 12 warned Peres against striking out in anger. It saw him tempted to unleash Israeli force against terrorist targets basically for political reasons, to demonstrate before the election that his government could be as unyielding as one led by Netanyahu.

By the next day, Israel gave warning that 40 villages in a buffer zone would be destroyed and advised their inhabitants to flee. Serge Schmemann wrote that: "Israel apparently hoped to create a massive refugee problem for the Lebanese government and for Syria...." He described "tens of thousands of terrified Lebanese civilians streaming north in jam-packed cars and vans." Peres' election, wrote Schmemann, was only seven weeks away. "His chances depend on his ability to demonstrate that he is capable of being tough with the Arabs."[28]

66 Building Relationships

Over the next day 300,000 villagers clogged the roads in flight before the air and artillery strikes. By the day following, the third day of bombing in a row, the numbers were hundreds of thousands more, while helicopter gunships hit Beirut and destroyed electric transformer stations in the Bekaa region. By the fourth day eight lanes of northbound traffic filled both sides of the main highway.[29] US and French diplomats had by now begun trying to end the fighting, as Palestinian refugee camps came under fire, rockets searing the Ein Hilweh camp on the outskirts of Sidon. Israeli planes bombed a power station northwest of Beirut, further reducing electricity in the capital after a strike on a transformer station on Sunday.[30]

On Thursday April 18, Lebanese civilians, fleeing artillery bombardments along the roads, sought shelter in a well-marked compound at Qana'a, belonging to the UN Interim Force in Lebanon (UNIFIL), the UN peacekeepers, in this case Fijian soldiers. Their officers fired red warning flares, signaling the Israelis to hold their fire, but in vain. Heavy 155 mm howitzer shells began to fall at about 14.00 hours, and continued for 90 minutes. One Fijian Blue Beret officer, holding a baby in his arms, looked down to see that he held only the upper half of the baby. The infant's body had been cut in two by shrapnel, and had inadvertently shielded the soldier. By the end of the barrage, 109 civilians had been killed.[31]

Ari Shavit, columnist for *Ha'aretz*, wrote an article, "How easily we killed them," which was adapted as an op-ed in the *New York Times* (May 27). He said that 170 civilians had been killed in Lebanon that month, mostly refugees, a good number of them women and children, "without shedding a tear,"[32] with "yuppie efficiency."

THE ELECTION

The effect of all this on the Israeli election (May 29) was that the Israeli Arabs, Palestinians with Israeli citizenship (20 percent of the Israeli population) simply abstained from voting for prime minister. Peres lost to Netanyahu by less than 1 percent of the total vote.

In the separate election for the rest of the 120-seat Knesset, both major parties lost heavily, Labor falling back from 44 to 34 seats, Likud from 40 to 31. The various religious parties, some entering the Knesset for the first time, rose from a combined 16 to a combined 24 seats. The right-wing Moledet party, which stood for expulsion of Palestinians from the land, fell back from 3 to 2. Two new parties entered the lists, Natan Sharansky's Yisrael B'-Aliya, the party of Russian immigrants, took seven seats, and the Third Way, an ex-officers' party opposed to the return of the Golan Heights to Syria, got the remaining four.[33]

THE NETANYAHU YEARS

The religious parties and the Russians, the main winners in this election, organized around their single issues and ambivalent about the major questions facing the nation, could have gone either way, to form a government coalition of the Right or Left. After Netanyahu's slender victory in the two-man race for prime minister, he had no trouble constructing a government to carry his extreme right-wing agenda.

I found myself unable to write to Netanyahu, the only prime minister since 1985 with whom I have not been in correspondence. A group of us from our Interreligious Committee had made another visit to the countries of the region in January, shortly before the election. One of those we met was Faisal Husseini, who told us that a Likud victory could delay the course of the Oslo process toward peace, but could not stop it. It seemed to me that Netanyahu made it the main objective of his three years as prime minister to retract the recognition of the legitimacy of the Palestinians as a people that was the heart of Oslo, yet he was not able to do it.

At first, Netanyahu tried to exclude his long-time rival, Ariel Sharon, from his cabinet. Sharon had refused to attend the swearing in of the new cabinet, but Foreign Minister-designate David Levy, on the day of the inauguration, announced that he would refuse the post unless a portfolio were found for Sharon.[34] After some hours of maneuvering, Netanyahu created, for Sharon, a new cabinet position that would turn out to be most powerful, a Ministry of National Infrastructure, which gave Sharon the power to construct bypass roads in the West Bank and Gaza to connect Israeli settlements with Israel proper, as well as control over defense industries, ports, energy, and the Lands Authority, which managed all state-owned lands.[35]

THE MATTER OF LEBANON

I was anxious to see the Clinton administration in Washington raise the plan I had first proposed to Rabin in 1992, to withdraw Israeli troops from their counter-productive occupation of southern Lebanon. I thought American insistence could nudge Netanyahu, for all his determination to give nothing to the Palestinians themselves, to wind up the explosive aggravation of the "security zone" in Lebanon.

Netanyahu would make his first visit to Washington as prime minister in July. Clinton by then was somewhat sheepish, having openly supported Peres all through the election and now facing a new election campaign himself in which he could not afford to be seen as leaning hard on Israel.[36] Secretary of State Warren Christopher had visited Israel late in June, urging Netanyahu to hold to agreements already made, but Prime Minister Netanyahu was totally unbending in what was his first press conference.[37] Netanyahu, perhaps as a way of mending fences with hosts who had openly campaigned against him, offered, in a speech before leaving Israel, to ease travel restrictions on Palestinians if security conditions would allow it.[38] Writing to Clinton, I asked that the topic of the Lebanon occupation be raised.

The subject did come up between Clinton and Netanyahu, but I remained in the dark as it was kept carefully out of the news. A *New York Times* editorial on the day of Netanyahu's arrival tried for a larger goal. It mentioned the three-year effort Washington had made to bring about the return of the Golan Heights to Syria, and urged a border deal in which Israel would return the Golan in exchange for full diplomatic recognition and a peace treaty with Syria.[39]

Netanyahu chose publicly to air his differences with Clinton, rebuffing the President's requests to stop settlement building.[40] Addressing a joint session of Congress the following day, he took the hardest possible line on return of any territory to Palestinians or Syrians, dismissing the principle of land for peace, to great congressional applause.[41] Palestinians were reported, next day, as distressed at his comments on Jerusalem, which he said he would never again allow to be divided between Arabs and Jews. Faisal Husseini feared Netanyahu had "made up his mind to go ahead with a declaration of war against the Palestinians." Things were so bad that Abu Ala (Ahmed Qurei), the principal negotiator of the Oslo accord, declared, "It is a dangerous step. If the Israeli Government wants to make the peace process fail, they should announce that openly, and not hold the Palestinians responsible."[42] Once Netanyahu had returned to Jerusalem, Shimon Peres said that his trip had "been in the wrong direction in every sense of the word."[43]

The Lebanon question opened up later in the month, with reports of the exchange of 45 Shi'ite prisoners and some 100 Hezbollah corpses for the remains of two Israelis, each side still sullenly refusing to give up what the other most wanted.[44] Two days later Foreign Minister David Levy was permitted to hold the first meeting of any member of the new government with Arafat.[45] But within the week, Sharon's new ministry reported plans for two new roads through the West Bank with access limited to settlers only, and two bridges onto the Golan Heights.[46]

Then on August 2 we heard of a "furtive" Netanyahu visit to Europe, in quest of Lebanese/Syrian guarantees over an Israeli withdrawal from southern Lebanon, but with the caveat that he entirely ruled out returning the Golan Heights as the price for a broad peace. The Israeli newspaper *Ha'aretz* of August 1 quoted the Syrian Vice President Abdulharim Khaddam as saying the plan was "a death trap aimed at the destruction of Lebanon."

Netanyahu, the report continued, had talked about this proposition with Clinton during his visit to Washington the previous month and had pursued it the previous week with Dennis Ross, the administration's Middle East envoy. The Iranians were strongly opposed. An unidentified diplomat traveling with Ross, after his meeting with Netanyahu, had said:

> Essentially they [the Syrians] are being asked to clean up Hezbollah, secure Israel's northern border and strain their relations with Iran all for the sake of the territorial integrity of Lebanon, which in the face of it is not a particularly attractive proposition to them. So this can't be easy.[47]

Provocatively, Netanyahu accompanied this proposal with the lifting of the freeze on expansion of existing settlements on the West Bank.[48] Soon he visited Jordan's King Hussein, asking him to broker his proposal with Syria. The prime minister spoke of wanting peace with Syria and brushed aside the suggestion that he wanted only to talk of his withdrawal from Lebanon. "We are prepared to engage in peace negotiations with Syria on all outstanding matters." Yet he was on record as having rejected any land-for-peace ideas, on the Golan or anywhere.[49]

A *Reuters* report the next day quoted the Damascus daily *Tishrin*, which on August 6 had said that Mr. Netanyahu primarily wanted to discuss Israel's security problems in southern Lebanon but not the possibility of withdrawal from the Golan Heights. "This talk does not mean anything for the making of peace," said *Tishrin*. The report continued:

> Mr Netanyahu, who held talks in Jordan with King Hussein ... said that his Government had submitted a peace proposal for Syria via the United States and was awaiting an answer. His adviser said the proposal spelled out Israel's terms for withdrawing its troops from Lebanon, in what he said would be a first step to peace with Syria.

Syria's Foreign Minister, Farouq al-Shara, had reportedly told the Syrian Cabinet, at its weekly session, that Israel was still refusing to conduct peace discussions on the basis of the land-for-peace principle, which had been the premise of the talks and the UN resolutions. Shara was quoted as saying: "If Israel is serious about reviving the peace process it is required to affirm its commitments and respect its pledges without any disguise."[50]

By now the plan had become widely known, had reached very high levels of discussion and acquired the name "Lebanon First." Reuters reported: "While King Hussein and Mr. Netanyahu met in Jordan on Monday, President Elias Hrawi of Lebanon held talks in Damascus with the Syrian President, Hafez al-Assad. Syrian officials said the two men discussed the Israeli proposal."[51]

The *coup de grace* came the following day. Syria's President, on a state visit to Cairo, declared that the Israeli proposal to resume talks between the two countries had not offered "the slightest hope of the possibility of a forthcoming peace." After his meeting with Egyptian President Hosni Mubarak, Assad said: "Lebanon and Syria first—at the same time, in the same steps."[52]

With that the prospect of ending the Israeli occupation of southern Lebanon, in which I had invested so much of my own effort for the past three years, was dead for the duration of Netanyahu's term. Whatever he actually meant by his proposal, he had convinced his neighbors that he would withdraw from the "security zone" only on the condition that Syria abandon all claim to the Golan Heights. This poisoned it entirely in the view of all the Arab parties to the conflict, reversing the whole intended dynamic. Henceforth the idea of "Lebanon First" became synonymous, for Syrians and Lebanese, with diplomatic blackmail.[53]

YEARS OF FRUSTRATION

The Netanyahu years remained essentially empty, despite what became more and more strenuous efforts on the part of US President Clinton to address the situation. Agreed elements of Oslo 2 failed to materialize. Netanyahu complained of Palestinian delay in revoking the suspect articles in the Palestinian National Covenant, while the promised dates for the transfer of more West Bank territory into the Palestinian Areas A and B passed without result. Prospects faded for maintaining the original Oslo schedule, which had called for a Final Status Agreement in five years.

Netanyahu's course eventually so alarmed me that I wrote, on Christmas Eve 1997, to President Clinton in the following terms.

Dear President Clinton,
    At present, I find myself more apprehensive about developments in the Middle East than at any time since the Israeli invasion of Lebanon in 1982. Hearing your own cautious hope that new life may be brought into the peace process there in the New Year, I thought I should express this to you. I have been traditionally an optimist on

the chances for peace there and in many other conflict situations, as you yourself have several times noted and acknowledged, and I felt my dim reading might count with you.

The relation between Israel and the Arabs, Palestinian and other, is currently headed for war, in my view. I hate that prospect, out of great love and concern for both Israeli and Arab peoples.

I think it self-deception to blind ourselves to that prospect of war. The war is likely to be nuclear, as it cannot be expected that the present government of Israel will refrain from using such weapons if under attack from Arab nations. I don't believe the war will happen out of concerted plan, but because the parties lose control under the grievous provocation of the events unfolding over the last two years.

Israel will win such a war hands down, but it will in the course of it have utterly destroyed the resident Palestinian population, all who do not escape into exile. Israel will thus be indelibly stained with genocide in the eyes of others, even of our European allies and many of our own American people. The war, however, will not be the end, but only the first of several wars that will end in the destruction of Israel itself. The United States, for its part, can expect a terrible harvest of terrorism over many years.

I do not believe this is an irreversible course, but it is the way things are going at present.

The fundamental accomplishment of the peace process between Israelis and Palestinians, for all the fears that have accompanied the Oslo process on both sides, has been the public and solemn recognition, by both parties, of one another's legitimacy as peoples, something neither had succeeded in articulating before. That was the genius of Yitzhak Rabin, Shimon Peres, and Yasser Arafat. There was reason to believe the peace could be built on that, and much progress was made.

From its inception, and consistently since, the Netanyahu government has set it as its most basic purpose to rescind that recognition. The only good news has been that they found this very difficult to accomplish. Every action, every refusal on their part has that aim. It has come to the point by now that I can see no reason for the Palestinian leadership to accede to any request to maintain the appearance of negotiation. The intention of Israel's present government is to take everything from them and leave them isolated and helpless in deprived bantustans. They ought not cooperate in that objective.

I recognize entirely the need for Mr. Arafat and his Authority to work incessantly against Palestinian terrorism. I believe, though, that this very concept has been shamefully abused, as the Netanyahu government has consistently invoked it as excuse not to fulfill its own obligations. I cannot say that Arafat or his Authority has been the source of any of the terrorism, while I can say with full conviction that this present government itself has been the source of repeated default on agreed obligations on the Israeli side. Arafat's very capacity to oppose or effectively police terrorism is progressively eroded by the demeaning treatment of Palestinians by the Netanyahu government. I cannot conclude other than that this erosion is deliberate policy, and that the objective is the war of which I warn, for the purpose of removing the Palestinians from the territory.

Mr. Netanyahu himself impresses me as not being smart, in ways that all earlier Israeli prime ministers have been. I believe he fails to foresee or understand the consequences of his actions. Mr. Sharon rather than he has become the true driving force of policy.

That he is unable to do other than he does because of his need for the support of such extremists as Mr. Sharon, Generals Eitan and Ze'evi, and the fringe elements of the settler movement, is simply untrue. He has always had the option of a government of national unity in which he could pursue a more peace-creative policy. He uses the threat of the fall of his government as blackmail on the United States. In recent statements from your administration I think I see much impatience with the Netanyahu government and even some glimmering of this view of the present situation, though you understandably shrink from seeing it in such stark terms. It would in any case be impolitic for you to say it in public as bluntly as I do here. I write this with as much love and concern for Jews and the state of Israel as you have yourself, and I do not question that you and your assistants also share fully my concern for the Palestinians and other Arabs. I understand the constraints under which you operate from an intemperate and one-sided Congress. I have great respect for the heroic work of Dennis Ross and many others in your administration, who genuinely work for peace, as you and your two Secretaries of State have clearly done, against all odds.

I mention foreseeable consequences—long-term terrorism—for the United States if the course of this Israeli government is not reversed. Our country will be held complicit in what is done for one basic reason, because of our condoning of the settlement policy by which this and earlier Israeli governments have tried to preempt any and all Palestinian claims by creating "facts on the ground." Our American administrations all recognized the illegality of these settlements until the time of President Reagan, whose administration softened the judgment to "obstacles to peace." It remained for your own administration to weaken this stance further, calling the settlement policy merely "unhelpful" and calling for only a "time-out" for what, in the view of all the other nations of the world except our own, that of Israel and Micronesia, is still illegal action contravening the Fourth Geneva Convention of August 1949. We make ourselves outlaws by not acknowledging that, and cannot but expect consequences. I write this though I have always argued to Mr Arafat and other Palestinians that it is a necessary test of Palestinian friendship for the state of Israel that they allow some Jews to live in peace in the territories so important to them, Judea and Samaria.

It is without pleasure that I write these dire warnings, but I believe I must, and I deliberately chose Christmas as the time to do it. I see it as within the capacity of the United States to reverse this threatening situation. My hopes and prayers are with you.

Clinton responded to this in person January 8, 1998, in a letter which pretty well ignored the dark expectations of my letter and must have been, in large part, a standard response to what he was hearing at the time, but is all the same a valuable index of his position:

Dear Raymond,

Thanks for sharing your views with me. The historic progress we have witnessed since September 1993 holds forth the promise of hope for all the people of the Middle East. For too long, conflict has robbed that region of its potential, and, most important, the lives of so many of its sons and daughters. Now there is an opportunity to define the future of the Middle East in terms of reconciliation and coexistence rather than confrontation and violence.

Since coming to office, we have worked carefully with the parties to the peace process to help them make progress. Those efforts continue today, and we are concentrating on restoring energy to the negotiations between the Israelis and the Palestinians so that they can deal with the difficult issues before them. A credible negotiating process is the best and surest way to make progress, and the parties need to have confidence in that process. For negotiations to succeed, both parties must exercise the leadership necessary to make difficult decisions.

As we have seen from bitter experience, there are still those who want to see the process fail, and they will go to any extreme to derail it. That is why it is so important that both sides do everything they can to prevent terror. Security and vigilance against extremists must be a full-time job. Violence and the threat of violence have no place in the negotiations. The progress already made in the peace process is substantial. We must actively safeguard that progress, forging ahead toward a comprehensive peace to include Israel and all its neighbors. The United States has an interest and a responsibility to help this historic process succeed.

Sincerely,
Bill Clinton

I was in fact more encouraged when I heard of a speech Arafat gave in Gaza, invoking the term *intifada* for the first time in some years. I wrote to him promptly on 19 January 1998, sending the message over the fax wires by way of Faisal Husseini at Orient House:

Dear President Arafat,
   Salaam!
   I hear that yesterday, speaking in Gaza, you raised the prospect of a renewal of the *intifada*. Since I have advocated all the years since Oslo that you needed the active mobilization of your public, you will understand that I find your statement very satisfying.
   Now that that word is out, it will be a major topic of questioning during your visit this week to the United States, from President Clinton as well as the public. Already I have heard it said on the radio this morning, "Arafat calls for a return to violence." It will be very important to counter that impression.
   Please do not give your enemies clubs with which to beat you. Mobilized but non-violent resistance by your people is a way to prevent violence, in fact the best way to carry out the clear responsibility you have to work against terrorist violence during this volatile period. The humiliations heaped upon the Palestinians by the Netanyahu government are constantly eroding your capacity to prevent terrorism. It is only by clearly leading a non-violent resistance, by a mobilized people, that you will be able to control it.
   Like the original *intifada*, this one should bring to your people the admiration of world opinion and of those Israelis who are working for the peace. Everything about it should be planned for that purpose. If the Israeli opponents of the peace, Sharon and the others, see the excuse for it, they will use their armed power to crush your people. The original *intifada* was a kind of relatively non-violent

resistance against which the Israeli Army was helpless, however much pain they inflicted upon your people. Every bit of violence now, even stones, but particularly guns or bombs, works totally against the true interests of your people. You need to make that fully understood among them, and be the leader of a resistance that is rigorously non-violent.

The other characteristic of the original *intifada*, which legitimized it in the eyes of the Israeli peace movement and others who care for the safety of Israel, was that while it rejected occupation and oppression, it was not a rejection of Israel, but the offer of real coexistence and even genuine peace between an Israeli and a Palestinian state. That too should be made amply clear now, that it is a way to peace, not to war.

You face enemies in the Netanyahu government, and will face them in parts of the American media and political structure that you will meet this week, who would see this reference to a new *intifada* as an opportunity to destroy you. If you use it well, making it plain that you and your people want the peace and the friendship of the Israeli people, not their harm, you can repeat the success of the earlier *intifada*. What you say during this week in Washington will be critically important in that regard. Hatred has no place in this. Your people's mobilized action, and your visible leadership of it, will be the more effective the more hatred is purged out of it entirely, and replaced by massive commitment to the peace of all concerned, both Israelis and Palestinians.

I wish you peace, and success in that great endeavor.

THE WYE PLANTATION MEMORANDUM

Only toward the end of Netanyahu's time did a faint glimmer of hope appear with the convening by Clinton of a new Israeli-Palestinian conference at the Wye River Plantation in Maryland.

The participants convened, with low expectations, on Thursday October 15, 1998,[54] Arafat and Netanyahu meeting President Clinton and his Secretary of State, Madeleine Albright. Clinton would spend a remarkable amount of time himself at this meeting, and much resented the delayed arrival of newly appointed Foreign Minister Ariel Sharon, who would not arrive until Monday, October 19, by which time the Clinton team had expected to have an agreement on a third Israeli handover of territory (after Oslo 1 and 2).[55] It was hoped that such a turnover, of perhaps another 13 percent of the West Bank, would at last open the way for final status negotiations to set the borders and status of Palestine, the fate of Palestinian refugees and the future of Jerusalem. When nothing of the sort was in sight by the Monday, Arafat began to speak of making a unilateral declaration of independence if there were no final status agreement by 5 May.[56]

Clinton, by now, was struggling to save the talks from total failure.[57] Back in Israel, a Hamas militant had chosen that Monday to set off a bomb in a bus station at Beersheba, which injured 67 people.[58] Serge Schmemann, reporting the conference alongside Steven Erlanger for the *New York Times*, described Sharon, who steadfastly refused to take the hand of Arafat, as bringing "muscle" to the table.[59]

King Hussein, visiting the United States for the treatment of his soon-to-be-fatal cancer, arrived at the meeting on Tuesday to take an active part in the rest of the negotiations.[60] On Wednesday, the Israelis threatened to abandon the talks altogether over two issues: they insisted that the Palestinians should extradite any of their people accused of terrorism to Israeli jurisdiction and that they should remove from the Palestinian National Covenant language calling for the destruction of Israel.[61]

Thursday's meetings brought a feeling of progress in dealing with the obstacles. Natan Sharansky, leader among Russian immigrants to Israel, spoke of a "clear breakthrough."[62] On the Friday, just before the onset of the Shabbat that would have brought a break in the negotiations, a pact finally emerged, all the participants appearing at a televised press conference to announce what became known by the very tentative name of the "Wye Memorandum." Described as a modest deal to rebuild trust between the sides, it contained assurances from the Palestinians that they would revise the Covenant and take steps to combat terrorism. Fourteen percent of what had been Area B, West Bank territory administered by Palestinians but under Israeli security control, would become Area A, fully controlled by Palestinians, with an additional 13 percent promised over the next twelve weeks. A joint Israeli-Palestinian committee would discuss further withdrawals. Further provisions promised a safe-passage corridor between Gaza and the West Bank, the building of a Palestinian airport in Gaza and the release of 750 Palestinian prisoners. Netanyahu, at the last moment, threatened to pull out of the whole deal unless Clinton would release Jonathan Pollard, the US Navy intelligence analyst imprisoned since 1995, when he had been convicted of selling classified information to Israel. His release had been a favorite Israeli cause ever since. Clinton refused immediate release of Pollard but promised "to review this matter seriously," and thereby saved the agreement.[63]

Serge Schmemann and Steven Erlanger, writing jointly in the *New York Times* on Sunday October 25, described three major crises that had occurred during the nine days of hard negotiation. Wednesday's pullout threat was the first, and the Pollard argument on Friday the third. Between them was an incident during Thursday's "Long Night." Clinton was sitting with Arafat and Netanyahu. He found the Israeli prime minister's treatment of Arafat so insulting that he suddenly slammed his papers down on the table and angrily walked off, exclaiming: "This is despicable." An unnamed diplomatic witness told the reporters how aides had made clear to Netanyahu that Clinton would return if his behavior improved. "Mr. Netanyahu relented, Mr Clinton returned, and the negotiations went into the crucial home stretch. 'People felt that was a turning point,' the official recalled."[64]

These years of disappointment for anyone concerned for the peace ended at last with the election, on May 17, 1999, of the Labor Party's Ehud Barak as new prime minister. The vote turned on disgust, among the Israeli electorate, with the stalemate created by Netanyahu. Continuing losses of Israeli soldiers in the "security zone" of southern Lebanon had become more of a burden than the public was prepared to bear, and Barak's promise that he would withdraw the occupying troops stood him in good stead in the campaign. In the two-candidate contest for prime minister, Barak took 56 percent of the vote to Netanyahu's 43.9 percent. Yet the voting for Knesset members left that body more fractured than ever, with an additional five new parties winning seats and the major parties with still slimmer representations than before. Likud, the main loser, lost 13 seats, retaining only 19, but the winning One Israel party, even as a three-way coalition of Labor, Gesher,[65] and Meimad,[66] lost 7 seats from what Labor had by itself in the previous Knesset, retaining only 27.[67]

Yet with Barak's accession to power the prospects for peace seemed better than they had been at any time since the Oslo Declaration had been signed on the White House lawn. Already we seemed much closer to millennial promises, hopes for healing the bitter wounds of this long conflict.

Part II
The Failed Negotiations

4
Sad millennium: the disintegration of Ehud Barak, May 1999 to July 2000

Purists told us the millennium would begin only in 2001. Those of us who paid at least some historico-critical attention to the dating of the birth of Jesus, on which the enumeration was based, knew it had come several years before. But for any of us who associated the millennium with the peace of Jerusalem and the land holy to the three Abrahamic faiths, millennial hopes began to blossom, after the three parched years of Likud, with the election of Ehud Barak. The hopes were destined to be so dimmed that Ehud Barak would get to Camp David the following summer a broken man. We need here to understand the reasons why, and they were three:

1. His effort to settle with Syria first, a project which roused Palestinian suspicions that he was trying to do an end run around them while reneging on formal agreements already made with them.
2. His losing out on that Syrian effort, coming away from negotiations over the Golan Heights with his own coalition and his prestige badly damaged.
3. His far worse failure over the withdrawal of Israeli forces from the "security zone" in Lebanon, which left him looking as though he had exposed Israel to defeat by an inferior force.

NEW CHANCES FOR PEACE

Israel always takes a long time after an election to form a government. Ehud Barak's victory had been convincing enough, but he still had to form a coalition government, like every prime minister before him. That task was more complex than ever now, because of the fractioned membership in the Knesset. There were now 14 parties sharing the Knesset's 120 seats, most parties' holdings being in single figures.[1] It seemed Barak could depend on his 26 One Israel seats, the Meretz[2] party's 10, and the Shinui[3] party's 6, then hope for a few more from the scatter of small parties. He had to include in his coalition either Likud, with its 17 seats, or Shas,[4] with its 19, if he was to have a majority—there was no way around that—and both prospects frightened parts of his real constituency. I thought he should be left some slack on that.

My own interest was to raise issues of the peace with him, since he had clearly been elected to achieve it. The issue, so familiar to me, of withdrawal from southern Lebanon had even been a feature of his campaign. The Israeli public had, by this time, become impatient with the slow trickle of casualties, and Barak had promised to withdraw from the "security zone" if he were elected. I was anxious, too, to raise the question of ethnic-religious discrimination exercised by Israelis against Palestinians. To raise the issue of racism in Israel was a delicate matter after all the years in which the assertion that "Zionism is racism"[5] had been used as a way of delegitimizing the whole enterprise of the Israeli state and society. But as much as any of us who were friends of Israel had to repudiate that, the actual discrimination and contemptuous treatment of Palestinians in Israel was a sore point that rankled more than most others and could not be ignored.[6]

I wrote to Barak about these things, on June 25, 1999, even before he had formed his cabinet and taken over the government, explaining first my long acquaintance both with Arafat and with his own predecessors and my basic concern for the peace of both peoples. I said how impossible I had found it to deal with Netanyahu, and how disappointed I had been at his wrecking of the chance to secure Syrian cooperation in a withdrawal from Lebanon.

Only on generous terms, I wrote, would Barak be able to win the peace with Palestinians for which he had been elected. Clearly he would feel pressure from many others who would want the settlement to be as minimal as possible. I told him I understood his leaving us in the dark about which coalition partner he would choose, Shas or Likud, that I could see the advantages to him of either, but that I was very apprehensive of the kind of machinations he would suffer from Sharon should he choose Likud. If the Palestinians received only isolated Bantustan-like fragments of territory, there would be no peace.

That said, I urged on him two basic perspectives. The first, one that I had long urged both on Arafat and Rabin, was that the Israelis and Palestinians needed an open border. I described to him the relation I had often spelled out to the others: how the Palestinians needed to accept the residence of some Israelis in "Judea and Samaria," but only those who were there to live in peace, not the settler fanatics who were there to displace Palestinians and impose the "transfer" on them. I explained my concept of the choice of citizenship, one and not both, for Israelis who lived in Palestine and for the Palestinians who should, reciprocally, be able to live in Israel. That perspective, I believed, would throw the entire question of settlements, of the forced annexation of territory by war, of national boundaries into a new light. Provision would have to be made for security in such an open-border arrangement, but the very openness of it would make that more attainable.

The second perspective had to do with racism. All of us who loved Israel had had to fight, over the years, the General Assembly's "Zionism is racism" proposition, which I had always seen as parallel to the Israeli proposition that Palestinian was a synonym for terrorism. Nonetheless, ethnic-religious discrimination was so widespread as to be all but universal in Israel, and the contemptuous dismissal of Palestinians had to be confronted as a damaging element in the culture. Things happened that would no longer be tolerated in the United States, in South Africa, or any civilized country. As special instance of this, I brought up the segregated housing of the West Bank settlements: no Palestinians need apply. If this were not tolerated, many of the most aggressive anti-Palestinian settlers would not choose to live there.

I concluded:

Mr. Barak, I ache for your peace and the peace of those others among whom you live. I have devoted my own activity for many years to fostering peace, not only in your part of the world but in Northern Ireland, in the Balkans and other places, none of them more dear to me than among your peoples. I wish you every success and blessing in the vital work that lies before you. If, by thinking and writing, by meeting and discussing with people, I can be any help in that work of peace, I will gladly do so.

THE NEW PRIME MINISTER

Ehud Barak's background was almost entirely in the army up to 1994, when he began to bring his soldier's role to the negotiation of the Israeli–Jordanian peace treaty and negotiations with Syria over the Golan Heights. The latter would remain a major interest of his as prime minister. Israel's most decorated soldier, he had held key command positions in the 1967 and 1973 wars. In 1972 he had been Netanyahu's superior in the elite unit that stormed a hijacked Belgian airliner at Ben-Gurion airport, killing the hijackers and freeing scores of passengers. The following year he led a commando attack on Beirut, killing several Palestinian leaders in their homes.[7]

In April 1983 he took charge of the intelligence branch at Israel Defense Force headquarters. He became Commander of Central Command in

January 1986 and Deputy Chief of Staff in May 1987. In April 1991, he assumed the post of 14th Chief of the General Staff and was promoted to the rank of Lt. General, the highest in the Israeli military. Following the May 1994 signing of the Gaza–Jericho agreement, Lt. General Barak oversaw the IDF's redeployment in the Gaza Strip and Jericho. He played a central role in finalizing the peace treaty with Jordan in 1994, and met with his Syrian counterpart as part of the Syrian–Israeli negotiations.[8]

He came to office with a strong mandate to pursue a peace settlement through the Oslo process, but appeared to conceive that task as a matter of Israel's deciding what it would give to the Palestinians rather than as something that Israel and the Palestinians would agree upon together.

As he came to office, Barak faced three areas of Israeli–Arab relations which he would juggle in turn during his term: decisions on a Palestinian state, peace with Syria, and extracting Israel, as he had promised, from its occupation of southern Lebanon.

Getting out of Lebanon would prove difficult, as no one in Syria or Lebanon was anxious to let Israel out of its Lebanon trap easily. When it came to the parallel tracks of seeking peace with the Palestinians and with Syria, Barak unexpectedly gave his attention first to Syria.

Even before Barak had formed his coalition and been sworn in as prime minister, he and Syria's President Hafez al-Assad exchanged compliments. Veteran British reporter Patrick Seale interviewed both, and the two interviews appeared in the same issue of *Al-Hayat*, a widely read London-based Arabic daily. Assad called Barak "strong and honest," and "a leader who can deliver if he chooses." Barak asserted: "The only way for a lasting and comprehensive peace in the Middle East is through an agreement with Syria. It is the cornerstone for peace." He said of Assad: "[he] has given the Syrian nation its new formula. He was capable of building a strong, independent and self-confident Syria." Barak concluded by renewing his pledge to withdraw Israeli troops from southern Lebanon.[9]

But on the same day the Israeli air force and the artillery of its allied Lebanese militia[10] opened fire on suspected infiltration routes by which Hezbollah guerrillas could penetrate into their occupied "security zone." An Israeli jet fired an air-to-ground missile into a valley near the village of Yater just southeast of Tyre. A ten-year-old Lebanese boy and his 70-year-old grandfather suffered shrapnel wounds in Qabrikha, half a mile north of the "security zone."[11]

Overnight this blew up into "Israel's most severe bombardment of Lebanon since 1996."[12] Decisions came, of course, from Netanyahu, who still served as prime minister, more than a month after the election, until such time as Barak would finish assembling his coalition. Israeli fighter planes bombarded Lebanon throughout the Thursday night, while Hezbollah retaliated by firing Katyusha rockets into northern Israel. Israeli bombers struck two power stations on the outskirts of Beirut, three bridges south of Beirut, and a power substation in the Bekaa Valley. Two Israelis and six Lebanese were killed. Four of the Lebanese were firefighters battling the blaze at one of the power stations, where ten others were wounded. It was a "severe step-up in the conflict in southern Lebanon at a moment of political transition in Israel."[13] Patrick Seale, the interviewer for the *Al-Hayat* article, blamed Barak for waiting so long to form a coalition, leaving Netanyahu free to sabotage his policy and tie his hands before he even entered the prime minister's office. Barak, Seale felt, could have formed a minority government right after his May 17 victory with the backing of 56 MKs and the tacit support of Arab members, inviting other parties to join his coalition later and keeping some cabinet seats open for them.[14]

Barak had his coalition, the fragile knitting-together of seven parties that controlled 75 of the 120 seats in the Knesset, by June 30, to be sworn in a week later, July 6. Likud had backed away from his offer of a "Grand Coalition" earlier that week, since Barak would not accept their conditions that Israel retain the Golan Heights and permit continued development of the Jewish settlements in Palestinian territory. That meant that Barak had to turn to Shas, with its 17 seats and its overriding interest in subsidies for its religious schools. Meretz, with its ten seats and secularization program, refused to join without assurance that the Shas leader, Rabbi Ovadia Yosef, would not himself sit in the Knesset. The determinedly secular Shinui party was left out. Two other religious parties were included: the traditional National Religious Party (reduced from a previous nine to only five seats) and United Torah Judaism (five seats), for whose votes Barak had to rescind his election-platform promise to include yeshiva students in the military conscription. A Center Party that demanded a written constitution within a year and Natan Sharansky's Yisrael B'-Aliya party, made up of Russian immigrants, each with six seats, completed the coalition. The inclusion of Shas made it highly combustible. Inclusion of Likud would have been at least as much so.[15]

On Friday July 2, Barak broke the silence he had largely maintained through the transition period. He telephoned Arafat, professing his intent to "continue on the path to peace of his mentor, Yitzhak Rabin," and promising a meeting soon after he presented his government to the Knesset. Through a spokeswoman, Marav Parsi-Tzadok, he rebuked President

Clinton for having said "I would like it if [Palestinian refugees] were free to live wherever they liked, wherever they wanted to live." Thus the issue of the right of return for Palestinian refugees came onto the table right away, as something "unacceptable to Barak."[16]

As foreign minister he re-appointed David Levy, the Moroccan-born Sephardic Jew who had been Netanyahu's first foreign minister but had then been ignored by Netanyahu and eventually broke ranks with the Likud party.[17] This would soon entail difficulties with Shimon Peres, who felt slighted at being passed over for this post.

On Tuesday July 6 Barak finally took office as prime minister, promising to move forward on both the Palestinian and Syrian tracks to peace and to pull Israeli troops out of southern Lebanon within a year. He had no apologies for having taken 45 days after his election before presenting his government to the Knesset, as he had had to form a coalition durable enough to carry out these tasks. A unified coalition he could not have, so he had built a large one instead.

He addressed the Knesset in stirring language, referring to himself as a "warrior" who "for ten years wore no other clothes but the olive uniform." He cited popular poet Hillel's words, calling himself one of the "gray soldiers whose hands are blackened from war and whose nostrils are filled with death." "Our tongue is dry from the march," he said, "and we cry love into the insides of your souls." As he spoke, Israeli Arab members, resentful at being excluded from his coalition, shouted catcalls: "How are you going to be the prime minister of everyone? Where are your Arab ministers?" Ariel Sharon poured out his scorn, and the media made much of Barak's reputed autocratic instincts, nicknaming him "Caligula" and "Ehud Bonaparte."[18] The period of office of this dedicated man, so shaped by his own experience, so committed to making the peace and doing it his way through what he felt to be his strengths, would develop from here with all the pathos of a classical tragedy.

NEGOTIATIONS ON THREE FRONTS

Syrian state television signaled to Barak on his inauguration day:

> Syria shares with Prime Minister Barak the same wish to put an end to wars and establish comprehensive peace in the region. The Syrian government is ready to match every step with a similar one and to resume peace talks from the point where they ended as soon as possible.[19]

Barak went, on the Friday of his first week, to Alexandria for a cordial meeting with Egypt's President Mubarak, but back in Jerusalem that evening he told an Israeli television audience his plans about transfer of territory to the Palestinian Authority. Netanyahu, in January, had suspended the Wye River agreement, accusing the Palestinians of failing to keep their part of the deal. In this way he had avoided a phased Israeli withdrawal from parts of the West Bank, the last of three scheduled in the agreement. Barak now told his television audience that he would like to combine this part of the Wye accord with a final agreement on such crucial issues as the status of Jerusalem, borders and the Jewish settlements. The Palestinians always objected to delays in carrying out the agreement, and Barak, while stating his preference, assured his listeners on Channel 2: "The Wye agreement will be implemented."[20]

On Sunday July 11, Barak met Arafat for the first time as prime minister, at the Erez Crossing on the border of the Gaza Strip. The meeting proceeded cordially, with an exchange of symbolic gifts. No mention was made of delay in fulfilling the Wye agreements or of recent expansions of Israeli settlements on the West Bank.[21]

But negative voices began to be heard about Barak. Palestinians were saying that there could be no peace without the return of Palestinian refugees to their former homes in Israel, but Barak insisted that no refugees could ever come back to the now Jewish state.[22] Here were the very themes that would eventually dominate the discussion, now showing themselves from the start of Barak's term.

Barak wanted Arafat to abandon his demand for full and immediate fulfillment of the Wye agreement. He wanted the United States, which he called his "major partner," to scale back its role in the region, act as a "facilitator," and stop acting as "arbitrator, policeman, and judge." Barak's hesitation about handing over control of territory was apparently grounded in fears of terrorism. This very fact actually gave the terrorists too much control over the peace process. Terrorists would know that they could stop any action that tended toward peace by making an attack.[23]

The Palestinians at this stage took every opportunity to be conciliatory. The high contracting parties to the Fourth Geneva Convention, representatives, that is, of the nations which had ratified that 1949 treaty on "the Protection of Civilian Persons in Time of War," would soon have a regularly scheduled meeting to assess compliance with the Convention and would, as always, point out that all the Israeli settlements on Palestinian land violated the treaty. The Palestinians, while wanting the message to be clear, were determined not to let it become confrontational with Israel, and asked that the meeting be terminated within the day of its opening.[24]

Barak made his first visit as prime minister to Washington from July 14 to 20. In a two and a half hour first-day meeting with President Clinton he professed Israel's readiness for "painful compromises and difficult decisions" with regard to Syrian claims to the Golan Heights. But he told Clinton that, while he would continue the withdrawal of Israeli forces from the West Bank under the terms of the Wye agreement, Israel would "never agree to return to the borders that existed before the 1967 war." Rather, "most" settlers would remain in the communities they had established on Palestinian territory.

He stressed again that he did not want the United States to be "policeman, judge, and arbitrator." He had, he said, "the mission of defusing a time bomb."[25] after the deterioration of relations that Netanyahu had brought about.[26] The message to Clinton, on all fronts, was to back off, but Clinton was so delighted to have Barak after his three years of sparring with Netanyahu that the two bonded thoroughly over the days of meeting.[27] Israeli warplanes, meanwhile, were raiding Hezbollah artillery batteries in Lebanon, after guerrillas had attacked an Israeli position within the "security zone."[28]

By the weekend, Barak and Clinton had spent some eight hours together. Barak outlined a plan to have a final status peace agreement within 15 months. Clinton pledged to contact President Assad of Syria and describe to him his "golden opportunity" to make peace with Israel. He made large new armament promises to Israel amid an ebullient atmosphere between himself and Barak.[29]

Yet back in the Middle East, the vast bedroom community of Maale Adumim[30] bore witness to the large-scale expansion and confidence that obtained in the Israeli West Bank settlements. Arafat had taken the 15-month target for an overall Middle East peace settlement reported in Barak's conversations with Clinton as meaning a 15-month delay before the Wye promises would be fulfilled. Barak sent assurances that he would move more quickly than that to complete withdrawals from the West Bank.[31]

Returned to Israel, Barak announced his acceptance of the Syrian formula, for negotiations on the Golan, to resume talks "from where they halted in February 1996." But Israel and Syria disagreed on what that point was. Syria spoke of a commitment from Prime Minister Yitzhak Rabin that, in return for peace, Israel would withdraw entirely from the Golan Heights. Israeli officials emphatically denied that any such commitment had been made. Barak meanwhile planned meetings with both Arafat and Mubarak to assure them that he was not giving Syria priority over the Palestinian track.[32]

The funeral of Morocco's King Hassan II presented the unusual spectacle of the Israeli prime minister, with a large official party, present among the official mourners from Arab states.[33] President Clinton attended too. To *Middle East International*'s correspondent Haim Baram it seemed that Syrian President Assad's absence was a careful avoidance of a meeting with Barak, which he felt President Clinton wanted to arrange at the funeral.[34]

Mixed signals followed. In Jerusalem, Knesset Speaker Avraham Burg showed lavish hospitality to his guest, Ahmed Qurei (Abu Ala, who had done much of the Oslo negotiating), speaker of the Palestinian Assembly.[35] Hamas had begun stirring against Arafat's apparent acquiescence to Barak's postponements of the land transfer promised at Wye.[36] At a second meeting of Arafat and Barak, again at the Erez Crossing into the Gaza Strip, the tone was full of bonhomie yet described as "frank," with Arafat repeating verbatim his previous demand for compliance with the Wye agreement. The prime minister, this time, proposed a two-week deadline to determine whether the Palestinians would accept his proposal to rewrite the time frame and the terms of Wye.[37] British reporter Graham Usher reported from Jerusalem on Palestinian unease over Barak's telling the world, from the time he was elected, that Jerusalem would be Israel's "indivisible capitol forever," ruling out any Israeli withdrawal to the borders of 1967, telling Arafat that he would have to accept that "settlement blocs" in the West Bank and Gaza would remain under permanent Israeli sovereignty, and that the solution for the 4.5 million Palestinian refugees "should be found in the countries where they are now living." Fulfillment of the Wye agreement, flawed though it was, would give the Palestinians full (Zone A) or partial (Zone B) control over 40 percent of the West Bank and civilian control over 96 percent of the Palestinians who lived there. Usher continued: "This hardly amounts to a state, but it would allow Arafat once more to dust down the threat of a unilateral declaration of independence should the final status talks snag."[38]

When Palestinian and Israeli negotiators next met, July 31, the Palestinian officials bluntly called Barak's request for changes in the Wye commitments unacceptable, and called the two-week delay for consideration a waste of time. It was "impossible to renegotiate such an agreement after it has gained official status," said chief negotiator Saeb Erekat. Barak, it was reported, was holding out on the third land transfer because it would leave some of the Israeli settlements isolated in the midst of Palestinian-administered territory. He feared this would create an opening for terrorist attack, which could derail the process again.[39] Negotiations simply broke off the following day, Sunday August 1. The tone hardened in ways reminiscent of the recriminations that had been the norm in Netanyahu's time.[40] Arafat, meanwhile, was hurrying around the Arab world seeking unity among Arab nations and Palestinian factions in the face of this Israeli insistence on rewriting the rules.[41]

The Washington administration put its influence on the side of Barak in this contest over the fulfillment of Wye obligations. Madeleine Albright determined to postpone her first visit to the region since Barak's election at least to the end of the month in order to help the Israelis persuade the Palestinians to accept changes in Wye.[42] By the following week the Palestinians had offered a minimal compromise. They would accept a slight delay in the transfer of land "if it comes within a package that ensures implementation of the Wye agreements."[43] Violence was beginning to escalate in this charged atmosphere. An angry Palestinian driver drove his car, twice over, into a crowd of Israeli soldiers, injuring eleven of them before being shot dead himself.[44] Hezbollah forces in Lebanon killed two Israeli soldiers and wounded six more after an Israeli car bomb had killed their regional commander, Ali Hassan Deeb.[45] Alarmed for the progress of their talks, Israelis, Palestinians, and Jordanians all mounted a concerted round up of Hamas.[46]

It was at this point that I finally wrote to Arafat, on August 13, feeling that the letter I had sent to Barak on June 25 required a parallel one to him. I always want, when I have written to one party to a conflict, to send copies to the other parties, leaving time enough so that the original addressee can have reflected on it. So I enclosed a copy of my letter to Barak but then took up the same issues in a way addressed more to Arafat himself, telling him that I followed with great interest the progress of initial negotiations between them, and Arafat's own dealings about implementation of the Wye agreement. But I wanted more to deal with the less particularized issues of which I had written to Barak.

The first, the concept of the two peoples, each with their own territories, accepting that some agreed number of the other people live among them, on the basis of a choice of citizenship but subject to the law of those among whom they lived, was one I had often written of before both to Arafat and to Rabin. I spelled it out once more, adding that nothing I heard from Barak's early statements, or had heard before from Shimon Peres, more alarmed me than the idea that the two peoples be separated, with closed borders between them. Even from an exclusively Israeli point of view, but more so from a Palestinian one, the border needed to be open, and both peoples able to move freely across it while respecting the principle that neither would set out to overturn the population balances in the other's state.

What was new in my presentation was a challenge to an Israeli supposition, often claimed by the settler movement, that the transfer of property rights, whether done justly (by purchase) or unjustly, entailed a transfer of sovereignty over territory. When Japanese or Vatican purchasers acquired property in New York or Los Angeles, no one interpreted this as meaning a transfer of territorial sovereignty. There was no justification in law for making Jewish purchases of property in Palestine any different.

Urging Palestinian welcome for some Jews to live in Palestinian territory, I wrote of the motives of settlers who had moved into the occupied territories. Hebron was the test case of religious motive for Jews to live there, because of the tombs of Abraham and the fathers, but the wrong Jews were there, with their shrines in Qiryat Arba to the most murderous of their heroes. Other Jews were there in friendship. Many of those living in the settlements encircling Jerusalem and Tel Aviv had come simply because of the financial inducements offered by a succession of Israeli governments. Those included some of the Israelis best disposed to peace with Palestinians. These, rather than those who had come out of hostility, were more likely to stay under the conditions I suggested. The presence then of Jews in Palestine and Palestinians in Israel would form a bond of friendship between the peoples, making most of the territorial demands Israelis had made on Palestinian territory unnecessary to them.

Dealing with the second perspective I had urged on Barak, the need to confront the anti-Palestinian racism prevalent in Israeli society while still fully repudiating the idea that Zionism of itself was racist, I put before Arafat the recommendation I had made to Barak, that Israeli society ought not tolerate the residential segregation that was enforced in the Jewish settlements on Palestinian territory, but should require that Palestinians be as free as Israelis to live there.

The letter had covered the same agenda as the one to Barak, of which I enclosed a copy for Arafat, but in a different way. I concluded:

> There is practical connection between these two ideas, the choice of citizenship for residents of either state and the non-acceptance of a strictly racist segregation in the settlements. Both will be inducements for the Israelis and Palestinians who have truly peaceful reason for living in one another's states, and disincentives for those who would want to live in the other's state merely as troublemakers. If these two basic principles could be realized in the final status, I believe they would beneficially transform the whole context for dealing with borders and settlements, and create opportunities for the

two states, Israel and Palestine, to live side by side in friendship and peace, open to one another.

Having put this before Prime Minister Barak, I thought I should spell it out just as explicitly to you, President Arafat. Like my letter to Mr. Barak, I will send a copy of this to President Clinton as well.

THE WYE 2 AGREEMENT

Gradually agreement came together on the Wye land-transfer issues. Both sides wanted to present an agreement by the time Madeleine Albright would arrive on September 1, but found they could not agree on the issue of prisoner releases. Netanyahu, at Wye, had agreed to free 750, but had not specified what sort of prisoners. Freeing a smaller number, he had seen to it that almost all were common criminals, or prisoners on the point of being released anyway, before he had suspended the agreement entirely. The Palestinians now wanted political prisoners released.[47]

Arriving on Thursday September 2, Albright found herself unable to overcome this standoff. She met Arafat and Mubarak first in Egypt, arrived late at night in Israel and went at once to a three-hour meeting with Barak that lasted into the early morning. There was still no deal.[48]

That same day, Ariel Sharon captured the leadership of Likud, defeating Ehud Olmert, the aggressively right-wing Mayor of Jerusalem. Netanyahu, after finally yielding the prime minister's office to Barak, had had to resign the party leadership because of a barrage of financial corruption charges.[49]

Prodded by Secretary of State Albright, the two sides finally reached the accord that would acquire the nickname "Wye 2" before the Shabbat began on September 3. Its central element was a plan to negotiate a conceptual "framework" for a permanent peace settlement by February 15, 2000, leading to the conclusion of a detailed agreement by September. From that time on, the rollercoaster course that would lead inexorably to the ill-prepared negotiations at Camp David in the next summer was determined.

Completion, in modified form, of the land-for-security agreement signed at Wye the previous year was also determined. The Israelis would now cede slightly more than 11 percent of the West Bank territory to partial Palestinian control, but in three stages: partly in that September (within ten days), partly on November 15, the rest on January 20. This land would be added to the 27 percent over which the PA already had full (Zone A) or partial (Zone B) control. The number of prisoners to be released would be 350, 200 within ten days, the rest in early October.

Nabil Sha'ath spoke of private "letters of assurance" from the United States as well.

The signing ceremony had to wait for the end of Shabbat, and would take place at the Egyptian resort of Sharm el-Sheikh on the Sinai coast. Secretary Albright spent her Saturday flying to Syria. Hafez al-Assad's initial enthusiasm for an agreement with Israel had waned by now, but she hoped, if negotiations with the Palestinians were a success, Assad would not want to be left out in the cold.[50] Mrs. Albright's talks in Syria appeared to yield no result. Assad still insisted on his formula that Israel resume talks from the point at which they had broken off in 1996. Itamar Rabinovich, former Israeli Ambassador to Damascus, had even written a *New York Times* op-ed of September 1, denying that Yitzhak Rabin had ever made the commitment the Syrians claimed, to return to the boundary of 1967. That had been the armistice line of the 1948–49 war, which had put the Syrians on the shore of the Sea of Galilee, with navigation rights on the sea and rights to the water. The then Secretary of State Warren Christopher had taken part in Rabin's 1967 dealings with the Syrians. The US State Department was consequently repository of the papers, and hesitant to reveal what they contained. The Syrians wanted President Clinton to intervene directly.[51]

The dispute went back to 1923, when these formerly Ottoman lands were being divided between the British Mandate of Palestine and the French Mandate of Syria. On British insistence, France had agreed to set the boundary 100 meters back from the Sea of Galilee shore, leaving all the water rights to the British. Israel now wanted that 1923 line, and negotiations for the return of the Golan to Syria stuck over this point.[52]

The Syrians had also required that Israel open a negotiating track with Lebanon. Consequently Mrs. Albright made a stop there, on her way back from Damascus for the Sharm el-Sheikh signing of Wye 2, the first time in ten years that a US Secretary of State had landed in an official plane in Beirut, to hold talks with Lebanese Prime Minister Selim al-Hoss.

Wariness and hope resulted from Wye 2. Barak and Arafat both faced deadlines of their own. Barak had set his 15-month limit with an eye to the end of Clinton's term as President. Israelis widely shared the conviction that Clinton, with his encyclopedic knowledge of every detail of the conflict and determination to bring reconciliation, was essential to the process. Arafat wanted his deal by September, two years late for the five-year promise made on the White House lawn in 1993, but on September 13, which was the date of the Oslo accord. He was anxious lest the Palestinian quest be sidelined by Israel's quest for peace with Syria. He feared that Barak wanted to settle with every other Arab party and leave the

Palestinians with no Arab support when their turn came. It was for this reason that he had agreed to modify the Wye timetable for the transfer of land, and agreed, as well, to submit a detailed list of all Palestinian security officials by September 13 and abide by a plan, to be thrashed out in a committee, for the collection of illegal weapons.[53]

The land transfers and the prisoner release followed even sooner than the ten days stipulated, 199 prisoners released on September 9,[54] and 7 percent of the West Bank, 160 square miles, transferred to partial Palestinian control on September 10. The land transfer involved no withdrawal of troops, as there were no Israeli bases in the area. There was little action on the ground, which was all hilly and sparsely populated. Many Palestinian officials, it was said, seemed unsure even where the new land was located. It touched and connected many existing Palestinian local government regions, from Nablus and Tulkarim south to Ramallah and Bethlehem. The actual changeover would take place the following Wednesday, when Israelis and Palestinians together would tour the land. The real meaning of the transfer was that now the Palestinian Authority would take over the land registries, issue building permits, and assume control also over antiquities, archaeological sites, and tourism. But Israel would continue security operations in the area.[55]

On September 13, a symbolic date since it was the sixth anniversary of the Oslo signing on the White House lawn, the first stage of the final status talks began ceremoniously, with Abu Mazen and David Levy meeting at the Gaza border. The Palestinians pointed out that this was the third renegotiation of what had been agreed before. Dennis Ross, the perennial negotiator for the United States, declared that a one-year deadline for a final status agreement was really unrealistic. "It's going to be very difficult."[56] Barak, on the following day, went to Maale Adumim, the largest of all Israeli settlements in the West bank and the one most threatening to the integrity of any Palestinian entity that would be established there. He declared it would "remain forever part of Israel," and said he considered it "part of Jerusalem."[57]

BARAK AND ARAFAT

In a determined show of cordiality, Barak invited Arafat to a midnight supper on September 16. The two habitual night owls talked, in a congenial atmosphere, for three hours into the morning, intending "to begin developing a working relationship and to discuss generally the negotiations for a permanent peace." Barak wanted to establish a pattern of regular meetings with Arafat.[58]

UN Secretary General Kofi Annan, in view of the increased negotiation activity, now appointed Norwegian Terje Roed-Larsen, the actual originator of the secret talks that led to the 1993 Oslo accords, as the UN special coordinator for the Middle East peace effort, his work to begin on October 1. The Israelis bristled at the thought of this appointment, protesting that the UN had expanded Larsen's functions beyond that of coordinator of UN activities in the region. This implied, declared Israel's UN mission, that the international organization had some role in the peace talks, and that was "unacceptable to the Government of Israel."[59]

Arafat, meanwhile, traveled to Washington for another session of what began to look like regular consultation with President Clinton. Meeting at the White House, they discussed how to bring the negotiations to a final peace settlement. Clinton, earlier in the year, had already offered to convene a summit conference if Israelis and Palestinians felt such a high-level meeting was needed to move the process along. When asked whether a Palestinian state should come of this, Clinton sidestepped, referring this question to the final-status negotiations. Arafat, throughout, sought Clinton's personal intervention, in contrast to Barak, who had forged a relation to Clinton but preferred that the administration keep at arm's length. Arafat, in Washington, spoke of approaching a "moment of truth," and called Barak "my new partner."[60]

But Barak, over his first three months in office, had outpaced even Netanyahu in authorizing new Israeli settlements in the West Bank. Since July, he had put out bids on 2,600 new housing units and five new bypass roads. Netanyahu had authorized only 3,000 new homes a year. These plans were made known by the Peace Now movement. Arafat, when he heard of them, described them as "destructive to peace." They were in line with the "master plan" for settlement expansion established by the Netanyahu government.[61]

How then was one to assess Barak's performance on settlements? Agence France-Presse reported, on October 12, that Barak had announced to the Settlement Council his intention to dismantle 15 of the 42 unauthorized settlements established over the past year. But when a couple of settler rabbis issued prohibitions against the "removal of Jews from Jewish land," he reduced to ten the number to be removed, "legalizing" the rest by decree. Five of those turned out to be unpopulated, and the settlers leaked the "compromise" agreement by which those "evacuated" from at least three of the five "populated" settlements would then be allowed to return to their outposts "in an orderly and legal fashion."[62] What was Barak doing? Was he trying at last to slow the pace of settlement against irresistible settler pressure, or had he deliberately reduced the effort to a charade? The question was more acute inasmuch as the Israeli army had recently seized some 10,000 hectares of arable and pastureland in the central and southern parts of the West Bank, 3,000 of them in the Hebron area "closed off" as a "training area" for the military. Hundreds more lay along the Green Line separating Israel from the West Bank in the Ramallah area, suggesting that Israel planned to annex a "security zone" strip, three or four kilometers wide, along that border.[63]

QUESTIONS OF RIGHTS, HUMAN AND NATIONAL

In mid-October the popular host of a Palestinian television talk show, Maher Dusahi, told on the air of having been arrested, jailed for 20 days, and tortured by Palestinian police after a guest on his program had denounced Arafat.[64] Official Syrian newspapers, meanwhile, accused Barak of "closing all routes" that might lead to a resumption of talks. Barak was denying that his predecessor Rabin had, in 1995, promised a return to the Golan border of 1967 in return for security measures from the Syrians, the agreement that had been "deposited" with the then US Secretary of State Warren Christopher.[65]

The contentious matter of the return of Palestinian refugees had by now become politically acute. Barak kept making successive statements that no Palestinian refugees at all would be allowed to return to ancestral homes in Israel. Arafat meanwhile was struggling to retain PLO political control over the terribly deprived refugee camps in Lebanon, where he was suspected of abandoning the refugees to their plight while he worked only for the rights of Palestinians still resident in their homeland.[66]

As November began, Barak and Arafat together met President Clinton in Oslo, where Arafat had received, jointly with Rabin and Peres, his Nobel Prize for Peace, "in a kind of multinational homage to the original dream of a permanent peace."[67] Clinton was concerned at the recent lull in negotiations. He won from Barak and Arafat a pledge to meet regularly over the next 100 days, up to mid-February. Each would appoint a team of negotiators, and they would meet up to three times a week in a "last sprint."[68]

Barak returned to lead a demonstration for the peace at the memorial to Rabin at the place of his murder in Tel Aviv.[69] But even as he did, the Palestinian Christian churches began planning joint protests against the building of a new mosque in Nazareth, in the shadow of the Church of the Annunciation. Arafat and the Palestinian Authority rejected the idea of putting the mosque so much in the face of the Christian shrine, but the Israeli government, which seldom granted Palestinians permits to build anything at all, had uncharacteristically authorized this mosque. The Christians, and the PA, saw this simply as an effort to sow division among Palestinians.[70] This issue would boil along for some time to come.

Trouble continued in Lebanon. Hezbollah guerrillas attacked the militiamen of Israel's surrogates, the South Lebanon Army, with mortar shells, wounding four in the heaviest fighting in weeks.[71]

From Rome came the first announcement that Pope John Paul II would visit Israel and the Palestinian territories for the last ten days in March.[72] But when the cornerstone for the Nazareth mosque was laid, the Vatican directly criticized the Israeli government for its decision to authorize the building.[73]

Barak's fragile governing coalition suffered during November, when Shas paralyzed the Knesset, threatening to pull out because of perceived slights. The loss of Shas's 19 seats would have reduced Barak to a minority government.[74]

Late in November the Palestinian Authority arrested seven prominent Palestinians from among 20 who had signed a statement accusing the Arafat administration of "tyranny and corruption." Three more were arrested the next day. Nine of the signers were members of the Palestinian Legislative Council with immunity, and there was discussion of taking that immunity away.[75] Many Palestinians complained that Arafat was "opening the door to opportunists who are spreading corruption throughout Palestinian society."[76]

Palestinian patience was wearing thin. A protest by 200 demonstrators against the expansion of Jewish settlements turned violent, as young Palestinians shot stones from slings and set tires on fire in the streets. Four demonstrators were injured as troops fired the familiar Israeli rubber-coated steel bullets at them.[77]

THE GOLAN FIASCO

Madeleine Albright at this period made a little-reported low-profile visit to Damascus. Most people regarded her mission as fruitless, assuming that the ailing Hafez al-Assad had given up on negotiating with Israel. The whole process seemed frozen in Damascus, and Syria was blamed for the impasse.[78] Everyone would be surprised when this effort suddenly blossomed.

Barak had hit heavy weather in his Knesset when he described Israel as a "democratic and multicultural state." A storm of protest rose at once as the watchdogs of the Right, the Russian immigrants, and the religious parties insisted that Israel as a state must value one culture above all others.[79] But Barak persisted, pledging to halt the expansion of settlements on the West Bank for a "moratorium of several months." More than that he dared not do, hesitating, in the face of his opposition, to call a real freeze. Gadi Baltiansky, his official spokesman, placated the settlers by declaring that "work already in progress" would go on. Barak's declared restriction on settlements was hailed, all the same, as major progress. At this point Mrs. Albright appeared on the scene to brief Barak and Arafat on the unexpected results of her mission to Syria.[80]

President Clinton, next morning (December 8) announced that Syria and Israel would reopen their talks about the Golan after a full four years of hiatus. Barak, he said, would be in Washington the following week as chief Israeli negotiator. Hafez al-Assad, too ill to take that role himself for Syria, would come on the scene only to sign a finished agreement, but would be represented by his long-time foreign minister, Farouk al-Shara. Never before had Israelis and Syrians met at such a high level.[81] Assad's illness, Barak's vows, and Clinton's hope for a legacy all contributed to what seemed a strong chance for success in this negotiation. Assad desired to finish what he had started in 1991 at the Madrid Conference.[82]

But there were risks as well. While Barak's allies rejoiced, his political foes rallied to hold on to the Golan. Ariel Sharon described the offer as "a big victory for Syria," saying that Barak had promised Israeli withdrawal to the 1967 line. Israeli residents on the Golan held emergency meetings to oppose return of the territory to Syria.[83]

In the Knesset, Barak got no encouragement for his venture with Syria. He won a vote, but tepidly, after six hours of hefty debate: 47 for, 31 opposed, and 24 abstentions. Three parties of his governing coalition refused their approval: the Sephardic Orthodox Shas, the National Religious Party, and the Russian refugees of Sharansky's Yisrael B'-Aliya. Barak promised that he would submit any agreement over the Golan to a popular referendum, the first in Israel's history. Sharon predicted that he would lose the referendum and the right wing geared up to stifle the proposition there.[84]

Things were brighter in Syria. Farouk al-Shara, foreign minister for the last 15 years, had always excoriated Israel in every statement. Now he "was seen as embodying his country's hopes for a swift peace." Damascus had shown a "gentler face" after all the years of tirades.[85]

Celebration filled the air even before the parties met. The *New York Times* headed its December 15 editorial "Israel and Syria speak of peace," despite noting "the narrow margin of approval Israel's parliament gave." *Middle East International*'s writers had as much assurance, Patrick Seale even titling his article "Where do they go from here?" as if it were a done deal.[86]

The parties arrived in Washington on December 15. French reporter Charles Enderlin narrates how Martin Indyk, now assistant secretary of state, climbed on board the Israeli plane on the tarmac to greet Barak before he descended. "I can't do it," said Barak. "What?" responded Indyk, "What do you mean? You were ready to do it, you were ready to have us convene the Syrians!" Barak answered, "Well, this law just passed in the Knesset. My people wouldn't understand. It's all too quick, and they will not understand.... I have to prepare my public for a full withdrawal from the Golan, and I have to take time." Indyk came down from the plane, met Secretary of State Albright and chief negotiator Dennis Ross, and said: "Houston! We have a problem!"[87]

The White House put a good face on the situation, hoping that "Maybe the dynamics of the negotiation will make him change his mind after all."[88] Clinton, Barak, and Shara all greeted this dawn of new peace talks after a halt of four years at an East Room press conference, Clinton and Barak both brief and unspecific. In Damascus, where Barak's step backward was not yet known, the government encouraged optimism without limits.[89] The bad news came from Jerusalem, where two cabinet ministers, heads of parties, Yitzhak Levy of the NRP and Natan Sharansky of Yisrael B'-Aliya, were in full revolt, threatening to pull their small but influential parties out of the coalition. All NRP members had opposed the proposition the previous Monday. Only the support of the ten Arab legislators and a few other left-leaning members from outside the coalition, on which Barak could count, assured that the proposal would have the needed 61 votes for a majority in the Knesset, but because Barak had committed himself to submitting the decision to a popular referendum, a narrow Knesset majority and a bitterly divided cabinet was bound to create difficulties.[90]

What was at stake here? The Golan Heights serve as a sort of artillery platform overlooking Galilee in Israel, and Damascus to the north. Some 17,000 Israeli settlers lived there, mainly Labor Party people who had responded to the call, when Israel first captured the Heights, to set themselves up as defender communities. Another 17,000 Druze citizens remained, their loyalty firmly with Syria. They had successfully resisted, over the years, in a campaign of civil disobedience, efforts to impose Israeli law on them. The 130,000 Syrians who had been driven from their homes at the time of Israel's conquest were now, with their descendants, more than 400,000 displaced persons anxiously awaiting their return. Families regularly stood shouting across the no man's land to their relatives on the other side, having no other way to communicate with them.

For Israelis, the Heights meant ski trails and vineyards. It seemed unlikely that Israel would agree to compromise its chances of peace for the skiing or the wines. But access to the scarce water resources of the region was the central matter of contention, as it had been for Britain and France when they drew the borderlines of their League of Nations Mandates in 1923, giving the British exclusive access to the Sea of Galilee and the upper Jordan. The border was just 100 meters back from the shore of the Sea of Galilee and the river, leaving the entire lakeshore on the British side. The actual sources of the Jordan, though, had remained in French hands. The Banyas source, at the foot of Mount Hermon, was well into the Golan, sure to return to Syria. Two other tributaries, the Dan and the Hasbani, arose in Lebanon, the Dan quickly crossing over into what was now Israel. Several other small streams drained down from the Golan into the Sea of Galilee.

But there was a rival line: the armistice line of 1949. The end of fighting in the Israeli Independence War had seen a defensive line that came down to the water in several places. It had marked the border up to June 4, 1967. The line was further complicated by the demilitarized zone patrolled by UN troops, which both sides to the conflict had hotly contested nonetheless.

There was a legal argument to be adduced as to which line should prevail. Security Council Resolution 242 spoke of the return of territory captured in 1967. That would give the advantage to Syria, in claiming all the land it had at that time. The Israelis argued for the 1923 British–French treaty line as legally definitive. But the question depended less on such arguments than on the desire of both sides to secure access to the water. The available water supplies could not truly meet the needs of either side, much less the combined needs of both, so many commentators argued an imperative need to develop desalinization programs as supplements, a thing that would best be done cooperatively.

The December meeting in Washington produced nothing more than talk of having talks later, which, President Clinton announced, would begin on January 3. Leaving the White House, Barak spoke of the conversation as "hard, but we're on the right track." Shara had no comment. Sandy Berger, Clinton's chief of staff, said they had "opened a gate" by this, the highest-level meeting between Syria and Israel in 50 years. He called the atmosphere "proper and cordial, but not warm."[91] In Ramallah, meanwhile, the Palestinians feared that Barak would use these talks with Syria as a pretext to slow progress with them. If he could settle with

Damascus, leaving them with reduced Arab support, he might squeeze more concessions from them.[92]

Few perceived how barren the prospects had become. Opinion polls in Israel at this time, ominously, gave only 41 percent of popular approval to the return of the Golan.[93] Barak, returning to Israel, made a reassuring late-night visit to Arafat, this time in Ramallah at the elegant home of Abu Mazen. They spoke of a long-delayed transfer of 5 percent of West Bank territory to Palestinian control happening within the week. Two other transfers remained pending.[94]

For three days up to Christmas, Israel and Hezbollah observed a rare and unannounced ceasefire, which the UN called the quietest period between them in two decades.[95] Goodwill gestures continued between Israel and Hezbollah, the Israelis releasing five Lebanese prisoners, the first such release since 1998, when Israeli had released 60 Lebanese in return for the remains of 40 Israelis. These five were among 21 who were said, by both Israeli and international human rights groups, to be held as "bargaining chips" for the return of four missing Israeli servicemen.[96]

Shas chose this moment to create a coalition crisis, announcing its intention to leave the government unless it received support for its schools, which were $36 million in debt. Their departure would leave Barak with a minority government of only 51 MKs, though the votes of small and Arab parties might keep him from falling.[97] Ariel Sharon, who had been rallying Golan settlers and Israeli rejectionists against Barak's plans, ran an op-ed attack in the *New York Times*, entitled "Why should Israel reward Syria?" He cited former President Gerald Ford as having promised in 1975 that any peace agreement with Syria would be predicated on Israel's keeping the Golan.[98]

Shas did not leave, at least not yet. The budget gave it most of the money it wanted, its spokesperson Yitzhak Suderi declaring: "It's a shame that we had to rock the government, rock the coalition, rock the world. But in the end that's why we won this battle."[99] For year's end, which coincided this year with the beginning of Ramadan, Israel released just seven of its 1,500 Palestinian prisoners. Some Knesset members complained of this release, saying it was surrender.[100]

Barak and Shara arrived in Washington on schedule on January 3. They had merely broken the ice in December. Now everyone expected them to go on a full-steam run at the issues that had bedeviled previous efforts: borders, security, normal relations. Ezer Weizman, the Israeli President, came to assist Barak. The party withdrew to the Clarion Hotel in Shepherdstown, West Virginia, 70 miles away from Washington, to be out of the glare of the press. But already Barak was insisting that security measures must be decided before giving any attention to borders. Clinton flew in by helicopter to welcome the Israeli delegation of 55 and the Syrian of 25. He announced that they would stay as long as it took to reach agreement.[101]

Clinton returned on the Tuesday, his visit already seen in terms of breaking what had promptly become an impasse, the Israelis and Syrians divided over whether Israeli security or the Golan borders should be the first topic. So much got through a news blackout. Clinton argued that four committees work simultaneously, on borders, security, water, and normalization.[102] This was agreed, but within two days it was evident that the committees were not meeting at all.[103]

Back in Israel, 20 rabbis issued a religious ruling that the Golan was a part of Eretz Yisrael and hence could not be surrendered in negotiation. American Orthodox Jews were out in force in Shepherdstown also, demanding that the talks be stopped, chanting "Traitor, go home!" to Barak, at the same time as Israel was formally transferring another 5 percent of West Bank territory to Palestinian jurisdiction, bringing the Palestinians up to full or partial control of 40 percent of the West Bank.[104]

Barak and Arafat had broken the deadlock over this transfer at their Ramallah meeting twelve days before. It had been meant to occur on November 15, the second of three scheduled transfers under the Wye accord. The Palestinians had rejected it then, saying the land offered was merely wasteland, but they settled now for no more than had been offered in November, putting "the relationship between us ahead of percentages," in the words of Israeli negotiator Oded Oran. Saeb Erekat commented: "Every moment we act as partners we find solutions. This is the key."[105]

Progress between Syrians and Israelis remained glacial. Clinton himself kept returning to try to induce agreement at least on an agenda. US officials back in Jerusalem were poring over the 20-year-old documents of Israeli negotiations with the settlers whom they had then evacuated from Sinai, thus breaking the Zionist taboo against ever abandoning a settlement.[106] By Sunday, Barak absented himself from the meeting to tour the nearby battlefield of the American Civil War at Antietem, commenting that more people had died there in a single day than in all of Israel's wars. Clinton gave a final, unsuccessful dinner, held meetings separately with both sides, and the Shepherdstown effort came to its frustrating close. Barak's concluding remark: "We won't sign an agreement unless it strengthens Israel's position."[107]

By the time the talks broke up, 100,000 rallied in Tel Aviv's Rabin Square to oppose a withdrawal from the Golan, trying to get a jump-start on any demonstrations by the Peace Now camp. Their banners, in

Hebrew, English, and Russian, read: "The Golan stays, Barak goes," and "I have no other land."[108]

Then began the leaks. *Ha'aretz* printed what it called a draft peace treaty framed by the Clinton administration.[109] On the vexing question of the border the draft bracketed each side's already well-known views.[110] As Joel Greenberg interpreted it, the leaked document suggested that Israel meant to keep its settlers on the Golan even after a military withdrawal, something Syria would not abide. The US media's inclination was to blame all the delay on Syria.

Talks had been scheduled to resume on January 19, a week after the failure at Shepherdstown, but by Monday 17, Damascus was demanding that its chief negotiating point, the position of the border, be settled at once. Further high-level talks were now postponed. Instead of Barak and Shara, both sides would send "experts" to Washington. The issue had gone on indefinite hold.[111] In Damascus, Syrian commentary insisted that Israel must first agree that Syria rightfully owned the Golan Heights. Only then could bargaining take place over other issues such as water rights, normalization of diplomatic relations, and security arrangements. Government spokespersons bitterly resented the leaking of the US working paper to the Israeli press. Damascus Radio intoned that "the Israeli side kept eroding the demarcation of the June 4, 1967 line," and that Barak was trying to make the talks a "labyrinth," entering into "negotiations for the sake of negotiations."[112] As the talks floundered, yet another Israeli soldier was killed in Lebanon, by a rocket fired near Sidon. Barak's promise to withdraw his troops from there by July relied on his coming to a peace agreement with Syria.[113]

The Lebanese front deteriorated still further while the talks with Syria festered. Killings mounted, of Israelis and Lebanese. Barak fretted for the resumption of the talks with Syria. The Israelis resumed air strikes, shutting down civilian life entirely in much of Lebanon. Arab and European nations loudly condemned the Israeli air raids on cities, describing them as a major blow to Middle East peace. "Guns do the talking," reported Michael Jansen from Beirut.[114] General Giora Eilad by now doubted that Israel would be able to withdraw from Lebanon by July but thought, in expectation of a peace pact with Syria, that it might be by the end of the year.[115] But shrewd Israeli reporter Peretz Kidron saw that already Israel was making preparations for an early withdrawal from Lebanon.[116] An aide to Hezbollah's leader, Sheikh Hassan Nasrallah, vowed that Hezbollah had no intention of halting attacks so that Israel could fulfill its promise to withdraw by July without further losses. Israel could not be trusted to withdraw if the pressure were relaxed.[117]

Ariel Sharon, anticipating that Clinton would still push the Israeli–Syrian track, began now a campaign to deny any Western aid to Syria as part of any deal. "I want to sound the alarm," he said, "before it is too late." His partner Silvan Shalom, in an effort to dilute the influence of Israeli Arab voters, pushed in the Knesset for a bill that would require a majority of all voters, not merely those who voted, in any Golan referendum.[118] The bill passed instantly, with a majority of 60–53, as three of Barak's coalition partners, NRP, Yisrael B'-Aliya, and Shas all cast their votes for it.[119]

Hezbollah was concentrating now on the South Lebanon Army (SLA), Israel's Lebanese surrogates, killing five SLA with a powerful bomb exploded near their jeep near Hasbaya.

The case was desperate enough that President Clinton, traveling in the subcontinent, announced that he would meet Hafez al-Assad in Geneva the following Sunday. He had been on the phone to Barak and Assad ever since the breakdown of talks in January.[120]

The meeting took place, as scheduled, but Clinton brought nothing to it other than Barak's proposals, none of his own, urging Assad's acceptance of a procedure and proposals that Syria had already rejected.[121] It was Clinton's first meeting with Assad in five years. He failed entirely to get the Syrians to resume talks with Israel. The Syrian President gave Clinton a lengthy lecture on border history, insisted that Israel return to the border of June 4, 1967, and that the border question be resolved before there could be discussion of security measures.

A dejected White House reported that it would be "impossible" to predict when talks would resume. The failure met with near despair—"very bad news"—by the diplomats involved, who had not imagined Assad could refuse the US President. They speculated that Israel, with no prospect of a Syrian deal, would now very quickly withdraw from its Lebanese "security zone." Madeleine Albright and Dennis Ross were dispatched together to explain the bad news to Barak.[122]

And so that adventure ended. How had it come to this? Amid all the tumult of violent events, some things become clear. Israel had at no time felt itself bound by law in any part of the negotiation, nor had President Clinton even hinted at any such dimension of the case.

The key decision had been made when Netanyahu determined that the question of the Golan should be the subject of a popular referendum of Israeli voters. The Knesset so ordered, Barak confirmed the decision, and Sharon and Shalom embroidered it with ever more difficult obstacles to any agreement. The whole matter had been subjected to the whims of Israeli popular opinion, despite its being a clear question of law, to which

Israeli government was bound and which it was competent to fulfill. No public opinion other than Israeli is understood to have such value.

Subjecting such a decision to the volatile whims of an easily panicked public has to be destructive. Both the Israeli and the Palestinian, as well as the Lebanese and Syrian publics have their share of rejectionists, people who want a victory over enemies and no peace. These people know perfectly well how to pull the Israeli public's chain, creating alarms that will paralyze the public every time. By doing so, the rejectionists can infallibly prevent anything. In this case, it was Ariel Sharon and his henchmen who sabotaged any possibility of reaching agreement over the Golan, and consequently of being able to withdraw peacefully from the occupation of southern Lebanon. But the same tactic is familiar to Hamas, to the Israeli settlers, and to anyone who wants to disrupt any stage of a development toward peace or reconciliation of the Middle Eastern parties. In fact every part of the process is subjected to that same absolute norm, that it be judged ultimately by what the Israeli public will bear. It is consistently a reason to ignore any considerations of law whatever.

REASSURING INTERLUDE: THE PAPAL VISIT

Western Christians hardly figure in the Israeli public scene. Christian Palestinians tend to be classified by Israelis simply as Palestinians, that population that has no other than a negative part in their life, whose needs and suffering they can ignore. Western Christians remain tourists, and even if, like many of the religious orders, they take up residence, they seldom take any part in the life of the country.

Pope John Paul II had long intended to visit the region, "the Holy Land," during the millennial year. Having witnessed, as a young man in the Second World War in Poland, the Nazi murder of Jews, many of them his own close friends, he had worked hard throughout his pontificate to heal the long-neglected wounds in the relations between Catholics and Jews. He had championed the rights of both Israel and the Palestinians. It had been a great event when, on December 30, 1993, the Vatican and the State of Israel established full diplomatic relations. Israel sent an ambassador to the Holy See and the Vatican raised the status of its apostolic delegate to that of nuncio (the Holy See's term for its ambassadors).[123]

In February, during what was Arafat's ninth visit to the Pope, the Vatican signed a pact with the PLO guaranteeing church rights in the expected Palestinian state. Freedom of religion and the status of Christian churches were promised and the Vatican recognized the "inalienable national legitimate rights of the Palestinian people," stating that "unilateral decisions and actions altering the specific character and status of Jerusalem are morally and legally unacceptable." The wording was taken as a reproach to Israel and a reaffirmation of Vatican support for a Palestinian state. This was not new, but it lent moral authority to the Palestinian cause, adding to the pressures on Israel. The Foreign Ministry summoned the Vatican's envoy to a meeting at which Israel expressed "great displeasure" at the inclusion of the Jerusalem issue and "other issues which are the subjects of Israeli–Palestinian negotiations on a permanent status."[124]

Early in March there appeared a first outline of what would become a sweeping papal apology for the historic failings of the Catholic Church, expected later in the month.[125] When it appeared, as a solemn prayer for reconciliation at a special mass in St. Peter's Basilica on March 11, it caused astonishment. The Pope apologized and begged forgiveness from victims and their descendants for many historic transgressions of the Church, including especially the perennial persecution of the Jews, the Crusades, and the Inquisition. The gesture, having no precedent in Catholic history, made a deep impression worldwide.[126]

The Pope would travel via Jordan. Competition had arisen about rival sites for the baptism of Jesus by John in the Jordan, and the Vatican gave reassurance that the Pope would visit both the Jordanian and Israeli sites.[127] As the day approached, the authorities had jitters over papal security on the trip, but Israelis and Palestinians were by now joining hands to protect him. Tourist revenues of $50 million were predicted. Rabbi Ovadia Yosef chose this time to compare Meretz leader Yossi Sarid, who had been recalcitrant about government funding for Shas schools, to the wicked Haman, enemy of the Jews in the time of the Persian king Ahasuerus (biblical book of *Esther*, 3:5–6). This had been the language used before the murder of Yitzhak Rabin, and the Shas guru would soon be charged in court with incitement to the murder of the Meretz leader.[128]

The Pope arrived at Tel Aviv's Ben-Gurion airport on Tuesday March 21, greeted by Israeli Prime Minister Barak and President Ezer Weizman, and telling how he had looked out, like Moses, over the Promised Land from the heights of Mount Nebo in Jordan the previous day.[129] On March 22 he visited Bethlehem, venerating the purported site of the birth of Jesus, cordially greeting Yasser Arafat and his wife Suha, who had come to meet him. He spoke extensively at the Dheisheh refugee camp in Bethlehem, where he deplored the plight of Palestinians. To finish his day, he said mass at the Cenacle, traditional site for the Last Supper.[130]

On March 23 the Pope visited the Holocaust memorial, Yad Vashem. His words were stirring, especially his repeated quotation from the Psalms:

> I have become like a broken vessel.
> I hear the whispering of many—terror on every side!
> as they scheme together against me, as they plot to take my life.
> But I trust in you, O Lord; I say, "You are my God."
> (Ps 31:13–15)

But it was not the words so much as the sight, broadcast live on Israeli television,[131] that touched the hearts of Israelis. Later, during the summer, I heard Rabbi Stephen Cohen describe the effect of this, and the Pope's later appearance at the Western Wall, thus: Jews had been so persecuted, so beaten about the ears for so many centuries by Christians, that they had trouble hearing the many much better things that the Pope and other Christians said in these recent years. The sight of the Pope there, at the Yad Vashem, at the Wall, had an altogether different effect on Israelis. Here at last was a man who cared, who understood Jewish suffering.

The afternoon's event was less successful. Leading representatives of the three Abrahamic religions assembled at a new hall erected at the Pontifical Institute Notre Dame, a pilgrimage hostel at the edge of the Old City walls. The Pope addressed them formally, the Chief Rabbi and the Grand Mufti took sharp verbal shots at one another's positions on the city of Jerusalem, and the Grand Mufti eventually walked out.

On Friday the Pope went to the Galilee, celebrating a mass attended by 100,000 people at the traditional site of the Sermon of the Mount. He delivered a homily on peace from which both Israelis and Palestinians felt a sense of endorsement.[132] The Pope went to Nazareth the following day, and was cheered by a mixed Muslim and Christian crowd, despite the still festering dispute over building a mosque in the face of the Christian basilica. It was a day of joy at the site that had been the source of so much tension.[133] The Pope concluded his day with formal courtesy visits in Jerusalem, to the assembled consuls general, to the Greek Orthodox Patriarch, the Armenian Patriarch, and the Grand Mufti.

The final day of the visit, Sunday, saw the crowning event, the Pope's visit to the Western Wall.[134] Approaching the Wall, as pilgrim, like a Jew, with no mention of Jesus, he prayed, head bowed, and inserted, in Jewish fashion, a paper bearing his prayer into a crevice between the massive stones. The paper was retrieved as soon as he left, this man who, escaping from a Nazi slave labor camp during the Second World War, had come home to find all his close friends and neighbors, Jews, simply gone. His petition was for forgiveness for all the harm that Christians had done to Jews throughout their common history. That done, he visited the Holy Sepulchre and departed.[135]

The visit had been a moment of light in the midst of the year 2000's descent into darkness. Deborah Sontag reported in the *New York Times* that, as soon as the Pope was gone, Israel resumed its normal discord. Ovadia Yosef was under the attorney general's investigation by now for his threats to the life of Yossi Sarid. That very day, Clinton had had his disastrous meeting in Geneva with Hafez al-Assad, and all hopes of peace with Syria seemed dashed. There were anxieties about another flare-up on the Lebanese border.[136] The following day would see a police recommendation that former Prime Minister Binyamin Netanyahu and his wife be brought up on charges of bribery, fraud, and theft while in office. His days in politics seemed, for the time, to have ended.[137] But one note of grace did come through that day. Interior Minister Natan Sharansky, a fair-minded man so often counted among the hawks of Israeli society, announced that the lands belonging to the Palestinian village of Kafr Kassem, which had been confiscated decades earlier to make room for the development of an Israeli town, would be returned, a significant step toward equality for Israeli Arabs.[138]

SOUTHERN LEBANON: EXTRACTION OR EXPULSION?

Israelis had good reason for their worries about southern Lebanon. Their Lebanese surrogates, the South Lebanon Army, were deeply worried by now that the Israeli withdrawal would mean their abandonment to the anger of their own society. Their defenses began to collapse and their members to throw themselves on the mercy of their fellow Lebanese.[139] Much effort went into denying these obvious facts. Ehud Barak declared that he foresaw no trouble in leaving Lebanon by the appointed date, and saw no need for a significantly larger multinational force (UNIFIL). General Antoine Lahad, Lebanese commander of the SLA, promised that his forces, a remaining 2,500 men, would not disband and flee, but would stay to "defend their land unto the death." He felt responsible for 70,000 to 80,000 Lebanese sympathizers in the area, and strongly opposed the Israeli pullout.[140]

Authorities in Lebanon were clearly worried about what would follow an Israeli withdrawal. For 22 years, since the Security Council had demanded Israeli withdrawal in its 1978 Resolution 425, the constant cry had been "Israel must go." Now Lebanon and its overseers in Syria began to fear the prospect. Syria would lose a bargaining chip when the Israelis went, their ability to deliver a peaceful Lebanon in return for the Golan. The Lebanese government foresaw with dread an increase in Hezbollah's political strength.[141]

Everyone assumed that talks with Syria would be halted until the new President, Hafez al-Assad's son Bashar, had solidified his position. Bashar, however, announced that time had not run out and it was not too late for a Syrian–Israeli deal.[142] This and the Lebanese track were inextricably entangled. Israel announced that it would free 13 of the 15 Lebanese detainees it had been holding as "bargaining chips," but by the following day this was held up again because of protests by the relatives of the lost Israeli airman Ron Arad.[143]

Cost estimates began to come in for Israel's pullout from Lebanon, set at $250 million, but that did not account for the relocation and settlement of SLA officers, said Amos Yaron, director general of the Defense Ministry.[144] Pressure on the SLA kept mounting as Hezbollah guerrillas blew up an Israeli-controlled outpost, killing at least one SLA soldier and wounding six, while two others, still buried in the ruins, were presumed dead.[145] Early in May, the foreign ministers of Syria, Egypt, and Saudi Arabia met at Palmyra, in Syria, to discuss the Israeli pullout and the problems it presented.[146]

The Israelis, meanwhile, in a misdirected blow at Amal, the other Shi'ite militia in Lebanon with which Israel truly had no quarrel, bombed the home of their commander, Abbas Hallal in the Islim al-Tuffah ("apple valley," opening to the coast midway between Tyre and Sidon), wounding his mother and five other civilians.[147] This venture opened up new fighting throughout the "security zone," the fiercest since that launched by Netanyahu the previous June.[148] Seeing the escalation, Barak ordered a sudden halt to all reprisal raids in Lebanon, declaring that all the Israeli attacks had been merely "accidents." His nemesis Sharon, however, called for a "thorough, systematic, and continuous policy to hit both Syrian and Lebanese interests in Lebanon."[149]

But the fight was now on. After this spate of violence, Israel began speeding up its preparations for withdrawal in case Barak should decide to do so before his self-imposed deadline of July 7. His senior military experts expected that they would do so under fire, some already advising Barak to do it as soon as possible. Some thought these hints of early withdrawal were merely aimed at Syria to remind them that time was running out to resume negotiations. General Lahad, however, was asking the Lebanese government for blanket amnesty for his soldiers.

Israelis had now begun to think of asking the UN to intervene on their behalf. The UN would be called upon to certify that Israel had indeed withdrawn from all Lebanese territory so that guerrillas could no longer legitimize their attacks on Israel's northern border. But Prime Minister Selim al-Hoss chose this moment to tell the UN's Terje Roed-Larsen that Lebanon considered a parcel of land on the edge of the Golan Heights to be Lebanese as well. There would be no dispute about the 1923 border between Israel and Lebanon, but this Golan question could be a problem.[150]

The Israeli side of the border became restive too. Residents of the northernmost town of Metullah went on strike, burning tires in the street and chanting "security, security!"[151]

Then came the avalanche. On Wednesday May 17, Israeli troops began evacuating outposts in southern Lebanon, "in preparation," they explained, "for an overall pullout from the area by July." Their handovers of positions appeared intended to let the SLA continue functioning after the Israeli withdrawal. The future of the SLA's fighters, however, looked now more dubious than ever. An Israeli officer was quoted as saying the handovers "do not signal a speeding up of the timetable." The guerrillas, of course, kept up their assault, shelling most heavily those outposts closest to the Israeli border. Barak announced a $400 million program for the improvement of sewage, water, roads, schools, and business incentives for the area, as a way to improve the morale of residents jittery at the signs of withdrawal.[152]

Fighting once again became intense, as two Israeli solders, two SLA, one Hezbollah guerrilla, four Lebanese civilians and one UN peacekeeper were killed.[153] Israeli warplanes pounded away at Hezbollah positions in return.[154]

Soon Hezbollah was advancing fast across southern Lebanon as the Israeli "security zone" collapsed. Israeli television showed them raising yellow flags emblazoned with Kalashnikovs over fortified Israeli command posts. The SLA abandoned its villages. Dozens of Israeli buses transported 1,000 SLA fighters and their families to a makeshift refugee camp inside Israel. Israel kept bombing the Hezbollah fighters and their triumphant followers, killing six civilians and wounding dozens, according to Lebanese officials. Tanks and troops welled up from within Israel to defend the border.

Barak found himself under pressure to pull the remaining troops out as fast as he could. This was no such orderly, staged withdrawal as he had intended. To his security cabinet he said, "There have been such moments, and there will be more in the future," pledging that he would pull all Israeli troops out "within a few weeks." When the cabinet continued trying to speed things up, he warned that forces in Lebanon "should not test our resolve by daring to fire at Israeli soldiers, and much less at northern border communities."

For the SLA, though, it had become a desperate scramble out of Israel's shrinking "security zone." Israeli planes were now bombing the Israeli tanks, artillery and armored personnel carriers that the SLA had left behind, so that Hezbollah would not get them. Sharon was still screaming that: "We must not unilaterally withdraw without first establishing quiet in southern Lebanon. That is the first thing that must be done. Unfortunately, the prime minister can't stand the pressure."[155]

And then it was all over. Headlines the next day proclaimed: "Israelis out of Lebanon after 22 years," and "Guerrillas ride through the zone in triumph." Before dawn on Wednesday May 24, Israel had abandoned the Crusaders' Beaufort Castle, their last outpost in Lebanon. Barak declared this the end of an "18-year tragedy" (counting only from the 1982 invasion, not that of 1978 and the Security Council demand for withdrawal in Resolution 425). Israel, he said, "has regained the initiative in the halting Middle East peace efforts."

Celebratory processions took place in Lebanon, people traveling with the Hezbollah units into the lands so long held by Israel, elderly women ululating, sprinkling cars with rose petals and rice as if at a wedding.[156] At the Fatima Gate, on the border, there was a crush of 3,000 SLA militia members and their families trying to flee into Israel, bitterly protesting their abandonment.[157]

After this convulsion in Lebanon, the political and military landscape had become uncertain. A surprising calm followed this rapid spasm. The Israelis issued stern warnings to Syria and Lebanon that they must control Hezbollah. Israeli soldiers felt a mixture of happiness and pain.[158]

A dangerous precedent had been set. Palestinians, disillusioned by the backward progress they had experienced all the years since Oslo, saw this as proof that a determined guerrilla assault could force the Israeli out of unlawfully occupied territory. Yasser Arafat was almost alone among them in asserting that this was not so, that Israel had left Lebanon by its own choice, and that Hezbollah had done nothing more than to hurry an Israeli decision already made. But in June, I was able to watch as a crowd of Israeli settlers stood besieging the Palestinians' Jerusalem headquarters, Orient House, on Jerusalem Day, the annual celebration of the 1967 capture of the city. The unarmed Palestinian guards who struggled to prevent the breaking down of the gates took up spontaneously the taunting deep chant: "Hezbollah! Hezbollah! Hezbollah!"

THE CRESCENDO OF PALESTINIAN DESPAIR

Amid all these shiftings and turnings, arrogance, and humiliations, what was the actual experience of Palestinians? I was in Jerusalem for much of this time and have, therefore, a different sense than what I normally got from following press at home.

One can follow this through day-to-day events, much as we have done with such episodes as the dealings with Syria over the Golan, the papal visit, or the extrication from the southern Lebanon "security zone." My own experience of it was largely in visiting friends during this period, old Israeli friends who are of the essence of the strong Israeli peace movement, the Palestinians who are their counterparts, seeing the lines of people waiting at the checkpoints, sensing the hesitation of either Israeli or Palestinian to go into one another's territory, witnessing house demolitions, often side by side with Israeli protesters who put themselves in front of the bulldozers and other engines of destruction.

I had arrived in mid-May, with a party of graduate theology students from a consortium of theology schools in the area of Boston, Protestant, Catholic, and Orthodox, to whom I and two other professors gave a workshop seminar on the conflict and its religious character for some three weeks, into June. We visited the biblical sites, but concentrated much more on meeting people in all the ordinary places of Israeli and Palestinian life. Things had not yet become violent, and the commitment to resolving the clash between Israel and the Arab world was still alive and well from the time of the Madrid and Oslo processes. Expectations were becoming frayed. A wariness was in the air.

Alongside the student workshop, I was engaged with a film crew from Boston College, making a documentary on the peace efforts of the two communities and peoples. We interviewed numerous Israelis and Palestinians, intelligent, activist people on either side. Their determination to bring about the peace was unmistakable, as was their frustration. By the time first the students and then the film crew had gone home to the United States, I stayed on, first to give a seminar on conflict resolution to an international group of my fellow Jesuits, then to take part in a further seminar in which some 35 Jesuits, from all parts of the world, who had taken a prominent part in the Catholic effort to heal relations with Jews, met people from every facet of Jewish life.

Israelis especially had a sense that they greatly needed US President Bill Clinton, who had come to know every facet of the Middle East situation with such precision, and was so ready to invest his time and his person that no successor, of either US political party, could be expected to do the things he could. That gave urgency to the work of negotiation, a deadline. But the Palestinians we interviewed feared that too many opportunities had been wasted, that they were being pressed into negotiations inadequately prepared. Basic affronts like the expansion of settlements, confiscation of land, the carving up of Palestinian territory into little Bantustan enclaves by limited-access roads connecting the Israeli settlements had been forced through by the Barak government, they felt, even far more extremely than they had been by Netanyahu. Was this the prelude to a restoration or was it preemptive action to prejudice any kind of resolution that could be made?

The settlers in the West Bank continued their adamant opposition to transfer of the three villages overlooking Jerusalem, thwarting the possibility that Abu Dis could become home to a Palestinian assembly. While we were there, we saw these fanatics trying to fence off, with barbed wire, areas in Abu Dis that were strategic only in the sense that they would prevent valued Palestinian access. They brawled violently with any Palestinians who protested, and of course enjoyed the protection of the police. Their barbed wire might be removed overnight, but they would return again, more disruptive than ever, each day.

Already at the beginning of May the Housing Ministry had announced that it would make "an exception" to the freeze on new settlement housing units: 200 new houses in Maale Adumim, the settlement most calculated to separate the West Bank into non-contiguous portions and cut it off from its Jerusalem core. This announcement cast a pall over the Eilat talks about "final status" issues. Militant settlers confronted Palestinian residents in Hebron, until Israeli soldiers had to remove scores of them from an encampment in the heart of a Palestinian neighborhood. One of their hotheads, Elyakim Haetzni, declared this the start of a "civil war," exhorting the soldiers to disobey orders to evacuate settlements, urging the settlers themselves to fight back, forming a private militia. The army seemed helpless to enforce any law upon them. Benny Kashriel, mayor of Maale Adumim, told the newspaper *Ma'ariv*: "The readiness for a fierce struggle grows every time more territory is handed over." Natan Sharansky described the handing over of Abu Dis and the other villages as an unacceptable "down payment" to the Palestinians, objecting that East Jerusalem would then become the final payment.[159]

The settlers aimed to take over high ground anywhere in the West Bank. Day after day, soldiers had to remove them from one hilltop near Nablus. When, in the Eilat negotiations, Oded Oran declared that a Palestinian state would indeed result from final status talks, Barak's office diminished the statement at once, saying that: "if there is a Palestinian state it will be as a result of negotiation."[160] It took a visit by Dennis Ross, renewing direct pressure from the United States, to reinstill any life into the Eilat effort.[161]

Things became so bad that it required a further Barak–Arafat meeting, the first since mid-March, the two talking for hours through the night

114   The Failed Negotiations

before agreeing that the talks should resume. The sides would meet now at an undisclosed location, hoping to address the status of Jerusalem, borders, refugees, and Jewish settlements before the time useful for negotiation (that is, before Clinton would be wrapped up in a new US election campaign) ran out.[162]

Intense feelings surfaced over the issue of Palestinian prisoners (1,650 at this time) as Israeli troops clashed with Palestinians rallying in the West Bank for their release. Rubber-coated steel bullets wounded six Palestinian stone-throwers. Barak meanwhile backtracked once again on his promise to transfer the three villages. Dennis Ross departed for Washington with mutterings about "much work remain[ing]" and "potential for progress."[163]

Angry protest erupted in Ramallah, another confrontation of stones and rubber-coated steel bullets—some protesters demanding release of prisoners, others calling on the Palestinian Authority not to abandon the refugees. It was another volatile week of frustration and violence. By May 15, four Palestinians had been killed by Israeli bullets in these riots and 400 injured. In addition, two Palestinian children had been killed in the northern West Bank town of Qalqiliya by a car driven by an Israeli settler. Palestinians believed these killings had been deliberate and no accident. For the duration of the first half of May, 650 of the 1,650 prisoners had been on hunger strike, several of them hospitalized and in urgent need of treatment. Any deaths among them would have brought about even wider fury. The rising young leader in Fatah, Marwan Barghouti, declared that there was no point in talking peace until the prisoners were freed. "All the agreements signed with the Israelis have stipulated that the prisoners should be released, but Israel has deliberately refused to release them," he insisted.[164]

So the peace talks had stalled. Israeli right wingers wanted to suspend the talks altogether because of the stone throwing. Barak found himself hamstrung by his political weakness. To keep Shas, with its 17 votes, in the coalition, he finally gave in to it over subsidizing the indebted schools.[165]

Confrontation became more serious on May 15, when for the first time in more than four years the Palestinian police exchanged gunfire with Israeli troops. The battle broke out first at the Beit El junction near Ramallah, at a time when chaotic clashes were occurring throughout the West Bank and Gaza. As crowds charged with stones and fireworks, the Israeli troops used first tear gas, then their rubber-coated steel bullets, then live ammunition. At this point Palestinian military police stationed on a hilltop north of Ramallah suddenly opened fire themselves. The Israelis responded with massive live fire in return and the fray continued for several hours. Late at night, enraged Palestinians attacked Joseph's Tomb at Nablus, shooting and throwing firebombs. One Palestinian was killed in this exchange. It was the anniversary of the Palestinians' 1948 disaster, the *Naqba*. Yet even as this went on Barak won Knesset approval for the transfer of the three villages to full Palestinian jurisdiction, an approval however that he would rescind yet again.[166]

These days were filled with the drama of Israel's precipitous withdrawal from Lebanon. That spectacle briefly quieted the turmoil in Palestine, but US commentator Milton Viorst pointed out nonetheless that the violence between the Palestinian Authority and Israel had shown a flaw in the Oslo plan. The Palestinians had agreed to forswear their right of resistance to occupation in return for vague Israeli promises to return the land. By now, as they saw the settlements growing, Palestinians were finding that too little was returned. Increasingly they believed the Israelis were acting in bad faith.[167]

A back channel of negotiation had meanwhile been created in Stockholm, with Dennis Ross on hand, to compensate for the fruitless negotiation efforts in the region itself.[168] Israel and the United States sought to portray these talks as making "significant progress," while Abu Mazen, representing the Palestinians along with along with Abu Ala and Hasan Asfur, found that "nothing of substance" had been accomplished in the two protracted rounds of talks up to May 21. "The ball is in Israel's court," he said, "and what is needed is an Israeli decision to come to terms with UN resolutions."[169] Late in May came the first anniversary of Barak's election. He found himself by now trying to put out fires on many fronts at once. At the West Bank city of Qalqilya Palestinian police held back demonstrators with nightsticks, but Israeli soldiers intervened all the same, wounding 20 with their rubber-coated steel bullets.[170] Jerusalem was emerging as an issue, its two images, as Deborah Sontag saw it, converging in a blur: the one "eternal, undivided capital" for Israelis, their own future capital for Palestinians, seemingly irreconcilable concepts, while in Stockholm the altogether non-secret back-channel negotiations considered seriously the ways to break this impasse. On the contested slopes of Abu Dis a new and modern governmental building had arisen, with a clear view of the Al-Aqsa Mosque and the Dome of the Rock. No one would quite willingly admit that it was intended for the Palestinian Assembly.[171]

In what seems now more like the later *intifada* situation, a firebomb cast into a passing car on May 21 critically injured a two-year-old Israeli girl. Barak responded by blocking all entrances to the Palestinian territories, declaring them unsafe for Israelis and tourists, and recalling his back-channel negotiators from Stockholm. This marked the end of a year of normalization. Because of the surging violence in the West Bank, in Gaza and in Lebanon, Barak cancelled a planned trip to Washington to consult with Clinton on the American-mediated final status talks. The last two weeks had produced an unpredictable shift on the ground. Palestinian frustration with the slow pace of the peace efforts erupted just as the negotiators had been getting down to the substantial points in Stockholm. The United States promised a Ramallah visit by Sandy Berger, the President's chief of staff, as a way to calm things down.[172]

Israel lifted the travel ban on Jericho on May 24. The Palestinians arrested three men suspected in the firebombing earlier in the week.[173] Barak was touring the country, talking prospects of peace in the nervous town of Qiryat Shemona on the northern border.[174]

By the month's end, Palestinian prisoners in Israeli jails ended the hunger strike that had gone on, by now, for some 31 days, some 500 prisoners living on liquids only for that time. This calmed the street demonstrations somewhat. The Israelis set up a more liberal policy on family visits to prisoners and let five of them out of solitary confinement. The suspended Stockholm talks, it was said, would now resume at an undisclosed location in the Middle East.[175] Barak had finally gotten to Clinton, startling the US administration by his willingness to relinquish the Jordan valley settlements that were Israel's buffer with Jordan. This constituted a breakthrough, as the Labor Party's Allon Plan had always seen these settlements as essential to Israel's safety.[176]

The Clinton meeting with Barak had taken place in Portugal. During the ninety minutes Barak spent with Clinton in Lisbon, reviewing the whole prospect of a Middle East deal before the Clinton Presidency would end, the two made their preparations to call a three-way summit at Camp David. Clinton would send his Secretary of State, Madeleine Albright, to the Middle East the following week. He was frustrated that the Israeli and Palestinian governments had not made more progress toward completing a final status accord by their self-imposed deadline of September 13. The main issues were still outstanding: the size and shape of a Palestinian state, the future of Jerusalem, the fate of the Palestinian refugees. Clinton was prepared to invest time, and believed that the withdrawal from Lebanon the week before had "transformed the political landscape in the region and created a new opening for a breakthrough."[177]

Barak's critics complained, all through this time, of his withdrawal from Lebanon, of his having handed over control, by now, of 42.9 percent of the West Bank to the Palestinian Authority, of his agreement eventually to transfer the three villages near Jerusalem. Realizing the danger he lived in from embittered settlers, Barak's security people tightened their watch around him.[178]

Madeleine Albright duly turned up as Clinton's emissary, her first visit to the Middle East in six months, to push the idea of the early Camp David meeting. After her visit to Arafat she would proceed to meet President Mubarak in Cairo, with the idea of reviving the talks with Syria: bad news for the Palestinians, who still saw traffic with Syria as a way of sidetracking them.[179] Arrived in Ramallah, Albright announced an agreement that Israeli and Palestinian negotiators would meet the following week in Washington to set the parameters for the Camp David summit. While she was there, the right-wing parties were introducing a bill in the Knesset to undercut Barak by dissolving that body and holding new elections.[180] Their success threw the government into turmoil, as seven Shas members, all of Sharansky's Russian exile members and the NPR, coalition partners all, voted against Barak. The vote was 61 to 48, with another 11 simply absent, enough to require that Barak invest his summer on the domestic concerns of his coalition.[181] It had become clear that Clinton's remaining months in office must now be devoted to winning a settlement between Israel and the Palestinians.[182]

Palestinian frustration was so high now that their own intelligence officers squared off in a shooting battle at their Gaza headquarters, 24 agents involved in this show of internal rivalry.[183]

On June 10, Hafez al-Assad, President of Syria for more than these 30 critical years, died.[184] With that, the landscape of the Middle East changed. Assad's officials hurriedly installed his son Bashar as successor President. British-educated and resident for some years in London as an eye doctor, Bashar had not been readied for the Presidency, as his father had groomed an older brother for the succession, turning to Bashar only after the brother had died in an auto accident. No one knew what to expect of Bashar. He would surely be under the influence of his father's advisers, who had installed him in place. The uncertainties in Syria consequently made the Palestinian talks all the more urgent for Clinton if he were to leave a heritage of peace.[185]

In mid-June Arafat came once more to the White House, where he had become one of Clinton's most frequent visitors.[186] He hoped for one more land transfer before the summit, which would then have given the Palestinians at least partial control over 80 percent of the West Bank on his entrance to these final-status negotiations, but Clinton sidestepped his request. Arafat had said, before coming, that he would not attend the summit without that further transfer. The atmosphere filled with tension, as Clinton had no desire for a summit that would collapse, but had already publicly committed himself to the summit during his Lisbon meeting with Barak.[187]

Summits are always risky things. Governments normally do not go into them without fully preparing the ground beforehand, so that agreements already made will simply be ratified, but Israel kept pressing Clinton now for a "working summit."[188] As a goodwill gesture, after the street uprisings of the previous month about prisoners, Israel now warily released just three. Palestinians, unimpressed, called it too little too late. And settlers were massing now outside the Knesset to protest any concessions on land, marching from there to Barak's residence.[189]

The rupture in Barak's coalition became more and more a hemorrhage. The Shas party declared itself out of the coalition, but left Barak some time to negotiate a reversal. Its issue had nothing to do with making peace or not making it. It wanted government to assume the debts of its ultra-Orthodox religious school system, remit its taxes and legalize its pirate radio station. It could be had back into the cabinet for money, but its fellows in the cabinet, the Meretz party, had sworn not to let it be given.[190]

The Meretz party, in order to keep Shas in the coalition, announced that it would pull its three ministers out of the cabinet (including its leader Yossi Sarid) but would continue to vote with the coalition in support of the peace moves. Barak promised to open a "continuous dialogue" with the settlers who protested regularly outside his office and residence, and urged his ministers and the peace negotiators to "visit the settlements and hear the settlers' concerns."[191] With that, and with a good dose of money, Shas returned to the fold, to a cabinet now without Meretz ministers.[192] It would not last for long. And as the tensions mounted, the Israeli army regularly practiced tactics for assault on Palestinians in a mock Palestinian village. Opposition leaders Sharon and Sharansky, meanwhile, made a regular practice of feeding leaks to the media to undercut Barak.[193]

As the date came closer, the Palestinians expressed more and more doubts about the hasty progress toward a summit. At month's end, they wanted just two more weeks to improve their position for a meeting a bit later. Barak, in reversal of his position the year before, when he had asked the Americans to stand back, asked anxiously now for their involvement to prod the process along.[194] But when Secretary of State Albright came again to see both Arafat and Barak, she reported back to Washington that the time was not right for a summit meeting, that there was need for more detailed preparatory talks.[195]

Tempers were rising on the Israeli Right, as evidenced by the arson burning of a Conservative synagogue in Jerusalem, an act Barak described as "awful."[196] Netanyahu's star had begun to rise again, despite all his legal troubles. A Gallup poll published in *Ma'ariv* showed him eight points ahead of Barak: Netanyahu 47 percent, Barak 36 percent, with 20 percent undecided.[197]

There was pressure from the United States, which urged instant action. But the PLO, by now, distrusting the rapid run to a summit, announced that it would declare Palestinian statehood by mid-September, whether or not a peace deal with the Israelis had been reached by that time.[198] Both sides were alarmed at this threat of a Unilateral Declaration of Independence. Yossi Beilin observed that a Palestinian state was meaningless if Israel did not recognize it. In a Palestinian opinion poll, slightly more than half expected nothing to happen in September, not a state and not a peace agreement.[199]

On July 5, Clinton issued the formal invitation. Barak and Arafat agreed to meet at Camp David the following week, Arafat only after receiving Clinton's full assurance that he would not be blamed if the summit did not succeed. He had told Albright, in Ramallah, that he went only reluctantly, and that more discussion was needed at a lower level. Abu Ala, speaker of the Palestinian Assembly, felt that Clinton had bent to Israeli pressure in calling the summit. He doubted that the meeting would achieve any of its aims. The status of Jerusalem appeared as the greatest sticking point. Arafat was not expected to sign any agreement that did not include Jerusalem.

Barak reportedly thought of conceding some Arab neighborhoods in Jerusalem to Palestinian control. Differences were narrowing as to the size of a Palestinian state. It was expected to be 90 to 92 percent of the West Bank, with 40,000 Israeli settlers to be evacuated. A settlement of the refugee question was mooted, with compensation financed by the international community. Sharansky, at a rally opposing territorial concessions to the Palestinians, offered to resign from the cabinet and withdraw his party from the government. If he were to resign, Barak would still have a majority, but a very slim one.[200]

And thus they came to the fateful summit, Arafat apprehensive, Barak hurried because he was losing support at an alarming rate, Clinton desperate to achieve the breakthrough before his term was up.

I had spent all these last weeks since mid-May in Jerusalem, returning to the United States on July 3. I had caught a sense of the temper of the place in both communities, and was thoroughly alarmed. Before I left, I made one more try, communicating through my good friend Issa Kassissieh, an officer of the Orient House negotiating team of Palestinians and close assistant to Faisal Husseini, to press the idea that Arafat could not represent the Palestinian cause all by himself, that he had no real political support from outside, not from the Arab nations, not from Europe, certainly not from the United States. He could bolster his power to negotiate only by the organized solidarity of his people. On this I had become a broken record by this time. I wrote June 25, 2000, as follows:

> It is hard to decipher, from outside, the American mediation of Dennis Ross, for whom I always have high regard, and the expected further visit of Madeleine Albright. Recent experience has so consistently shown that American urgings of peace, surely genuine, are built on the expectation that the Palestinians will concede to the Israeli demands in ways that President Arafat may not and ought not. That leaves little room to hope that a summit in Washington among Arafat, Barak and Clinton will produce the desired framework agreement on final status issues.
>
> The predictably angry Palestinian reaction is variously reported. The Jerusalem Post, always inclined to present the most drastic anti-Palestinian picture, quotes Arafat as saying that, if there is no agreement soon, he will leave the country for Cairo or Tunis and let Barak solve his problems with the Palestinians as he did with Hezbollah. I don't know whether he said that or not. If so, it may be only the expression of impatience and not a real threat. But meanwhile Police Chief Jibril Rajoub is quoted (in *Ha'Aretz*) to the effect that, if Israeli tanks come, they will not meet white flags of surrender.
>
> The situation may not be as bad as appears, but let me draw the worst conclusions from it, as hypothesis, as I comment on it.
>
> ***The Prospect of Resuming Open Warfare***
> Recognizing the high level of Palestinian frustration, which I regard as danger to you more than to the Israelis, recognizing also the readiness of Palestinians for further sacrifice, let me state the most obvious single factor. If open warfare were resumed, nothing is more certain than that the Palestinians would lose, sacrificing great numbers of dead, very probably with the drastic result that the remaining population would largely be driven from the country. This is not a formula for the restoration of Palestine but for its destruction. The rest of the world, the Arab world included, would weep and wring its hands, but nothing more would follow. Israel would become still more unpopular internationally, might even lose some American aid or sympathy, but the propaganda machines would be at work immediately to say it was all the Palestinians' fault for acting rashly.

Available Alternatives

Conceding what the Israelis and Americans urge is no genuine alternative. The people would rightly not accept any such agreement. Their rejection might even take the form of just such open rebellion as would bring about the same result—total defeat, great loss of life and utter destruction of the Palestinian presence in the land—as predicted above for a response of open warfare.

Other alternatives do indeed remain. One should never forget that, for all the crushing disparity of power between Israelis and Palestinians, the Israelis need an agreed peace, a genuine one and not one that will fall apart, as much as the Palestinians do. If they are denied that, they must negotiate further. Even the most recalcitrant and self-centered of their own public will understand that.

Two resources stand out as available to the Palestinian negotiators. Those, in my opinion, should be employed, even if things are less drastic than the current reports let us believe.

1. Arab Solidarity

The late President Hafez al-Assad understood the need for solidarity. He always urged against separate deals by the different Arab states, in the face of constant Israeli and American urging that all negotiations be bilateral, so that Israel, with its disproportionately greater power, could pick off the Arab states one by one.

Palestinians and Syrians alike have suspected, over the last two years, that the Israelis and Americans were playing off the two 'tracks,' Syrian and Palestinian, against one another. Israelis have always been able to plead that their diplomatic resources were strained when they had to deal with both at once. They have often enough denied that they were unable to field both teams at once, but they have still taken advantage of that argument. They should be met by both Syria and the Palestinians, not only at the same time but together.

The right thing for Bashar al-Assad to do at this point is to respond favorably to the new negotiation proposals, but make it clear, as his father often did, that he will come to no agreement in which the Palestinians do not share. Palestinians would do well, right now, to be talking as brothers to the Syrians, urging this upon them.

The late President Assad was no friend to President Arafat. His demand for a comprehensive settlement, though, was his best contribution to the Arab and Palestinian cause over all these years and should be appreciated. This is a new time, with a new President in Syria. Palestinians ought not hesitate to approach him and his advisers with good hope. Even if the structures of negotiation are now so rigidly set in bilateral form that there is no way of having the whole negotiation happen in one room, Syrians and Palestinians can so coordinate their work that it is effectively one negotiation.

2. *Palestinian Popular Mobilization*

I have tried, as bluntly as I could, to say how disastrous any attempt at armed resistance would inevitably be, resulting in catastrophic defeat for the Palestinians. It would not be good for Israel either, as it would leave Israel more than ever a foreign body in the Middle East. In the long term Israel would have no future, but that would not help the Palestinians, who would already have been destroyed.

A non-violent resistance, however, remains an available alternative, and would even promise success in achieving the true and necessary Palestinian goals that have eluded your work of negotiation. I'm sure that, in your study of the ways of negotiation, you have learned to recognize the Best Alternative To a Negotiated Agreement. As much as the agreement offered by the Israelis and Americans now is truly unacceptable, war, or even allowing the risk of war, is no good whatever as an alternative. This non-violent option may be the best alternative you have left.

It is not a first option, but a last. It is in fact much better if the situation is not as drastic as this week's news reports suggest, and there is time to prepare for this kind of resistance, as every bit of preparation time is valuable. The exercise of being prepared to resist injustice non-violently has value, also, in mobilizing a people, even if it never comes to the need to exercise this non-violent resistance in fact.

I have urged this on President Arafat consistently since 1991, when the Madrid Conference effectively brought the *intifada* to a stop. Without the mobilization of the Palestinian resident population, he lacks the power base he could otherwise have in his negotiation with Israel. Any mobilization now would have to be rigorously non-violent, not permitting even stone throwing, or it could be used to discredit the Palestinian cause and its leadership. But a fully non-violent mobilization, clearly under the leadership of Palestinian authorities, would have as much effect as the *intifada* had in its time, putting the agenda-setting initiative in Palestinian hands and winning the approbation of a world public and even of many Israelis.

It would also give President Arafat the only tool I know of to control those forces in the Palestinian public that are inclined to violence. He has often commented, and we who observe have agreed, that he cannot be expected to police Palestinians of a violent temper or terrorist organizations more effectively than the much stronger Israeli forces have been able to do. But if the Palestinian public is organized for non-violent resistance and understands well, from its leadership on down, that every act of violence is a betrayal of vital Palestinian interests, then public opinion will not tolerate violence from any organizations or individuals.

The Shape of Such Non-Violent Resistance
Let me state again that non-violent resistance is not a first step but a last. It is literally last, as it contains in itself a firm resolve not to resort to violence, or let the situation degenerate into violence, recognizing that violence could in fact only produce disaster for the Palestinians (and eventually for the Israelis as well).

It remains to explain what kind of steps a mobilized public could take. And if this is well understood, the public should be prepared and trained for it.

The first steps are simple enough. The negotiating team, and Arafat as President, can simply make clear that they do not accept those parts of a proffered agreement that are unacceptable. I would not find it sufficient that the negotiators alone declare this. Clear signs of Palestinian solidarity in this rejection of unjust terms should be given by formal resolutions of the Palestinian Legislative Council, endorsed by the President and stating those terms that the Palestinian people will not accept. These should be realistic and not overblown. You should not put yourselves in the position of declaring some things unacceptable that, eventually, you will accept, as then you would be expected to back down further. Hence statements of this kind should be very carefully crafted.

Popular street demonstrations against unacceptable proposals should also be encouraged. These constitute, in fact, valuable occasions for training the public in the discipline of non-violence. It should be clear that fully peaceful demonstration has the approval of Palestinian authority, and that any and every lapse into violence is a hindrance to the Palestinian cause and thus an act of betrayal of the people.

Rely upon the Israelis, especially their military and the settlers, to misbehave. There will in fact be violence, but it must all be Israeli violence, none of it Palestinian. The people will suffer in this situation, but you know very well that they will suffer far more in any alternative that involves violence on their part rather than violence by the Israelis alone.

The readiness of Palestinians to sacrifice for their freedom is not in doubt. Very often people understand the value of sacrifice if they have taken a violent stand, but feel that it is merely weakness if they respond without violence. About this, Palestinian leadership will have to instruct people insistently that their sacrifice is a true service to the interests of Palestinians if they make no violent response, and damage to those interests if they do. Armed Palestinian police, especially, have to know this.

If people respond to Israeli police, army or settler violence with violence, it will all be blamed on the Palestinians, and will only serve to give the Israelis the excuse for further demands. Palestinian leadership, without ever disavowing responsibility for peaceful demonstration and effective leadership of it, will have to reiterate this constantly. In this way the Palestinian authorities will actually gain credit with their own people for their effective leadership.

It is very useful to instruct people, when they are assaulted, simply to sit down in the street and, if the Israeli authorities are so inclined, let themselves be carried off to prison. The rest of the public may not then be indifferent, but through further demonstrations should flood the prisons to the bursting point, still without violence.

All this will be a preliminary stage of mobilized resistance. It is especially important that the people learn the effectiveness of their non-violent stance during this period. The international press and electronic media should be informed carefully every time such a peaceful demonstration is to take place. There is no need to try to manipulate them. The news people will understand the moral equations of this situation instantly when they see peaceful demonstrators assaulted by force. It will make good copy for them, as did the *intifada*. Legions of further press and electronic reporters will begin to arrive as soon as this development shows itself.

At some point the Israelis will crack under this pressure, and the Palestinians will win what they need. When that will happen is uncertain. The Israelis will understand as well as you do that the Palestinians lose as soon as they respond to violence with violence. They will be trying to provoke you, knowing that that is their only chance to win. The reporters, too, will be waiting for that, and will readily report it if you allow it to happen. That is the importance of discipline among the Palestinians.

A further stage may begin if the Israelis decide simply to take what they want from you without consent. They are already doing this, of course, with every confiscation, house demolition or settlement. If they escalate this to any new stage, in response to peaceful popular demonstrations against unjust demands, then it is time to escalate the non-violent resistance campaign as well.

Blocking of roads, not with barricades but with masses of people sitting down, is one way. These should be primarily West Bank and Gaza, everywhere in Area B, where it will be maximum inconvenience to Israeli settlers, preventing their freedom of movement. Rely on the settlers, once again, to respond excessively and with violence. Be sure the media are there. Those who attack you will add to their own disgrace, and their every attack will be a further defeat for them. They will end by being so discredited that you will get Israeli agreement to remove all those among the settlers whose purpose in being in your territory is to create violence and trouble for you. Logistically, there are places where you can organize such actions better than others, but you should see to it that no Israeli can go on with the ordinary things of life without having you, your suffering and your rightful demands in his face.

They may come to arrest Arafat himself and others of the leadership. Neither you nor he should be worried at that. There was a time, years ago, when the world might have reacted to Arafat's arrest with the indifference they have shown to Abdullah Ocalan's over the last year. But this is Arafat who has been to the White House, who shook the hand of the martyred Rabin, who is recognized by the American President as a partner for peace, who has won the Nobel Prize, who has led his people to negotiations for peace with Israel, and who would be arrested for the use of peaceful means to achieve that. The world's media and all the chanceries and diplomatic channels of the world, and many of the Israelis too, would resound like a booming drum to Arafat's arrest in those circumstances. He could only gain by it, in the hearts of his people and in the success of his efforts for their rights. He should go to it smiling with grateful dignity. The spectacle of Arafat taking off for Cairo or Tunis while his people suffered what could only be defeat would not be a dignified one, but this would be a way of winning.

In all of this you would have Israeli allies. Those Israelis on the Left who have felt they were virtuous in arguing for minimal concessions to you against others who wanted to give you less, would become far more conscious of the true needs that must be met. They would prepare their state not merely for negotiations of Israelis with other Israelis, but for true negotiations with you. And those most resistant to you would learn that they cannot have the peace they crave without granting you your rights, nor take what they want without regard to you.

But you would have to keep in mind, and keep it always in the minds of your people, that they could lose all the advantage of this by any reversion to violence.

I hope I have not played the schoolmarm in spelling this out in such detail. In the 1980s, when the Palestinian cause seemed so desperate, I visited and corresponded with President Arafat regularly, working in close concert with Ambassador William Wilson and Stanley Sheinbaum as we sought to establish the initial US/PLO dialogue. When that proved to be so ineffective I maintained contact with Arafat, I hope helpfully, often through his nephew, Dr Nasser al-Qidwa, in New York, as well as with the White House and the series of Israeli Prime Ministers.

Since the Oslo breakthrough, when it became easy for Arafat to communicate directly with all these people himself, I have tended to hold back, for the most part only writing to urge him to patience in various crises, and I sense that his expectations are mostly from his meetings with the Rosses, the Albrights and the Clintons.

But now, his contacts with the world of Israeli, American and international diplomacy seem to be calculatedly used against him and the interests of his people, his struggle with them like punching at pillows. It is for that reason that I come forward again with proposals that, I hope, may be of genuine use to him. As always before, I do so out of concern for both peoples, as I foresee disaster for Israel too if its people get the things they so thoughtlessly seek.

When I hear Palestinians speaking, they often seem so discouraged, sure that they are going to get nothing from all this negotiating and that the Israelis will take everything from them. I think they have forgotten the lesson of the *intifada*, that they won a great deal, won their way to the table, when they acted so. Stopping the *intifada* was taken as part of the deal when preliminary agreements were signed, and surely it was what the Israelis most wanted, as they were losing continuously as long as the *intifada* went on. Circumstances have now required that any renewed mobilization of Palestinians be even more rigorously non-violent than was the *intifada* itself, or it will be self-defeating. But the people have been demobilized and reduced to passive observers of what was decided about them by others since the *intifada* ended. That is a demoralized state in which to leave them, and it deprives the Palestinian leadership of their strength. Their very determination is turned against the leadership itself as they worry that the leaders will agree to things they cannot accept.

The Israelis, too, are suspected of being unwilling to concede anything of value to the Palestinians. There are all shades of opinion among them, of course, but they are not all so hard-hearted as that. But with the full weight of demanding public opinion upon them, they are negotiating with a side that has no power counters to balance theirs. They too suffer from that obvious disparity of power. It leaves them unable to move, even when they are willing.

With that level of apprehension, confident that Faisal Husseini would put my letter to Issa before Arafat, I left for home. But as the Camp David meeting got under way, I continued to use this link through Orient House to put further thoughts before the negotiators in Maryland.

5
Camp David

HIGH STAKES

Most US observers missed the dim auguries as the Camp David meetings approached. The Clinton administration and the US media remained determinedly upbeat, denying the cumulative bad news much as they had earlier about the negotiations with Syria over the Golan, taking a "go-for-broke" stance and expecting these talks to bring a final end to the 52-year-old conflict. Elsewhere people saw more clearly how close the relations of Israelis and Palestinians were to breakdown, the implications of a collapse of the Oslo process apparent to all concerned.[1]

Barak relied on the insistent approach of the United States. In his desperately weakened condition, he wanted to push things to a conclusion before he lost power altogether. He proclaimed that he would try to forge the deal for which the Israeli public had elected him, and proclaimed that, if he failed, the conflict would "disintegrate into Belfast or Bosnia."[2]

Clinton appeared to have decided that he could not make things worse by forcing the parties into an end game. If he succeeded, he would finish his term in glory. If he failed, the risk to himself would be minimal.

For Arafat, the stakes were highest. His lifelong struggle for a Palestinian state, which he had come to see as living alongside and at peace with Israel, depended on this effort at Camp David. He approached it more skeptically and cautiously than the others. He acted against the advice of his senior advisers, who thought the necessary groundwork had not been laid for these talks to reach a compromise on any major issue.

Among the most important of Arafat's advisers was Akram Hanieh, editor-in-chief of the Palestinian daily *Al-Ayyam*, who was close to Arafat throughout the summit and who, soon after, published in his paper a detailed account of what happened. That narrative becomes, therefore, a major source for the events that followed.

In advance of the summit, Hanieh described the lunch meeting in Ramallah during June at which Arafat had told Madeleine Albright:

"Madam Secretary, if you issue an invitation to a summit, and if it gets held and fails, then this will weaken the hope among the [Palestinian] people in the possibility of achieving peace. Let us not weaken this hope." When, on July 4, Clinton called to say that Barak had new offers he would make at a summit and did not agree to any preparatory talks, Arafat tried three times to clarify to Clinton his concern about these expected consequences, but Clinton, relying on recommendations made by Albright, Ross, and Sandy Berger (White House national security adviser), called the summit anyway.

The Middle East, Hanieh judged, was about to witness "a new adventure in American diplomacy." It seemed, as he read it, that the US peace team was attuned only to vibrations coming from the Israelis. He saw the joint US–Israeli assessment as "yet another proof of the short-sighted understanding of the uniqueness of the Palestinian question."[3]

Yet Arafat would gain much if he were to succeed in a high-stakes summit presided over by Clinton. His only alternative was UDI, a unilateral declaration of independence. The decision the previous year to extend the deadline of the Oslo process once again, but only to September 13, 2000, pressed him in that direction, and a vote of the PLO's Central Council had authorized him to do so, though in deliberately vague terms that left him ways to escape it, when they met in Gaza on July 2–3. But a UDI would clearly be accompanied by violence, by Israeli annexation of whatever West Bank land had not yet come under full Palestinian rule, perhaps more, and by complications for the acceptance of Palestinian positions in the international community. So Arafat gambled.

PALESTINIAN STARTING POSITION

The PLO Council had laid down a Palestinian consensus on the outlines of what they would consider a just solution to the conflict with Israel, thus setting at least a starting position for the negotiations. The points, in order of their appearance in the communiqué, were first, the right of return "or adequate compensation" for Palestinian refugees, in line with UN General Assembly Resolution 194;[4] second, Israeli withdrawal to the 1967 borders in accord with Security Council Resolutions 242[5] and 338;[6] third, removal of Israeli settlements from all occupied Palestinian territory; and fourth, the establishment of East Jerusalem as the future capital of an independent Palestinian state. Arafat would bring with him, besides his negotiating team, a delegation of 50 other Palestinians, including representatives of dissident factions. Hamas and the DFLP quietly declined this invitation. On July 9, PLO Executive member Yasser Abed Rabbo confirmed that any agreement would be put to a Palestinian referendum "like for the Israelis."

This communiqué, meant as empowerment of Arafat to deal at the conference, received unanimous approval of the Council, despite the fact that delegates belonging to the Popular Front and Democratic Front factions had asked that "the present peace process should be reviewed," and even Hamas, which had no seats on the Council and had refused to attend even as observer, had muted its response.

And while the official PLO position discouraged any "partial or vague agreements" or another mere interim accord, two models were offered as a way to break an anticipated impasse. One was a "horizontal agreement," by which Israel would grant Palestinians some form of self-government in Jerusalem in exchange for deferring the issue of sovereignty, and Palestinians would agree that the right of return for the 1948 refugees would apply for now only to the West Bank and Gaza, postponing the issue of return to their homes or compensation to a later stage. The other was a "vertical agreement," by which Israel would recognize a Palestinian state and the Palestinians would maintain security cooperation in return for postponing all final status issues to another day and another set of negotiations. This would allow Arafat to realize the objective of a state without having to sign away any of the national issues. It might also give Barak a stay of political execution, as most Israelis were obsessed with security but not much concerned about Palestinian statehood. And Clinton could boast a peace achievement of sorts before the US Presidential election in November.

Distrustful Israeli military analysts were saying already that they believed Arafat really preferred to achieve independence "through friction and blood." They used other demeaning characterizations: that he "wants to appear as both the pyromaniac and the fireman."

Abu Ala believed that nothing would be accomplished in this atmosphere, and said that Barak was trying to escape from negotiations and jump to a summit "because he thinks he can force deals."

Even before his departure, it was clear that Barak could not bring his main cabinet ministers with him. Sharansky told reporters he would resign, with his party, on Sunday. Housing Minister Yitzhak Levy of the NRP also talked of quitting. Shas leader Eli Yishai was undecided on whether to travel with his Prime Minister. Barak still thought he would be able to bring his foreign minister, David Levy, internal security minister, Shlomo Ben-Ami, attorney general, Elyakim Rubinstein, and some security advisers. Arafat planned on bringing Abu Ala, his economic adviser Mohammed Rachid, senior negotiators Abu Mazen and Saeb Erekat, and security chief Mohammed Dahlan.[7]

I worried that my June 25 letter to Issa Kassissieh might not have reached Arafat's attention, so I wrote directly to him, using e-mail for speed, on July 6. I congratulated him on holding firm against signing agreements, under US and Israeli pressure, that could only have harmed his people, reminding him of the statement by US President John F. Kennedy during the Berlin crisis of 1961: "Any treaty of peace that adversely affects the fate of millions will not bring peace." I stayed with my familiar theme of his need for full mobilization of his people in a disciplined non-violence. Their protest, their rejection of any unfair proposal for peace, should be unflinching and organized, but so disciplined that there would be no violence, not a shot, not a stone. Every instance of Palestinian violence, I wrote, would be used as propaganda to discredit their cause in world opinion, losing the sympathy of those who could press the Israelis to offer something just. The Israelis themselves, I wrote, had no such discipline and would exercise a kind of violence that would be counted against them even by their own public. His people would succeed only to the extent that he held the line against any violent Palestinian response. He should remember that the Israelis needed a genuine and lasting peace as much as did the Palestinians, who would succeed if their rejection of inadequate proposals were both firm and non-violent.

US and European publics, I wrote, were constantly exposed to smooth articulation of Israeli positions, which were represented as the only reasonable ones. That was a great part of their strength, and they were regarded as the more convincing any time the Palestinian response was angry and sounded less reasonable. There should be careful and moderate presentations of Palestinian needs, with his most capable people, who had demonstrated their appeal to Western publics, constantly out before the cameras and microphones, giving background interviews to reporters, never less than the Israelis, full of reason and without rancor, but explaining Palestinian suffering and needs to the foreign public that was so important to them.

BARAK'S TROUBLES

Quickly it became apparent that Barak's condition was even worse than we had expected. On Sunday July 9, the eve of his departure for Washington, his coalition crumbled. Shas, with its 17 members, the NRP, and Sharansky's small Russian immigrant party all walked out, calling a vote of confidence for the following day. Barak defiantly told them that the collapse of the coalition would not affect his trip to Maryland, as he relied on his mandate for peace from the electorate. He had now only 42 seats in the 120-seat Knesset. He reckoned that he could stretch this to 52 with the help of three small parties: a liberal Russian immigrant faction, a secularist party, and a trade unionists' party.

Shas leader Eli Yishai claimed that he had joined the coalition to make the peace, because it was important to him and his party, but that he must know the road. He didn't know Barak's "red lines," he complained. Barak replied that the "red lines" were well known, but that revealing them in more detail would weaken his negotiating position. His foreign minister, David Levy, of his own party, chose this moment to announce that he would not join the delegation, in protest at what he regarded as hard-line positions of the Palestinians and their "threats of violence."

Meretz officials, who had actually left the cabinet to keep Shas in, were furious at the Shas defection. Former trade minister Ran Cohen exclaimed:

> All through the years we have heard of the moderate stand taken by Shas because Rabbi Ovadia Yosef, their leader, he puts foremost the saving of human lives—that saving lives is more important than territory. Now Barak comes along and with tweezers goes over every detail, every settlement, every road, every section, measures as exactly as possible in order to save lives, to prevent returning to the killing of Jews and Arabs in a continuation of 100 years of war. And the Shas people … say they are about to quit? For what?[8]

Barak survived the vote of confidence, just an hour before leaving the Knesset for the airport. The count was 54 to 52, with seven abstentions and seven absent. He had the support of most Arab members, of the rigorously Orthodox United Torah Judaism party and the secular, anti-Orthodox Shinui party. As he departed, Barak spoke over the jeers of the opposition:

> From here, from united Jerusalem, the eternal capital of Israel, the greatest leaders of Israel went out to meet the greatest and most important decisions in the history of our nation. I wish to depart today from Jerusalem to Camp David in order to complete the labor of peacemaking that was begun by Menachem Begin and Yitzhak Rabin.

Likud banners asserted: "Barak is traveling to the summit defeated and alone!" Sharon goaded the prime minister in the Knesset:

> I regret that the person who wanted to be the Prime Minister of everyone became in just one year the Prime Minister of almost no one, except maybe himself. You don't have a majority of the Knesset. You don't have the support of the people.

Mohammed Dahlan, hearing of this, wondered aloud: "Is he really capable of making a peace agreement after the disintegration of his government last night?"[9]

But in Washington the Clinton administration kept up its brave front of optimism, even in the face of the stunning political drama in Israel. "Clinton praises Arafat and Barak as leaders with the vision, the knowledge, the experience and the ability and the sheer guts to do what it takes." He spoke thus in response to Barak's insistent request.[10]

A FIRST POSITION PAPER

Seeing all this disarray, I wrote, on July 7, what would be the first of several background analytic papers. They all went first to the Palestinians through the rapid e-mail service of friends who could reach the delegation, but I put them also before the Israeli and US teams. This first one dealt with some matters of legal confusion on which I feared the Palestinian negotiators might be pressured to accept readings that had no real standing in law. Law, and the observance of law, was becoming more and more a focus for my own considerations on the conflict, and would become increasingly prominent in what I would write as the negotiations went on. The paper was as follows:

The Israeli–Palestinian Camp David Meeting
A Few Legal Questions
Raymond G. Helmick, S.J.
July 7, 2000

UNSCR 242:

Palestinians worried last week when Israeli Attorney General Eliakim Rubinstein offered his opinion that Resolution 242's prescription of the return of territory conquered in 1967 did not apply to the Palestinians, because there was no Palestinian state at the time the resolution was passed.

Rubinstein's disclaimer fails to meet the real objective of Resolution 242. I trust that everyone is aware of the flaw in the more traditional Israeli argument (Begin at Camp David) that the resolution calls only for "withdrawal from territories...," and does not say "*the* territories," which Begin understood to mean that withdrawal from some territory (Sinai) fulfilled the requirement, and there was no need to withdraw from all of it. This interpretation is already refuted by the fact that the English and French texts of the resolution have equal legal force, and the French reads "*des territoires....*" But in fact, Begin himself had recognized in 1967, when Resolution 242 was first passed, that the real demand on Israel to return the territory, *all* the territory, came at the very beginning of the resolution, in the appeal to Article 2 of the UN Charter, which prohibits any acquisition of territory by force (rather than by agreement). The Rubinstein argument fails the same test. The Palestinians, consequently, as the *resident population* of the territories captured in 1967, have legal right to them. It is not the case that these territories belong to the Israelis, to give them or not to give them to the Palestinians, but instead they are Palestinian territories illegally occupied by Israel. The Palestinian claim is primary. This has to be recognized if Resolution 242 is seen as the legal basis for negotiation.

And it applies as much to East Jerusalem as to anywhere else in the West Bank or the Gaza Strip.

The Israeli Claim that Property Ownership by Jews Transfers Sovereignty over Territory to the Israeli State

It has become a commonplace of Israeli understanding of the law that, when an Israeli Jew acquires property rights over a piece of land in the Palestinian territory, that automatically gives the Israeli state a sovereignty claim to that land. This has been the basis for Israeli claims in Hebron, for the various bits of property that Mr Moskovitz[11] keeps acquiring or pretending to acquire in East Jerusalem, to any of the settlements, Jabal Abu Gnaim/Har Homa being a case in point. No such claim would ever be recognized in any other country. Property acquired, for instance, in New York by Japanese, German, or Vatican interests entails no such transfer of sovereignty claim.

VIOLENT ATMOSPHERE BEFORE THE TALKS

That very day, July 7, witnessed the killing of a 33-year-old Gaza woman and serious injury to her husband, two children, and a driver. The family was passing the Jewish settlement of Kfar Darom in the Gaza Strip in a taxi shortly after midnight when Israeli soldiers manning an outpost sprayed them with gunfire. The army at first claimed the soldiers had come under fire and were shooting at "terrorists," but that turned out to be so clearly a fabrication that the government offered a half-hearted apology and called it instead a mistake by the soldiers. Palestinian officials and media saw this instead as "cold-blooded murder" and blamed it on "the venomous anti-Palestinian incitement" among Israeli soldiers and the settlers. Palestinian security officials urged the government to remove the "trigger-happy" soldiers from the settlement and put the killers on trial, a request that, as nearly always in such cases, was ignored.

The incident did not stand alone. Two West Bank boys were killed on consecutive days by exploding Israeli army munitions, and on July 5, 16-year-old Khalil Abu-A'ram died after stepping on a landmine near Yatta in the Hebron district while grazing his flock, the third Yatta boy to die in similar circumstances in three years, during which several other children and shepherds had been mutilated by such explosions. The villagers believed the mining of their fields was a deliberate policy of the Israeli settlers to drive them off their lands. B'Tselem, the Israeli human rights group, had documented 83 such incidents since 1987, killing 33 Palestinians, 25 of them children, and injuring 90 others, including 69 children. All these episodes contributed to poison the atmosphere between the parties about to meet at Camp David.

Clashes were not in fact limited to those between Palestinians and Israelis. Ill feeling and rivalry between different Palestinian security forces occasioned an outburst of violence in Ramallah.[12]

Seeing all this popular turmoil, I was apprehensive of the Camp David approach, an effort to have the political leaders agree on the resolution of all the problems while their people were in such drastic disarray. So I wrote once again on July 9, this time much more extensively, in an effort to catch the leaders before they left for the summit. I called the paper simply "Observations on the Camp David Summit."

> As the summit approaches, I recognize that the Palestinian team, like the Israelis and the Americans, already has its overall strategy planned. I hesitate for that reason to interfere, but I am conscious that the negotiation is at a dangerous impasse, from which it needs to be set free.
> **A Fundamental Fallacy:**
> I regard it as a basic error to believe that peace between peoples can be achieved simply by agreement between governments. That

concept has bedeviled the treaty agreements between Israel and Egypt, between Israel and Jordan, both of which are agreements between governments but not between peoples, who still remain basically estranged. The weaknesses that block their successful implementation, like that of much else in international peace policy, are: 1) a failure to attend to the deep need for healing from victimization of the parties to the conflict, 2) strategies that impose foreign recipes for peace that are not internalized by the peoples concerned, and 3) strategies that appeal to the political hierarchy as the exclusive decision makers.[13]

This negotiation is too important to leave it prey to such errors. It should confine itself, therefore, to the more modest task of preparing the most favorable ground for developing a sustainable reconciliation between the peoples. The time scale has critical importance. Negotiators need to leave room for a process far more time-consuming than agreement between the leaders, and the governments concerned must then provide that process with adequate technical and financial support.

The Objective:

The parties all profess, in apparent good faith, that they come to this summit to make peace between their peoples. It seems less clearly realized that this is incompatible with any objective of winning victories over one another. Those are games for children.

The feeling of haste, that everything must be done while a non-repeatable window of opportunity remains open, also obscures that objective of creating a genuine peace. It is true that President Clinton, soon to end his term, brings both skill and commitment to this task that cannot be expected of any of his likely successors. It is just as true that either Prime Minister Barak or President Arafat could be damaged in his ability to carry the process forward if they fail to bring their peoples a feeling of success. The proper conclusion from that is that positive conditions for further progress, at the more important level of the peoples, should result from this meeting. A "deal" that pretended to bridge the chasms of expectation while only papering them over would in fact be the betrayal of any such possibilities.

A proposal hovers over these negotiations: that the two peoples should be effectively separated in the final status agreement. I would regard this as a disastrous proposal. Surely it cannot work for Jerusalem if the city is to remain united, as everyone wishes, after an acceptable sharing system is worked out. For the rest of the territory of the two states that must stand side by side if there is to be real agreement, separation would mean building in a perpetual situation of enmity, exactly the thing that should most earnestly be avoided. It would also entail making permanent all the checkpoints and crossings and the cutting off of Palestine from communication either with Israel or with the rest of the world.

The Israelis, too, have lived ever since 1948 caged in their tiny territory, unable to go where they will in the Middle East. If they lower the barriers, and have an open border between the internationally recognized territories of Israel and Palestine, then both they and the Palestinians will have access to the whole land. The Israelis will gain a welcome in the rest of the Middle East, and both peoples will be let out of their cages. This should be clearly seen as objective in these talks, that the border set between the Israeli and a Palestinian state remain open.

Such an objective will need the additional time of which I wrote above. For the time it will take to build mutual esteem and friendship between these two peoples, in place of the dismissive contempt Israelis commonly show to Palestinians at all levels of society and the raging anger that is still the common Palestinian response, due provision will have to be made for mutual security (Palestinians needing this at least as much as Israelis). Exaggerated or paranoid provision, of course, will only exacerbate the problem. The objective has to be the eventual removal of separation, not its permanent maintenance.

Effects of this Definition of Objective on the Final Status Issues:

Over recent days I have written of legal issues that should have determinative value in these negotiations. Security Council Resolution 242, in its appeal to Article 2 of the United Nations Charter, clearly prohibits the acquisition of territory, in this case the West Bank, Gaza, or East Jerusalem, by right of conquest. That is the fundamental meaning of any nation's treaty acceptance of United Nations membership. Any changes have to be the result of free agreement, and may not be dictated by either side. This does not mean that no change may ever be made, but it does mean that the Palestinian right to this land is primary. It is for them to agree to any changes of status, and they might reasonably expect concession of other territory to replace any they might agree to yield.

General Assembly Resolution 194, on the Palestinian right to return to the homes from which they fled or were expelled, or alternatively to full compensation, was also accepted by Israel from the beginning as the condition of its own acceptance as a member of the United Nations.

If then the objective of the negotiation is defined as suggested above, a proper strategy for the Palestinian side would be:

1. *It should hold fast to its legal right to this land, which may not be taken without its explicit and free agreement.*

    There is likely to be heavy demand on the Palestinians to neglect this principle on the basis of the need for haste, to come to agreement before the favorable moment passes. This is a kind of principle on which the Palestinian side needs to be immovable. Otherwise the entire agreement will be decided by the weight of superior force, American as well as Israeli, and the Palestinians will inevitably be cheated.

    On the other hand, if the objective is truly peace, the Palestinians have no need to be inflexible in the matter of territory. They might properly insist that they should be adequately compensated for any territory they might agree to yield, in view of what has transpired since 1967, by other genuinely habitable territory from the Israeli side. All this should clearly be a matter of agreement, not force. The Palestinians ought to remind themselves constantly that Israel needs an agreed peace with them as much as they do with Israel, and is consequently not in a position to force such issues as this.

2. *It should recognize the true importance for Jews, Israeli and others, that some Jews should be able to live in their ancient traditional homeland, "Judea and Samaria."*

    On this, Palestinians ought to show flexibility, again on the basis that their objective, and that of their Israeli counterparts, is truly a sustainable peace.

    If the principle of prior Palestinian right to these territories is to be upheld, and the importance for Jews that some of them be able to live there accepted, then it should be clear that Jews, even though they may want to retain their Israeli citizenship and voting rights, would be living on Palestinian territory and under Palestinian law. Adequate protection should be guaranteed to them, and for an agreed interim this might have to be provided by Israeli forces, but the objective should be to replace this with a truly credible Palestinian guarantee of their safety within an agreed time.

The trouble is that many of the wrong Jews are presently living in settlements on the Palestinian territory. Their objective is to drive

Palestinians away and usurp their rights. It is as much in Israeli interest as in Palestinian interest to remove these troublemakers if the Israelis genuinely want peace. Responsibility for removing them rests with Israel, which improperly tolerated, and often connived at, their settlement in the first place. But the technical recognition that Jews living on Palestinian territory were subject to Palestinian jurisdiction would by itself be a strong inducement for those Jews whose intention is anti-Palestinian to leave the territory. Likely enough, the Israeli government would have to enforce their recognition of this rightful Palestinian jurisdiction over them, even forcibly remove them, as happened years ago in Yamit, if they refused. But the right Jews, those who came in friendship to live among Palestinians in places sacred to Jewish memory, should be made welcome, though by agreement this should not be in such numbers as to distort the demography of the land.

Hebron in particular should be a test of Palestinian generosity in this regard. The Jewish settlers there at present have every intention of creating havoc and disrupting Palestinian life in the place. Israel has the responsibility, which it ought to have discharged long since, to discipline them, require their recognition of Palestinian rights and remove them if they remain intransigent. But the Palestinians have the responsibility to respond with friendship to Jewish religious needs in this place so important to both.

If this perspective is accepted, the question of transfer of sovereignty over territories on either side of the 1967 line will be seen much differently. Currently there is talk of Israel's retaining territory along the edges of the West Bank on which the most populous Jewish settlements have been built. Those in fact are not the areas of greatest traditional interest to Jews, whose religious associations are rather with areas central to the West Bank. In those, the option should simply be acceptance of some reasonable number of Jewish residents under Palestinian jurisdiction, retaining their Israeli citizenship if they chose. The matter of demographic balance would basically be adjusted of itself when those settlers unwilling to live under Palestinian jurisdiction returned to Israeli territory, and the need for actual border adjustments (with proper territorial compensation to Palestinians for any territory they conceded) would become minimal.

Any concession on Jewish residents of Palestinian territory, of course, should be reciprocal. It should be balanced with acceptance of Palestinian returnees to Jaffa and Haifa and the other places from which Palestinians were driven in 1948.

Here again, there should be agreement that the numbers will not be such as to upset the demography that has been established during the years of Israeli statehood. That is a part of the reciprocity. The firm legal provision of General Assembly Resolution 194, on which the Palestinians should not compromise, envisions a general Right of Return, but does also provide the alternative of compensation in the case of those who do not wish or are not able to return.

Preserving the basic demography should not, in fact, be a great problem. The number of Palestinians who will want to return, after all this time, to Green-Line Israel, will be limited. Many even of those who want to return will prefer to go to Palestinian territory. It would be useful to do a survey of the Palestinian diaspora to find how many would actually want to return to what is now Israeli territory. My expectation is that this would relieve a lot of the anxiety that Israelis now have about their state being swamped by returning Palestinians. I don't believe there is any way that would happen.

The question of Jerusalem works differently than these other territories discussed here. Basically the same principles apply, but it is a far more emotional question both for Israelis and for Palestinians and therefore has to be dealt with separately. Rather than make this paper excessively long, I will postpone that to another paper soon.

Jerusalem was in fact, even this early, on everyone's mind. Faisal Husseini, who knew Jerusalem better than any other of the Palestinian leadership and enjoyed more of its people's trust than any other, wrote an op-ed article published on July 9 in the *Los Angeles Times*. It was simply a falsification, he wrote, to think of Israelis as keeping the city unified while Arabs wanted to divide it. The city had five constituencies, all of which had distinct rights: the adherents of three great faith traditions, Judaism, Christianity, and Islam, and two peoples, Israeli and Palestinian. To reach a peaceful resolution to its troubles, one must devise a way to ensure that all five of these constituencies have a role in the administration of Jerusalem and its holy sites. No single group should be able to claim either religious or political exclusivity in Jerusalem. All the city's residents, not just Jewish Israelis, should have a say in how Jerusalem is run.

Since Israel's capture of East Jerusalem in 1967, Husseini continued, all decisions about land use, housing and development had been made by Israelis. Palestinian Christians and Muslims had had no say and had suffered as a result. Moreover, Israel had imposed a military closure that systematically prevented Palestinian Christians and Muslims from entering Jerusalem. In the Palestinian view of Jerusalem, such actions could not occur because administration of the Old City would be shared and followers of all three religions would enjoy unimpeded access to their holy sites. As Jerusalem was the spiritual center for all three monotheistic religions, no one should have a monopoly over the Old City, and no one should act there unilaterally.[14]

THE LAW QUESTIONS COME TO THE FORE

The talks had actually begun, on July 11, before I wrote again. Worldwide television had been full of Clinton ushering his two smiling guests through the rustic grounds of Camp David, of the elaborate show of courtesies as Arafat and Barak stood back for each other before entering the door. Before flying by helicopter to the presidential retreat from the White House, Clinton had spoken of his hope for a spirit of "principled compromise," adding: "Of course, there is no guarantee of success. But not to try is to guarantee failure." The little dance at the door before the two leaders entered Laurel Cabin was actually a contest of symbols: who would enter first into the crucible of decision-making, each trying to make the other enter first. But from that point on, a rigorous news blackout was enforced.[15] People as far away as the residents of Ain el-Hilwe refugee camp outside Tyre held their breath—along with the rest of the 200,000 desperate Palestinian refugees in Lebanon.[16] Jerusalem's streets filled up with demonstrators for and against Barak and his peace endeavor.[17] On the op-ed page of the *New York Times*, the Likud's Limor Livnat inveighed, for her US audience, against putting any trust in Arafat who, she said, was no Sadat. Israel, she believed, could not afford to give up any least bit of what it had in its possession.[18]

I had reflected more on those questions of international law, which, I feared, had been sidestepped throughout the process, without which I saw little prospect that the talks at Camp David could succeed. The negotiators had entered into isolation now, but I felt confident I could still get these papers before them through the good offices of Faisal Husseini, whose Orient House functioned now as practically a foreign ministry for the Palestinians. I was conscious of how crippled Barak had now become as a negotiator and of the constraints under which Arafat labored. I emphasized the anxieties alive among these two peoples who would have to live with any agreements that came out of Camp David and the vital role of law in bringing them about. In Jerusalem, relative equilibrium had been maintained over the rival religious claims to the Temple Mount/Haram al-Sharif for 33 years through the fact that Moshe Dayan had put the platform under the jurisdiction of the Islamic *waqf*,[19] while the rabbinate had contended that *halakha*, Jewish law, forbade any Jew from going onto the Mount until the conditions were right (the reconstruction of the Temple, with the arrival of the Messiah). Barak inquired of the two chief rabbis how they would see the negotiations he was now entering. He found there was no easy solution for the issue. The rabbis did not believe that Jewish sovereignty over the Mount could be relinquished, but thought the *waqf* would never dare to relinquish the claims to the Mount that they held on behalf of the Arab world and Islam.[20] Such were the perils of disparate religious law. How would the laws of nations or an actual process of negotiation then affect them?

Expectations at Camp David Summit
Raymond G. Helmick, S.J.
July 12, 2000

As I read the news reports of the opening of the Camp David meetings, I am impressed by their hopefulness. Expectations differ between Israelis and Palestinians, and of course with the Clinton administration hosts. Palestinians at home demonstrate quite effectively, asking that President Arafat and his team not compromise where they should not, while Israelis demonstrate competitively in the streets, for and against the peace effort and Prime Minister Barak.

At the crux of the public expectations is that each side will "compromise." Most commentary takes that as meaning territorial compromise, i.e., that the Palestinians give up more territory than they already have, and that the Israelis decide how "generous" to be in what territory they "concede." The supposition of that is that all the territory is Israel's to give or to keep. As I wrote in a memo of July 7, the true legal position (as in Security Council Resolution 242, basing itself on Article 2 of the United Nations Charter) is the very opposite: that the territory belongs rightfully to the Palestinians, and that any change can occur only by their agreement in the light of present circumstances.

A more realistic understanding of the compromises required from each side would emphasize not what each side gives up, but that they **give each other real reason to believe their future will be one of peace.** That includes not only land, but guarantees of peace, and that in fact is the original formula of SC Resolution 242: land for peace.

Land for Peace

The 242 formula requires *of Israel* that **territory captured in the 1967 war be returned**. That holds despite all the Israeli efforts over the years to say that the requirement has been met by returning *some* territory and it need not be all. If that were the case, the Israelis would not be at Camp David now. *Of the Arab nations* (for all the omission to include the Palestinians themselves in a formal way) it requires **peace**.

This distinction should be clearly maintained in the negotiations, that the Israelis are required to return land obtained, and held to this day, simply by the use of force, in defiance of the treaty obligation Israel entered into when it first joined the United Nations and accepted the Charter, with its Article 2. Security Council Resolution 242 represents in fact a compromise restriction on that Article 2 obligation: that territory must be returned *in exchange for peace,* rather than simply by reason of the Article 2 obligation itself.

After the 1956 invasion of Egypt, Israel, Britain, and France had been required to withdraw from all the captured territory, not in return for some other benefit but simply by the Article 2 obligation. The same was true of the 1978 (and 1982) Israeli invasions of Lebanon, as dealt with in SCR 425, or the Iraqi invasion of Kuwait. SCR 242 modifies that position, and requires the return of land *only in exchange for peace.*

As in the previous Israeli negotiations with Egypt and Syria, which led to treaties, and those still anticipated with Syria and Lebanon, **the Arab party's role is not to yield up territory but to agree on the terms of peace**. That holds good for the Palestinian team at Camp David as well. **Defining the terms of that peace, rather than further compromise over territory, is the way the Palestinians should give the Israelis real reason to believe that their common future will be one of peace.** This should be understood as a matter of principle in the negotiations, even if, in the course of the negotiations, some *agreed* compromises or exchanges of territory might be made.

The issue of a Palestinian Right of Return, as specified in General Assembly Resolution 194, should also not be compromised, though once acknowledged by Israel its implementation should then be a matter of finding what is actually feasible. In my memo of July 7th I speculated on how many refugees would actually want to return (it would be good to have a genuine survey), and what practical conditions should be agreed as to how an acknowledged Right of Return should be implemented: what compensation for those who could not or did not wish to return.

Terms of compensation, of course, should be equal to what Israelis would expect themselves. The models should be, for instance, what Jewish settlers in Golan would get when the territory is returned to Syria, or the full compensation expected from the Swiss banks for gold they had taken for themselves in the period of World War II. The Israelis, of course, haven't got that kind of money for compensating Palestinians adequately, so where it would come from would have to be found, just as has been thought in the case of Israelis who would leave the Golan.

Content: What the Palestinians May Offer as Assurance of Peace

My impression is that the Palestinian team, understanding that they ought not to relinquish territory beyond what has already been taken from them, have seen these Camp David negotiations more in terms of what pressures, about territorial concessions, they must resist. It is equally important that they think in terms of **what assurances of a genuinely peaceful future they offer to the Israelis**. As I mentioned in my memo of July 9th, this should be the central understanding of the objective in these negotiations: that both sides are there *to make the peace*, not to win victories over each other or to humiliate the other.

Not being privy to any details of what is under discussion at Camp David, I can only pick up the generalizations I hear in public. There are two of these that I see as especially important, and in the negotiations you will surely hear others.

1. A frequent Israeli demand is that there be a **declaration that the war is over**, that there will be no more violence permitted or endorsed by Palestinian authority. The ability of the Palestine Authority (or State) to guarantee that will of course depend on a) the fairness and acceptability of the eventual agreement to the Palestinian population (an unfair agreement will simply not produce real peace), and b) the effectiveness of the Palestine Authority (State) in asserting its genuine leadership of the Palestinian cause. But the Israeli *public's* need for genuine assurance on this point should be taken most seriously by the Palestinian team and granted after full discussion. It in no way precludes peaceful demonstration against injustices.

2. Israelis still need assurance of **Palestinian recognition of their legitimacy as a people**. I have heard this expressed by theologian/philosopher Rabbi David Hartmann, whom I greatly

respect, as a wish that Palestinians, and President Arafat as speaking for them, would say "The Jews have come home." When he asked that, I felt he had not heard properly, because I believe the Palestinians have in fact said it: that it is the genuine meaning of the Palestinian readiness to accept a two-state solution; that it was even the essential meaning of the *intifada*, that the Jewish State of Israel was accepted in the very act of the Palestinians' demand for a state of their own alongside it and rejection of occupation; and that the genuine meaning of the Oslo Declaration of Principles was the mutual recognition by the two peoples of one another's legitimacy. Nonetheless, even if the Palestinians have said it, the Israelis have not heard it. It therefore has to be one of the peace-making objectives of the Palestinians to make that recognition intelligible to the Israeli public.

What is lacking here may be only a matter of warmth. In my memo of July 9, I mentioned how the peace treaties between Israel and Egypt and between Israel and Jordan had only been agreements between governments, and not between peoples, who remained deeply estranged. The expression "Cold Peace" has often been used for the arrangement with Egypt. Peace between Israelis and Palestinians ought not be cold, though a recognition of the time it will take to enkindle real warmth and friendship is the basic reason I am reluctant to see too hasty a process, one that would not really involve the peoples. What governmental leaders can do is only to prepare the ground, provide the most favorable circumstances in which the mutual esteem and cordial relations can be built up between their peoples. The process is incomplete without that.

As an illustration of that need for reassurance I cited the article by Ari Shavit that had appeared that very day, July 12, in *Ha'aretz*, asking that Palestinians recognize the Jewish/Israeli people. That Shavit should ask this now seemed to me a matter of deafness, as it had been given before, but the article witnessed how little that had penetrated Israeli consciousness, much as had David Hartmann's plea that Palestinians concede that "The Jews have come home." This was the very same issue I had discussed with Arafat and the members of his Executive as long ago as those meetings in March, 1986, on the three pre-conditions for US or Israeli dialog with the PLO, for which I had worked so intensively from then until the dialog with the United States had begun at the end of 1988. I cited also Rabbi David Rosen's comment, speaking to our Jesuit group just shortly before this, on how Jews, having been boxed on the ears (by Christians!) for so many centuries, had trouble now in hearing the more conciliatory things that were said to them. It was of this that I asked the Palestinian negotiating team to be conscious. The Jews too—who now oppressed them—had suffered, not as recently as they, but in a very real way.

THE MEDIA HUSH

The US administration stretched a news blackout over Camp David once the talks began. Deborah Sontag, perched on the edge of the conference at Frederick, Maryland, did write of the startlingly changed atmosphere as two persons, Israeli and Palestinian, Avraham Burg and Hanan Ashrawi, appeared on the US television program *Crossfire*, addressing each other with warmth and good-humored banter in a way that could never happen on Israeli television, but that was as close as the news came to Camp David.[21]

HANIEH'S READING

Akram Hanieh had researched the background of the Camp David mountain retreat meticulously, and describes the early impressions of the Palestinian team. He found the atmosphere highly artificial and thought it manipulative that they should be isolated there under heavy pressure from lofty figures in the US administration.[22] He felt that for all the US officials, even for Clinton, who had invested much effort in understanding Arafat, the rules were: 1) that Washington would always exercise its role according to the needs, requirements and concerns of the current Israeli government; 2) that Washington would always accept the main Israeli demands as facts that could not be discussed; and 3) that the United States would always demand equal amounts of "flexibility" and "concessions" from both the Palestinian and the Israeli sides, ignoring the fact that the Palestinians were victims of Israeli "aggression," or that the land Israel offered to give up was Palestinian land occupied by military force.

From those three "rules," Hanieh drew three conclusions: 1) that the US administration, at the summit, destroyed the terms of reference for the peace process, as defined in Madrid in 1991, namely Security Council Resolutions 242 and 338 and the principle of land for peace; 2) that the US team held itself to Henry Kissinger's pledge never to take or present any position on the Arab–Israeli conflict without prior coordination with Israel—this a conviction on the basis of which the Palestinians understood every idea presented by the United States as coming, in fact, from the Israelis (often enough things that the Israelis had raised unofficially hours before the United States presented them as their own ideas); and 3) that the United States would exert pressure only on the Palestinians, never on the Israelis, who were "treated like a spoiled baby that should be pleased."[23]

These were Hanieh's perceptions as he took part with his colleagues in close consultation with Arafat. How far they represent the view of the rest of the team is hard to say, but they bespeak a gloom and apprehension that must have weighed heavily on the negotiators.

The day after their arrival we heard that Barak and Arafat had held an impromptu private meeting, with neither Clinton nor Madeleine Albright present. The official State Department briefing gave no hint of what they said, but the fact of their meeting seemed a highly positive sign. It contrasted with the behavior of Menachem Begin and Anwar Sadat at the earlier Camp David meeting 22 years before, when the Israeli prime minister and Egyptian president had met only in President Jimmy Carter's presence. Barak, deprived of the company of his foreign minister, Levy, now widened his delegation by the inclusion of Dan Meridor, formerly of the Likud, now chairman of the Foreign Affairs and Defense Committees of the Knesset. Clinton was away elsewhere, but Madeleine Albright spent an hour "grappling" with Barak on the "tough issues" of borders, settlers, refugees, and Jerusalem, which somehow had never been mentioned in the scanty press briefings of the last three days.

THE BEN-AMI DIARIES

The man who would eventually replace Levy as foreign minister, Shlomo Ben-Ami, kept a diary that constitutes another basic contemporary source for the mood and perceptions of the negotiators. On July 13 he records that he told Barak that the United States had accepted, for the first time, the principle that 80 percent of the settlers would remain under Israel's sovereignty. He saw that as an historic shift in the US position, since the United States always insisted that settlements were illegal and an obstacle to peace. He had argued that the summit would enter the pages of history as the event that legitimated the settlements, and Jewish Jerusalem as the capital of the state of Israel, two values which they would never lose.

He told too of his one-on-one meeting with Clinton, in which the President told him already that he was very angry with the Palestinians for not coming up with substantive proposals, but merely listening while he was asking them to move forward. Ben-Ami narrated how he and Lipkin-Shahak had met Muhammad Rashid, Arafat's Kurdish financial adviser, and Muhammad Dahlan, his security chief in the Gaza Strip, junior members of the Palestinian delegation, who claimed that the senior Palestinian leadership was backing away and dodging responsibility. The two Palestinians, as Ben-Ami understood them, made it clear that they were the only ones who were willing to make tough decisions and to work both with the Israelis and with Arafat, trying to influence Arafat.[24]

This effort by Israeli negotiators to deal separately with junior members of the Palestinian team would eventually become a sore point, as the Palestinians saw it as manipulating them and trying to go behind the backs of the senior decision makers to produce disunity in the Palestinian team. It is not certain that Ben-Ami was correct in his assumption that these two junior members were eating out of his hands, but the suspicion of it goes a long way to explain the reluctance Arafat would show, much later, in putting them in positions of great influence in the Palestinian Authority.

BACKGROUND NOISES

No one had visited Clinton and had his welcome to the Oval Office more often (twelve times) than Yasser Arafat. Clinton had taken Arafat's side often, as during the Wye negotiations, when he sensed that Netanyahu had insulted Arafat and had left the table abruptly, implying: "I'm not going to tolerate this." Now the President would find out if this investment could be made to pay in a peace settlement. His relation to Barak was more recent, but he kept emphasizing to Arafat that Barak was taking political heat by being here, and was "the best Israeli leader Arafat could hope for."[25]

Reporters hung out in the small towns around Camp David, kept at a distance. Those of us who were interested hung on every word. We heard the UN's Terje Roed-Larsen report that most of the claimed Israeli violations of the Lebanese border, disputes that had so far delayed UNIFIL's taking up positions at the border, had now been rectified. Reporters had retreated back to Washington for lack of news, and reported a lull in the talks, which they expected would lead to a whirlwind of decisions by the time Clinton would be leaving for a Group of Eight conference in Japan the following Wednesday. The US officials present kept emphasizing to the Palestinians that Barak "represented their best hope for a conciliatory peace partner."

Now, as anxiety grew among the privileged settlers, they resorted to violent attacks on West Bank Palestinians. Clashes became daily affairs, the worst of them happening in the center of Hebron, where the few hundred Jewish settlers lived among 160,000 Palestinians. On July 15 to 16, settlers rampaged through four Arab neighborhoods close to Qiryat Arba and in the center of town, stoning shopkeepers and bystanders, smashing the windshields of cars, and injuring many people. Three Palestinian cameramen who tried to film the marauding settlers were badly beaten by Israeli soldiers. Palestinian refugee activists from the Qalandiya refugee camp, north of Jerusalem, went wild in turn, torching three Israeli buses that were on their way to bring Israeli settlers to an anti-Barak demonstration in Tel Aviv. The drivers all escaped, but the Israeli army sealed off the camp while it searched for the perpetrators.[26]

Ben-Ami, meanwhile, was recording in his diary acrimonious sessions between the US and Israeli negotiators and their Palestinian counterparts. Ben-Ami himself had presented the Israeli proposal on borders in Clinton's presence. Sandy Berger, the White House chief of staff, had lashed out at the Palestinians for being unwilling to act as Clinton requested. Ben-Ami demanded of the Palestinians that they reply to his territorial proposal with a methodical counter-proposal of their own. He would not accept a demand for the 1967 borders as a serious response. Clinton then said that he accepted the Israeli position regarding borders and their refusal to accept the principle of returning to the borders of 1967. He commented on how the issue of settlements here was very different from the one on the Golan, and emphasized the importance of including 80 percent of the settlers under Israel's sovereignty.

It was on July 15, as Ben-Ami's diary reported, that he presented Israeli maps and so on, and Abu Ala presented the Palestinian position. Abu Ala talked still in terms of 1967 borders, international legitimacy, and so on. Clinton was sitting in front of Ben-Ami, who observed how "this red head was fuming." Suddenly Clinton lashed out at Abu Ala in what Ben-Ami considered a very degrading style. He yelled at him: "Sir, this is not the Security Council, this is not the General Assembly. You can give your lectures there, but don't waste my time. I have a lot at stake here as well." Clinton, thought Ben-Ami, saw the Palestinians as not fulfilling a promise he had received from Arafat, to come up with practical proposals. He accused the Palestinians of not having come to the summit with sincere intentions. Then he got up and left the room.

HANIEH'S DOUBTS

Akram Hanieh, meanwhile, bellwether of the Palestinian team, recorded an opposite and equally negative reaction to what was happening. In the Fourth Paper of his *Al-Ayyam* series he complained that none of the Israeli delegation were peacemakers. To him, they were only local politicians trying to protect their seats in the Knesset, all eager to separate themselves from any concession or breakthrough that Barak came up with, acting as though the very word "moderate" was an accusation that every Israeli negotiator had to avoid so that his popularity would not go down in the opinion polls.

Barak himself, Hanieh felt, came to Camp David with the deal all tied up in maps and proposals, expecting as a matter of course that the Palestinians could not but agree to 100 percent of what he offered. Hanieh saw the Israeli establishment as steeped in its mythologies and its occupation mentality; unable to see the Palestinians as peace partners with whom they should deal as equals. They failed to refer to any of the references in international law, launching their proposals without any interest in international resolutions, especially those resolutions (242, 338) that were the very basis of the peace process.

The Israelis, in Hanieh's view, simply excused themselves from real negotiation despite the sessions that would last tens of hours. Israeli positions would never come from themselves, but only be produced through the lips of US officials, seemingly supposing that they could impose their predetermined peace formulae on the Palestinians through US support. This was especially strange since the Palestinians knew that the Israeli security establishment had presented their political leadership with a very different assessment from that.[27]

Hanieh would go through the specifics of what had been discussed on each of the outstanding issues: refugees, land and borders, security, and Jerusalem.[28] More important, though, is the process his account and Ben-Ami's reveal.

The Palestinians were convinced that Camp David was an effort to coerce them, that the Israelis had decided to use Arafat's familiarity with Clinton and his awe before the massive power of the United States to leave him no options but to accept whatever they chose to give him. Whether or not that was actually the case, the fact that the Palestinians believed this explains much of the behavior that Israelis and US officials observed in them, their digging in defensively against what they saw as really an assault.

Were they justified in reading the situation so? Much in Ben-Ami's account truly confirms that Palestinian reading. Clinton's temper tantrums and browbeating when he did not get his way are case in point. The President, in fact, seems to have been trying to get more for the Palestinians rather than less, to nudge the Israelis, though ever so gently, to add more to the pot. Still, the ultimate criterion for him was what the Israelis would decide, with no impulse to look instead at obligations under international law.

Clinton, of course, would be baffled when the Israelis, astounded as much as he was that the Palestinians did not simply take what was offered, did in fact add more to what they had told him were their absolute red lines. But that the Palestinians, whom he was trying to help, should not understand that here naked power was the actual rule puzzled and infuriated him. To his mind, they just would not let themselves be helped.

That the game they were playing, one in which the abandonment of law would leave them helpless before the arbitrary demands of military forces more powerful than themselves, had any legitimacy did not occur to him. Having all that power, and meaning to do with it as much good for them as the Israelis would accept, he could not conceive that they not simply take advantage of as much shelter as he chose to provide them. And so, as much as they might be ready to negotiate the realities once the legal obligations were acknowledged, he took every reference to their rights under international law as a refusal to treat seriously the things he was offering under the rules of simple power.

Ben-Ami, who would later become the one among the Israeli team who would most urgently argue that the Palestinians had in fact made concessions and offered true proposals, and would understand better how the different context of Taba would allow them to negotiate with more freedom, reveals in his diary things that directly confirm those Palestinian suspicions.

From the earliest entries of his diary, Ben-Ami argues very contentedly to Barak that Israel has now won, as concessions *from the Americans*, things they could not lawfully have without Palestinian agreement: the occupied land on which 80 percent of the Jewish settlers lived in the West Bank, and the Israeli position on Jerusalem as their capital. (It is worth noting that he does not take it that the United States has agreed to Israeli possession of the whole of Jerusalem, but to West Jerusalem as capital of the state of Israel.)

He had commented, also, on Barak's refusal to carry on with the Stockholm preliminary negotiations, to make the already agreed land transfers before the summit or to hand over the three Jerusalem-area villages, that the reason was Barak's determination not to have those previously agreed assets already in Palestinian hands before the negotiation happened at the summit, but to make them bargain for them all over again at the summit and thus wrest more concessions from them. And that Clinton should fly into fury when the Palestinians balked at accepting what was effectively a diktat was, at the time he wrote his diary, welcome enough to Ben-Ami.

The effort to hive off younger members of the Palestinian delegation and make them pawns of the Israeli positions struck Ben-Ami, at least at the time of writing (July 13), as quite legitimate. That the Palestinians should take this attempt to create division among their own negotiators as reason for them to dig their heels in deeper did not occur to him.

CHINKS IN THE NEWS BLACKOUT

By Sunday July 16, the news blackout had left reporters, who had to put something in their papers, reduced to providing background on the lead players, from the United States, Israel, and Palestine, and their "chemistry." But that day Clinton broke the silence himself, when the *New York Daily News* tabloid reached him by phone at Camp David to ask his thoughts on a rumor that Hillary Clinton had once, years before, made a remark that could be taken as anti-Semitic. Hillary was running for election as senator for New York, where such a rumor could hurt her badly, and questions about it brought Clinton to the phone.

Asked if he were satisfied with the Camp David talks, he responded: "Good, it's hard. It's like nothing I've ever dealt with, all the negotiations with the Irish, all the stuff I've done with the Palestinians before this and with the Israelis, the Balkans at Dayton." Of the leaders: "They know if they make a peace agreement, half of their constituents will have to be angry with them for a while." He attempted to be upbeat about prospects, but concluded: "I would be totally misleading if I said I had an inkling that a deal is at hand. That's just not true. But we're slogging."

With that little bit of meat to chew, reporters opined that they would not know what was coming of the talks until Tuesday, the eve of Clinton's departure for Okinawa, which would set a kind of deadline. One official who had spoken with the participants, contacted by phone, said: "It is impossible to know where it's heading. That's the good news!" Back in Tel Aviv, tens of thousands of West Bank settlers had congregated on Saturday night, marching against Israel's taking part in the negotiations at all. This capped days of Rightist protest against leaked proposals to cede small Israeli settlements deep in the West Bank to eventual Palestinian control.[29]

By Tuesday July 18, expectations had dropped lower with the approach of the supposed deadline. The White House remained committed to reaching an agreement by then and spoke of shifting into high drive for the last 48 hours. Yet some US, Israeli and Palestinian officials, in imitation of Clinton's breach of the blackout, were now leaking to reporters their feeling that additional summits might be needed. What the White House called "an agreement," they said, could include anything from a modest declaration of principles to a full-blown accord. The Israelis muttered that Barak "is not going to stay forever at Camp David," that he had taken "giant steps" while Arafat had remained unyielding.[30]

On Wednesday we heard that Clinton had delayed his departure for Japan by a day to remain with the talks. Members of the Israeli delegation were phoning their contacts in the press at home now to say that the Jerusalem question had been heavily discussed since Monday, and hinting that progress had been made on this most intractable issue. The news blackout was obviously crumbling. Arafat was reported to have phoned his headquarters in Gaza to say he was on the verge of packing his bags to go home. *Ha'aretz* said the negotiators had focused on a package of US-negotiated proposals on "the core issues of borders, refugees, and Jerusalem." One Israeli had exclaimed on the phone: "I was astonished by the degree of progress in the last few hours." There was talk now of incorporating the Israeli bedroom communities (among them Ma'ale Adumim and Givat Ze'ev) into the legal entity of Jerusalem, while placing areas populated by Palestinians (such as Beit Hanina and the Shuafat refugee camp) under Palestinian control. The negotiators had not yet dealt with the Old City. Arafat, reportedly, had stood firm on Jerusalem, insisting that no agreement could come without Palestinian control over the Al-Aqsa Mosque and the Church of the Holy Sepulchre. The negotiations had now gone on for eight days.[31]

THE CRUNCH

Crisis came and was rebuffed on Wednesday night. The Thursday papers, on July 20, carried pictures of Clinton meeting separately with Arafat and Barak, under headlines that read: "Clinton leaves peace talks; Arafat and Barak stay," and "Pact is elusive after a tense, seesaw day." The turnaround had been dramatic. Clinton's spokesperson, Joe Lockhart, had announced baldly that the talks had failed, but 90 minutes later Clinton himself said the talks would remain intact. Both Barak and Arafat had sent letters to Clinton saying they were pulling out. Clinton told how "We thought it was all over. Then we discovered nobody wanted to give up. And that should be encouraging."[32]

It was Clinton who had actually performed a walkout. He said his leaving was not brinksmanship, but it was. That the talks had been reborn after the announcements of failure, with no guarantee of success, underscored the milestone that had been reached in Middle Eastern history: that Palestinian and Israeli leaders had at last confronted, in each other's presence, the monstrously difficult question of Jerusalem.[33]

My own access to people at the talks was now much easier to the Palestinian than to either the Israeli or US officials. I could rely on Faisal Husseini and his office to get things through to the Palestinians at Camp David, but had to invent stratagems to get them to the others. All the same, when I saw the talks at this crisis stage, I wrote again, this time urgently, on the Jerusalem question.

Jerusalem
In the Final Status Negotiations
Raymond G. Helmick, S.J.
July 20, 2000

After last night's dramatic developments at the Camp David Summit, with a first announcement that the talks had concluded without result, President Clinton's departure and the Israeli–Palestinian decision to continue the effort, it remains as difficult as ever for an outsider like myself to discern what is going on.

Most reports and speculation agree, though, that the issue of Jerusalem has been the obstacle, and that in fact the question of sovereignty over the Holy Places, particularly the Al-Aqsa Mosque and the Holy Sepulchre, had assumed central importance.

Early Israeli comment, when the talks seemed ended and before it was announced that they would continue, tended to assign blame to the Palestinians for "failing" to accept Israeli positions. Palestinian comment was more tempered even at that stage, pointing out that their side remained open to further negotiation. Outside commentators pointed out the progress that had been accomplished insofar as the issues of borders, refugees, and even Jerusalem had been brought into serious discussion at a summit level, where it had not been possible to raise them before.

The two sides presented the actual sticking point differently. Commentators close to the Palestinians emphasized Israeli refusal to concede Palestinian sovereignty over East Jerusalem, as a capital for the Palestinian State. Israeli commentators instead spoke of the amount of progress that had been made on many issues, including the offer of some level of autonomy for Arab neighborhoods in East

Jerusalem, but stressed that Israel would not agree to any part of what had been discussed and offered between the two sides unless there is a total package, all issues agreed and a declaration that the entire conflict is over.

That the two sides feel prepared to negotiate further in these circumstances is, to my mind, very encouraging. At the risk of presumption, since I lack so much information on the state of the discussion, I want once again to offer some outside thoughts. The priorities may look different to someone, like myself, who has not been engaged in the day-by-day exchange, and that different perspective could have some value.

Sovereignty in Jerusalem:

Two things cause me some apprehension as I hear discussion of the final status of Jerusalem. The *first* is the *religious direction* the negotiation has taken. The *second* is the *emphasis on sovereignty as a priority, apparently more than the openness of a shared city*. I have no doubt of the importance and legitimacy of the interests represented by each side as they take their stands on both these issues, but I would like to see them placed in a context that would relate them better to the issues of an overall agreement on the relations of the two states that will exist here, Israeli and Palestinian.

Sovereign Control of Holy Places::

Palestinian statements for several days have laid stress on sovereignty over the Al-Aqsa Mosque and the Holy Sepulchre. The Western Wall is just as clearly of supreme religious importance to Israelis. I note with satisfaction the emphasis that Palestinian statements for quite some time have placed on the *five elements* that must be accorded their due place in the final status: the *two peoples*, Israeli and Palestinian, and the *three faith communities*, Jewish, Christian, and Muslim. All this is entirely legitimate, and the two sides need to find agreement about all five elements. It is so much a part of my own consciousness that the title of the university course I teach at Boston College on the Middle Eastern conflict is "Two Peoples, Three Faiths."

Religion, though, brings its dangers of exclusiveness and the exacerbation of conflict issues, something I am especially conscious of as a clergyman, a Catholic priest of the Jesuit religious order. I expect religious motivations, from all three faith communities, to offer resources for healing conflicts as well, but their history of destructive involvement in this and other conflicts leaves me very wary.

I would like, for that reason, to see the religious element in this issue carefully contained and separated from the two secular issues involved in the status of Jerusalem, which are: 1) the legality of Israel's hold on East Jerusalem territory, and 2) the aspiration that Jerusalem should be the capital for both of the two states, Israeli and Palestinian.

Separating the question of sovereignty over the Old City, as location of the major holy places of all three faiths, from that of the rest of Jerusalem, East and West, can best accomplish that purpose.

General Assembly Resolution 181, the 1947 partition resolution, prescribed an international status for Jerusalem, without ever really establishing what international authority should govern it. That proposal was superseded by the events of the 1948 war, which divided the city between opposing forces, and has since lost the international support it once had. More recent proposals of a shared sovereignty over Jerusalem have been more attractive to Palestinians than to the successive Israeli governments, all of which have insisted on an exclusive Israeli possession of the whole city, which they saw as "united" despite all the evidence of difference between its Israeli-resident and Palestinian-resident areas.

Shared sovereignty over the city as a whole is difficult to define. There are also suggestions of a shared sovereignty for the Old City alone. The best formula for this is *not allowing the Old City itself to come under any one exclusive sovereignty.*

Under what sovereignty should it then come? Israelis will not consider the United Nations or any other foreign national power or combination of powers appropriate.

Because this is primarily a question of the right of access for members of all three faith communities that regard parts of the Old City as holy, I would suggest that the Old City be governed by a body answerable to the two state authorities, Israeli and Palestinian, and the religious authorities of the three faith communities: the Rabbinate, the Waqf, the Vatican, and the Ecumenical Patriarchate. A municipal authority could be designated by consensual agreement among these parties, and no restriction permitted on free access of believers to any of their holy places. The particular interests of the two states and the various religious authorities in particular quarters and places within the Old City could be recognized, and no interference allowed to their rights in those places.

This would effectively separate the religious issues involved in sovereignty over the Old City from the secular issues regarding the rest of Jerusalem. The Old City is of particular interest to the two States only because of these religious considerations. It is not what either State would regard as its capital. Hence a different approach to Old City sovereignty than that which obtains for the larger population centers in Jerusalem could have appeal to both sides.

Sovereignty and Openness in an Undivided Jerusalem:

The governing legal principle for the city should be the same as for the all other territory which Israel acquired by force in the 1967 war: return of territories (*des territoires!*) in exchange for peace as prescribed in SCR 242, with reference to the prohibition of such acquisition of territory by force in Article 2 of the UN Charter.

That means that territory beyond the boundary of June 3, 1967, is presumptively Palestinian and can only be exchanged or conceded by their agreement.

Circumstances have changed sufficiently since so that some agreed changes are in order, what is written above about the Old City being a case in point, but Israel has no right to assume possession by force.

Israel has boxed itself into the position of claiming sovereignty over the whole municipal territory of Jerusalem as its united and eternal capital. But the boundaries of that municipal territory have already been treated by Israel as changeable ever since 1967. A wide variety of optional plans, all predicated on redefining the municipal boundaries, have come under discussion even in recent times.

For that reason, it should be possible to define the presumptive borders according to the legally binding line of June 3, 1967, and to negotiate whatever changes can gain mutual approval from there. Abu Dis stands out as a neighborhood clearly a part of the Jerusalem conurbation that is not within the municipal boundaries as presently defined. As much as Abu Dis, in the Palestinian view, is not identical with Jerusalem or any adequate substitute for it, there is no reason not to regard it as a part of the city.

Even as Israelis have discussed handing over Abu Dis and other areas to full Palestinian control (Area A), they have spoken of calling it "Al Quds," the Arab name for Jerusalem, to distinguish it from Israeli Jerusalem. All the other Palestinian-inhabited neighborhoods of East Jerusalem could just as easily be designated as parts of a municipality called Al Quds, under Palestinian sovereignty, and leave Israel in sovereign control of all that is called Jerusalem, having been under Israeli sovereignty on June 3, 1967.

This of course is a purely legal disposition of the territory, and will surely not satisfy the Israelis. Some territories now occupied by Israeli settlements *to the West* of the city are part of the West Bank. Those might well be conceded, by agreement and not by force, and preferably *in exchange* for other territory that Israel would concede to the Palestinians from Green-Line Israel, perhaps in the neighborhood of the Gaza Strip.

But the plan throughout the time of Israeli occupation of the West Bank was to seize control of Palestinian territory by establishing settlements as "facts on the ground," in particular encircling Jerusalem with a ring of settlements, all in plain contravention of international law. None of that should be accepted as *fait accompli*.

At this point I went into the argument I had often raised before about the need for Palestinians to concede, through negotiated agreement, the importance of allowing some Israelis to live in the territories holy to Jews in memory of the ancient kingdoms, and for the Israelis to make this a reciprocal acceptance of some agreed and limited return of Palestinians to Jaffa and Haifa, but always with the proviso that the border should remain an open one.

This is particularly clear in the case of Jerusalem. Israeli Right-wingers treat every suggestion for the sharing of Jerusalem as if it were a proposal to *divide* the city, to set up walls, fences, and checkpoints as it was before 1967. No Palestinian, to my knowledge, has in fact proposed any such separation. The Palestinians and Israelis who for some years have studied the question of mutual rights in Jerusalem have all, without exception, sought for ways to share rather than divide the city. Concentration now on rights of sovereignty in parts of the city should not be allowed to compromise that objective. Whereas, in fact, the city is so divided in practice that Jews hesitate to enter Palestinian neighborhoods and Palestinians to enter Jewish neighborhoods, the goal should be that the entire city be open to all its citizens, of both states, without checkpoints or obstacles, whether social or physical.

To relate this to the overall shape of a peace agreement, that should also be the objective of the entire agreement, that boundaries of two states should be agreed and recognized, but that the borders be open. Anything less than that will simply foster continuing estrangement between the two peoples and lead to repeated and continuing conflict.

It may well be, in the neighborhood of Jerusalem, that some temporary security arrangements for Israeli-inhabited neighborhoods would have to be agreed for a set period of time. That too should be negotiated freely, with respect for the other side's genuine needs. But it should be recognized that any such arrangement is temporary, and that the objective is to remove it in due time.

Whatever is done in any part of these negotiations, however, should be an effort to solve problems, not to invent them. The objective is to make peace.

PAUSE, AND SECOND TRY

The crisis had left the negotiators exhausted, and with Clinton gone, the energy drained out of them. The talks were described in the press as stalled but alive. "Squirreled away in their cabins in the woods, the Israelis and Palestinians tried to recover from the rollercoaster drama of late Wednesday night when, within the space of an hour and a half, the summit meeting died and was reborn." As the conference teetered on the edge of uncertainty, the prospect of violence loomed should they fail. The Israelis said they had stayed only because Clinton had asked them to, while US officials claimed that Barak had taken the initiative rather than go home empty-handed. People cited Shlomo Ben-Ami as having persuaded him to do so.

The Palestinians felt strongly that an unfair effort was being made to portray them as the spoilers, as being intransigent. They took this as new evidence that the United States was permanently biased in favor of Israel. Arafat began, from this time, to say he could not recognize an Israeli annexation of East Jerusalem, yielding sovereignty forever, without a formal mandate from the Arab and Muslim world. Israel, he believed, was seeking exactly that in exchange for giving the Palestinians some degree of control of Palestinian neighborhoods that would be short of sovereignty.

Back in Jerusalem, Sharon was declaiming on Israeli television: "Barak has set a dangerous precedent. We'll have to work hard to reverse the decisions he made in the last nine days."[34] Arabs in Jerusalem were following the reports of discussion about their city with a mixture of rising anticipation and extreme anxiety that concessions might be made that failed to meet their most basic needs.[35]

Israeli hopes soon rose. On July 21, Barak phoned his environmental minister back in Jerusalem, Dalia Itzik, to say that chances of success had risen to a 60 to 40 level. Clinton, too, told reporters in Okinawa that he was hopeful, and made arrangements for an early return over the Saturday, so that he could resume negotiations early on Sunday evening. The Palestinian mood remained pessimistic. Abu Mazen had returned home, not out of pique but to attend his son's wedding. He gave a somber account over Voice of Palestine radio. The US officials were talking now, and revealed that Barak and Arafat had met on Thursday night for the first time in five days, seated at dinner on either side of Madeleine Albright, but that no word was exchanged between them.[36]

The Sunday papers blossomed with pictures of Clinton and his daughter Chelsea boarding the plane in Japan for his early return. He spoke of being encouraged by the Group of Seven leaders at the conference to pursue the Camp David effort to a successful conclusion, and told of an encouraging fax he had sent to Madeleine Albright, who had tried to keep the flagging discussion alive in his absence. "Whether we get an agreement or not," said Clinton, "they have tried. They have really been out there working!"[37] Back in Maryland, the negotiators were in a "waiting for Clinton" mode. Over the Saturday's Shabbat observance the Israelis hinted that the impasse might be broken. Arafat still insisted that he had no mandate from the Arab world to do anything less than regain sovereignty over all East Jerusalem.[38] Commentary emphasized that the Holy City was going to prove the toughest element in the conflict to resolve.[39]

With Clinton's return on Sunday afternoon the talks began to race toward their crucial point. Richard Boucher, the State Department spokesman, set the tone, saying: "We are not here for an unlimited period of time." Egypt's President Hosni Mubarak had traveled to Saudi Arabia to ensure support for Arafat in the debate over Jerusalem. The Pope, in his weekly Sunday address, exhorted the leaders to adopt the long-held Vatican position that a special international status be extended to the holy sites in the Old City of Jerusalem. Barak had spent the day touring the battle site at nearby Gettysburg with Madeleine Albright. He was said to contemplate deferring a final decision on granting shared sovereignty over East Jerusalem and some neighborhoods adjacent to the Old City, but the Palestinians were saying that such ideas were not sufficient to allow Arafat to make a deal.[40]

Clinton plunged at once into the nitty-gritty of issue-by-issue deliberation. He met, from the time he arrived late Sunday afternoon, almost to dawn on Monday with Israeli and Palestinian negotiators. A picture of him in Tuesday's *New York Times* showed him at a table, poring over mountains of paper, with Aba Ala and Nabil Sha'ath, Elyakim

Rubinstein, and Oded Oran. Nothing would be agreed until everything was agreed: that was the principle. Israeli negotiator Lipkin-Shahak, on the phone to an Israeli reporter, said: "It's either zero or 100. There is no middle ground."[41]

BLAME

Catastrophe struck on Tuesday night (July 25). The headlines blared: "Clinton ends deadlocked peace talks. Barak praised, Arafat said to show less flexibility over Jerusalem."

Clinton and the other US mediators made it clear that it was Arafat who balked at the end, and over Jerusalem. Returned to the White House, the President praised Barak for his willingness to make hard compromises. "I would be making a mistake not to praise Barak, because I think he took a big risk. The Prime Minister moved forward more from his initial position than Chairman Arafat, particularly surrounding the question of Jerusalem." He said the discussion had been "really unprecedented" in raising issues that "had long been considered off limits." Israelis and Palestinians had never before discussed Jerusalem in face-to-face encounters. "Under the operating rules that nothing is agreed until everything is agreed, they are of course not bound by any proposal discussed at the summit. However, while we did not get an agreement, significant progress was made on the core issues."

Looking back in retrospect, nearly four years later, we may question the compatibility of those two statements: that nothing was achieved, and that significant progress had been made.

No side announced any immediate plans to resume talks. Arafat's declared intention to declare independence unilaterally on September 13 imposed the next serious deadline on the process which had seesawed from hope to despair and back again since the Oslo agreements had been signed in 1993. The participants, for all their labor, could issue only a bare bones "Joint Statement" which, against all the warnings, was merely another Declaration of Principles:

1. The two sides agreed that the aim of their negotiations is to put an end to decades of conflict and achieve a just and lasting piece.
2. The two sides commit themselves to continue their efforts to conclude an agreement on all permanent issues as soon as possible.
3. Both sides agree that negotiations based on UNSCR 242 and 338 are the only way to achieve such an agreement, and they undertake to create an environment for negotiations free from pressure,

intimidation and threats of violence. [This can only be taken as ironic comment on what had happened.]
4. The two sides understand the importance of avoiding unilateral actions that prejudge the outcome of negotiations and that their differences will be resolved only by good faith negotiations.
5. Both sides agree that the United States remains a vital partner in the search for peace and will continue to consult closely with President Clinton and Secretary of State Madeleine Albright in the period ahead.[42]

Barak, like Clinton, laid the full blame on Arafat, adding ominously that Israel was prepared for "every possibility." He added, though: "The vision of peace suffered a major blow, but I believe that with good will on all sides it can recuperate."

Arafat said nothing on departure, but Saeb Erekat and Abu Mazen put an unexpectedly positive face on what had happened, saying it had laid the groundwork for an agreement by September 13, Erekat adding: "What happened at Camp David are seeds that will grow very fast."

Cooling down a bit from his first disappointment, Clinton allowed that, in some respects, it was hardly surprising that the summit meeting, with its qualities of an almost brutal showdown in close quarters, had not produced what he wanted. "This is like going to the dentist without having your gums deadened," he said. Barak, before leaving, added: "We are ready to end the conflict. We looked for an equilibrium point that will provide a peace for generations, but unfortunately Arafat somehow hesitated to take the historic decisions that were needed to put an end to it!" Saeb Erekat, meanwhile, declared: "The prospects for agreement on all permanent status issues are stronger than at any time in almost nine years."

Who was right? We have to read all these statements in the light of what the failure meant to each participant. It was Clinton, the super-negotiator and persuader, who had broken things off. His place in history was at stake here. With the ever-destructive election campaign season close approaching, this must have seemed a last chance to consolidate it. He had just rushed back through eleven time zones from arduous meetings in Japan, and proceeded without rest through two full nights and the intervening day. That his phenomenal patience and endurance had snapped in the face of ongoing disappointment should cause no surprise, nor should his resentment at those whose resistance would not yield.

Barak faced personal political disaster as the result of the failure. For that reason he had increasingly considered wider concessions during the last stages of the meeting. He had incurred mountainous resentment from the most articulate spoilers in the Israeli political system. Now he returned with nothing to offer those who had supported him in his labors. It had to be clear that his career in government was over and that his successors would not be promoters of his aims of peace. We need not wonder at his need to point the finger of blame.

Arafat and the Palestinians had come only reluctantly to Camp David, mostly because all other courses, especially that of UDI, seemed so bleak. Having warned that the prospects of success were slight, and determined that they would not abandon the essentials of their position under pressure, they had received promises that they would not be blamed should the venture fail. Arafat is not good at addressing a Western public. Erekat and Abu Mazen made their statement in dread that the world would take a report of failure as evidence that the Palestinians had not really tried. Their public too would be crushingly disappointed. They had feared that Arafat would give in too easily. That he had not was reassuring to them, but prospects for the future looked empty.

The United States was unremitting in its continued pressure on the Palestinians as the ones who must yield. Everyone's behavior was judged on how far they would concur with Clinton's wishes. Sandy Berger, the White House chief of staff, vouchsafed to the press that "Barak was more willing to think out of the box, far more willing to consider, though he never accepted, solutions that would have broken the logjam. Arafat, on the other hand, while he did make some compromises on Jerusalem, was not prepared at this point to crack open his traditional positions." Berger's idea of the best chance for the future was that the summit would provoke a reassessment within the Palestinian delegation, a group of about a dozen of Arafat's top political and security lieutenants. Did this mean that he really placed his hopes on provoking disunity among them?

Filling in details, US officials told how prospects had fallen apart just after midnight on Monday, the second all-night session Clinton led after his return from Japan. On Sunday and Monday nights Clinton had worked with negotiators from both sides. Progress was reported on the borders of a Palestinian state, on the fate of the 3 million Palestinian refugees, and on security arrangements. In what turned out to be a last effort, Clinton met Arafat shortly after midnight. By then Barak had made what the administration regarded as considerable concessions, relinquishing to Palestinians control in the outer and inner suburbs of East Jerusalem. US officials declined to go into precise details, but in the last week of summit talks, according to Israeli reports, US proposals had been put forward on concepts of shared sovereignty in East Jerusalem. Barak was considering these ideas, which represented a radical departure from the established Israeli policy that Jerusalem was the eternal, undivided capital of Israel. Effectively, Clinton kept floating ideas on behalf of Barak, who thus made no clear commitment to them himself.

Said Barak: "We believed the ideas raised by the President were far-reaching and deserved a kind of positive response by Arafat."

The Ben-Ami diaries for the night of July 24–25 fill in a little detail at this point. He himself had spent time with Clinton up to the time when, between 9 p.m. and 1 a.m., Clinton met again with both teams. When Ben-Ami had discussed with the President the sanctity of the Temple Mount, Clinton had seconded him with the statement that "not only the Jews worldwide but the Christians support this notion as well."[43]

When Clinton had obtained Barak's assent to a set of proposals over the sacred Mount, he sent George Tenet to persuade Arafat to do the same, but Tenet encountered Arafat's argument that he could not alienate the Haram al-Sharif without the consent of Muslims throughout the world.[44]

When, after midnight on Monday, Clinton spoke with Arafat, he could not move the chairman from his position that East Jerusalem should be the capital of the new Palestinian state. The question of sovereignty over the holy sites in Jerusalem was at the heart of the problem. An administration official explained it thus: "Think of Jerusalem as four concentric circles: outer suburbs, inner suburbs, Old City, and the religious sites. As you move into the center, the issues become more intense, historical, religious." There was surprising convergence on how different parts of the city would be managed, but severe disagreement on the notion of sovereignty.

CIA Director George Tenet then tried to persuade Arafat to accept Clinton's proposals. Ben-Ami, in Clinton's presence, expostulated to Saeb Erekat: "You are barely 4 million Muslim Palestinians and pretend to represent 1 billion Muslims regarding the Temple Mount." Clinton's proposals, he told him, were historic, and he then appealed to the familiar argument about lost opportunities. That amounted, once more, to the "all or nothing, take it or leave it" proposal that the Palestinians had heard so often in these days. He added that Arafat was placing the Muslim agenda before the national Palestinian agenda, and added: "Your national agenda is held hostage in the hands of the Muslim agenda and you will pay a heavy price for this."[45]

One official depicted Clinton's last conversation with Arafat. "The President described once again what was at stake: gaining a state, international legitimacy, and international economic support." Conversely, if Arafat let an agreement pass, he could declare a state on what would be 40 percent of the West Bank, and the Israeli reaction would be strong, possibly the forcible annexation of all the Jewish settlements.

When Arafat refused, Berger, Albright, and Dennis Ross met one of the Palestinian negotiators. They discussed, for one last time, the possibility of Arafat accepting a partial agreement that would deal with the shape of a Palestinian state, refugees, and other matters, but would put the question of Jerusalem aside for the time being. This did not appeal to Arafat either. He felt he would lose leverage over Jerusalem, according to the administration account, if he settled the other issues first.

At 3 a.m., Arafat sent one of his negotiators from his cabin to Clinton with a letter. Politely he thanked Clinton for his efforts, but said he would not accept the proposal on Jerusalem as it stood. In the morning, Clinton then met separately with the Israeli and Palestinian leaders. The sessions focused on where the peace process would go now. This brief meeting of all three leaders together was only the second formal session at which all three had met throughout the exercise, though they had been at dinner together several times.

All were drained by their exhausting discussion and to some extent pleased to get out of their long confinement. Barak had referred to Camp David as a prison. Clinton and Barak stressed the danger of violence as September 13 neared, Barak saying: "We meet at the end of an important stage of the peace process and at the threshold of an era of uncertainty," Clinton added: "Every day things go past it will put more pressure on the Palestinians to declare a Palestinian state unilaterally and more pressure on the Israelis to have some greater edge and conflict in their relations as a result of that." And in echo, a threat of violence was reported from Sheikh Ahmed Yassin, the Hamas leader back in Gaza: "This failure is another indication that the only choice we have is resistance. Only by force are we able to retain our rights."[46]

For myself, I felt impelled to write encouragement at this point. I felt sure that it had been a mistake to break off negotiation at this point, basically that Clinton himself, for all his skill and goodwill as a negotiator, had faltered under the pressure of sleeplessness and frustration and failed to pursue the goal when it was so nearly within reach. Even on the day this news first broke, before hearing all the bloody details I wrote, particularly for the Palestinians, but circulating it to the Israelis and the administration as well:

Adjournment of the Camp David Negotiations
Raymond G. Helmick, S.J.
July 25, 2000

Disappointing as the termination of the Camp David talks may be, there is no reason to lose heart at this point. A great deal is gained. The question of Jerusalem, on which the Israelis have never agreed to negotiate before, has been opened. We on the outside don't yet know what was agreed about borders, settlements, and refugees, but apparently substantial progress has been made there too. And as with the question of Jerusalem, the taboo has been breached. More will follow.

This remains true despite the Israeli statements that nothing is agreed until all is agreed. Palestinians have good reason to hold to that principle too. Statements that the Israelis will not hold to things they have agreed while at Camp David need not be taken too seriously. The international community, and President Clinton in particular, will hold them to those things and allow no regression.

Threatening elements are only from the extremists, both Palestinian and Israeli. Everyone knows who they are and what their motives are. Hamas calls for a Palestinian return to armed struggle. Every responsible Palestinian must realize that such regression would lose his people everything that has been gained in these last weeks, would in fact lose the Palestinians the entire struggle. The Israeli General Mofaz pictures Palestinians as about to storm Israeli settlements, and boasts of arming the settlers still further and authorizing them to kill any Palestinian who assaults the settlement perimeter fences. Palestinians need to give the lie to any such expectations. President Arafat returns with his standing bolstered among Palestinians, who need not fear that he will give away what is precious to them. At this point, it should be made clear to all Palestinians that he has been gaining the things they need by his steadfast diplomacy, and that it could be lost by rash or violent action on their part. If he is to prevent Hamas and other extremists from wrecking Palestinian chances, he must assert this kind of leadership and demonstrate the success it has had.

I have been insisting, in my own writings, for quite some time on the need for mobilization of the Palestinian public behind the open and explicit leadership of the Palestine Authority. Any demonstrations or demands by Palestinians, now more than ever, need to be recognizably organized by this authority, and no one be permitted to violate its prerogatives with stupid or counterproductive action.

But the main pressure Palestinians can exert on Israel just now is their solidarity behind that leadership. Provocative action can currently only harm them. The leadership needs to make it public why they have refused certain concessions that were promoted as "compromise" at Camp David, and why they will remain steadfast in those refusals.

You can be sure the Israelis will have an election now. Netanyahu, Sharon, Sharansky and others will be in the extremist anti-peace camp as surely as are the settlers and the Kach people who are talking of assassinations of both Barak and Arafat and the destruction of the mosques now. I expect that, by itself, will mean that Barak wins. The condition of that is that the Palestinians, all through the electoral process, keep demonstrating to the Israeli public, and to Barak, that for all their insistence on legal principle and their own rights they are offering peace. That is what the Israeli public will vote for. Palestinians should all be aware that it was Hamas and the bombers who elected Netanyahu before.

I would be proven wrong in my expectation that the extremism of the Israeli Right would lose them the election and that Barak could yet win the inevitable election by winning the peace. Yet it would take the provocative action of Ariel Sharon in September to change that prospect. Wrong too in the expectation that Clinton would be left in charge of the negotiation by a successor President. That would have been so had the successor been Albert Gore, but strange things happened in that election too.

AFTERMATH

Both Barak and Arafat, as they returned home, pledged to continue working at their halting quest for peace despite the breakup at Camp David. Both received homecomings that, while orchestrated events, illustrated the difficulties they would face in forging any compromise on Jerusalem.

Barak faced a somber, subdued ceremony staged by his close political allies at the airport. As he rode into Jerusalem, the road was lined with protesters, many in the knitted skullcaps favored by the settlers, holding signs that said such things as "Barak, you are weak!"

At the airport he had been close to tears as the army band played the Israeli national anthem, "Hatikva." He hugged those in the line of his supporters, including a delegation of bereaved parents from the Four Mothers movement, saying:

> I went there knowing there is no peace at any price, but there is also no peace without a price. A painful, difficult and heart-wrenching price. Today I return from Camp David and look into millions of eyes in whose name I went and say with a pained heart: we have not succeeded.

But already the narrative of a failure brought about solely by Arafat's fault began to take shape, as Barak intoned at the airport:

> We did not succeed because we did not find a partner prepared to make decisions on all issues. We did not succeed because our Palestinian neighbors have yet to internalize that in order to obtain a true peace some of one's own dreams must be conceded; one has to give, not only request. But I look today into the eyes of millions in whose name I was sent and say we did everything we could. We turned over every stone; we exhausted every possibility to bring about an end of the conflict and a safer future for Israel. And we still hope.

Arafat himself received a hero's welcome on his arrival in the Gaza Strip, precisely because he had refused to compromise on Jerusalem. Looking worn and tired, he was hoisted on the shoulders of his supporters. A crowd of 5,000 turned out and hailed him as a modern-day Saladin,[47] a title that would not really serve him in good stead.

Saeb Erekat declared his intention to resume negotiations with his Israeli counterparts as early as the following Sunday. Despite Israeli premonitions of violence, the day remained quiet, the Palestinians determined to prevent any clashes. Nabil Sha'ath promised: "There will be no violence from the Palestinians, not unless Israel makes violence, or the settlers turn to it."[48]

Clinton, back at the White House, contented himself to say that more time was needed. "If there is going to be an agreement here, it must be one that meets the legitimate interests of both parties."[49] James Baker, the former secretary of state and architect of the Madrid Conference, saw encouraging signs that both sides had moved toward peace on some issues, in fact everything other than Jerusalem. He took it as a challenge to see if they could build on their accomplishments or would slide back to recriminative violence. There was no point, he said, in criticizing leaders for not making a deal that they could not make except at the risk of losing the support of a majority of the people they represent.[50]

The two leaders started to plan their next steps, as details of Clinton's last-minute proposals began to leak out. Both spoke of putting the failed Camp David behind them and moving ahead with a renewed peace effort. On Thursday they confirmed that the negotiators would meet on Sunday at the border of the Gaza Strip, saying that the ideas Clinton had floated at Camp David, including proposals the Palestinians had rejected, had carried the peace process further than ever before. Less than 24 hours after their return, Barak and Arafat were laying out travel plans that suggested both believed some form of agreement, perhaps only partial, and possibly excluding the deal-breaking issue of Jerusalem, might yet be possible in the weeks and months ahead. Their decision to return so quickly to the table reflected a recognition that the negotiations at Camp David, particularly the new US ideas, had swept the historic rivals into new political terrain that they must now explore, and from which neither could easily retreat. Graham Usher, writing from East Jerusalem, saw them as largely a revisiting of proposals that had been made as far back as 1995 by Abu Mazen and Yossi Beilin, now presented as a US bridge in what was called, to save it from being a formal proposal, a "non-paper."[51]

The plan put forward by Clinton had included a complex mosaic of jurisdictions in East Jerusalem. Gilead Sher, one of Barak's top aides at Camp David, said Clinton had proposed that Arafat have a presidential office in the Muslim Quarter of the Old City, which Israeli commentators felt would allow the Palestinians to claim they had fulfilled their pledge to establish the capital of their new state in Jerusalem. Other Israeli officials said the US proposals had provided for some Palestinian quarters in East Jerusalem to be annexed to other Palestinian territories outside the city and expanded to establish a new city, to be known as Al Quds, the historic Arabic name for Jerusalem.

Sher and Erekat both saw continuing possibilities in these proposals. A meeting had already taken place, it was revealed, on Wednesday between Israel's deputy defense minister, Ephraim Sneh, and Tayib Abdel Rahim, a senior aide to Arafat. They had discussed joint efforts to prevent outbreaks of violence either by Israelis or by Palestinians discontented by events. Thus, in the wake of Camp David, much contrary to the dismal narrative that would be circulated months later, there was a flurry of diplomacy and hope.[52]

Yet the clouds of disillusionment too continued to gather, as Amos Oz, one of the most inveterate peace voices in Israel, took up the

170 The Failed Negotiations

ominous sobriquet given to Arafat on his arrival: Saladin! Oz had doubts now, after his long espousal of a two-state solution, whether there could actually be peace with the Palestinians. He raised the specter of the "right of return," an element which in fact seems not to have been a major obstacle during the actual talks at Camp David, where the Palestinians had thus far shown understanding that it would have to be negotiated so as not to undermine the demographic character of Israel, but Oz read it in terms of the Saladin image, and felt Arafat was seeking not just the right to a Palestinian state, which he supported, but the destruction of Israel.[53] By year's end, this cry of "right of return" would become a clamor among Palestinians who, by now, felt that every right was being taken from them, and an issue whose resolution had seemed clear would become one of the greatest obstacles.

Others on the Israeli Left judged as harshly. Two eminent philosophy professors, Avishai Margalit and Menachem Brinker, founders of the Peace Now movement and venerated gurus for its rank and file, maintained that Barak had offered tremendous concessions at Camp David. If an ungrateful Arafat rejected that generosity, the whole Israeli peace movement must turn against him. That sentiment had pervaded the Israeli media even through much of the negotiating period.[54]

On the Friday, Clinton made a move destined to stir the worst fears of betrayal among the Palestinians. Anxious to shore up Barak's crumbling political base, the US President went on Israeli television promising that, as a concrete reward for the peace, he considered moving the US embassy to Jerusalem.[55] A disgruntled Arafat, starting off on his diplomatic tour, first to see President Jacques Chirac in Paris, complained now at the way both Barak and Clinton had heaped all blame on him for the failure of the Camp David talks. He referred to them as the "big lies" that were being told. Hanan Ashrawi spoke of a "fundamental American bias." The Palestinian media concluded that Clinton had tilted so dramatically toward the Israelis simply as a way to help Hillary Clinton in her senate campaign in New York, after she had been accused, quite irrationally, of an anti-Semitic remark. The White House was deeply offended at this and called it ridiculous.[56]

The atmosphere was becoming ugly. In Hebron, a rumor spread that the 7,000 Hebron area settlers would, according to the suggestions made at Camp David, be among the 40,000 who would have to live under Palestinian rule in any final peace pact. The settlers responded militantly, expressing their resentment that outsiders, including journalists, should regard them as extremists.[57]

Yet Barak had begun to make headway in consolidating his government. Thanks to complex backroom maneuvering, it seemed he would survive, after all, a vote of confidence in the Knesset and keep his battered coalition together for the next three months. The Sunday meetings between Israeli and Palestinian negotiators had shown that the peace effort was still alive. There was question whether Foreign Minister David Levy, who had refused to accompany Barak to Camp David, would now remain or would resign and return to his Likud roots. Levy had a long history of changing sides, often for reasons of purely personal pique. During Camp David he had made a sympathy visit to hunger strikers who were protesting the talks. But after meeting Barak he decided to stay in the cabinet for the time being but to abstain in the confidence vote on Monday. Likud, though, said it would not join any government of national unity, but was determined to topple Barak, whom it accused of lying to the people and breaking his promises to the public not to surrender any part of Jerusalem.[58] The future at this point was mystery.

6
Negotiations continue, August 1–September 28, 2000

QUANDARIES IN ISRAELI OPINION

Barak did get through his vote of confidence, but not without suffering a new humiliation the same day. The legislators gave him 50 votes for to 50 against—it would have taken 61 to have ousted him that Monday, July 31—with eight abstentions and twelve members who simply disappeared from the chamber as the vote was taken. But the Labor Party had nominated Shimon Peres for President, and the Knesset decided to punish Barak by electing Likud member Moshe Katsav instead, in the process humbling the veteran leader Peres as well. On a first ballot, Katsav had 60 votes to Peres' 55.[1]

Yaron Dekel, Israel Radio's chief political analyst, commented: "The only thing that is sustaining the Prime Minister is that the Knesset members do not want, at this time, to go to elections within 90 days," many of them fearing for their own seats.[2]

The Katsav victory signified much more trouble to come for Barak. Somehow he would need to get through just a little more rancor in the Knesset before it would recess, after Wednesday, for its 90-day vacation, but Sharon, having formed what he called a "Jerusalem coalition," warned that he could interrupt the recess if Barak tried to "sneak" any peace agreements through while the Knesset was away. "We will stand our ground," he pledged. "We can call the Knesset at any time." And in truth it could be done by the petition of 25 members, easily obtained by the opposition.[3]

David Levy chose this time of Barak's troubles finally to quit his post as foreign minister, after all his separation of himself from Barak and his policies. Levy, known for his keen sense of which way the wind was blowing, had been threatening to resign unless Barak formed a Grand Coalition government, bringing in the Right. Expecting his departure, Barak remained unfazed, even cocky, crossing the Knesset chamber with bouncy step after Levy's fiery speech, to clap him on the back and shake his hand. This was the last Knesset session before the recess. Said Barak: "In a few more weeks the dust will settle. We may have three months to try and consolidate either the peace negotiation or the government." Yossi Sarid, head of the Meretz party with its ten seats, wanted to see time gained to allow for the achievement of peace with the Palestinians, but the Likud's Limor Livnat warned: "Don't try to pull any fast ones while the Knesset is on recess."[4]

REFLECTING ON WHAT HAD HAPPENED

I had been pondering my own response to all these events ever since the Camp David failure. I had been able, during the period of the talks, to get my own thoughts directly before the Palestinian delegation, but had far less certainty, despite my efforts, that they had reached the US or Israeli officials. I had learned long since, of President Clinton, that he was very good with paper, having often heard back from him directly or through his former national security adviser Tony Lake. I sent him a long letter dated August 4:

> Dear President Clinton,
> Christ's Peace!
> A great deal of gloom has descended over the Israeli–Palestinian peace process, unnecessarily to my mind. I watched with much admiration as you nursed the process along over the two weeks at Camp David, and realized anew how essential your role as accomplished mediator has become, here as in Northern Ireland and elsewhere.
> I felt, though, that you had yourself lost patience, understandably enough, at two critical points. The first was when you announced, before leaving for Japan, that the summit had ended without result. The parties continued, to your evident satisfaction, and had the time to overcome their own feelings of frustration. The second time was after Arafat turned down the offer made him about Jerusalem. You apparently drew the conclusion that his intransigence was the problem and the process altogether blocked. I would venture that this conclusion, which has produced the gloom among Israelis and Americans, need not hold....
> You have become increasingly open to Palestinian needs and suffering over your time as President, more so than any previous President of the United States, while never losing the commitment to the safety and well-being of Israel that you share with your predecessors. Nevertheless, I feel that you saw the political predicament of Prime Minister Barak more clearly than that of the Palestinians in this instance. ...I think you should be open to the consideration that your proposal contained elements that were simply impossible for either the Palestinians or any other Arabs to accept.

The most significant result of the Camp David summit was that the taboo questions of Jerusalem and refugees were addressed for the first time by the governments. That is solid accomplishment, and not the end of a process.

I should say, in this context, that I have been in close contact with the Palestinians before and during this process, as I have been over many years with both Israelis and Palestinians, while always keeping successive US administrations informed of my actions. During June this year, when I was in Jerusalem and often seeing Faisal Husseini and others at Orient House, I found that there was a feeling of discouragement throughout the Palestinian public, much like that which afflicts Americans and Israelis now. I urged that they ought not be so pessimistic, as the Israelis needed peace with them, a genuine peace that would truly meet the needs of both sides, as much as they needed just such a peace with Israel. I quoted to them a saying of President John Kennedy, who said in 1961, in the context of Soviet actions over Berlin, **"Any treaty of peace that adversely affects the fate of millions will not bring the peace."** That is fundamental.

Two very basic matters of legal principle govern Palestinian responses to all offers made to them. They are not simply matters of stubborn obstructionism.

The first is the rejection of the acquisition of territory by force, i.e., Israeli taking of Palestinian territory by force. That of course is the content of Security Council Resolution 242, which we so often simplify down to the formula "land for peace." That equation refers to Israel returning land, and the Arabs providing reliable assurance of peace, not further compromises about territory in which the Palestinian or Arab side is required to surrender more.

Resolution 242 rests on the most fundamental of all obligations entered into by every nation that has accepted membership of the United Nations, Article 2 of the UN Charter, by which all member states have renounced such acquisition of territory by force. That is the basic underlying purpose of the United Nations treaty as such. It was enforced on North Korea when it invaded South Korea in 1950, on Israel, Britain and France when they invaded Egypt in 1956, more recently on Iraq when it invaded Kuwait in 1990. SCR 425 prescribed it when Israel invaded Lebanon in 1978, a prescription that has only recently been met after twenty-two years. Resolution 242 already compromises Article 2 of the Charter in that it lays down a condition—that the Arabs guarantee Israel peace—before requiring the return of captured territory, but it allows no further compromise on the principle.

At this point in the letter I went once more over the familiar ground of former Prime Minister Begin's unsuccessful effort to read "return of territory" as meaning only some of the territory, and thinking that the return of the Sinai to Egypt would suffice.

The practical question is whether the Palestinians are going to adhere rigidly to this formula—return of all territory captured in 1967—or whether they will recognize the practicalities of the situation, in which there have been large demographic changes since that time. My sense, from extensive conversations with them, is that there is every readiness to deal with the practicalities, but not without a recognition and acceptance of the underlying legal obligation. If the Palestinians were to compromise on the legal obligation as such, they would stand in a quagmire, with no legal defense against anything the Israelis chose to do or decide. The Israelis would be licensed to determine all things by force of their military superiority, and the obvious disparity of power would leave the Palestinians no recourse. This is what the Palestinians have been unable to accept in the proposals made to them at Camp David.

The United States, which has sought to be honest broker between these parties, has a damagingly compromised record in this matter. From the beginning, in 1967, we defined the encroachment of Israeli settlements on the captured land as illegal, as in fact the rest of the world still does. At a later time we softened that language and called the settlements merely "obstacles to peace," and more recently still we have weakened the language further to call them merely "unhelpful." That has crippled our diplomatic stance even as we urge on the Israelis their Oslo commitment not to take actions that predetermine the outcome of what they have engaged to negotiate.

I have myself urged on the Palestinians for many years that they recognize the importance for Israelis that some Jews be able to live in what, in their history, are the territories of Judea and Samaria. That does not mean that their settlements there are legal, but it does mean that a Palestinian offer of peace should include some acceptance of Jewish presence in these territories, though only if the underlying legal principle of Article 2 is acknowledged.

And once again I covered familiar ground, the recommendation I had made long since for agreement from both sides to accept the residence of some of the other's citizens on its territory, but under their law. I acknowledged that openings had been made at Camp David in this respect, both in the readiness of Palestinians to accept annexation of some small amount of West Bank territory that included the bulk of the Israeli settlers, provided that land equal in extent and value be conceded to the Palestinian state as well, and in their acceptance that some agreed number of Jews should be allowed to live in the ancient Judea and Samaria territories, but under their jurisdiction. I continued:

> There is a second basic matter of legal principle without which the Palestinians truly cannot accept a final agreement with Israel, and that is the right of return for their refugees. Acceptance of General Assembly Resolution 194 was the explicit condition for the original acceptance of Israel into the United Nations, and that resolution has been consistently reaffirmed since, and up to the time of the Oslo Declaration of Principles even by the United States. Prime Minister Barak has had understandable reluctance to contemplate anything that would basically disrupt the demographic relation of Jews and Palestinians in Israel, and the obvious question about a Palestinian right of return is whether it would have that result....
>
> Should we fear, then, that the Palestinians, in return for Israeli recognition of their right of return, would try to transplant every descendant of a Palestinian refugee of 1948 back in Green-Line Israel? In no way. What matters is the recognition of what happened in 1948, and the principle of GAR 194, with its alternative provision for compensation to those who will not in fact return. Given that recognition, it is my clear sense that the Palestinians are prepared to be reasonable. The actual terms could be agreed on in advance of formal Israeli acceptance of the right of return.

And again I raised my long-standing suggestion that an actual survey be made of how many Palestinian refugees would want to return, and whether to Israel itself or to the area of the new Palestinian state.

> Behind all this is a fundamental need for an Israeli recognition of the human equality of Palestinians. Some of the more extreme religious elements in Israel basically reject this, and their insistent voice makes it politically difficult for an Israeli government to deal with it. But without it there will not be peace.

On the basis of a supposition of inequality, it is taken for granted, even much too often in American policy, that it is Israel's right to determine, by itself and without any consultation, what Palestinians will get and what not. It is assumed that what Israel took by force in 1967 is hers to grant or not to grant to Palestinians. The basis of that supposition is force and force alone. In law, the right of the 1967 residents of the land is primary, so that it is for the Palestinians to agree or not agree, in negotiation, what Israel may have of land that was taken in 1967. There is no reason to doubt that they will negotiate this matter realistically and responsibly in view of demographic changes since. They deserve land in return, so that they too have a place to live.

Putting this in terms of the actual numbers of Israelis and Palestinians who would come to live, by agreement, in one another's states, I raised again my argument for an open border:

> In that case, the border could be kept open. Closing it, the "separation of peoples," is a physically impossible project in any case, and could only lead to permanent enmity between the two peoples. But with an open border, each people would have its defined territory, internationally recognized, its own government and all the institutions of its nation, but all Israelis and Palestinians would, at the same time, have the use of the entire land. The Israelis, who have been confined, like the Palestinians, to their tiny bit of territory, would gain access to the entire Middle East....

Jerusalem, I argued, was the crux of the problem: negotiating sovereignty over Jerusalem. And with that I gave the President a full review of the proposals I had made in my paper on the status of Jerusalem during the days of Camp David, not knowing in fact whether he had come to see that paper or not. I argued as strenuously as before for separating the dangerous religious questions from the secular question of the rest of Jerusalem by confining those religious questions within the walls of the Old City, as well as for the principle of keeping the borders open. I concluded:

> Mr. President, I have been at pains throughout this exercise to find ways that a final status can be agreed without recourse to violence. I understand, and have represented this regularly to my Palestinian contacts, that a peremptory unilateral declaration of independence by the Palestinians would likely result in such violence. It is my

expectation that such a declaration would not be made if there were clear signs of progress.

I should point out, though, that the regular Israeli statements that they would, in case of the unilateral declaration, forcibly annex substantial parts of the West Bank and other Palestinian territory, amounts precisely to the one thing most contrary to their obligation as members of the United Nations and treaty signatories to its Charter: the seizure of territory by force. I have yet to hear American voices raising objection to this.

I wish you well in your vital task of fostering agreement and peace between Israel and the Palestinians. You have a better chance of accomplishing it than anyone else. I have the greatest respect for the strenuous and skillful efforts you have made.

In Christ,
Raymond G. Helmick, S.J.

REVIVING HOPE

Freed from the daily adversarial sessions of the Knesset, Barak set off for Egypt, seeking a consensus of the Arab nations about East Jerusalem. He set as his objective some swift, workable deal, after Camp David had opened up the taboo subjects that would combine both symbol and substance for both sides. Prospects were actually quite positive. Kamal Abu Jaber, the former Jordanian foreign minister, commented: "The Jews and Muslims are in a Catholic marriage with no possibility of divorce. Everyone realizes that the problem now is how to engineer arrangements to satisfy at least the minimum requirements of both sides and to live together." Abdel Moneim Said, director of the Al-Ahram Center for Political and Strategic Studies in Cairo, added: "There is a growing linkage for the region between having conditions of peace and the possibility of development. In addition, there is no one in the Arab world, except for some fundamentalists, who would deny any more the legitimacy of Israel. So we are all transforming from an existential struggle of 'us and them' to how we are going to be living with them."

A number of Arab officials, during these Cairo talks, addressed the refugee issue as a soluble thing. An arrangement on what numbers could return, based on the principle of what was actually practical in the interest of both Israeli and Palestinian states and their peace, required only that the Israelis should accept on principle that Palestinians had a right to return if they had fled or been forced from their homes in 1948.[5]

Even in Lebanon things had begun to settle down. Having determined that the Israelis had fully withdrawn their forces, the UN finally deployed its peacekeepers on the border, their numbers expanded from 4,000 to 6,000.[6] Not many days later the Lebanese Army itself would also enter the south of the country for the first time in 22 years, to the restrained response of the Hezbollah forces there.[7]

Former US President Jimmy Carter wrote of the progress that had already been made on the question of Jerusalem during the long-ago Camp David negotiations of 1978. The protagonists of that time, Prime Minister Yitzhak Shamir and President Anwar Sadat of Egypt, had accepted a paragraph that they saw as basically resolving the issue. It acknowledged the city to be holy to Islam, Judaism, and Christianity; guaranteed free access to all parts of it; permitted the holy places to come under the jurisdiction of their own religious representatives; and approved a municipal council with balanced representation of the inhabitants to supervise all community functions and to guarantee the integrity of the various cultural and educational institutions. A present solution, Carter believed, could be built on that foundation. Though neither side found difficulty with the wording, the paragraph had not been included in the final declaration of 1978 only for fear that it might make the already controversial text unacceptable to the Knesset of that time.[8]

Important at this time was the article Orient House director Faisal Husseini gave to the *Los Angeles Times*, objecting to the way Arafat was classified, by both Clinton and Barak, as the obstructionist for his stand on Jerusalem. Husseini cited how the UN Security Council had unanimously condemned, with the concurrence of the United States, Israel's efforts to change the legal status of the city after 1967, and how the international community had continued to decline recognition of Israeli sovereignty over any part of Jerusalem, East or West. For the 30 years since, Israel had ignored international opinion and had undertaken construction of settlements on a massive scale, at the same time placing strict limits on Palestinian construction in Jerusalem. It had imposed a permanent military closure on Jerusalem and enacted legislation to force Palestinians to emigrate from the city. Now, as if it were a "compromise," Israel offered Palestinian residents of Jerusalem a small degree of control over municipal matters in Arab neighborhoods in East Jerusalem, in return for Palestinian agreement to Israeli sovereignty over the entire city. Husseini continued:

> We Palestinians do not seek to divide Jerusalem; the city already is divided. Instead we recognize the interests of the Jewish people to

Jerusalem and seek to share the city. In negotiations at Camp David and elsewhere, we have expressed willingness to reach an agreement that would give Israel sovereignty over all of West Jerusalem in exchange for recognition of Palestinian sovereignty over East Jerusalem. We have proposed establishing an open city, giving all Palestinians and Israelis, as well as their visitors, free access to all parts of Jerusalem, with each side retaining the ability to regulate access from the city to other parts of its territory.

We also have been willing to consider establishing special arrangements for the Holy City that would not only guarantee access to Jewish, Christian and Muslim holy sites but also would satisfy all concerned interests and promote peaceful relations among the city's diverse ethnic and religious communities.

Thus, we Palestinians have not been unwilling to compromise on Jerusalem.

Israel demands sovereignty over all of Jerusalem. We seek sovereignty only over East Jerusalem. Who is being inflexible?[9]

Later, after everything turned cataclysmic with the outbreak of mutual violence after September 28, the narrative would gain standing among much of the Israeli and US public that all had been lost at Camp David, that further negotiation had been stymied by Palestinian bad faith at that time. It did not look at all like that during these weeks that followed the adjournment of the July talks. I was sufficiently encouraged so that I wrote next to Prime Minister Barak on July 9, enclosing a copy of the letter I had sent a few days earlier to President Clinton.

> Dear Prime Minister Barak,
> Shalom!
> You have followed a courageous course in your peace efforts of this summer. I have had a lot of contact, myself, with the Palestinian negotiators before and throughout the Camp David sessions, and have more recently written my observations to President Clinton, urging him not to lose hope after the inconclusive finish to the July summit, but to expect more. I will be writing again to Mr Arafat soon after sending this letter to you, urging the viewpoint that I have tried to impress on him in all my many meetings and correspondence over the last fifteen years. I have always put that in the context of SCR 242: that while responsibilities about territory are placed particularly on Israel, it is the responsibility of the Palestinians, as of all the Arabs, to give reliable assurance of peace....

Writing to the Palestinians and to President Clinton I have put great stress on the legal obligations of SCR 242 and of the "right of return" GAR 194, as things that the Palestinians cannot let pass. I find them ready to recognize the existential problems these raise for Israel and to negotiate the practicalities, reasonably and responsibly, once the basic legal principles are acknowledged. I have written of those, and of thoughts I have on the sharing of Jerusalem among those actually resident there. But first I want to put a more general consideration before you, relying on the fairness I recognize in you to see it....

The experience of the Oslo period, these seven years, has been devastating for Palestinians. The problem has not been merely with Baruch Goldstein, or the efforts of the Netanyahu government and the settler movement to renege on Oslo, but with an underlying mentality that expressed itself in the policy of closures. That mentality... is intricately interwoven with and successfully clones military, economic and ideological institutions of the State.

The reason for all of this is the focus on security for the State of Israel and on the private security of its citizens, a reasonable and necessary consideration of course. I note that among the principles agreed at the end of the Camp David meetings was the security, equally, of both peoples, Palestinians as well as Israelis. I am not sure what everyone meant by that or whether its implications were well enough understood. A security system—closures, separation of Palestinian jurisdictions into what many people call Bantustans, checkpoints, economic isolation, restrictions on every part of life, being treated as strangers in their own native land—that is simply onerous on the Palestinians is a way for Israel and its citizens never to have security for themselves. It is self-defeating. I have heard Hanan Ashrawi—old friend and a frequent voice now on our media—describe this as a "mentality of occupation," an assumption that all the decisions were for the Israelis to make, because you are so obviously the stronger and even controlling party....

You have apparently dealt with much of this at Camp David. It is hard for those of us listening attentively from outside to know just what was said and done there. Up to now, everything has been based on the fact that Israel was in possession and had the stronger military power. In law, the Palestinians enjoy an equality of rights, and that seems much more recognized as a result of this process of negotiation. That might easily be construed as Israel losing and then Palestinians gaining through the process, but it is not so. Israel gains immeasurably as it comes close to a genuine peace. Not to have the peace, and to live with the enduring resentful hostility of the Palestinians and all your Arab neighbors is loss for Israel.

Eventually, if Israel tried to survive as simply fortress against the whole surrounding Arab world, Israel's material superiority would fail and the nation be tragically lost. People know that, even if they seldom say it. And you, having taken these significant steps toward a really genuine peace over the opposition of so much of the political establishment, will have the people with you if you produce the kind of agreement that will truly assure the peace.

The weaker parties in the Israeli political spectrum are those who abandoned your coalition just as you went to Camp David. When you have your agreement and they come objecting to this, that or the other point in it, you are in a position to ask them: "Where were you?"

That much said, I enclose here a copy of the letter I recently wrote to President Clinton....

I do understand, as you do, that a unilateral declaration of independence by the Palestinians would have destructive results, for them as much as for you. I understand why Mr. Arafat feels he must set such a deadline. It is years late, and his people have suffered so much disillusion through the whole Oslo period. Nonetheless, my impression is that he will delay such drastic action if there is sign of solid progress and his people can believe it is not merely another evasion.

Were it to come to a unilateral declaration, though, I hope Israel would have some better response planned than a unilateral seizure of Palestinian land. That would be yet another act of sheer military force, precisely the thing that Israel, like every other nation, renounced in signing the Charter of the United Nations.

I wish you well in your important work. You have my prayers as well as any thinking I can do that might be helpful to any of you, the parties.

Sincerely yours,
Raymond G. Helmick, S.J.

That this letter had the prime minister's attention was soon confirmed, by the response sent on his behalf from the head of the Bureau of the Prime Minister and Minister of Defense, dated August 17:

Dear Prof. Helmick,
    On behalf of Prime Minister Ehud Barak, thank you for your letter of August 10, 2000 and copy of your letter to President Clinton. It is

gratifying to know that there are those who spend tremendous time and energy focused on matters of global importance, and we appreciate your sharing your thoughts about the peace process.

Your good wishes and prayers are likewise much appreciated, and serve to encourage the Prime Minister in his efforts to bring an end to the one hundred years of conflict and bloodshed.

May the coming months bring peace, security and prosperity to the people of the entire region.

Sincerely
Haim Mandel-Shaked

NEGOTIATION CONTINUES, WITH DEADLINES

The two sides were meanwhile holding secret talks to try to get the negotiation process back on track. In the actual meetings, it was still slow going, with Jerusalem the major stumbling block (not, interestingly, the refugee question!). Yet polls showed that the Israeli public was not at all up in arms about Barak's published Camp David offerings on Jerusalem, and that 40 percent of Israelis were prepared to give up Arab East Jerusalem without even finding out what they would get in return.

It was widely believed that all the negotiators, US, Israeli, and Palestinian, knew, though they would not say it in public, what the solution would be. The good news seemed to be that, if the parties could share Jerusalem, they could share the Middle East.[10]

Barak consolidated his shaky control of foreign policy during these days, replacing the ambassadors to Britain, France, and South Africa, all of whom were David Levy loyalists, and firing Yitzhak Meir, his ambassador to Switzerland, an appointee of the National Religious Party, which had walked out of the coalition because of the peace negotiations.[11]

The *Ha'aretz* editors, at this time, took alarm at suggestions coming from within the Rabbinate to insist on building a synagogue on the Temple Mount, in the midst of the mosques. The Chief Rabbinate, toying with these concepts, had tried to make them harmless, the coexistence of Jewish and Muslim worship on the Sacred Mount:

> Under the surface, however, new winds have begun to blow. An ever-growing circle of religious Jews has come to see the Third Temple not as a distant dream, but as an event that will soon be upon us, requiring real preparation. Priestly robes are being woven; holy vessels are being fashioned; red heifers are being bred; words are being uttered that sound hostile and threatening to Muslim ears. These new winds

are liable to drag simple-minded people into acts of rashness that could be catastrophic.

The editors concluded: "Israel has a national, historical and religious interest in safeguarding the physical—and archaeological—wholeness of the Temple Mount. Restricting Muslim activity on the Temple Mount or holding Jewish prayers there is not in our interest."[12]

Settler violence, too, had grown to new dimensions since the news had spread of what Barak had offered as Palestinian borders at Camp David. In Hebron, the only city divided between areas of Israeli and Palestinian control, even Chief of Staff Lieutenant-General Shaul Mofaz, who would in later years always place the blame for violence on Palestinians, recognized the dangers the settlers presented. Speaking with the IDF paratroopers on duty in the city he had said, "The frictions here can ignite the whole of Judea and Samaria."

Mofaz had been commander in the West Bank in February 1994, when Baruch Goldstein killed 29 Muslims at prayer. Now he spoke of an atmosphere of growing extremism that, to a large extent, had been created by settlers in the Jewish enclave. Many brawls broke out because of provocations started deliberately by the settlers. Street fights (so far, without shooting) had recently become almost a daily occurrence. The Palestinian reaction was much more bitter now than it had been in the past.[13]

Ha'aretz editorialized about this danger, adding that police and soldiers too were prey for the settlers. Only last month, two policemen and five soldiers had been hit by rocks thrown by settler children, and a soldier was slapped by the father of a settler youth the soldier wanted to restrain. Hebron had not been a quiet place to live for many years, and the concept of Jewish–Arab coexistence had been distorted there by deep-rooted hatred and mutual disgust. Violence had been commonplace ever since Kiryat Arba was established after the Six-Day War. Given the daily routine of violence, it took an unusually violent incident, like the massacre perpetrated by Baruch Goldstein at the Tomb of the Patriarchs, to draw the kind of attention from government that would result in action.[14]

The White House, all this time, had seen the September 13 deadline for a unilateral declaration of independence by the Palestinians as a looming threat. Clinton wanted another summit meeting, but only if he could be sure that the Israelis and Palestinians would settle all the outstanding issues. He saw the window of opportunity narrowed, further, by the late September onset of the Jewish religious holidays, which would last into early October, bringing the time close to the late October return of the obstreperous Knesset. The administration had concluded that Barak would not be able to hold up long after that. Barak's poll figures were dropping precipitously.[15]

Ariel Sharon now came up with a new surprise bit of obstruction. Pulling together a much depleted gathering of Knesset members, he got them to pass, 39 to 1, a resolution calling a special session to contest the impending peace talks. Only a third of the Knesset's 120 members attended, but they tentatively set August 28 as the date for a special session to debate the resolution that any attempt by Barak to renew the peace talks without new elections would be invalid.[16]

President Clinton tried to modify the effect of his announcement about moving the US embassy to Israel into Jerusalem in an interview with the London-based Arabic daily *Al-Hayat*, making it contingent on the conclusion of an Israeli–Palestinian peace, and converting it into a clear signal that the United States would recognize a Palestinian state established as a consequence of negotiations. He continued:

> Jerusalem is really three cities. It is a municipal city like any other with problems of environment, traffic control, and city services. It is a holy city which embodies the values of three great religious traditions and which contains religious sites sacred to three religions. And it is a political city that symbolizes the national aspirations of Israelis and Palestinians. Resolving the issue of Jerusalem means dealing with all three of these dimensions in a way that harms no one's interests and promotes the interests of all. And I believe it can be done.

And, he said, the outcome would not produce winners and losers: "What is fair and just for Palestinians and Arabs must also be fair and just for Israelis. There cannot be a winner and a loser in these negotiations. We must have two winners or we will lose the peace."[17]

Back in Jerusalem, though, the Temple Mount faithful had made their annual effort, on the day of *Tisha B'av*, commemorating the destruction of the Temple, to march through the Mugrabi Gate, above the Western Wall, onto the sacred platform to proclaim the end of the mosques and the rebuilding of the Jewish Temple. This year, with all the emotion gathering about the safety of the Al-Aqsa complex, the occasion was more fraught than usual. Jerusalem District police commander Yair Yitzhaki had secured from the Muslim authorities governing the platform, the *Waqf*, a promise of free access for the march, as had happened several times before. But when dozens of Palestinians streamed toward the entering procession, *Waqf* officials, fearing clashes, came to the gate and barred the unwelcome visitors despite their earlier agreement. Yitzhaki closed the compound to all visitors, and when it was reopened, announced that the ban would be reinstituted, possibly along with stronger measures, if the *Waqf* again refused Jews entry to the Mount.[18]

Arafat had returned from his three-week tour of European, Arab, and Asian capitals on Saturday August 12.[19] Hosni Mubarak had told a Cairo weekly, during Arafat's visit, that Egypt would not stop him from reaching a deal over the disputed city "if it's compatible with his Palestinian people's demands."[20] On August 16 it came out that, while in Jakarta, Arafat had told Indonesian President Abderrahman that he was reassessing the advisability of a Unilateral Declaration of Independence. He would ask the PLO's Central Council (a 129-member policy-making body) to make a decision on this when it met in the Gaza Strip early in September. In the interim, for the first time since Camp David, teams of the senior officials were to meet late in the afternoon of August 17 for substantial exchanges on Jerusalem and other issues. Dennis Ross was expected to arrive on that Thursday, earlier than had previously been announced.[21] Ben-Ami had also told the Labor Party political committee that an effort would be made to convene a new summit meeting early in September, but that it needed a "pre-agreement" that would clarify the positions of both sides.[22]

Arafat was left by this time with few options. He could give in to the US–Israeli urgings, which in his people's eyes would be capitulation, or he could declare Palestinian independence, with dire results predictable, whether he did it on September 13 or later. Somehow he needed a third option to escape this dilemma.[23]

On August 17 I wrote my promised letter to Arafat, spelling out, in a way adapted for him, the same sort of proposals I had sent to President Clinton and Prime Minister Barak:

Dear President Arafat,
    Salaam!
    During the Camp David summit meetings I wrote my observations on the proceedings several times to Orient House, and since then I have written both to President Clinton and to Prime Minister Barak what I thought necessary to bring the process forward, letters of which I sent copies for you. I had much admired the way you held fast when offered proposals that did not meet fundamental Palestinian needs. Yet I found it encouraging that you and Prime Minister Barak had opened up the questions that had previously been untouchable: Jerusalem, borders, refugees, and their right of return. Good progress was made.

Today I read Meron Benvenisti's column in *Ha'aretz*, in which he rightly observed that these questions could not be solved by clever "creative solutions," which he compared to alchemy. This is familiar to me, from working with people in the conflicts of Northern Ireland, the Balkans, Lebanon and many other places, where clever ideas never provided solutions to problems. Instead, real progress toward peace was achieved only when people decided that was what they wanted. The ideas will always be available when that point is reached.

I feel sure that you and your people are truly determined to find the way to solve the problems of your conflict with the Israelis now. For all Mr. Barak's trouble with his Knesset, I believe his people too will back him if he comes to them bringing a genuine peace agreement with you. I argued, in one of those position papers I sent to Orient House, that you could not expect to resolve the long-term animosities among the two populations during a conference. But the leaders can set out firm agreements on the basic legal relation between their peoples. You and the Israelis have good reason to do that now....

I was glad to see you withdraw somewhat from the idea of a unilateral declaration of independence on September 13. You have rightly complained, always, of unilateral Israeli actions. This is no time to imitate them, when actual mutual agreement is within reach. Your position is stronger now than it has ever been, because the Israelis so deeply need agreement with you.

Throughout this time I have endorsed your legal claim to all the Palestinian land captured in 1967, in view of Security Council Resolution 242 and of Article 2 of the United Nations Charter on which it is based, and also to the right of return of refugees in view of General Assembly Resolution 194, whose acceptance was the condition of Israel's membership in the United Nations. Those legal entitlements stand in reciprocal relation, though, to the Palestinian and Arab responsibility to offer peace. That is the requirement of SCR 242: land (to be returned by the Israelis) for peace (from the Arabs).

In other conflicts that had involved seizure of territory by force, the offending country was required, under Article 2 of the Charter, simply to return it....But SCR 242 is different, and has been accepted as the legal basis for your situation: the Arabs, and you the Palestinians, are required genuinely to offer peace in return for restoration of the land to you, its rightful possessors.

It is not for the Israelis to make concessions to you of something that is theirs. The land is rightfully yours. Anything to be conceded to the Israelis, beyond their strict rights, must be the result of agreement and accommodation by you. But accommodation has to be made if there is to be peace. And accommodation has to be made in the matter of right of return also, so that there may be peace.

Concretely, you will never have peace on the basis of an arrangement that means destruction or fundamental disruption of the Israeli state and society. Israel, or Mr. Barak speaking for Israel, may no more grant that than you may allow Israel to devastate the Palestinians and their right to their land....

Those are the things that you yourself recognized in leading your people to the prospect of peace, that you and I discussed in our several meetings in Tunis and Kuwait in 1986 and in much correspondence since, that were the basis of the PNC resolutions that endorsed peace overtures to Israel in the 1980s and your statement to the UN General Assembly in 1988, that were fundamental, as a matter of realized Palestinian public opinion, to the *intifada*. They were the basis too of Palestinian participation in the Madrid Conference of 1991, the Oslo Declaration of Principles of 1993 and all you have done to bring about the peace since. They remain the constants of your relation to Israel.

All of this means, in relation to the right of return of refugees, that a way must be found both to have full recognition of their right to return after the wrong done them, and a way found to keep the demographic character of the Israeli state and its territory. The refugees unable to return must receive full and adequate compensation. We hear it rumored in our American press that you were offered a really large sum of money as compensation for the refugees, without any acknowledgment of their right of return and refused it. I feel you were right to refuse it. You (they) should receive that money, but only with acknowledgment of the right of return.

And once again I advocated a formal survey to see how many Palestinian refugees would actually return, whether to Israel or to the Palestinian state.

Formal agreements could be made in advance with the Israelis to regulate this. I would not expect them to agree to a generalized recognition of that right of return without knowing first what would happen as a result and that it would not mean dismemberment of their state. But I would not settle for anything less than a recognition of the wrong done and the right of return, with compensation for those who did not return.

Coming to the questions of Jerusalem and the borders of a Palestinian state, I reviewed matters on which I had written to Arafat before, but with special caution on the topic of religion as an element of danger that should be confined within the walls of the Old City and not allowed to leak out and infect consideration of all the other issues of a secular political nature, much as I had done in the letters to Clinton and Barak, of which I attached copies for Arafat. I concluded:

> I know you have given much thought to all these questions, and the ideas I offer here should not be taken as disparaging other possible solutions that you may be considering. What I regard as important for me to say is that a solution will be found only if both you and the Israelis truly want one, and not if either of you is governed by suspicion and determined to find reasons to say that nothing will work. I greatly admire the hard work you and Prime Minister Barak and your many trusted associates have put into this work of seeking a peaceful solution. My conviction is that it is within reach.

THE REFUGEE QUESTION COMES TO THE FORE

Dennis Ross appeared on the scene on August 18, the day after I had sent that letter (by e-mail) to President Arafat. Ross' mission was to break the impasse over Jerusalem. If he succeeded in narrowing the gap, Clinton was prepared to meet Barak and Arafat separately in New York during the opening of the UN session next month.[24] It remains notable at this period that Jerusalem always figured as the real problem, so much that we are left wondering what was then the status of the refugee question. Was it a question of principle, open to discussion of the numbers who could return, or had it become a demand for wholesale return of the entire population? That it figured so distantly in the discussion at this time argues that it had not become a deal-breaking issue at all.

Barak made news, the day of Dennis Ross' return, by referring explicitly, for the first time, to a Palestinian state.[25] Barak embarked now on a new course, the promotion of Israeli civic reform, informing his supporters that he would try to limit the privileges of the religious estate. We would hear more of this as the summer wore on, but when he first raised this banner over the weekend of August 20, the ultra-Orthodox, who by now had all become his opponents, were enraged, and his own supporters surprised.

No one had succeeded at the task of separating religion and state in Israel since, during the war of 1948, David Ben-Gurion had made his bargain with the religious parties, of privileges for their support. Every Israeli government had had to have the religious parties as coalition partners, and always at the price of increasing privilege. It seemed to his supporters that Barak was trying to realign Israeli politics most fundamentally, consolidating the power of the secular forces, in an attempt to set the stage for new elections.[26] By the end of the week Barak called for a pact with Likud if Arafat should balk at endorsing the Israeli plans. Though Sharon rejected this offer out of hand, it was taken as a threat to the Palestinians that the Prime Minister could get along well without them, and at the same time a threat to the religious parties who had quit Barak's coalition in protest at his peace plans.[27]

As Israeli worry over the right of return question grew, I wrote once more to Barak on August 21:

Dear Prime Minister Barak,
   Shalom!
   When I wrote to you about the negotiating process on August 10th, I enclosed a copy of what I had written a few days earlier to President Clinton. More recently I wrote to Mr Arafat as well, and felt you should have a copy of that also.
   You may feel as you read this series of letters that I espouse the Palestinian side on the questions that stand between you, because I regularly call for an initially strict adherence to the legal demands of SCR 242 on territory and GAR 194 on the return of refugees, though always with the proviso that, once the principle is recognized, the practical details should then be reasonably and responsibly negotiated.
   I would feel as much concern for and even identification with the Israeli cause on these issues. I do firmly believe, though, that Israel, in its formal diplomatic stance and eventually in its public opinion, needs to recognize the deep hurt that has been done to the Palestinian people, what they so often refer to as their "disaster" (*naqba*) in 1948 and their further loss in 1967, the two definitive moments in your common history to which the UN resolutions relate. That seems to me necessary for the soul of the Israeli people.
   There seems to be great reluctance to accept the moral suppositions of these two major judgments of the international community,

both of which Israel has formally accepted without acknowledging their clear implications, as if acknowledging them would taint the whole enterprise of the Israeli state and society. As I see it, an embrace of the legal principles animating those two resolutions would remove basic ambivalences in Israelis' self-understanding and enhance the respect in which Israel is held throughout the world. Short of that Israel, this precious possession and self-expression of the Jewish people after their long dispersal, will forever remain, in the eyes of most of the world and especially its neighbors, a rogue and outlaw state.

People fear, of course, the consequences of an acknowledgement of Palestinians' right of return, that it might utterly disrupt Israel's demography, as in fact the origins of Israel did the Palestinian demography and as the settlement policy all the years since 1967 has attempted to do to the demography of the West Bank. I saw Elia Zureik's August 10 article in the *Los Angeles Times*, which argued for accepting every refugee who wished to go back to the 1948 situation as the meaning of a Palestinian Right of Return. But Zureik stands apart from the responsible Palestinian leadership in this. My sense, from talking extensively with them, is that they are prepared to negotiate a realistic, responsible outcome.

For some time I have argued to Mr Arafat that this should be done in advance, so that you know what the demographic result would be from a clear acknowledgment of GAR 194. I would think that should have priority as a matter to be agreed in the negotiation.

The 1949 truce line as the boundary envisioned in SCR 242, also, has status as the presumptive border between Israel and Palestine, and the settlement activity since 1967 carries a stigma of illegality that practically the whole of international judgment affirms. If Israel will not acknowledge that, it will not come to terms of peace with either the Palestinians or the Arab world.

Once again, if the legal principle is once accepted by Israel, I see the Palestine Authority as willing to make responsible practical adjustments to recognize what has happened—the "facts on the ground"—demographically. It is only fair that they should have territory in compensation for any territory they concede in that context.

I have argued to them myself, for many years, that they need to recognize and accept the importance, to Jews, of Jews being able to live in Judea and Samaria, and should make agreements that some numbers of them, such as would not constitute an assault on Palestinian demography, be able to live within the Palestinian state, under its jurisdiction but retaining their Israeli citizenship. This should be a reciprocal arrangement, balanced by Israel's acceptance of some Palestinians back into its territory, under Israeli jurisdiction but able to retain their Palestinian citizenship, again only in such numbers as would not undermine Israeli demography. If this were the basic pattern, it would minimize the need to annex settlement bloc areas to Israel (in return for other land in exchange).

Since many of the settlers have moved into the West Bank in explicit hostility to Palestinians, it is unlikely that they would remain under those circumstances. The many peaceful settlers would more likely remain, and their numbers would likely come out practically equal to the Palestinians that Israel has already proposed to allow back for family reunion. Evenhanded treatment like this would truly be the guarantee of sustainable peace between your two peoples. Interim security arrangements, such as the joint patrols you have already mounted successfully in many places, would doubtless be necessary, but their duration could be limited.

That applies as much to Jerusalem as anywhere else. You have already opened the question of Jerusalem, which until Camp David was closed. The reality, as you know, is that Jerusalem is actually a divided city. There will be no comfort, or perhaps even safety, for Jews in East Jerusalem or Arabs in West Jerusalem until their right to self-determination and governance is recognized in the places where each lives. That in fact will open the city so that each can enter and be at peace in the other's area and the city will at last be united. There is no need for any crossing points or border checks. The whole city can be made available to both peoples, and both gain....

` In writing to Mr Arafat, I stressed what I would also repeat to you, that solution of these problems is not a matter of having bright ideas but of really deciding that you want a solution. No number of bright ideas will serve if the two sides don't want to end their quarrel, and the bright ideas come easily when they do. You have taken a very daring gamble that your Israeli public, like yourself, truly wants to see an end to this conflict. I believe and hope you are right, and that they will support you when you bring to them a credible agreement. I admire your courage, too, in taking on the secular reform of your society just at the moment when your parliamentary position is at its weakest. I think you deserve, for that, to carry the votes of all the secular public that would otherwise go to Likud in an election—I've no idea whether that will actually occur or not. But this matter of the peace is success or failure for the whole Zionist enterprise of the Israeli state and society, at the moral and existential levels. I urge you not to hold back on the things that would make for your peace.

Should we suppose, then, that as of late August, a month after the end of the Camp David talks, the parties had abandoned hope and believed that the chance to negotiate the peace had been lost? By no means. The chance was seen as precarious, and Israel and the United States were both determined that it was Palestine that must give in, but no one gave up, and both Israel and the United States in fact kept coming up with new modifications of their proposals. Barak warned of "tragedy" if the Israelis and Palestinians should fail to reach an agreement. By now he no long treated his Camp David proposals as "null and void" without full agreement, but referred back to them with new confidence, encouraged in this by his acting foreign minister, Shlomo Ben-Ami.[28] Yet even as he took his steps the quiet voice of Sheikh Ahmed Yassin, the Gaza leader of Hamas, raised the threat of that tragedy against which Barak warned.[29]

An Israeli mistake over this weekend illustrated how much cooperation was actually available to Israeli forces and the Palestinian police. In a botched raid on the West Bank hideout of Mahmoud Abu Hanoud, a suspected perpetrator of bombings that had killed 27 Israelis far back in 1997, three Israeli soldiers were killed by "friendly fire." Jabril Rajoub, the Palestinian director of West Bank security, responded at once that, if the Israelis had only informed their Palestinian counterparts that they had located Hanoud's hideout, the two security forces could have worked together and avoided that bloodshed. Everyone knew what a diplomatic catastrophe it would have been if, as first reported, the soldiers had been killed by Palestinian police fire. It became clear that the fire had come from the Israelis themselves, who even took pains to praise the security cooperation of the PA, which they considered crucial to secure the cessation of terrorist attacks.[30] Subsequent investigation showed that the Israelis' error had been in planting their own people too thickly on the ground, including undercover agents on rooftops. This had led both to the deaths of their soldiers and the escape of Hanoud, who was then in fact captured by the Palestinians. They proposed to prosecute him themselves.[31]

THE UN AS FORUM

President Clinton now prepared a diplomatic whirlwind in New York for the annual opening of the UN General Assembly. He arrived in Manhattan on Monday September 4, declaring that this might be "the last real chance" to jump-start talks between Israelis and Palestinians. Dennis Ross and CIA Director George Tenet had both been dispatched to the Middle East to try out new formulations. National Security Adviser Berger added: "There needs to be some flexibility that could indicate we have some chance of getting real momentum here. If we are not any further than we were at Camp David, it will be tough to get this done."[32]

Clinton planned to hold separate meetings with Barak and Arafat in New York—trying to impress upon them, especially on Arafat, a sense of urgency. The two sides seemed to remain both closer to and farther from a permanent peace agreement. Jerusalem stood before them. Several Israeli and US proposals offered ways of sharing sovereignty, but Arafat still insisted on full Palestinian sovereignty over the Haram al-Sharif. Madeleine Albright had spent 45 minutes with Barak, who was losing hope that Arafat would give way on this demand. But Arafat appeared ready to postpone the September 13 deadline for UDI. Palestinian experts expressed this in terms of Arafat's seeing the UN Security Council resolutions as already presenting a compromise "that calls for Israeli withdrawal from all territory occupied in the 1967 war, which included all of East Jerusalem." Ghassan Khatib, a Palestinian political expert, explained: "He has been fighting the extremists by the argument you have to abide by international legality—not more. How can he tell them to live with less?[33]

When Clinton addressed the UN, on Wednesday, he spoke of a new and threatening age of civil wars. He had met the previous evening, separately, with Barak and Arafat, having warned that "like all life's chances" the moment for accord "is fleeting and about to pass."[34] White House spokesperson Joe Lockhart said no breakthroughs had been achieved in Clinton's meetings with the Middle East leaders, "But the process is not broken down, it is ongoing." Both Barak and Arafat, of course, addressed the Assembly on the theme of peace.[35] Various *Ha'aretz* correspondents commented on Barak's establishing a close relation with Sharon during this meeting. His first phone call from New York was to Sharon and he kept Sharon's Likud liaison in the delegation, MK Meir Sheetrit, close to him and his plans at all times. Israeli reporters felt he was holding this as a threat over Arafat's head, and perhaps preparing a Grand Coalition with Likud should the talks fail.[36]

As the week of the UN opening wound down, the White House began to feel the chance for a solution of the Middle East problem slipping away. Clinton, his aides said, would not give up abruptly, but there would be no more Middle East meetings that week.[37] Nevertheless, Clinton, on Friday, made a last brief visit to Barak (going to his hotel in deference to the Sabbath) hoping to bolster the prime minister's position at home, where he would face a rambunctious Knesset when it reconvened in late October. Arafat left New York on the Friday for Gaza, where he would meet the Palestine Central Council. Nabil Abu Rdaineh was quoted by *Reuters* as saying that Palestinian and Israeli negotiators would resume the Middle East talks at mid-level next week.[38]

Jerusalem correspondent Haim Baram now saw Barak's tenuous coalition reduced to just 24 MKs in his own One Israel party and six from the rapidly disintegrating Center Party, two of whom, ex-Likudniks Dan Meridor and Roni Milo, had actually dissociated themselves from Barak's "excessive concessions" to Arafat, while a third, Yitzhak Mordechai, who had actually been Netanyahu's defense minister, faced criminal proceedings for alleged sexual harassment. That meant Barak could only count on three of his Centre Party MKs. The eleven Meretz MKs would vote for his peace process, but had small commitment to Barak himself. His turning toward civic reform and limitation of Rabbinate privileges, burning his bridges with the religious parties, was taken as a bid for the votes of the rising Shinui party, right wing but determinedly against the influence of the Orthodox.[39]

ARAFAT POSTPONES THE DEADLINE

Hamas and Islamic Jihad, meanwhile, had announced that they would boycott the Palestine Central Council meeting, expecting it to defer the Unilateral Declaration of Independence and endorse a continuation of the peace effort, which these bodies rejected.[40] And indeed, when the Council gathered for its two-day closed meeting its 129 members, accepting Arafat's wish, did postpone the declaration, resolving to meet again on November 15, which would be the twelfth anniversary of the original declaration of Palestinian independence by the Palestine National Congress of 1988 in Algiers.[41]

Camp David's sense of urgency, however, had withered by now. The Palestinian population sank to new depths of discouragement. Said Muhammed Saffin, a security forces officer: "The Palestinians are ready to explode at any minute. We feel like a soldier at the border waiting for the order to pull the trigger. By the end of the year, there will be no logic to waiting any longer. People will only get more radical." Twenty-year-old Heba Hassan granted, reluctantly: "Everybody knows that you can't call it a state if only one party declares it. As a member of the third world, we can't make our decision alone. There are so many countries that have influence over this deliberation." Retired Kamil el-Solh mourned: "Nothing ever happens. Since 1948, nothing has happened. We are a stateless people. Care of—that's our address. Care of what? Care of who? Who cares?"[42]

Palestinians had to be terribly worried, too, at the actual expansion of settlements that they saw taking place on Barak's watch, even as they were told this was the prime minister striving for peace. The first quarter of 2000 had seen an 81 percent increase in construction in the settlements, according to the Central Bureau of Statistics (CBS). The figures showed that in the first three months of the year 2000 work began on 1,000 new buildings, compared with 550 in the last quarter of 1999. The ascending numbers corresponded to Ehud Barak's rise to power—in the months of May and July 1999, construction work had begun on 720 new buildings in the settlements. Construction fell between the months of August and October 1999, with only 550 new buildings. The upward trend however returned with the onset of the new millennium.[43]

At the same time, the Barak government carried on a grim policy of deporting Palestinians. *Ha'aretz* correspondent Gideon Levy commented, in this regard:

> Sometimes it's hard to believe that the hand is the same hand and the head is the same head: At a time when the prime minister is bringing up very daring ideas in the negotiations with the Palestinians, and especially insisting on defining the "end of the conflict," his government and its institutions are sticking to a policy toward the Palestinians which is so cruel that it raises great doubts as to the purity of the government's intentions. From Israel's point of view, the policy of conquest is continuing as usual, and it will not end a moment before an agreement is signed.[44]

One glimmer of hope broke through, as it was reported that offshore gas deposits in the seas off Israel and Gaza would soon be opened, opening visions of joint ventures that would relieve some of the stress on the deconstructed Palestinian economy.[45]

There was irony in the revelation at this time that Yossi Beilin and Abu Mazen had constructed a plan as long ago as 1995 that offered an agreed solution to most of the problems that now vexed the negotiators, including practically every feature on the status of Jerusalem. In that draft agreement, Israel had unambiguously recognized the right of the Palestinian refugees from the war of 1947–49 to return to the Palestinian state, and also acknowledged their right to compensation. At the same time, the Palestinians declared that the refugees' right of return was "impractical" and accepted as de facto that the refugees would not be allowed back to Israel proper.[46] The plan had not been shown to then Prime Minister Rabin, who had been murdered within a week of its actual completion, but it did receive the approval of Yasser Arafat. In the few weeks since it had come to light, it had become the Bible of the US administration as both Clinton and his national security adviser, Sandy Berger, believed these understandings could save them a lot of effort in discussions that would eventually yield almost exactly the same results.[47]

It turned out that Abu Mazen himself, just before the beginning of the Camp David talks, had phoned Sandy Berger at the White House and suggested the use of that document as a basis for the permanent arrangement. Since then, there had been hanging in Berger's office a map of the final arrangement drafted according to the principles defined in the "safe and recognized borders" section of the Beilin–Abu Mazen plan. This section, incidentally, had appeared only in the final version of the agreement and was not even included in the version of the document published in *Newsweek* magazine.[48]

At the UN, the Clinton administration moved to reopen the peace talks between Israelis and Palestinians at an informal working level in New York. Secretary of State Albright played down prospects that they could make substantial enough progress to lead to an accord in the near future, saying: "Camp David was a watershed. We started to talk of issues that were never talked of before."[49]

Talks resumed in earnest on September 20, after much indecision over whether they should be held or not. Senior Israeli and Palestinian negotiators held what the Israelis described as a "businesslike" session. The day before, Barak had actually halted the talks scheduled for this week, only to renew his commitment to them in the evening.[50]

People talked now of what would happen after the US election, when Clinton would no longer be there as President with his intimate knowledge of every detail. Bravely, the negotiators asserted that they would continue, whoever was elected in the United States.[51]

A glitch developed in US participation, as Martin Indyk was relieved of his post as US ambassador to Israel. His security clearance was lifted pending State Department investigation of whether he had mishandled classified material. Indyk, originally an Australian citizen and pillar of AIPAC, the chief arm of the Jewish organizational lobby in the United States, had been hastily granted US citizenship in order to be inserted into the National Security Council as desk officer on the Middle East, effectively AIPAC's man in the Clinton White House, and had subsequently held high posts in the State Department before being made ambassador to Israel. His departure left a gap in the role of the United States in the negotiating process, as he had always been a close partner to Dennis Ross.[52]

MIXED RESULTS

Even at this late date, Israeli settlement building continued apace, to the growing despair of all Palestinians. Clearance had been given in these days by Israel's Defense Ministry for the construction of another 1,400 housing units in the settlements, and for the drafting of new zoning and construction plans for the settlements. Under the Barak government, permission had been granted to convert 40 temporary outposts into permanent settlements, "legalizing" the illegal by decree.[53]

On September 25 Barak hosted Arafat to a cordial late-night dinner in his private country villa at Kochav Yair, attempting in this way to improve the strained personal relationship between them. It was their first meeting since Camp David. Gadi Baltiansky, Barak's spokesman, said afterwards the meeting had been held "in a very good atmosphere and a positive spirit." Barak had earlier said there was no point in meeting Arafat unless he agreed in advance to consider the US proposals on Jerusalem, but he had agreed to drop his precondition at the urging of the United States and the more dovelike of his Israeli ministers, especially Yossi Beilin.[54]

After this meeting, the Israeli and Palestinian negotiators expected to fly to talks in Washington in the next few days. US mediators had prepared working papers summarizing the points of concord and divergence. *Ha'aretz* said that Albright had informed Barak and Ben-Ami over the weekend that the United States would hold off on presenting the document.[55]

In the Knesset, the Likud members of the Constitution, Law and Justice Committee endorsed a bill to "secure" Jerusalem's current border by requiring a majority of 61 Knesset members before any authority in Jerusalem could be handed over to the Palestinian Authority. MK Shaul Yahalom said that the passage of the bill in the committee should signal to Barak and his government that they must immediately halt all negotiations involving territorial or municipal compromises in Jerusalem.[56] The technique was the long-practiced one that had been used to prevent any resolution of the dispute with Syria over the Golan.

On Wednesday September 27, Attorney General Elyakim Rubinstein, handed down his verdict on the bribery, fraud, and theft charges against former Prime Minister Binyamin Netanyahu and his wife Sarah. Netanyahu could now say he was acquitted of all charges. It was evident that he would now reenter the political ring and challenge Ariel Sharon's leadership of the Likud Party.

With that, we come to the crux of the whole development since Camp David. Was the peace effort to be accounted a washout? That was the subsequent judgment, expounded by Sharon; echoed by both Barak and

Clinton in the disappointment of their last days in power; believed, the following year, by a great proportion of the Israeli and American publics, and espoused fervently by the Bush regime in the United States. The persistent effort to maintain the process, despite uncertainty about its result, argues strongly against that.[57]

The argument, in effect, was that there could be no progress unless Arafat gave in on the one specific issue that was of most special interest to the Israelis, as Jews, and also to the Palestinians, as custodians of the sacred space for all the Muslim world: control of the Temple Mount, the Haram al-Sharif. Negotiation never ceased about this. It was so much expected that a resolution would be found on this key difficult point that the opponents of any agreement at all remained in a state of perpetual agitation all summer long for fear of it. Arafat never left the negotiation—it was Clinton, after all, who called off Camp David when he got frustrated beyond his limit to endure.

This presented the essential dilemma for those Israelis who wanted no peace settlement that would involve the creation of a Palestinian state and their loss of the settlements in the lands they had expropriated since 1967. On September 29, even after Sharon had manufactured a catastrophe for the peace process, Yoel Marcus published an article in *Ha'aretz* that must have been prepared before he heard of Sharon's action, predicting that settlement of the dispute was inevitable:

> Yours truly wishes to declare here that the new year of 5761 on the Hebrew calendar will be the year of the agreement with the Palestinians. Am I absolutely certain? You bet I am. Is this my final, irreversible assessment? The answer is yes. Why? Because both sides have no other option but to arrive at a peace settlement.[58]

What could the right wing do to avert such a result?

AN ARTIFICIAL CRISIS

Ariel Sharon had manipulated the Israeli public all his public life, creating panic among them by the exercise or provocation of violence any time there was a threat of progress toward resolution of the conflict. Now he found his predominance among the opponents of a peace resolution threatened by Netanyahu, who was vindicated now, however dimly, by his absolution from the corruption charges brought against him. Sharon chose this as his moment of sabotage, to bring the entire quest for peace to shipwreck.

200 The Failed Negotiations

On September 28 Sharon approached the Temple Mount, the area of the mosques, from the gate above the Western Wall, the usual entrance for tourists. It was no special thing for an Israeli to visit the Mount. Ordinary Israelis did it frequently, as tourists like the many Western Christian visitors, despite the halakhic injunctions of the rabbinate that prohibited observant Jews from treading there, for fear that they would step upon the site of the Holy of Holies. That meant effectively that only the non-observant went there, and basically not to pray. Muslim fears were only that Jewish fundamentalists would come to destroy the mosques and take over the holy site to rebuild the Temple. These received encouragement to do so from all the crazier fringe of Christian fundamentalists in the United States, who saw the re-establishment of the temple as precondition for the return of the Messiah.

Sharon was no ordinary Israeli, nor a tourist. He came to the Temple Mount leading a group of right-wing Israeli legislators and accompanied by 1,000 armed soldiers and police, many from the start in full riot gear, anticipating that their presence was bound to cause disturbance, more than had been present the day it was conquered by Israelis in the 1967 war. Police helicopters clattered overhead.

The program of his visit was to assert Jewish claims of total possession of the site, in direct, though private, violation of the many agreements Israelis had made not to undertake actions that would prejudice the territorial outcome of negotiations. He used the occasion to criticize Barak's "concessions" on Jerusalem, as well as to upstage Netanyahu by the vehemence of his opposition to negotiation.

He stayed for over an hour, while indignant young Palestinians, shouting "Allahu Akbar" and trying to break through the police lines, progressed to stone throwing. The police answer was with the familiar rubber-coated steel bullets. The predictable violence left many Palestinians and more than two dozen of the police injured. Rioting spread soon to the surrounding streets and even to Ramallah, where more Palestinian protesters, hurling rocks and firebombs, were severely hurt by the rubber-coated steel bullets.

Sharon left proclaiming sanctimoniously: "I brought a message of peace. I believe that Jews and Arabs can live together. It was no provocation whatever." With the vast security operation organized for his visit, he had asserted Israeli sovereignty over the Temple Mount. Faisal Husseini countered: "Israel has no sovereignty here. They have military might, they have the power of occupation, but not sovereignty." Sharon's visit, he proclaimed, was "a direct attempt to derail the peace process, and an attempt to inflame the whole region." All this turmoil overshadowed an overnight bombing that had occurred in the Gaza Strip. Two roadside charges there had detonated near a convoy of cars headed for the Israeli settlement of Netzarim, due to become a daily flashpoint throughout the oncoming new *intifada*, killing one Israeli soldier and wounding another.[59]

The affair was far from over. The following day, the Muslim Friday day of prayer, saw renewed agitation on the platform of the mosques. Heavy Israeli military units were brought into the vicinity of the Dome of the Rock and Al-Aqsa Mosque. The soldiers fired live ammunition into stone-throwing crowds of protesters, leaving four dead and at least 200 wounded.[60] The second *intifada*, a human-made crisis provoked with full deliberation, had begun.

7
Through the blood of the *intifada* to the Taba negotiations, September 29, 2000–February 8, 2001

VIOLENCE EVERYWHERE

The following days witnessed escalating mayhem. We all had to wonder whether the negotiation process and the prospect of peace had been dashed altogether by Ariel Sharon's newest bid to set the Middle East ablaze.

September 30, the third day of the disaster, added a further 16 Palestinian dead and hundreds of wounded to those, now counted as five, already killed the day before, making a total of 21 deaths already. Upheaval extended all the way from the northern fringe of the West Bank to the bottom of the Gaza Strip. Eight Palestinians had died demonstrating at the entrance to the Gaza Strip settlement of Netzarim. This included a first major iconic image of the uprising, as 12-year-old Muhammad al-Durrah's death was caught on camera by a French television team.

The little boy was sheltering, in terror, with his father for fully 45 minutes behind a concrete stanchion, while his father shouted to the Israeli soldiers to hold their fire. The camera caught the moment when the child took a bullet in the stomach and crumpled. The father, struck by four bullets, barely survived, and an ambulance driver who tried to come to their rescue was also killed. Veteran Israeli television journalist Roni Daniel saw this image for the first time as he was actually delivering his newscast on Saturday night. "I lost my voice," he said afterwards. "I've been doing this for many years, and I'm not exactly a vegetarian. But my brain went dead, and my tongue went limp. To see a little boy killed before your eyes...." The image played on Israeli and Palestinian television repeatedly that day and for days to come.[1]

KILLING ISRAELI ARABS

By the fourth day the Palestinian death toll had doubled, to 40, and a first Israeli policeman had died, shot down by a Palestinian police officer who had been his companion on a joint patrol.[2] Rage grew in Israeli Arab villages as well, with riots and strikes in Jaffa, in many small villages of western Galilee, but especially in Nazareth and the area around it. A first Israeli Arab had been killed on Sunday at Umm al-Fahm, his death followed by fierce struggles in the city square and the burning of a local bank.[3] By Tuesday October 3, five Israeli Arabs had died in clashes with the police. The funerals of two of them in one village drew 30,000. The funeral was a political demonstration with black flags, PLO flags, and Syrian flags accompanying the coffins.[4]

These killings of Israeli Arabs touched a particularly sore point, as they had always been treated with contempt as second-class citizens. That the state should shoot them down so nonchalantly symbolized the tenuous place held in Israel by non-Jewish citizens, and government soon realized that it could not afford to alienate further this 20 percent bloc among its citizens.[5] An effort was first made to explain any dissidence among them as something plotted by Arafat,[6] but that would not wash. Soon questions arose as to who had ordered Israeli troops to fire so wildly at Arab citizens of Israel, and the fingers pointed at Barak himself and at Shlomo Ben-Ami, who besides being foreign minister still held the security portfolio.[7] By Wednesday October 4, when the Israeli Arab death toll had reached ten, comparison was made between the killings of Israeli Arabs and the far more tender treatment of riotous or murderous Jewish settlers.[8] Violent demonstrations, with hurling of rocks and petrol bombs, had marked the protests this same week at the meetings of the International Monetary Fund and the World Bank in Prague. Police there knew how to break up the riots without bloodshed. Israeli police knew that too, as could be seen when Shas mounted violent demonstrations over the jailing of Aryeh Deri, or in the riots organized on Bar-Ilan Street in Jerusalem by members of the ultra-Orthodox Jewish community, some of whom hurled rocks at police officers; and during the closure of major traffic arteries and intersections by angry workers, the police never once fired a shot, not even a rubber-coated bullet.[9]

JOSEPH'S TOMB

A flashpoint of violence developed around the tomb of the biblical Joseph in Nablus, a town fully under the authority of the Palestinians. Religious Jews maintained a yeshiva within the tomb, protected by Israeli soldiers but under Palestinian Authority guarantee. On the first Sunday after Sharon's provocation an Israeli police officer died of gunshot wounds within the religious site. As fierce fighting followed, with heavy Palestinian casualties, some ranking army officers called for abandonment of the site, but the issue was contentious. Joseph's tomb, a "bone in the throat" to the Palestinians, had seen deadly tumult at other times of great strain. Twelve soldiers, all of the obscure Druze sect, the only non-Jews regularly accepted into the Israeli Army, remained there,[10] but early on the following Saturday, October 9, Barak ordered them withdrawn, in an indication that he wanted to stop the confrontations. Responsibility for guarding the tomb was handed over to the Palestinian authorities.[11]

The effort met with no success. At 3.00 a.m. on the Sunday morning hundreds of young Palestinians, many of them members of the Tanzim, Fatah's youth group, arrived to tear the ancient structure apart, stone by stone, with sledgehammers, pickaxes, and their bare hands. By the time Palestinian police moved to restrain them they had burned the compound, reducing the shrine to charred rubble. The police chief's comment: "We lost 18 martyrs here and 170 people were wounded. There are people here who have lost their brothers. What do you expect?"[12]

Barak, in reaction, issued a 48-hour ultimatum, demanding of Arafat that he restrain all violent protest. Otherwise Israeli forces would employ "all available means" to quell the riots. It was hard for Palestinians to envision what "all available means" would be, given that tanks, artillery, helicopter gunships, heavy warplanes, and mass machine-gun attacks were already in common use against them by the Israeli forces. They responded with ridicule to the suggestion that the army had been showing restraint over these first nine days. Ahmed Qurei queried: "Barak is giving ultimatums today to the Lebanese, the Syrians, and now to the Palestinians. But who started this conflict?"[13]

THE SETTLERS ARE HEARD FROM

Even as these events took place, Israel's right wing went wild. Mobs of Israelis from the segregated neighborhood called Nazaret Illit, Upper Nazareth, descended on the Arab neighborhoods of Nazareth proper— with the police intervening on their side. Settlers attacked Arab villages, like Kifl Harith, Dir Istiya, Salfit, Bidiya, and other villages near the large Ariel settlement, as well as al-Azariya, one of the three edge-of-Jerusalem villages that had been in the eye of the storm, demanded by the Palestinians all through the talks before Camp David, near Ma'ale Adumim. That they occurred in Area C of the West Bank, wholly under Israeli control, made these attacks by settlers especially deadly, as the settlers had been heavily armed by the army for their "protection" while the Palestinians were completely unarmed and had no recourse to aid from the Palestinian Authority. The army (whether in Israel itself or in the West Bank) consistently waded in on the side of the attackers.[14] Riots of this sort accounted for another ten deaths of West Bank Palestinians and Arab citizens of Israel on the night of Yom Kippur, October 8.[15] Nazareth saw more deaths the following day.[16]

Palestinians made their own attacks, firing now on Jewish settlements in the Ramallah area, whereupon the army positioned tanks about the city for possible retaliation. As the Shabbat ended, Israeli settlers in this area began blocking roads and stoning Palestinian cars as they passed. In the Gaza Strip, Palestinians fired on a bus heading for the town of Rafah, wounding eight Israelis. At this, Barak closed down the Gaza airport.[17]

Eventually there is a sameness to the reports: more deaths day by day, escalating confrontations, increasingly heavy weapons on the Israeli side—artillery, helicopter gunships, antitank rockets, lobbed grenades, air-to-ground missiles, tanks—and growing Palestinian rage. Palestinian deaths consistently outnumbered those of Israelis, in these early days by huge proportions though eventually over the next several years it would balance out at three Palestinians to each Israeli dead. But from the start there were regular complaints about excessive Israeli force.[18] As Israeli columnist Aviv Lavie put it: "Our victims are stories, theirs are mere numbers."[19] By the end of the week, the Security Council passed its Resolution 1322,[20] condemning this extreme Israeli use of force by a vote of 14 to 0 with one abstention, the United States abstaining on this occasion rather than exercising its more usual veto over resolutions unpalatable to Israel.[21]

FINGER-POINTING

Who would take the blame? At the outset, everyone from the *New York Times*' Joel Greenberg[22] to the Arab marchers in their thousands in the streets of Cairo and Beirut, recalling the 1982 massacres of Sabra and Shatila in Lebanon,[23] to spokesmen of the Israeli Left like Meretz leader Yossi Sarid,[24] to US State Department spokesperson Richard Boucher ("We ... were quite concerned that the visit by Sharon to this site risked creating tensions, and in fact it did")[25] placed the responsibility squarely on Sharon. Madeleine Albright spoke of Sharon "clearly undermining the peace process."[26] Columnist Akiva Eldar commented: "The ten days of awe and reflection between the New Year and Yom Kippur won't be enough for Ariel Sharon. First, he needs to ask for forgiveness from the Almighty for having desecrated the holiest of sites."[27] Military commentator Ze'ev Schiff, too, agreed that "the riots on the Temple Mount were triggered by a provocative act on the part of Israelis, namely Likud Chair, Ariel

Sharon, and other Likud MKs, who visited one of the most sensitive points in the dispute with the Palestinians at the worst possible time."[28] Even Ben-Ami, the minister of security, asked the reason for the mounting Palestinian riots, called them "a reaction stemming from Palestinian frustration over Sharon's visit to the Mount."[29] With tension over the negotiations at its peak, and the issue of the Temple Mount at the crux of the dispute, it was clear to all that Sharon's visit was meant to assert a total Israeli claim over the holy site.[30] The uprising was already called the Al-Aqsa *intifada*. Sharon's action had put religion at the dangerous epicenter of the Israeli–Palestinian conflict in a way it had never been before.

Soon, however, Prime Minister Barak took the tone that the riots were the work of the Palestinian Authority.[31] Army officers enthusiastically took up this chant,[32] and Foreign Minister Ben-Ami promptly chimed in. In a television interview on the Friday, the day of the first Palestinian deaths, he had unambiguously placed the brunt of the blame on Sharon. Hearing Barak's cautious excuse, though, that the deaths had begun only on that day, a day after the Sharon visit, Ben-Ami revised his account on the Saturday, adding "It's hard to say that there were not at least some Palestinian Authority forces behind this matter."[33]

Behind all this finger-pointing lay the question: how could Sharon have mounted such a huge military operation, to muster his 1,000-strong armed escort for the September 28 adventure on the platform of the mosques? In no way could he have done this without authorization from Prime Minister Ehud Barak and his Security Minister Shlomo Ben-Ami, who was also acting foreign minister and chief negotiator.[34] Before long Palestinians would begin to describe the Sharon provocation as actually the work of Barak and Ben-Ami themselves, what Saeb Erekat would come to describe as Barak's "exit strategy" from the negotiations.

Quickly the tide of Israeli interpretation shifted, until Aviv Lavie could write, in a *Ha'aretz* column, that in recent days facts and opinions had become so entangled in Israeli media reports that one could no longer distinguish between them. Lavie continued, that this accepted interpretation served Israel's political interests, so that it was not hard to guess how the account had reached local journalists. Perhaps, thought Lavie, there might be some truth to this view—he did not see Arafat as a leader built of the most righteous human components. And yet the accusation ought not to be presented to the public as a fact without thorough evidentiary grounding. "Would anyone dare to hurl comparable accusations at Ehud Barak?"[35]

THE OUTSIDE WORLD TRIES TO HELP

With President Clinton, UN Secretary General Kofi Annan and others calling urgently for a halt in the violence, Madeleine Albright announced on the Monday after Sharon's foray on the mount, October 2, that she would arrive Wednesday in Paris and would meet both Barak and Arafat to search for a way out of the bloodletting. The death toll stood now at 55, almost all Palestinians so far.[36]

The Paris talks proved stormy. Albright spent from 10 a.m. on Wednesday to 3 a.m. on Thursday, struggling to find a way to stop the violence, but failed to reach an overall agreement. At one point Arafat left the meeting, saying of Barak's treatment of him: "This is humiliation. I cannot accept it." Albright at this point ordered the security guards to "shut the gates," so that the Palestinian leader could not leave the compound in central Paris. According to the account of a Reuters correspondent, Albright ran after Arafat, urging him not to leave. The gates closed in front of Arafat's car, and he got out and returned to the meeting.

In the end, Barak headed angrily home for Israel, refusing to join Albright and Arafat in going to Cairo for further talks with President Mubarak. In a closing meeting with French President Chirac, the Israeli prime minister said that Arafat could "choose between the road to an agreement or the sliding down to violence."[37]

Back in Jerusalem, Sharon was unapologetically denying that his visit had anything to do with the breakdown into violence. He adopted the Barak/Ben-Ami explanation that the whole thing had been engineered by Arafat from the start. Seeing that his rival Netanyahu had been driven to the fringe of the political stage by the tumult Sharon had created, some Israeli commentators were beginning to say that competition with Netanyahu was Sharon's only motive, one they interpreted as quite innocent, for his Temple Mount adventure.[38] And as Israel shut down for Yom Kippur, both sides braced for the worst.[39]

Much discouraged, I wrote once again to Arafat at this stage, on October 7, still on my familiar theme of the need for non-violent mobilization:

Dear President Arafat,
    Salaam!
    Excuse me if I intrude upon you once again.... I have no doubt of your commitment to bring about a just peace agreement, and have challenged the efforts to portray the present calamity as something planned by yourself or other Palestinians. Like most of the Palestinian commentators, I do not believe this rage among your people is something you can turn on and off like a tap....

As I read the accounts from many sources, it seems that the Palestinians appear to most Westerners as the victims in this affair, as indeed they are. It alarms me, though, to anticipate that this understanding could be reversed overnight if the Hamas or any other rejectionist organization began to set off massive bombs, as they might at any moment now. International sympathy would revert to the Israelis at once, and all Palestinians be seen again as "terrorists."

Raising, as I had so often, the appeal for a disciplined non-violence, which was not the same as non-protest, I continued:

I don't believe the chance to return to negotiation…has disappeared. It will disappear, though, if Israelis begin to be seen as victims, or suffer large casualties from terrorist attacks. I've argued several times this summer that the most non-violent side of this will win. The Israelis are already losing heavily through lack of restraint.…

Israelis, even many of those who have traditionally been the peace activists, are very ready to believe that you are the manipulative instigator and controller of angry and violent protests that are in fact the result of the people's frustration and are beyond your control. You can only master what is outside your control by something better. I am asking that you plainly and openly organize and call for a disciplined and dignified protest, altogether non-violent.…

With this, I went into an exposition of some recognized conflict-resolution theory, the priority for the Palestinians of dealing with the anxiety of Israelis.

I've written earlier that the public which you and your people most need to address is the Israeli public. It is not, in fact, the public of the European or the other Arab countries. You need to stand firm, not agreeing to what you know is injustice, but let that Israeli public know that you are not their enemy, have no wish for their destruction or loss, and demand of them only that they grant you your rights. Overcoming their anxiety is the only way you have to combat their racism, their assumption that their desires and needs are important but that your people and their desires and needs are not.

These very days are the critical times. They could bring your people real success, or they could bring new disaster. I apologized, when I began, for intruding upon you again, but I would feel delinquent if I did not try to press these thoughts on you.

BARAK TURNS TO SHARON FOR HELP

The violence, after this first dreadful week, moved ahead on its own momentum. A politically devastated Barak tried now to reform his coalition, making overtures to Likud for a Grand Coalition, an improbable venture.[40] This thrashing about on his part to save his own political career would henceforth affect the prospects for continued negotiation.

On October 9 (the day after Yom Kippur) hundreds of Israeli Jews rampaged in Nazareth, attacking Arab homes and setting off a melee in which police killed two more Israeli Arabs.[41]

When, on October 11, Palestinians stoned the funeral procession of a slain American-born Jewish settler, it set off hours of gun battles. Meanwhile Arafat released 20 Hamas prisoners. Soon we would be hearing of his arrest policy for militants as a "revolving door."[42]

COULD ARAFAT STOP IT?

Some Israelis recognized at this stage that the situation had actually got out of Arafat's control. Danny Rubinstein argued in *Ha'aretz* that the religious character of Sharon's challenge to the Muslims left Arafat and his security forces only a drastically limited authority to check the outbursts. We were not yet into the era of suicide bombers, yet Rubinstein foresaw it clearly. It lacked only bloody enough assaults by the Israelis to unleash the readiness of radical Muslims to die when their religious sensitivities were hurt, as had the Shi'ites of Lebanon. It needed no such organizations, even, as Hamas or Islamic Jihad to release such emotions. But such bloodlettings were now beginning, and were carried out by the Israeli army rather than by fanatics like Baruch Goldstein.

The PLO itself had seldom generated such fanatic responses in the past, Rubinstein observed. The flags turning up in the demonstrations and riots of these days were the green banners of Islam rather than the Palestinian national colors.[43]

LYNCHING AT RAMALLAH

New fury broke on October 12.[44] In the midst of the funeral procession for a victim of the violence, two Israeli soldiers, out of uniform, were discovered in an unmarked car. The crowd took them for undercover agents, though Israeli explanations after the fact claimed they had entered the city by accident. Palestinians believed they had come to the funeral on an assassination mission. In a scene reminiscent of a similar one in Northern Ireland some years earlier, when a car with two plain-clothed British soldiers had been discovered in the midst of an emotion-laden funeral, the crowd pulled the Israelis from their car and began beating them. As Palestinian police tried to intervene, angry youths dragged them into the police station, where they continued to pummel and stab them. Dramatic photos circulated round the world as the body of one Israeli soldier was pitched through the flowered curtains of an upper-storey window to a mob below, which proceeded to stomp on his corpse and parade his mutilated body through the streets, and an exultant young Palestinian appeared at the window waving his bloody hands.

Israelis blamed the Palestinian Authority directly, and Arafat in particular, for these cruel deaths. They destroyed the Ramallah police station where the deed had taken place with rockets, and went on to Gaza to demolish another police station and the transmitter for the Palestinian Authority's radio station, on the grounds that it was "inciting" the Palestinians to such atrocities. Helicopter gunships, tanks, and heavy warplanes fired on both Ramallah and Gaza, though the Israelis described their attacks as "limited" and "symbolic" only. Palestinians saw nothing symbolic in them. Saeb Erekat told reporters: "If this is not war, I don't know what else it is."[45] In Manhattan, 15,000 gathered in the midtown streets near the Israeli Consulate General to condemn the Palestinian outbursts and rally behind Israel at this critical moment in its history. Raw emotions were exhibited even among New York's top politicians.[46]

By the following day Israel was still in shock. Helicopter gunships continued their shelling all over the West Bank and Gaza in widespread retaliation raids.[47] In Jerusalem, a huge cordon of Israeli soldiers prevented Palestinians from gathering for the usual Friday prayer at the Al-Aqsa Mosque.[48]

Two weeks into October, the death toll standing now at some 100 persons, mostly Palestinian, President Clinton called for an immediate summit. He demanded to meet both Barak and Arafat in Egypt. Kofi Annan, meanwhile, kept shuttling back and forth between Jerusalem and Gaza City.[49]

Veteran reporter David Shipler, experienced in both the Israeli and the Arab reality, saw Israelis and Palestinians pulled toward the black hole of their conflict. They had been there before, a place so dense in passion that it emitted no light by which they could truly see the other's legitimacy as a people.[50] Here was one of my own certainties being shattered. Since Oslo, with its mutual, public and solemn recognition by both peoples of one another's legitimacy, I had believed this was an accomplishment no one could take back. I had seen Binyamin Netanyahu devote his whole three years as prime minister to the effort to retract that recognition of the

Palestinians' legitimacy as a people, and altogether unable to accomplish it. But already, this new and violent *intifada* was wearing heavily away at that bedrock mutual acknowledgment of one another by these two peoples.

RE-ENTER CLINTON

Could it get any worse? The death toll now stood at seven Israeli Jews, twelve Israeli Arabs, and 80 Palestinians.[51] The indomitable Clinton was on his way to Middle East talks, still hoping to bring about a truce.[52] In Cairo, people came out in droves to make blood donations and give financial aid to the suffering Palestinians.[53] And in Gaza, the Tanzim youth group, huddled around the wreckage of Arafat's bombed-out headquarters, began to form itself into an armed militia.[54]

At Sharm el-Sheikh, both sides made their promises to Clinton to work to stop the violence, the Israelis to pull back from the Palestinian areas, the Palestinians to curb the riots. No one much believed either side.[55] Blood boiled in the West Bank and Gaza. The prospects of a ceasefire were utterly unclear, and there were yet more deaths.[56]

To *Ha'aretz* columnist Akiva Eldar it seemed that the legacy of Yitzhak Rabin was now dead. He quoted Barak's boast, that "In contrast to the last two governments, I haven't conceded anything to Arafat. I simply looked into the possibilities." The implicit criticism leveled by Barak concerning his predecessors' Oslo policies marked a turning point. They amounted to the final nails in Rabin's coffin.[57]

BARAK'S "TIME-OUT"

The obstacle to further negotiation was still Barak, with the uncertainties of his minority coalition. Directly after the Sharm el-Sheikh summit and the truce, he began telling his confidants that he did not believe the Palestinians would abide by its terms, and therefore expected the violence in the territories to continue. Should that be so, he saw no possibility of resuming negotiations on a final-status agreement.[58]

By Friday October 20, the report was that Barak might halt the peace effort altogether in order to revamp his government. Already, in three days since the truce, ten more Palestinians had been killed in gun battles. Barak was deep in conversations with Sharon about a government of national unity, the "Grand Coalition" of Labor and Likud, which would have put paid to any hope of further negotiation. Survival in government had assumed greater priority than peace, as it so often does.[59] In New

York, the UN General Assembly had adopted a resolution which condemned Israel for "excessive use of force," with US Ambassador Holbrooke denouncing it as "one-sided, unbalanced" for lack of enough condemnation of Palestinians.[60] He dismissed the General Assembly itself as a "useless body."[61]

The weekend found the Israelis making contingency plans for the event of total breakdown. Deputy Defense Minister Ephraim Sneh had charge of planning, and talked of a big fence to physically separate the two peoples, with Israel determining the borders unilaterally.[62]

Unilateral separation, a wall between Israelis and Palestinians, was the favorite topic as Barak conducted his unity-government talks with Likud. It came up against objections from both the Israeli and the Palestinian sides. Israelis saw the physical impracticality of such a wall. If it were intended to prevent Israelis from coming into any contact with bomb-toting Palestinians, any geographical point of such contact would have to be sealed off, the safe passage from Gaza to the West Bank would be abolished, a fortified wall would have to be built in the heart of Jerusalem. The United States was firmly opposed, Clinton arguing against it in telephone conversations with Barak, who yet urged it in the expectation that Arafat would now make his Unilateral Declaration of Independence on November 15.[63]

Barak, by this time, had formally declared what he called a "time-out" in the peace process.[64] At the same time, he had finally realized that he had to heal, so far as was now possible, the rift he had created with Israel's Arab citizens. He announced an official inquiry into the killing of 13 Israeli Arabs.[65]

Death tolls were getting seriously out of hand. Israeli army policy in this fourth week of the uprising was systematically to target even unarmed demonstrators with live ammunition or worse. This resulted in the deaths of at least another 20 Palestinians over the weekend of October 20–22 alone, including seven aged 16 or younger. As many as 700 demonstrators or innocent bystanders were wounded as the use of rubber-coated steel bullets gave way now to live rounds fired from M-16 rifles and heavier submachine guns. A total of 127 Palestinians had been killed by soldiers or marauding settlers by late October, 19 of them under 17 years old, and over 5,000 wounded since Mr. Sharon's escapade of September 28.[66]

Ha'aretz reporters were convinced at this time that Barak was doing all he could to avoid another summit.[67] He had to worry at this time about the reemergence of Binyamin Netanyahu, who had announced the end of his own personal "time-out" from political life to challenge Sharon for the leadership of Likud, adding new venom to the political scene.[68]

DEATH TOLLS

For all the Israeli anxiety about attacks and bombs, most of the casualties at this stage were still Palestinian. The era of the suicide bombings had not yet come, and bus bombings were still a memory from earlier periods of turmoil. On a typical day, October 24, two 16-year-old Palestinians were killed in clashes with the army, one in Jenin, one in Gaza, while another 13-year-old from Khan Yunis died in a Gaza hospital of wounds suffered four days before. An additional five Palestinians were seriously injured, but there were no Israeli casualties.

Wednesday October 25 brought an appearance of calm over the West Bank and Gaza, as tensions seemed to ease.[69] Clinton, still chafing at Arafat's failing to bring the trouble to a standstill, "walked to the edge," in David Sanger's expression, of putting the blame on him for the whole breakdown. For Barak he had only the warmest praise. He still wanted to bring both to visit Washington the next week.[70]

For the Friday prayer day, October 27, several Arab organizations prepared a "day of rage." It resulted predictably in four more Palestinians shot dead, in various places about the territory, and that of course meant four angry funerals for the following day. Roadside bombs exploded near Hebron and near Bethlehem. The death toll stood now at 137, all but eight of them Arabs, whether Palestinian or Israeli Arab.[71]

GILO

Emotion at the four funerals spilled, as expected, into yet more violence. But another phenomenon had presented itself in the last few days as residents of Gilo gathered at the sharply defined edge of their township, some with binoculars, to stare and point across the steep defile that separated them from the hillside Bethlehem suburb of Beit Jala. Bursts of ineffective small arms fire had come through the night from Beit Jala, aimed at Gilo but unable as yet to get across the valley between them.[72] In Beit Jala, Bethlehem, and Beit Sahour, residents had already experienced the first constant overflights of helicopters at all times of day and night as this storm gathered. They responded more in anger than in fear.[73]

Gilo, in the mind of Israelis, is simply a large Jerusalem neighborhood. It was built, though, very soon after the 1967 Israeli conquest, on newly captured West Bank land, yet within the new metropolitan boundaries that the Israelis drew for Jerusalem. In Palestinian eyes, therefore, it is simply a settlement and, like all the Israeli settlements on conquered land, illegal under the Fourth Geneva Convention.[74]

214 The Failed Negotiations

Beit Jala is a prosperous town of large, well-kept and comfortable stone houses on the outskirts of Bethlehem, home to a population that mingles Christians, both Greek Orthodox and Latin Catholic, and Muslims, as well as the Catholic-founded University of Bethlehem. It quickly found itself surrounded by a cordon of tanks, dug in on the hillside, their turrets pointed toward their town. The army responded to the initial fire with shells from the tanks and rockets from helicopter gunships.[75] Over the months and years to come, this confrontation would escalate until it engulfed all of Beit Jala and Bethlehem itself.

A cult of death began to take root in the desperate towns and refugee camps of the Gaza Strip. Martyrdom in the cause of liberation, or resistance to the Israelis and their attacks, came to be seen as a privilege, celebrated in the ritual of funerals as stretchers carrying the bodies of the dead were carried through the streets through shouting and gesticulating throngs.[76]

THE KNESSET RETURNS

As the month ended, Barak found he had no unity government with Sharon and Likud. Sharon's stated price for a coalition had been outright veto power over any diplomatic initiatives whatever. The fickle Shas party, though, offered Barak a "safety net"[77] to save him from the instant dismissal of his crumbling government when the Knesset returned from its three-month recess, a promise that they would not join a confidence vote against him while violence still reigned.[78]

On the following day, as the Knesset reconvened, seismic changes stood in evidence, in Israeli–Palestinian relations, from the time it had recessed, right after Camp David. As illustration of the difference, Barak had ordered that day a missile attack on the offices of Fatah and on the personal security forces of Arafat. In a hint that he might want to re-engage with Arafat, Barak was rumored to consider sending Shimon Peres, with whom Arafat had shared the Nobel Peace Prize, to him. Leah Rabin, widow of the murdered Prime Minister Rabin, had upbraided Barak on Sunday for not making use of Peres.[79]

The constant Israeli air strikes still meant disproportionately more Palestinian casualties than Israeli, yet as October ended two Israeli guards at a government office in East Jerusalem had been shot, one fatally, by a Palestinian. An Israeli resident of Gilo was found, bound and stabbed to death, in nearby Palestinian territory. In an emergency meeting with his top military and security officials the prime minister ordered what he called "pre-emptive pinpoint" strikes by helicopter gunships on Fatah offices in Ramallah and Nablus and the headquarters of Arafat's personal bodyguard, Force 17, in Gaza.

This produced only more defiance, Arafat himself declaring: "All these things cannot shake one eyelash from the eyes of a Palestinian child holding a Palestinian stone to defend holy Jerusalem, the capital of the Palestinian state." Deaths totals now were at least 154 in just over a month of fighting.[80]

"Pinpoint" attacks, understood by the Israeli military as a way to minimize casualties, proved less accurate than claimed, the rockets aimed at the Fatah offices in Ramallah and Nablus destroying nearby houses and the place of worship of a small Samaritan sect.

When an Israeli reserve officer was killed by Palestinian fire at an army outpost outside Jericho Israeli helicopters attacked the headquarters of the Palestinian intelligence service in Jericho in response. And ominously, the Gilo neighborhood came under much heavier fire than previously from both Beit Jala and the nearby Al-Ida refugee camp. Here too the Israelis responded with machine-gun fire and missiles and, in the evening, employed helicopters.

A great deal of gunfire broke out in Hebron as well. In Nablus, settlers shot two Palestinian residents, and there were other exchanges of fire all over the West Bank and Gaza, in at least a dozen places.[81]

All this made November 1 a day of special consternation for Israelis, but the incident that really galvanized their attention was a car bomb in Jerusalem's Talbieh neighborhood. Only one man was lightly injured, but a Jerusalem bomb was something new in the *intifada*. Barak said the car bomb was a direct consequence of Palestinian Authority leniency and the PA's release of Islamic Jihad prisoners.[82]

Shimon Peres had just spent the night of November 1–2 with Arafat at the Erez Crossing Point between Israel and the Gaza Strip, working out a ceasefire on the basis of the Sharm el-Sheikh agreements after the chaotic day. Barak and Arafat were both to address their publics by radio at midday announcing an end to the violence, which by now had included massive shelling of the casino complex in Jericho.[83] After the car bomb, the radio addresses were postponed.[84]

The next day, October 2, a more serious car bomb killed two Israelis near the open-air Mahane Yehuda market in Jerusalem, one of them Ayalet Hassbacker, the 28-year-old daughter of former NRP cabinet minister Yitzhak Levy. It was Friday, a prayer day, and two more Palestinians died in confrontations with the Israeli army, though Barak acknowledged Palestinian efforts to calm the extreme situation.[85]

MORE WASHINGTON MEETINGS

Clinton would persist in his quest, even as his Presidency came to an end. Two days before the election for his successor, which would take place on Tuesday November 7, he predicted that Arafat and Barak would both be coming to Washington within a few days, by which time he would be a "lame duck." The toll was now up to 183 deaths, still mostly Palestinian, and Clinton would leave office on January 20. Little more was expected than that he might calm things down.[86]

The day after the election, with the outcome still uncertain, Dennis Ross announced that he would resign with the end of Clinton's administration. The President appointed a commission, to be led by George J. Mitchell, the former Senate leader who had had such remarkable success in dealing with the Northern Ireland conflict, to inquire into the causes of the current violence in the Middle East, along with Warren Rudman, former Republican senator from New Hampshire, former President Suleiman Demirel of Turkey, Foreign Minister Thorbjorn Jagland of Norway, and former NATO Secretary General Javier Solano of Spain. The picture of Israeli rockets and tracer fire directed at Beit Jala remained unchanged.

At the UN, the Security Council decided to hold a closed meeting on Friday to hear Arafat and Israeli Ambassador Yehuda Lancry debate a Palestinian proposal for a UN protective force in the West Bank and Gaza. US Ambassador Holbrooke threatened to veto any new resolution condemning Israel. The Israelis argued that, if the Palestinians wanted to discuss violence, they should simply approach Israel by the channel of peace talks.[87]

As Arafat prepared to meet Clinton on Thursday November 9, the Israelis made the first of the "targeted killings" that have become so much the hallmark of their policy since. As assassination target, they chose Hussein Obaijat, a local Fatah paramilitary commander who, the Israelis believed, had organized shooting attacks on Israeli soldiers. They fired a missile from a helicopter gunship at his car, killing not only Obaijat but also two middle-aged women passers-by. The attack would establish a regular Israeli pattern from this time on: summary execution on suspicion only, without regard for "collateral damage" deaths of other civilians at the scene.[88]

News of the assassination hardly helped at Arafat's meeting with Clinton, which yielded no progress. Washington insiders talked now of a "political process" rather than a "peace process." Arafat commented: "My tanks are not besieging Israeli towns." Clinton, never flinching from the effort, was trying to gauge whether a last-chance peace drive was feasible.[89]

At the UN, on Friday November 10, Arafat asked the Security Council to send a 2,000-strong multinational force to insert itself between Israelis and Palestinians in the West Bank, Gaza, and Jerusalem, in light of the more than 200 deaths in the last 40 days, mostly Palestinian. Consideration of a Security Council Resolution was expected by Monday.[90]

The 56-member Organization of the Islamic Conference, meeting in Qatar, bitterly denounced Israeli actions.[91] Little was expected of Barak's meeting with Clinton in Washington, where people now talked only of preventing disaster. It was understood that Barak was preparing for a "clean break" with the Palestinians, including outright annexation of the settlements.[92] Clinton himself argued to Barak that Arafat was in fact more than willing to renew serious negotiation, but could not break through the prime minister's insistence that Arafat had to stifle all violence among Palestinians before he would talk to him.[93]

THE SWELLING TIDE OF DEATHS

Monday's death toll was four Israelis and only two Palestinians, for Israelis the worst one-day toll since the fighting began.[94] The Israeli army at once ordered a clampdown on movement and scoured the West Bank and Gaza for suspects. Israeli soldiers shot down two youths near their home in the Gaza Strip.[95]

I found I had become so dismayed myself as the deterioration continued that, for over a month, I had written nothing, had hardly thought anything about the Middle Eastern situation beyond how devastating it was. When, quite often, I had wanted to do so, I had felt simply helpless. To my surprise, I received a prompting from my friend Issa Kassissieh, Faisal Husseini's right-hand man at Orient House, asking that I do some more thinking, analysis, and feedback.

The Palestinians, Issa told me, still believed that their real ally was Israeli public opinion, even as their image was distorted and the victim became the victimizer in the eyes of the world's media. They sought concrete ideas to communicate with Israeli society. "I believe at the end they are after peace," wrote Issa, "but we have to give them the trust and confidence. And of course vice versa. After all, both of us are stubborn."[96]

I found myself out of the mode for thinking constructively, and struggled to put together some ideas in response. I reverted to my long-standard line, on the need for rigorous non-violence, but added that I didn't believe either the US officials involved, Clinton and his assistants, or the Israelis understood, however much they longed for peace, what it might cost.

Even when they brought to it their best will, they still felt they could impose their own idea of a solution by preponderance of military force. The Palestinians, as a result, had never really been partners to a negotiation process, but had been expected simply to take whatever the Israelis offered them and say thank you.

` I promised to put my thoughts together soon and write an analysis I could send to all the parties, but it would not be until early December, when serious negotiation began again to come within reach, that I would manage to formulate what has, ever since, been my basic understanding of the situation.

A poll of Palestinian opinion, published at this time by the Bir Zeit University, showed disillusionment with the US role in negotiations. Commitment to peace with Israel was strong as ever, yet 80 percent supported the uprising and military attacks, even including suicide bombings, understanding this not as attack on Israel but as war of independence.[97]

Measurement of Israeli opinion at this same juncture showed Israeli citizens raising their voice to ask if Israel should be sacrificing its citizens, its soldiers, and its hope for peace to defend the settlements. The Israeli Left had been largely silent since the *intifada*, stunned by the violence. But now they began to speak again of their old recognition that settlements were an obstacle to peace and a provocation for the present violence. Some women of a grassroots organization—Four Mothers—that had pushed for Israeli withdrawal from Lebanon were regrouping to advocate withdrawal from the territories.[98] Amira Hass, the one Jewish reporter for *Ha'aretz* who made a point of actually living among Palestinians to see what their experience of Israeli suppression was really like, wrote at this time of the cruel and total disruption of life brought about by the constant heavy military pressure on civilians by the Israeli army. "We have to ask the question," she wrote, "asked by one of the senior Fatah officials, 'Don't they understand in Israel that they are turning us into Hezbollah?'"[99] Meanwhile, LAW, the Palestinian Society for the Protection of Human Rights and the Environment, an affiliate to the International Commission of Jurists (ICJ), Fédération Internationale des Ligues de Droits de l'Homme (FIDH), World Organisation Against Torture (OMCT), and member of the Euro-Mediterranean Human Rights Network, provided day-by-day records of the incredible death and devastation brought upon Palestinians, even at this early stage, by the Israeli military action.[100]

Brigadier General Benyamin Gantz, portrayed as the "resolute commander of Israeli forces in the West Bank," commented: "We are much stronger than they are. We could really clean this area out. But what then? We can cope with it militarily speaking. But it would take us to a point where everybody would lose." He added; "If I were to use all my force, I could probably wipe out Beit Jala in a matter of hours. Should I do that? I definitely don't want to do it."[101]

It was clear, though, by this time that the Israeli government had extended its aims to the destruction of what remained of the Palestinian economy. The *Ha'aretz* staff, in a joint effort, tracked this campaign.[102]

On November 17 Arafat issued ceasefire orders to all Palestinians, those who recognized his orders and those who didn't, repudiating all resort to violence in an effort to get back to the negotiating table.[103] Doubts were surfacing at high levels in the Israeli media about the extremes of military action against the Palestinians. *Ha'aretz* editorialized:

> While the public debate in Israel continues on the question whether the current policy of restraint should be maintained, reports are piling up on the suffering of Palestinians in the West Bank and Gaza Strip who believe that Israel is not pursuing a policy of restraint at all but, quite the contrary, is treating them with murderous cruelty.[104]

Barak informed Clinton that he would be open to "international supervisors" if an Israeli–Palestinian peace agreement were reached, to oversee its fulfillment. The Israeli army said that the number of shooting incidents had declined from previous days (this even though at least six more Palestinians had been killed just since midnight). What they meant was that, for the first day, no shooting had come from Beit Jala toward Gilo.[105]

But on the Monday a powerful roadside bomb ripped apart an armored school bus used by the children of settlers at Kfar Darom, killing a teacher and a maintenance man and dismembering several children. Israel medics evacuated the five worst cases, children missing limbs, to hospitals outside the area. The evening saw the most extensive air strikes yet, as Israel bombarded military, police and media targets throughout the Gaza Strip in retaliation. Each time the diplomatic efforts increased, a terror attack would succeed in scuttling, even if only temporarily, the closed-door conversations.[106]

The US State Department now issued the most severe warning to Israel by the Clinton administration since the fighting had broken out seven weeks before, describing the retaliation for Monday's bombing of the school bus, which it called a "heinous attack," as disproportionate. Israeli response was angry, complaining that the United States, as Israel's chief

220   The Failed Negotiations

ally and its major security partner, was trying to be "too even-handed" in its approach to the violence.[107]

On Tuesday November 21, Egypt recalled its ambassador, breaking off Israel's longest-standing and most productive relation in the Arab world. Hosni Mubarak, incensed by the Monday bombing of Gaza, abandoned the efforts to play the mediator between Israel and the Palestinians on which he had staked his reputation.[108] Sharon was calling publicly for the "liquidation" of Palestinian security chief Mohammed Dahlan, expressing consternation that he had not been killed in the air raids.[109]

Wednesday November 22 witnessed another bus bombing, this time in the coastal city of Hadera, killing two Israelis and wounding scores as a powerful car bomb exploded next to the bus during rush hour. The interior of the bus was entirely engulfed in flame. Barak declared that Israel would "get even" for this "barbaric" attack that took the current violence into the country's heartland. Gazans shuttered themselves up in their houses in anticipation of yet another Israeli bombardment.

Earlier that day Israeli soldiers had shot dead four Palestinians in southern Gaza, at a roadblock that had been set up to capture one of them. Five more Palestinians had died in a variety of other clashes, establishing a new benchmark of eleven deaths in one day, the most in a single day since the earliest days of the uprising. In Jerusalem, right-wing protesters packed the city center, vowing support for the settlers in the occupied territories and opposition to Barak's policy, which was still described as military "restraint." US Secretary of Defense William Cohen, arriving that day from Cairo, expressed hand-wringing US anxiety about the mounting violence, and Arafat, in Cairo, denounced the United States for supplying Israel with weapons: "The weapons used are American; American helicopters, American fighter planes, American armored cars, American missiles, American shells, American bombs."[110]

A NEW START?

All this while the American Presidential election still hung in the balance. It was referred to the Supreme Court on Sunday, November 26.

Respected voices in the United States were rising at this stage reminding us all that the fundamental underlying problem was the Israeli settlements. Former President Jimmy Carter wrote of the illegality of all the settlements as something that had been recognized by all parties, even then Prime Minister Menachem Begin, in the Camp David meetings of 1978, on the basis of Article 2 of the United Nations Charter, which prohibited an acquisition of territory by force, and Security Council Resolution 242.[111]

Barak provided a shock to the political system when, on Tuesday November 28, he called for early elections in Israel, pre-empting the initiative of his opponents, who had been ready to bring him down by a non-confidence vote.[112] In Washington, the lame-duck Clinton administration saw this as a chance for Barak to go for broke for a peace settlement in the brief remaining time, since without it he would have no chance in the election.[113] There was no strength left in the US government, it was felt, to promote such an outcome because of the country's own contested election.[114]

To hold an election under such conditions of crisis and war seemed to many an invitation to yet further disruption. Barak promptly cancelled a brainstorming session on how to return to the table and devoted his time to internal political issues, but the violence, unsurprisingly, would not be put aside.[115]

Speaking on November 30 to an assembly of newspaper editors, Barak presented his plan for a peace deal to be made more slowly and in steps. It would be incremental, starting with an immediate handover of more territory to the Palestinians, another 10 percent, with the possible recognition of Palestinian statehood, but postponing for up to three years discussion of the crucial issues of Jerusalem and refugees. The Palestinians would have most of the Gaza Strip but only 40 percent of the West Bank, and that separated into more than a dozen segments. Saeb Erekat responded that Palestinians would return to the table only for "full permanent status negotiations, including Jerusalem, settlements, refugees, and borders."[116]

I had finally found myself coherent enough to produce a letter I had long been mulling over. The straits of these last two months had clarified for me what had long been a concern, that the destroying element in all the process of peace seeking we had seen was disregard for international law. The letter I wrote to Arafat that day, December 1, fulfilling the promise I had made to Issa Kassissieh on November 13, remains the fullest expression of my own outlook on the negotiations.

> Dear President Arafat,
> Salaam!
> The conflict situation between Palestinians and Israelis appears to have become routine now, two months after Mr Ariel Sharon's initial aggressive visit to the Haram al-Sharif. The political context, on the Israeli side, has meanwhile changed, with the calling of new elections....
> I have been watching this situation as closely as I can from a

distance over this time.... As I see it, the Israeli public is still ready for a peace settlement, over 60 percent of them according to opinion polls that I would expect to be accurate, despite their evident alarm over the way things have developed in these last months. Their right-wing ideologues have tried to raise apprehensions about Israel's conceding one thing or another—amounts of territory in the West Bank, Jerusalem, right of return for refugees. Nevertheless, for this substantial part of the Israeli public, the issue appears to be none of these things, but simply whether an accord will truly bring peace or not....

I have always believed that Mr Barak meant what he said, from the start of his earlier election campaign, that making a genuine peace was his real priority. I never have believed that he understood the full requirements for that, namely that Israel accept the rule of law in its relation with your people.... Hence the excessive force, none of which could be exercised without his approval, with which the Israeli military has responded to the Palestinian outbursts of defiant rage. That rage itself, inasmuch as it is uncontrolled, has been the weakness of the Palestinians.

How then can this situation be directed in a way that leads to a just peace both for Palestinians and Israelis?

The most basic requirement is that the Israelis accept and submit themselves to the rule of law. I truly commend you on having insisted on this throughout this year's negotiations. It has been neglected by the State of Israel ever since its founding in 1948. Instead, successive Israeli governments have always assumed that their relations with Palestinians, and in fact with all the Arab world, would be determined by preponderance of military force. United States governments have, despite occasional mild misgivings, concurred with the Israelis on this ever since 1967. It goes by the name of *Realpolitik*, and is total renunciation of the rule of law.

It is to the great credit of Mr Barak, and of President Clinton, that this total reliance on force has not been the principle of this year's negotiations, and in fact President Clinton, throughout the bad years of the Netanyahu government, recognized and, within rather timid limits, opposed this outlaw character of Israeli policy.

This year's negotiations have, instead, been based on recognition, by Israeli and American governments, that great wrong had been done to Palestinians, and that some major concessions must be made to your people as the price for peace. Both genuinely feel that what they offered was so impressive that you should have accepted it. The flaw in their policy is that it has not been based on the rule of law. That has meant that you and your people have never been a true party to this negotiation, which has instead been a negotiation merely between Israelis and Israelis, between those who wanted to concede something, those who wanted to concede more, and those who wanted to concede nothing at all, with the Americans concurring and urging acceptance of the outcome on you. The underlying supposition has been that everything was for the Israelis to concede, and that you had no right other than to accept what they offered.

The law suppositions that must fundamentally be recognized are as follows:

1. **Article 2 of the Charter of the United Nations**, according to which every nation that has accepted membership in the organization has renounced any acquisition of territory by force.
2. **Security Council Resolutions 242 and 338**, which are plainly and explicitly direct applications of Article 2 of the Charter, requiring the return of territory captured in the 1967 war in exchange for peace. After all the efforts in Prime Minister Begin's time to restrict this requirement to some of the territory, it is by now evident that it means all the captured territory, including East Jerusalem, although the Jerusalem question is still complicated by the provision for international status envisioned in GAR 181.
3. **General Assembly Resolutions 181 and 194,** authorizing the establishment of the two states in Palestine, one Jewish and one Arab, and then specifying the right of refugees to return to live in peace, or, if unable or unwilling to do so, to receive due compensation. Recognition and acceptance of these two General Assembly Resolutions was actually a specified condition for the admission of the State of Israel into the United Nations in 1949.
4. **The Fourth Geneva Convention of 1949**, which explicitly outlaws the colonization of occupied territories, as well as the expulsion of citizens from occupied territories and the violation of their human rights. I see frequent Israeli arguments against the applicability of the Fourth Geneva Convention, including the observation that it has not been invoked in other cases in which its provisions have been violated. That, of course, is no valid argument against its applicability. It is rather a reason why it should have been invoked in the other cases. Its meaning, in this case, is that all the Israeli settlements on occupied territory, including those in Gaza as well as the West Bank and all parts of East Jerusalem, are strictly, and have always been, illegal. That

applies also to settlements on the Golan Heights. It has been a fundamental defect in the legality of American policy that, after maintaining until 1981 that those settlements are illegal, it has, since the administration of President Ronald Reagan, described them merely as "obstacles to peace," and since 1993, under the Clinton administration, has described them merely as "unhelpful." It has been clear to all the rest of the world, throughout this time, that they were and remain strictly illegal.

5. **Security Council Resolution 1322** of this year, which defines the military response Israel has been making since September 28 as excessive force. This is, by comparison with the other items listed, a peripheral matter, painful as the armed assault on the Palestinian public has been. The charge, and the Israeli responsibility, is serious. But it is really not worthwhile, in my view, to let prospects of peace be lost because of demands for punishment of these abuses. Demand for international protection of the Palestinian public from these assaults is reasonable, but the insertion of international forces is not the only way to accomplish that. If the State of Israel can be brought in any other way to recognize that it is subject to the rule of law, that would suffice to end this unjustified brutality.

That catalogue of the decisions of the legal obligation that had binding force on Israel was the most original element in this letter to Arafat, one that I would soon repeat to Barak and to Clinton. The rest of my letter urged on Arafat, as a matter of strategy rather than of ethics, that he must win the trust of Israelis before he could expect that they would accede to the demands of international law. His own people had little reason to trust the Israelis after the record of broken promises, massive military attack, and continuing colonization that they experienced, but they should realize how little the Israelis trusted them in turn. The greatest weakness of the Palestinians in their current critical situation, I argued, was their unbridled rage. I compared this with their success in the 1985 *intifada*, which had been visibly characterized by its relative non-violence and its direction against occupation but not against Israel. I continued:

> It has been my own experience, in dealing with many conflict situations, that people are motivated and empowered by their indignation against the affronts visited upon them, so long as this helps them make plans how to end those affronts and they retain a confidence in their own ability to address the evil. But when they succumb to their own feelings of frustration, their indignation turns into hatred,

and their confidence in their own ability to solve the crisis turns to cynicism, even to disbelief in their own leadership. Those are crippling obstacles to their own purpose. Palestinians right now are becoming so nihilistic in their rage against Israeli injustice that they risk losing everything. It is the task of Palestinian leadership to relieve the frustration of their public and restore the sense that they are capable, through mobilized and calculated resistance to the occupation, necessarily non-violent if it is to be successful, of winning their rights.

Recognizing the importance of such leaders as Marwan Barghouti and Mohammed Dahlan, who seemed at this stage to be escaping from Arafat's orbit of authority, I urged him to win their support for the non-violent strategy I always put before him. But I reminded him, too, of the assurance the Israelis would need that their acceptance of the rule of law would not work to their ruin.

> You must remember, President Arafat, the conversations and correspondence you and I had between 1985 and the end of 1988, when you gave your formal acceptance in Geneva to the three famous preconditions for dialogue between the PLO and the United States and it was accepted, disappointing as was the immediate outcome of the resulting dialogue.
>
> You needed then to know what would result if you publicly accepted the three preconditions. Would you simply be told that it didn't matter, that nothing was changed, that the question of refugees was already settled by the famous agreement of Cyrus Vance with Moshe Dayan that Palestinian refugees were offset by Jewish refugees from Arab countries and nothing remained to be settled? I spent all of three years working at that question...as to what response your acceptance of the three preconditions would receive. Without that, though you were in fact ready to accept the preconditions, you felt you would have played your "last card" in vain and so betrayed your people's hopes.
>
> The Israelis are in a comparable position now. Even though their defiance of law has been flagrant all this time, they need to know in advance what would be your response, what would actually happen, by free negotiated agreement, in all these areas if and when they acknowledge and submit to the rule of law. Their communal racism would have to be broken through to acknowledge you as their equals in rights, but they would also need to know that their acceptance of

that and of all the consequences of the rule of law would not be the destruction or unacceptable disruption of their state and society....

I would develop these ideas further in letters to Prime Minister Barak and President Clinton, attaching copies to each of what I had written to the others, but not until a bit more than a week later. Most basically, I was trying to deal with the disparity of power that had necessarily to negate any effort at agreement that could be made between Israelis and Palestinians. Whatever agreement might be signed under that disparity of power could only be seen—by the powerless side—as a diktat. It could never be accepted by the Palestinians as truly binding them, as it would not be just. If, however, the underlying assumption of the negotiations were that of international law, the process would not, as some Israelis might fear, be prejudiced against Israel, as the law is there for the protection of both parties, and will protect their genuine rights and interests. It will not protect their dealing unjustly with their partner, as for instance by letting them retain the territories they have unjustly settled with their own population, but it will protect them from injustice to themselves.

It is also not true that the law would predetermine all matters and leave no room for negotiation over the critical issues of land, of borders, of settlements, of the status of Jerusalem, of refugees. The law would preclude determining any of these issues by force, or by pre-emptive action made possible by military predominance. It would still, though, permit changes in any of these matters to be made by mutual agreement, freely negotiated between equal parties in accord with the genuine interests of both.

What reliance on the law and its just implementation would accomplish is to overcome the disparity of power that is the ultimate nemesis to any genuine agreement, and allow both parties to come to agreements that would fully bind both and lead to a reliable and sustainable peace.

PROGRESS TOWARD RENEWED NEGOTIATION

The day I wrote that letter, December 1, was the first Friday of Ramadan. Deadly street clashes continued, despite the movement both sides were making toward each other. Only Palestinians resident in Jerusalem were allowed for prayers at the Al-Aqsa Mosque on this solemn day of prayer. Entrance to the city from Bethlehem or from the north was blocked off. Palestinians who managed to reach Jerusalem were barred from the Old City.[117] But the following days saw greater quiet. On Monday December 4, the Israeli Army actually removed angry Israeli settlers who were blocking the roads in the Gaza Strip, yet they also fired rockets into the heavily populated Dheisheh refugee camp in Bethlehem. Israelis had become preoccupied now with the politics of their election.[118]

American concern for Middle East peace made an appearance on Wednesday December 6, when 101 American rabbis called for the sharing of the Temple Mount. They saw no reason to require exclusive Jewish sovereignty over the plaza that was of such importance to two religions.[119]

Momentum for further negotiation suffered a setback on Thursday December 7, when Arafat, emerging from his car to address a crowd in Gaza, flourished a sub-machine gun. The moment was broadcast repeatedly on Israeli, Palestinian, and world television for the rest of the day.[120]

Violence surged the following day, another Friday of Ramadan, December 8, the anniversary of the beginning of the so much more successful *intifada* of 1987. This was another "day of rage," proclaimed from the mosques. Ten Palestinians were killed before the day was over.[121]

On Sunday December 9, Ehud Barak stunned the Israeli political world once more, stepping down from his elected position as prime minister, thus forcing an early election, not for the Knesset as a whole but for the office of prime minister alone, by early February. Such a vote was required within 60 days of the prime minister's resignation. People still expected that there would be a general election in May—it would not in fact happen.[122]

PLEADING FOR ADHERENCE TO THE RULE OF LAW

It was time for me to complete the task I had undertaken in writing to Arafat on December 1, and to write also to the Israeli prime minister and US President, enclosing for them copies of what I had written to Arafat. To Barak I wrote, on December 10:

Dear Prime Minister Barak,
    Shalom!
    Your announcement yesterday that you would call a new election for prime minister within two months came as something of an earthquake....
    It pleases me that you frame your bid for reelection as Prime Minister within the intention to proceed with the peace efforts. I have always credited you with meaning, as you promised, to make this the major priority of your time in office. It has been difficult to maintain that confidence over these last months. I

have heard repeatedly Saeb Erekat's conjecture that the Sharon escapade on the Temple Mount and the subsequent heavy repression of Palestinian protest has been your "exit-strategy" from the peace endeavors of the summer. I vigorously resist accepting that explanation, yet I cannot but recognize that Sharon would have been unable to bring his thousand-man heavily armed escort onto the Mount for his provocative assertion of possession without authorization from you and from Mr Ben-Ami.

Stressing, then, the centrality of Sharon's provocation to all the violence that had followed, I wrote that Barak and Ben-Ami ought to have seen that beforehand, and had at the least made a grave mistake in authorizing Sharon's action. The treatment of Palestinians since had not been as equal human beings, but marked with extremes of violence, which I compared with the disciplined avoidance of violence by US police who had confronted riots against the WTO meeting in Seattle or the Czech police who faced much the same over the IMF meeting in Prague. I wrote not to scold him, but to describe what I saw as the things that would prevent any success in efforts to reach a peace settlement. Excessive force toward the Palestinians would bring no openings toward peace, but for Barak there was no political future if he did not come to his own Israeli public in two months' time with a credible formula for future peace.

I cited then the same list of binding obligations in international law that I had sent to Arafat: Article 2 of the UN Charter, Security Council Resolutions 242 and 338, General Assembly Resolutions 181 and 194, and the Fourth Geneva Convention, including the new Security Council Resolution 1322, as I had to Arafat, only because it was so new, copying the whole list just as I had sent it to Arafat. And I argued for the rule of law as the only thing that would overcome the disparity of power, making whatever agreement was reached actually binding on the Palestinians, as no diktat could be.

I acknowledged, as I had to Arafat, how necessary it was that the Palestinians let him know what he might expect from them as agreements if he relied, under law, on negotiation rather than the force so readily available to him. Israelis might well contest the applicability of some of the items I had listed as features of the rule of law, as they habitually did of the Fourth Geneva Convention, but they then needed to accept the judgment of the international community and not shelter behind American vetoes. I continued:

I know that Israelis have worked on a supposition that the world, the "international community," hates them and will judge unjustly. There is a reason for the hostility that Israel faces, and it is precisely this assumption of immunity to the rule of law, and mistreatment of the Palestinians on that basis, which accounts for it. I submit that this hostility would fall away if Israelis made it clear that they truly meant to abide by those rules to which they and other nations have sworn themselves.

This had been a heavy letter, filled with accusations. I closed it with all the assurance to Barak that I could muster:

I give you my negative judgments here with great affection. I wish only the best for you and for your people, as also for the Palestinians and all those others who will be affected by your actions over these next two months.

I wrote next to President Clinton, enclosing this time copies of what I had written both to Arafat and Barak, that same December 10. I didn't repeat, this time, the catalogue of binding judgments in international law that I had given them, but tried instead, more briefly, to spell out the nature of those obligations:

Dear President Clinton,
    Christ's Peace!
    The situation between Israelis and Palestinians has deteriorated far beyond what you, more even than others of us, must have hoped. Personally I think it unfair to blame you, as some have done, for rushing the negotiation, at Camp David, faster than it could be made to run. I sent you, at the time, my assessment of what had happened (letter of August 4), and copies of what I wrote then to Prime Minister Barak and Mr Arafat (letter of August 22). Both of them sent, through aides, kind acknowledgments of my letters. I've written to both of them again, twice to Arafat, and as I believe I should always inform you of anything I send them, I enclose copies of those letters.
    The underlying fault I find in the United States role in the summer's efforts, as I have written to both, is that it has not followed or insisted on the rule of law, which, I believe, is the only basis on which true agreement can be reached between these parties. I won't repeat, in this letter, all that I have written to them, but as regards United States policy, this has been the besetting fault that, for many

years, has voided all American efforts to mediate peace in the Middle East.

As I wrote to them, successive Israeli governments, ever since 1948, have taken it for granted, and made it the basis of their policy, that Israel would be exempted from the laws that govern other nations, and that the questions between it and the Arabs, including especially the Palestinians, would be decided by the preponderance of military force. That is directly contradictory to the treaty obligation Israel and every other nation that has become a member of the United Nations incurred by accepting Article 2 of the United Nations Charter. Israel was also required, as the condition of its receiving membership in the United Nations early in 1949, to subscribe to General Assembly Resolutions 181 of 1947, which authorized its own creation as a Jewish state in Palestine *along with* the creation of an Arab state, and 194 of December 1948, which authorized the return of all refugees from what was the War of Independence for Israelis and the *Naqba* for Palestinians to return to their homes *to live in peace*, or if unable or unwilling to do so to receive due compensation.

The 1967 Security Council Resolution 242, which everyone cites as the legal basis for any genuine settlement of the conflict, reinforced in 1973 by SCR 338, draws explicitly on Article 2 of the Charter as the basis of its demand for return of conquered territory, though this time with a condition not applied when other countries were required by international judgment at the UN to return captured territory (e.g., North Korea, Israel in Lebanon—SCR 425—or Iraq in Kuwait). Israel was required to return land only in exchange for peace (i.e., treaties with the countries it had fought in 1948).

A further legal obligation which Israel, as an occupying power, incurred from 1967 was adherence to the Fourth Geneva Convention, according to which it is forbidden to expel citizens from the occupied land, violate their human rights, or most notably to colonize their territory with its own citizens. All these provisions have been notoriously and increasingly violated ever since 1967. Israel commonly argues that the Fourth Geneva Convention, to which it gave its free assent, somehow does not apply, but the Security Council has several times (notably SCR 242 and 1322) based its demands on Israel on the judgment that the Fourth Geneva Convention does indeed apply.

Since 1967, though, the United States has, with only occasional hesitations, concurred with Israel in exempting it from the implementation of all these rules of law, providing the shield of its veto in the Security Council against repeated efforts by nearly all other nations to enforce them. With full determination, on my own part, to protect Israel from harm, I believe our country has in this way done a terrible disservice to Israel, to its safety and to its moral standing among the nations, while also doing grave injustice to the Palestinians.

This year's negotiations have been different. I credit you, Mr President, with having recognized, to a degree that none of your predecessors have, the right of the Palestinians to have a country of their own, with due guarantee of Israel's safety, and the need of Israel, for its own good, to facilitate that. We could see it in your standing with Prime Minister Rabin, in your repulsion from the negative policies of Prime Minister Netanyahu, and your support of Prime Minister Barak in his giving full priority, for his time in office, to establishing a lasting peace with the Palestinians. Prime Minister Barak himself also deserves full credit for his efforts in this regard. But the defect in the effort, as seen especially at Camp David this summer and in the judgments you and the prime minister stated of its apparent failure, was that it was not yet based on the rule of law. Instead, you and Prime Minister Barak judged between you that the offers he made to the Palestinians this summer (or, more accurately, discussed) were more than generous, better than anything any Israeli Prime Minister had offered before, and that it was simply wrong-headed of Arafat not to take what he was offered and be satisfied.

In practice, that meant that the Palestinians were never really parties to the negotiation. Like practically everything that had preceded it, this was a negotiation between Israelis and Israelis, between those who wanted to offer something, those who wanted to offer more or less, and those who wanted to offer nothing at all. It recognized, with American concurrence, no other right for the Palestinians except to take what they got and say thank you.

I've been over this ground in my letters to both Prime Minister Barak and Mr Arafat, which are enclosed here, and will not bore you with further repetition. Questions of trust are central here for both sides, and there is an initial requirement to stem the tide of violence that has engulfed both since the day (September 28th) when the despicable Mr Sharon made his provocative heavily armed incursion onto the Temple Mount/Haram al-Sharif. It would be the height of irony if he, for his trouble, became the arbiter of whether the Middle East goes on to peace or enduring warfare.

You meanwhile, President Clinton, have long proven yourself the best mediator, the most committed to breaking through to agreement and peace and the most skillful, that we have had in the Presidency, certainly in my (69-year) lifetime. That is saying much, given that Jimmy Carter preceded you in the office. If you don't make this work, neither one of your likely successors is likely to do it. There is small time for it. I really believe that this rule of law principle is the key to it. That is not abandonment of the Israelis. It is their one hope of reaching the peace.

In Christ,
Raymond G. Helmick, S.J.

Finally, on this same December 10, I wrote once more to Arafat, having promised that each of these correspondents would receive copies, which I enclosed, of what went to the others. It was once again my accustomed plea for a disciplined mobilization of his people for a rigorously non-violent protest against continued occupation, without malice toward the Israelis. Only by the success of such a campaign, I wrote, could he win his own people's support against the violence, fatal to their own cause, of Hamas and the other rejectionists on the Palestinian side.

REOPENING OF NEGOTIATIONS

Both Arafat and President Clinton worked steadily from this point to reopen the negotiating process within the narrow window of opportunity that remained. For Barak, his own election appeared to loom larger than further work on the peace. Continued negotiation would be judged insofar as it would contribute to his election chances. For the remainder of his time in power he would vacillate between proceeding with the negotiations and calling them off. That indecision was the worst of all choices he could make, and doomed his electoral chances altogether. Setting up a race for prime minister alone, separated from a Knesset election, clearly made it a referendum, not necessarily on the peace process itself, but on its conduct by Barak.[123]

The long-awaited Mitchell Commission, established two months earlier to investigate the outbreak of violence and seek ways to avert further bloodshed, had finally arrived in town, with the death toll now well over 300. Its members spent the afternoon with Barak and the evening with Arafat, on December 11—the day the US Supreme Court threw the US election to George Bush. Another Palestinian was killed that day outside Nablus under contested circumstances, Israelis and Palestinians giving incompatible reports, exactly the kind of case the commission would have to investigate. Authority to proceed in the search for peace had become wobbly for Israeli or US governments or for the Palestinians.[124]

On Thursday December 14, as more killing went on, Arafat sat down in the Gaza Strip with senior Israeli officials Shlomo Ben-Ami, the foreign minister, and Gilead Sher, Barak's chief of staff, in an effort to revive the peace talks. Amnon Lipkin-Shahak, minister of transportation and tourism, was expected to join the following day. The Israelis were willing now to moderate their demand for total cessation of violence as pre-condition for any further talks. The mood was suddenly more optimistic.[125] In another high-level meeting that day Ben-Ami emerged convinced that Arafat truly wanted to reach an accord before Clinton left office.[126]

By Sunday December 17, Barak and Arafat had both agreed to send their negotiators to talks in Washington. Arafat received eight MKs of the Left parties in a genial meeting at the beachside in Gaza. For the first time since Sharon's incendiary escapade in September, both sides were dropping their conditions for resumption of negotiation, opening the talks even as the shooting continued—the toll now beyond 330. Arafat, speaking to press and cameras, asked: "If it is necessary, why not? But we have to prepare for this meeting, to have a strong foundation." Uri Savir concurred: "My sense is that, given the time line, Arafat is ready to give it a try."[127]

On Monday December 18, the Knesset decided that it would not disband to allow a new election of its own members. Only a prime minister would be elected, and the date would be February 6. The choice would be between Barak and Sharon.[128]

By Wednesday December 20, talks were under way again in Washington. Clinton met negotiators for both sides for 45 minutes at the White House, carrying forward a process he had started with a phone call to Barak ten days before. These sessions had begun on Tuesday night at the Bolling air force base and were expected to continue through Saturday. Within the month remaining to Clinton's term it was hoped that a three-way summit could be convened. Arafat, people presumed, would rather deal with Barak than Sharon.[129]

The assassination phenomenon continued to agitate opinion. On Thursday December 21, Israel publicly admitted, on radio and television, hunting down and killing individual Palestinian militants as a matter of policy, "liquidations" in the generals' parlance. Ephraim Sneh called them "our eliminations," and said: "Let them accuse us all they want. You can't beat terrorism with symposiums at the university."[130]

The element of violence that has caused more dread among Israelis than any other during all the years of *intifada* made its appearance on Friday,

234 The Failed Negotiations

December 22: a suicide bombing, such as had been seen occasionally in previous years but had not marked this uprising as yet. This bomber turned up at a roadside café near a settlement in the Jordan valley, killing himself and wounding three Israeli soldiers. Elsewhere in the West Bank three more Palestinians were shot dead in other incidents that day, bringing the death toll to at least 341.[131]

The five-day search in Washington for common ground between Israelis and Palestinians ended on Saturday December 23. Clinton sent the negotiators home, giving them until Wednesday to say whether they felt they could make progress, but also giving them a document that would be the shaping of diplomatic activity over the next month, his suggested "parameters" for resolving the conflict.[132]

THE CLINTON PROPOSALS

Christmas itself was bleak. The city of Bethlehem, which had anticipated hosting record numbers of visitors in this millennium year, stood dark and quiet at the time of the midnight mass, a pathetic victim of violence. Its 1,800 hotel rooms had all been practically empty ever since early October. "Martyr posters" were almost its only decoration for Christmas. Bethlehem, Beit Jala, and Beit Sahour all came under shelling.[133]

Christmas, however, would see the dawn of serious new hope from Washington. Lame-duck President Clinton chose that day to reveal publicly the extensive set of proposals for a peace accord between Israel and the Palestinians that he had given privately to the two teams a couple of days before. These would govern the process of negotiation that culminated at Taba in the following month.

Israel, he proposed, would cede sovereignty over the Temple Mount. The Palestinians would give up the right of a general return to Israel proper. A Palestinian state would cover 95 percent of the West Bank. He laid out a timetable to govern the development of security arrangements over a number of years.

On the refugee question, Clinton's proposal offered return to the Palestinian "homeland," that is, the new Palestinian state, eliminating the prospect of a large wave of refugees returning to Israel proper. Israeli news reports said that Israel would agree to absorb tens of thousands of refugees, but Clinton mentioned no number. An international program would be established, with Israel taking part, for compensation and resettlement of refugees in third countries.

For accepting only 95 percent of the West Bank, the Palestinians would be compensated with a part of the Negev.

If an agreement were signed, both sides would declare "an end to the conflict," meaning that no more claims would be made by either side. It appeared that Clinton had the backing of Barak, whom he had briefed a week earlier.

The wide-ranging proposals were intended as a basis for a comprehensive, end-of-conflict solution to be reached before January 20, the day George W. Bush would be sworn in as Clinton's successor.

The proposals caused an immediate sensation. Ehud Barak said, on Israeli television: "It is not at all easy for us to accept them. The natural tendency is of course to want to make many changes in them." But "I believe if Yasser Arafat accepts things as they were presented by President Clinton, we are compelled to accept them."

Arafat said that his side was thoroughly reviewing the outline, but: "There are a lot of obstacles." US administration officials had met with Arafat two weeks before in Morocco and found in him a new urgency and a recognition that, if an accord were not reached now, even more violence than in the last few months would follow.[134]

This news was such that I could not refrain from writing again to Arafat myself that very day, December 26, again by rapid e-mail:

Dear President Arafat,
Salaam!
Tomorrow, Wednesday, when President Clinton is looking for responses from you and Prime Minister Barak to his proposals of last week, is a critical day for the relation between your peoples and the hopes for a just peace.

When I wrote to you on December 1, taking the line that any true agreement must be based on the rule of law, citing various key international judgments from Article 2 of the UN Charter through the recent Security Council Resolution 1322, I suggested that the Israelis needed to know in advance what would result from their acceptance of that rule of law.... I would reaffirm that now, in the context of the following.

I don't know whether this last-minute intervention by President Clinton will succeed or not. I hope it may, and would not want to see you act on it other than in those terms of the rule of law.... But I am concerned that your response to the Clinton proposal should be positive. I believe you should be stating those principles of the rule of law as fundamental conditions, but the conditions on which your answer to Clinton is yes. My point is that, if this initiative of President Clinton's fails, it should be because the Israelis say no, not that you say no. Your proposal, inclusive of all necessary conditions, should be a positive one, to them and to President Clinton.

That means assurance that Israeli acceptance of the Right of Return proclaimed in General Assembly Resolution 194 will not entail practical dismemberment of the State of Israel.... It is not the objective of the Palestinians to regain all the land lost in 1948, but to have a State in the West Bank and Gaza, and satisfaction of the rights of those who suffered injustices ever since 1948.

With best wishes,
Raymond G. Helmick, S.J.

The Clinton administration did indeed expect that responses would be qualified, yet positive enough for Israeli and Palestinian leaders to come to Washington for intense negotiations. Nabil Sha'ath, after meeting with Arafat and his advisers, gave assurance that the leadership would deliver a letter to the US consulate in Jerusalem on Wednesday detailing its reservations about the proposals. It would be, he said, neither positive nor negative. Barak said: "If Arafat says yes, we will not be able to fail to negotiate at this dramatic time for President Clinton. This answer, like the Palestinians', was taken as a 'Yes, but...'" An official in Washington described the Clinton proposals as "parameters and options," adding: "There is still a lot to be negotiated." The United States expected Barak and Arafat to come to Washington for separate negotiating sessions that officials expected to be very tough.[135]

Barak, after meeting late into the might with his advisers, prepared to accept the Clinton proposals "as a basis for discussion, provided that they will stay, as they are, a basis for discussion for the Palestinians." Nevertheless, he sought "clarification," always a useful qualifying word in such dealings, "concerning matters of essential interest to Israel."

Clinton of course, as always, was working the phones, speaking to all parties. The Palestinians had not yet issued a clear-cut reply, but forwarded a list of questions and objections.[136]

The Palestinian hesitation was over the lack of full detail in the Clinton proposals. In many ways they found them too vague. The US plans had, in fact, not yet been presented in writing, but the newspapers were full of complicated details of supposed plans.[137]

The choices were clearly among the most painful of Arafat's enduring career. Like Barak, he had to know if his people would accept the deal or believe it was good. Surely the extremist groups like Hamas would oppose it. The Knesset was not in session now, but the Likud leaders were circulating objections for MK signatures.[138]

More detail of Clinton's proposals was emerging by now. In East Jerusalem, Arab neighborhoods and the Haram al-Sharif plaza would come under Palestinian sovereignty, the Jewish neighborhoods under Israeli sovereignty. The area beneath the plaza would either be kept under Israeli sovereignty or else recognized as an area sacred to Jews where Palestinian sovereignty would be restricted and no excavations allowed. The Western Wall and the Jewish Quarter of the Old City would come under Israeli sovereignty, and Israel would have a corridor through the Armenian Quarter to the Wall.

Refugees would be able to return to the Palestinian state, not to Israel. Israel would allow an agreed number into its territory under arrangements to unify families. Most refugees would be absorbed into the countries of their present residence with international financial support.

As to borders, 95 percent of the West Bank and all of Gaza would come to the Palestinian state. Israel would annex clusters of Jewish settlements on 5 percent of the West Bank, and the Palestinians would receive in exchange territory in the Negev near the Gaza Strip.

With regard to security, the Palestinian state would not keep heavy weapons. Israel would be permitted to keep troops in the Jordan valley for six years, against threats from the East, and to send in forces in the case of an immediate threat. An international force, including Israelis, would be stationed along the Jordan border to monitor the crossing into the Palestinian state.

An "end of conflict" statement was integral to the proposals.

Responses expected from both sides had become murky by Friday December 29. The Palestinian Authority, wary of being cornered again by a powerful Israel backed one-sidedly by the United States, was willing to negotiate "under international sponsorship." Their response was expected to be positive in tone, but not an outright acceptance. Barak would offer a conditional acceptance. He took a very tough line on Israeli television, saying he would not concede sovereignty over the Temple Mount and rejecting any repatriation of refugees.

The accompanying violence did not stop. By now at least 346 had been killed.[139]

By the weekend all sides seemed to be resisting the Clinton plan. The US still hoped that Arafat would clarify his position. Popular opposition was swelling in both communities. Barak had backed away from the central point on Palestinian sovereignty over the Temple Mount. The Israeli Army was objecting to the provisions about the Jordan valley. The Fatah organization marked its thirty-sixth anniversary by totally rejecting the US plan as "originally an Israeli plan for a settlement that aims to cancel our national rights based on international law." Yet behind the scenes negotiations were still proceeding, and no one had yet expressly dismissed the idea of reaching an accord. In Washington, officials were not giving up.[140]

Arafat traveled to Washington to present his reservations to Clinton in person, bearing with him an explanatory letter.[141] The letter, a position paper, is not well known. It produced some consternation at the time, witnessed by stiffness at the obligatory photo-opportunity and grim faces at the exit, yet it was not a rejection of the Clinton "parameters" but an effort to point out where they failed to meet basic Palestinian needs in order to supplement them. The full text was published in the Palestinian paper *Al-Ayyam*.

The letter set out from the start to state why the US proposals, without clarification, failed to meet required conditions for a lasting peace. They would lead to partitioning the Palestinian state into three cantons, divided by settlements and exclusive access roads, break Palestinian Jerusalem into separate islands, divided from one another and the Palestinian state, and would require the Palestinians to give up the refugees' right of return. They included no practical security arrangements for Palestine in its relation to Israel and, in general, seemed to cater to Israeli demands while ignoring the basic Palestinian requirement, a viable state that could survive. In the Palestinian view, the Final Settlement Accord should include not just general political principles but a full account of details, mechanisms, and timetables for ending the conflict, supported by clear and effective international guarantees.

The letter took exception to Clinton's provision that, while Israel would annex 2 to 6 percent of Palestinian land in the West Bank, the compensation to the Palestinian state would be only 1 to 3 percent. The Palestinians insisted on equality in this exchange. In addition, when the Clinton proposals spoke of geographical contiguity, they actually provided it only for the Israelis, not for the Palestinians. In that connection, the Palestinians objected to the concept of "settlement blocs," which would entail the annexation of substantial portions of West Bank land between settlements, whereas the built-up settlements themselves occupied only about 2 per cent of the whole West Bank. Other vague provisions, such as leased land, muddied the nature of the US proposals, and the lack of maps made them difficult to judge. It was not clear whether the percentage counts of West Bank land that would go either to Israel or the Palestinians included occupied East Jerusalem, the areas of Jewish shrines or the Dead Sea. Palestinians had to fear that the outcome would give Israel control over extensive parts of the land, robbing the Palestinian state of any durability or connection to its own international borders. The Clinton proposals seemed to leave room for Israel to claim over 10 percent of the West Bank and even to annex all unoccupied land, to the detriment of contiguity in the Palestinian state. Areas vaguely proposed as compensation for the valuable agricultural land Israel wanted to annex were largely arid areas currently serving for toxic waste disposal.

Coming down to particulars, the letter specified objections in the Jerusalem proposals, where the formula "Arab areas to Palestine and Jewish areas to Israel" did not provide for territorial contiguity. That and the dispositions for Arab sovereignty over the Haram al-Sharif and Israeli over the Western Wall needed further clarification, particularly on whether the Western Wall was seen only as the area used for Jewish worship or continued on into the Muslim Quarter to include the tunnel that had figured in so much controversy in Netanyahu's time. The Palestinians were much concerned, too, that the character of Jerusalem as an open city be maintained.

On remaining issues the Palestinian letter raised its specific reservations. With regard to the refugee question, the Palestinians were unwilling simply to let the right of return be forfeit, or to let the Israelis be sole judges of what would be done. With regard to security, they found the proposals one-sided, attending to Israeli security but not to that of Palestinians. They welcomed the proposal for international forces to replace the Israelis over three years, but saw no need for the Israeli Army to remain a further three years, even under international supervision, in the Jordan valley or maintain its three warning stations there for a further ten years. Three years seemed an excessive time to allow for Israeli withdrawal from the Gaza Strip, especially when contrasted with Israel's success in absorbing a million immigrants from the former USSR in less time.

The letter criticized the failure of the US proposals to address such issues as water, compensation for the damages caused by the occupation, ecology, future economic relations, and other bilateral issues vital to the establishment of a comprehensive and lasting peace. The letter concluded with a firm commitment to ending the conflict as soon as possible on the basis of Security Council Resolutions 242 and 338 and in keeping with international law, but emphasized the particular difficulty of the refugee problem.[142]

Arafat's meetings with Clinton in the afternoon (for two and a half hours) and evening (another hour) left US advisers bewildered just because of the number of questions raised, but the outcome was in fact quite positive.[143] On reflection, US officials realized that Arafat had accepted Clinton's plan as a basis for future talks,[144] and that this Palestinian acceptance, qualified and conditional as it was, might well open the door for the Israelis as well to go ahead with it.[145] The Israeli reservations were at least as heavy, as was witnessed when the Chief Rabbinate reacted to these events by issuing a decree to the effect that Jewish law forbade the giving up of Israeli sovereignty over the Temple Mount.[146]

Gilead Sher, the senior negotiator on the Israeli side and Barak's chief of staff, had begun to say, by Friday January 5, that there was now too little time left to broker an accord. The dragged-out procedure of the last ten days had resulted in both sides agreeing to Clinton's framework with many reservations. In the next few days, the White House would decide whether to keep struggling with the possibility of resolving the differences. Sher had spent Thursday night and Friday with Dennis Ross and had met Clinton in the evening before returning to Israel.[147] The time pressure was all the more menacing as various opinion polls now showed Sharon with anywhere from 18 to 28 points' lead over Barak.[148]

On Sunday January 7, Clinton gave a farewell address at New York's Waldorf Astoria to the Israel Policy Forum. He spelled out in plain words the proposals that, as he revealed, he had first made to the Israeli and Palestinian negotiators on December 23 at the White House. Jerusalem, he told them, must serve as the capital of the two states, Israel and Palestine. He did not elaborate on his ideas for the Temple Mount/Haram al-Sharif, but spoke of the need for mutual respect for the religious beliefs of Jews, Muslims, and Christians. An international presence in Palestine should provide border security along the Jordan valley and monitor the fulfillment of the agreement by both sides. The Forum, a group representing the more liberal end of the American Jewish spectrum, warmly greeted his speech. To the Israelis, he said: "You discovered that your land is also their land, the homeland of two peoples. There is no choice but for you to divide this land into two states for two peoples and make the best of it."[149]

The opposition mustered its forces in Israel. On Monday January 8, tens of thousands of Israelis rallied at the Jaffa Gate against what they saw as US proposals to divide Jerusalem.[150] Barak was declaring that he was not willing to "sign over" the Temple Mount to the Palestinians, Arafat that he could not agree to a US plan "that deprives the refugees of their rights."[151]

The arrival of Dennis Ross on Thursday January 11, produced a flurry of negotiating activity. Senior officials of both sides met late at night, Ben-Ami cutting short a visit to France and meetings with Albright and Jacques Chirac in order to be present. Only nine days were left to the Clinton Presidency and already what lay beyond him seemed a gulf. A round of negotiations in Washington seemed possible, the US officials turning up the pressure by saying that Clinton's blueprint would expire once he stepped down.

Ben-Ami, Amnon Lipkin-Shahak, and Gilead Sher met for four hours with Saeb Erekat, Yasser Abed Rabbo, and Ahmed Qurei at the Erez Crossing on Friday, with a second round scheduled for Saturday. Ben-Ami, not for the first time, commented that Israel's blockade of Palestinian cities was counterproductive and of little security value. "The blockade turns Palestinian territory into a boiling pot. You can't humiliate both the masses and their leaders."[152]

The clock was ticking. The Clinton team tried to instill a sense of urgency in the face of the bleak prospects with the next US administration.[153] The Bush people were already talking of scuttling Clinton's policies as soon as they got into office.[154]

Arafat and Shimon Peres met for three hours in Gaza City on Friday January 13. Abed Rabbo described this as "serious talk, very serious—it's the most serious one in a very long time." The two discussed their differences on land and other issues, in many cases spelling out positions for the first time.[155]

Yet the death of another Israeli sufficed even now for Barak to cancel the peace talks for a precious day. The precedent set by Arafat himself years ago, when he suspended the peace process after the Baruch Goldstein massacre at the Hebron mosque, had become the norm for Israeli governments ever since. But despite the mutual recriminations, both sides were expected to resume contacts on the Tuesday in a last-ditch attempt to come up with a document outlining areas of agreement and dispute before President Clinton left office on Saturday, or at least before the Israeli election that loomed on February 6.[156]

Campaign advertising for that election had shifted into high gear on Israeli television. Barak was trailing badly, as Sharon preached the healing of rifts. Some Labor Party stalwarts were suggesting that Barak stand down as candidate in favor of Shimon Peres, and in fact Peres fared much better then Barak against Sharon in the polls.[157]

On Wednesday January 17, masked gunmen murdered the head of Palestinian television, 54-year-old Hisham Mikki, as he sat at a beachfront restaurant in Gaza. The Palestinians blamed "collaborators" with Israel, but Israel denied any involvement. Hours after the murder, Arafat met Ben-Ami in Cairo in an effort to move the peace process forward. There was no breakthrough, but the talks were described on Israeli radio as "deep and detailed."[158] But on Thursday Israeli television reported that Arafat had proposed, at his meeting with Ben-Ami, that the two sides begin intensive talks immediately. Barak convened his advisers to consider the idea, and they were expected to say yes.[159]

The violence had not let up. When the bullet-riddled body of 16-year-old Israeli Ofir Rahum was found in Ramallah, it turned out that he had been lured over the Internet to meet a Palestinian girl, who was reported then to have exulted over this death. Profound grief was manifested at the young boy's funeral next day, but the police were uncertain whether they were investigating a crime of passion or a nationalist attack, or possibly something that blurred the lines between them. Sure to his habits, though, Barak postponed by a day the meeting to deliberate on Arafat's proposal of marathon peace talks. He was waiting, too, for Foreign Minister Ben-Ami, who was off in Turkey that day.[160]

TABA, AT LAST

William Jefferson Clinton, master negotiator on whom both sides had relied throughout these many years, yielded his Presidency of the United States to George Walker Bush on Saturday January 20, 2001. Only on Sunday evening, with Clinton out of office, did the critically important talks, based on his Christmas Day "parameters" recommendation, get under way in the Egyptian resort town of Taba. High-level Israeli and Palestinian negotiators would search now, without US mediation, for the "final status" deal that had evaded them last summer. After the couple of weeks of on-again-off-again preparatory talks, casting off gloom and doom, they embraced the possibility of a comprehensive agreement. Ben-Ami, Beilin, and Lipkin-Shahak would lead the Israeli team. Barak and Peres would remain behind in Jerusalem, on call in case momentum should build up in such a way as to require their presence. Ahmed Qurei, Saeb Erekat, and Yasser Abed Rabbo would represent the Palestinians, while Arafat would travel to Egypt to be on hand for consultation.[161]

With their assistants, the negotiators sat at a long banquet table set for 42 people in Taba. The Palestinian negotiators arrived with their suitcases and bulging briefcases, set for the ten-day stretch. The Israelis preferred to return to Jerusalem to brief Barak and the Cabinet after three days, but were also ready for lengthy, substantive negotiations. Gilead Sher, who had joined them, saw the expectations as low, "only for delineating basic lines, guidelines if you will, for continuing the negotiation as it will be renewed after the elections."

Peres, in Jerusalem, warned of the danger of overreaching, and worried about the meeting producing "a comprehensive failure." Barak highlighted the differences between sides, taking a hard line to his Cabinet, to whom he promised he would: 1) never accept the right of Palestinians to return to their former homes in Israel; 2) not sign any document that would give Palestinians sovereignty over the Temple Mount; and 3) that 80 percent of the settlers in the West Bank and Gaza would remain in place under Jewish sovereignty.

Saeb Erekat told reporters: "It is clear that the negotiations will fail if this mentality rules the Israeli delegation." The Palestinians, fearing press leaks, bristled at the news that the Israelis planned, for security reasons, to re-cross the border every night to sleep in Eilat.

The discussions at Taba went through a first day on Monday, but on Tuesday the killing of two Israelis shut them down. Two Tel Aviv restaurateurs and an Israeli Arab friend were seized while visiting Tulqarem in the West Bank. Their Hamas kidnappers videotaped the whole incident. They let the Israeli Arab go but shot the two Israelis dead. Barak called his negotiators back to Jerusalem, calling the attack "horrendous." Ephraim Sneh commented that the break was "a pause, not a suspension. At a time when there is a glimmer of hope, it would be a mistake to stop because of a few nasty terrorists." Yet Barak insisted that the Palestinian Authority had indirect responsibility for the murders by reason of letting terrorist squads be at large in areas of Palestinian responsibility.

Ahmed Qurei expected the talks to resume next day. The negotiators, he said, were "continually haggling over fractions of land" that would either be annexed by Israel or incorporated into a Palestinian state. The formula for the division or sharing of Jerusalem was creating the most visible rifts. The Barak government had said in advance that it would negotiate within the Clinton parameters, which called for Palestinian sovereignty in Arab neighborhoods, but on Monday, unexpectedly, the Israeli officials revived the idea of some sort of joint sovereignty for the historic city center and its holy sites. The Palestinians quickly rejected this and reiterated their demand for sovereignty over all Arab districts and religious sites in East Jerusalem. The "holy basin" was discussed, an area larger than the walled city itself, including religious and archaeological sites just outside the walls.[162]

The postponement of talks lasted a full two days. The killing of the two Israelis had broken the momentum of discussion. Barak predicted that the negotiation would last "several more days," but "with the intention of resuming them" after the election on February 6. Yet Sharon, as his steamroller bore down on that election, derided the very thought of such talks. Yossi Sarid had come down to Taba now to join in the process. Representatives of the UN and the European Union were in Taba to monitor the talks, but no US officials.[163] In Washington the word was that the new

244   The Failed Negotiations

Bush team was tiptoeing around, evading the Middle East question, not a participant at all. Barak and Arafat both took pains to keep the new secretary of state, Colin Powell, informed, but no one else in the administration was listening.[164]

The talks resumed on Thursday, but with little remaining hope for a full accord after the 48-hour hiatus. Little time remained for a comprehensive, detailed settlement that would include the demarcation of borders and the compensation or repatriation of refugees.[165] The electoral campaign remained lackluster, with the violence continuing and only eleven days left. Sharon led Barak by 16 to 18 points in the polls.[166]

On January 27, as the Shabbat evening approached, Barak called a halt. The negotiations concluded after a week of stop-and-start work. The senior Israeli and Palestinian officials joined in saying that they had "never been close to reaching" a final peace accord, but had simply lacked sufficient time to conclude one before the Israeli election on February 6. Both sides said that Barak and Arafat would likely meet in Stockholm within days, their first meeting since the dinner at Barak's home just days before Sharon set off the violence in late September.

Ben-Ami described the talks as "the most fruitful, constructive, profound negotiations in this phase of the peace process." He hoped the two sides would pick up again after the election, though like everyone else he expected Barak to lose. Ahmed Qurei spoke of the genuine effort at serious negotiations, and believed it could help to restore trust between the two sides. The Palestinians also hoped to resume negotiation after the election, even with Sharon. George Bush spoke for seven minutes to Barak on the phone of his "desire to see peace in the region based on a secure Israel."

Miguel Moratinos, who had monitored the Taba meetings on behalf of the European Union, said: "The atmosphere at the outset was extremely warm, and extremely serious, with a real political will to strike a deal." Yet the Palestinians felt that the Israelis had been internally divided about their own aims. Tempers had flared when the Palestinians said the Israelis were toughening their positions. Gilead Sher, the Prime Minister's chief of staff, had frequently left the room to confer by telephone with Barak in Jerusalem, and had always left word that nothing decided in his absence could be taken as the position of the Israeli government.

A Western diplomat added, after speaking with both delegations: "Barak decided that making the concessions Israel would need to make would be suicide politically." The negotiators were striving to ensure that future negotiations would start from where these had left off. They wanted to create a detailed, permanent record of the talks' progress, "a kind of formal or informal 'deposit,' as was done with Syria and elsewhere, for the collective memory of the two societies," said Moratinos. Ben-Ami regretted: "If we had quality political time, we could have definitely reached an agreement."[167]

SHARON

And so it was over. Some interesting recriminations followed. Dennis Ross told of having warned Ben-Ami, then responsible for security in Israel, the day before Sharon's visit to the Temple Mount of what would likely follow. "I can think of a lot of bad ideas," he had said, "but I can't think of a worse one." The Palestinian Authority released a document saying that Ross himself was architect to a policy that substituted process for substance. The United States, it said, had failed to realize that negotiators could not succeed while Palestinians lived in misery and Israeli settlers, with "green lawns and swimming pools," remained occupiers of Palestinian territory.[168]

Arafat had gone on to the World Economic Forum at Davos, Switzerland, where he delivered an impassioned denunciation of Israel's "savage and barbarous war" against the Palestinians. That did it for Barak, who declared that he would not meet Arafat in Stockholm or anywhere in Europe, as the EU diplomats were urging him to do. He suspended Israel's participation in the peace effort altogether until after the February 6 election.

Shimon Peres was present for Arafat's Davos speech as well, as the Palestinian leader intoned: "The current government in Israel is waging and has waged for the past four months a savage and barbaric war as well as a blatant and fascist military aggression against our Palestinian people." These two, Arafat and Peres, had stood together, along with Yitzhak Rabin, to receive the Nobel Peace Prize after Oslo. Peres responded: "I must admit I came prepared for a wedding, not a divorce," and urged Arafat to build on what had happened at Taba so as to conclude a peace agreement in the coming weeks. "Let us restrain our voices and see the horizon."

The two finished with a handshake, to a standing ovation from the political and business leaders of the world. But that horizon was filled now with Ariel Sharon, and a practical void in the United States. In the polls, at that point, Peres stood neck and neck with Sharon, while Barak was still behind by 16 to 18 points.[169]

Peres, of course, did not replace Barak as Labor candidate. Barak settled that by February 1, painting Peres in ugly colors as other Labor politicians denounced one another. By this time Barak was a full 20 points behind Sharon in the polls. Ben-Ami, himself another possible substitute candidate, bewailed: "This election is supposed to be a referendum on peace but it isn't. Are we discussing issues? Very little. Everything is personal.... The candidate is mute on substance.... The media are magnifying banalities to suggest a family feud."[170]

Sharon easily bested Barak when the election came, taking 62.5 percent of the vote to Barak's 37.4 percent. The election had the largest victory margin but also the smallest turnout of any in the nation's history, only 62 percent bothering to vote, as against the 80 percent who had voted in 1999. The Israeli Arabs had sat on their hands.[171]

But with no separate election for a new Knesset membership, Sharon had to deal with the fractured Knesset he inherited from the 1999 election. It is doubtful that he could long have survived politically with only the right-wing and religious parties in his government. Immediately he began casting about for a Grand Coalition, a unity government with Labor. Barak had already been looking for this himself since October. Now he announced his departure from politics,[172] setting off a feeding frenzy among other Labor politicians who would like to succeed him. If Avraham Burg had won the post, it was feared he might prevent a coalition with Likud.[173] But Barak took his resignation back when Sharon offered him the defense ministry in a unity government, asking Shimon Peres to serve as foreign minister and dangling before him the illusory possibility of reopening negotiation with the Palestinians. Yet when Arafat got on the phone to Sharon and suggested such a resumption of talks, Sharon answered him: "This matter is in your hands," and reinstated Barak's earlier policy that a total cessation of Palestinian violence must precede any further peace dealings. The Labor Party, with its talk of coalition, was truly providing the only means by which Sharon could survive in government. Among its leaders, Yossi Beilin and Shlomo Ben-Ami recognized this and objected from the start, saying a unity government would deadlock over the peace issue, and that deadlock would lead to increased violence on the West Bank and Gaza.[174]

Not surprisingly, Palestinian violence increased as hopes dimmed, and Israeli counter-measures escalated, even before Sharon took over his post. In the atmosphere of rising violence, Peres, the great enthusiast for a Grand Coalition within the Labor Party, claimed that 80 percent of the party wanted it.[175]

It was not until March 7, after yet a third turn-around by Barak, who turned down the defense ministry to resign again from political life,[176] and an appeal to the 1,700-member governing body of the Labor Party,[177] that

Sharon could present his Grand Coalition government and take office. He promised that he would provide security for Israel and its citizens while fighting diligently against violence and terrorism. Seven parties took part in his coalition, giving him a majority of 73 seats in the 120-member body.[178]

Already Colin Powell had been rebuffed when, visiting the region for the first time as secretary of state, he called for an easing of the blockade on Gaza.[179] It took Sharon less than a week before he was blockading Ramallah, his first major action against the Palestinians after his inauguration, blocking off streets with trenches and mounds of earth, establishing checkpoints backed by tanks and armored personnel carriers. Sharon claimed this was nothing new, that he was simply foiling a car bombing in Jerusalem after members of a group plotting it were arrested.[180] We would soon see how successfully Sharon's policies would make Israel safe for its citizens.

Part III
Aftermath

8
The web of civility dissolves: early February to September 11, 2001

THE JESSE JACKSON VISIT, JULY 2002

In late July of 2002 I spent several days in the Middle East, traveling this time as one of a delegation with Rev. Jesse Jackson. We were several American Christian clergy, among them representatives of the World Council of Churches and the (American) National Council of Churches, with Rabbis Steven Jacobs and Leonard Beerman, both of Los Angeles, and Dr. Nazir Khaja, past President of the American Muslim Council. This was the sort of group that had a near guarantee of a cordial reception both from Israelis and Palestinians.

Our arrival was on a Saturday afternoon, and by the time we had made our way from the airport and got settled into our hotel, the Notre Dame Hostel close by the northwest corner of the Old City, the Saturday sunset had come and the Shabbat rest was over. Israeli television invited our Rev. Jackson to be interviewed early in the evening, and we all walked down the Jaffa Road to get to the studio.

The deserted street gave us our first sign of how changed was life in the Jewish city. Where were the people who would normally be out on a Shabbat evening? Hardly anyone was in sight. People feared, in this terrible time, to come out to public places.

Everything in Israeli life confirmed this. Friends I had met on an earlier visit during January that year, many of them strong peace activists, had told me how getting on a bus raised the prospect of the last moments of one's life, and that they went all lengths to stop their teenage children from riding buses, from going to movies, dances, markets, or eating places. No one could lead a normal life. Fear of violence, especially now of the suicide bomber, on a bus, in a car, walking along the street, entering the restaurant or theater, tracked every step.

A fierce anger resulted from this, welling up through Israeli society and affecting attitudes toward every Palestinian. The Palestinian had lost all human attributes and, in ordinary Israeli perception, represented only danger.

Our Jackson group went out to Ramallah to see Arafat and request that he come out with us to the courtyard of his headquarters and make the renunciation of terrorism that he is so often asked to give (and in fact does quite regularly), in Arabic and in front of the international press. That was done, but on the way we had a good look at Palestinian life under the curfew that had been their regular experience since March of 2002.

The Kalandia checkpoint, which we had to pass on the way into Ramallah, had long lines of people and vehicles waiting many chaotic hours under the broiling July sun with no amenities of any sort—no shelter, no toilets. We of course had the red-carpet treatment. An Israeli army jeep led our small bus through the maze of streets, first to Saeb Erekat's home and then to the Arafat Muqada (HQ). We would not have been able to get there without this escort, since most streets were cut off by deep trenches and heaps of rubble, and you had to know which were open to find your way.

No one was out on the street in this city of some 140,000. Had people come out, they could be shot for breaking curfew, even in this place that had been transferred to their own authority and then reoccupied. Windows were closed. No cars could be seen, as everyone knew that a car left on the street would be rolled over and flattened by a tank. There was no regular water supply, for drinking or any of the obvious needs such as flushing toilets in houses full of many small children, no electricity to provide air conditioning to these middle-class dwellings, and the temperature that day was 104 degrees Fahrenheit.

That had been the basic experience of Palestinians in this or other West Bank cities, that July of 2002, for far more days than not since the previous March. Some cities, like Nablus, had had it without interruption, other than for a few hours of shopping time, for as much as nine weeks as of that time. When, a day later in our Jackson visit, we went to Bethlehem, the curfew was lifted for that one day by reason of our presence, and that allowed the students of Bethlehem University, in these last days of July, to complete the final exams of their semester that should have been taken in May.

The Palestinian experience of violence through this time has exceeded that of their Israeli neighbors by far. Most of the deaths of those first months of *intifada* after Mr. Sharon's September 28 adventure into early 2001 had been Palestinian. Once suicide bombs developed as response to the tank, artillery, rocket, and helicopter gunship pounding by the Israelis, we began to hear of more numerous Israeli deaths and the numbers settled eventually to approximately three Palestinians killed for every Israeli, but it would be some time before that ratio was reached. For much of the first year most of the deaths were Palestinian.

In Palestinian towns this meant heavy armored assaults at any time, tanks firing heavy artillery into houses, frequent house demolitions, and the devastation of whole urban centers by concentrated artillery. It meant assassination runs by helicopter, multiple rockets fired into crowded civilian places with small concern by Israeli army or authorities—or public—about the multiple killings of unarmed civilians that normally accompanied each of these extra-judicial killings of suspects. To an extent unimagined by Israelis, no Palestinian's life under these conditions is ever for a moment safe.

While this goes on, Palestinians see more and more of their land confiscated and new colonies of their enemies encroaching further and further into territory they have lived in and cultivated for countless centuries. Add to this the calculated humiliation that makes up the fabric of life for every Palestinian, harassed at every turn by Israeli soldiers, teenagers or in their twenties, who take out their own disgruntlement by brutalizing those subjected to their control. The abasement of their fathers, witnessed as a constant of their lives by horrified children, drives them to frenzied hatred of those who inflict it.

One begins to see the depth of despair that characterizes Palestinian life. Economic life, as much as it is devastated for Israelis, hardly exists for Palestinians any more at all. Israelis wonder where the suicide bombings come from, but have little sense that it results from this despair.

THE NARRATIVES

Both sides have narratives that intensify the emotions that these hard circumstances inflict on each. For Israelis, the story is that Arafat turned down the generous offer made at Camp David by Barak for no other reason than that he had decided on staging a violent uprising instead. During our Jackson visit we met the responsible Labor leadership in the coalition government. Shimon Peres, foreign minister at the time, told us that story twice in the course of three-quarters of an hour's conversation. Defense Minister Benyamin Ben-Eliezer also told us the story twice as explanation of why he, after trying for years to be a friend and cultivate Arafat, now saw no hope of progress so long as Arafat remained the Palestinian leader. Rabbi Michael Melchior, the always generous-minded minister of religious affairs in the government, and with him Rabbi Michael Rosen, the genial diplomat who, more than any other, brought about the establishment of diplomatic relations with the Vatican and was the chief Israeli sponsor of the Pope's visit to Israel in March 2000, also told us twice over this same story of Arafat's malfeasance in turning down a good offer in favor of terrorism. When challenged on it, as a distortion of what happened at

Camp David and after, they showed themselves both puzzled and indignant that anyone should question it.

But the story is instructive as to where the priorities need to be for Palestinians who wish to return to the serious negotiation of their freedom and peace with the Israelis. Their first needs are to disabuse the Israeli public of that false narrative that so much further embitters Israeli anger toward them, and then to persuade Israelis that it is not their program, as Palestinians, to kill them. On the Jackson trip, we had the opportunity to talk of these things at some length with Arafat and his whole cabinet.

The Palestinians have a narrative too, one that may also be exaggerated but which has much concrete evidence to support it. Added to the sense of betrayal that all the years of further confiscations and destruction of their land, the growth of settlements, new isolation of their cities and villages, and deconstruction of their economy and institutions have brought upon them since the Oslo development gave them hope, their story is this. Ariel Sharon, leader of all those Israelis who want no reconciliation with Palestinians but desire instead to take away from them all they have left, deliberately set flame to the combustible tinder of frustration and despair in Palestinian society by his calculated action of September 28, 2000. The subsequent boiling over of Palestinian outrage, in the violence that has escalated ever since, had exactly the effect Sharon had planned, as a power bid for himself. It panicked the Israeli public to such an extent that it elected him to crack down on Palestinians.

But the narrative does not end there. Instead, far from trying to restore calm and end the outbreak of violence, Sharon, in this narrative, continued to stir the pot every time there has been any chance of calming the storm. Instances of this are legion, but the outstanding instances have been in November 2001, and July 2002 (just days before our visit that month). On both of those occasions, the leadership of the various militant factions, Hamas, Islamic Jihad, and the Al-Aqsa Martyrs' Brigade, have agreed, at the bidding of the Palestinian Authority, to put an end to suicide bombings and attacks on Israeli civilians in Israel proper. And on both occasions, within hours of the Israeli government's knowing that this agreement had been made, Israeli forces have made assassination attacks, killing multiple innocents in the process, and shattering the agreements in a single blow.

Is this actually the case? Alex Fishman wrote about the episode of November, 2001. He is the far from dovelike security commentator of the Israeli daily *Yediot Aharonot*, a paper that has basically put its own seal of approval on the policy of "targeted killings," as carried out by both the Barak and Sharon governments. Fishman himself has close contacts in the army and the security services and writes from within the military and security establishment's own terminology and way of thinking. He writes of "the liquidation of Mahmud Abu Hanoud, the so-called 'No. 1 wanted Hamas terrorist,'" questioning what makes a terrorist number one, two, or three. Closely associated with the Abu Hanoud assassination was the death of five children killed by an IDF explosive charge at Khan Yunis. Israeli army analysts had no doubt that they had now, as a result, to prepare with dread for a new mass terrorist attack in response.[1]

The same pattern was repeated in July, 2002, when Hamas leader Sheikh Ahmed Yassin made an unprecedented public call for a ceasefire with Israel. That call was the culmination of long, patient negotiations between the Palestinian Authority and the Hamas leadership, aimed at achieving a ceasefire between the Palestinians and Israel, putting an end to suicide bombings and paving the way to a resumption of some kind of political process. Within hours the Sharon government sent an F-16 fighter-bomber to launch a 500 pound missile in the middle of the night at the sleeping inhabitants of an apartment building in Gaza, killing the Hamas military chief Salah Shehadeh but also 14 other persons, nine of them children, and wounding 140 others. The attack had all the marks of deliberately sabotaging the anti-violence accord between Hamas and the Palestinian Authority. Deputy Defense Minister Dalia Rabin-Pelosof resigned from the government in protest, charging the Sharon government with destroying the life work of the late Yitzhak Rabin, her father. Even the Bush White House noticed that something was wrong with this and gently chided the Sharon government.[2]

Does the Sharon government, then, want to prolong the violence, and does it calculatedly time its own violence to provoke more from the Palestinians themselves? This is certainly the general Palestinian conviction, and there is much to speak for it. Even when there has been a formal *hudna*, or truce, maintained for a full nine weeks by Hamas, Islamic Jihad, and the Al-Aqsa Martyrs' Brigade in the Autumn of 2003, the Sharon government maintained a regular drumbeat of assassinations, without compunction at the killing of numerous innocents ("collateral damage") until these organizations were goaded into new suicide attacks. An undeclared six-week stilling of Palestinian violence later in the year met exactly the same fate. Throughout, even when the Palestinian bombings were at their height, the margin of three Palestinian deaths to every Israeli killed has been maintained.

Among Palestinians, this narrative, coming on top of their disillusionment at the disappointment of all their hopes during the Oslo years, breeds a profound despair. The Fishman article in *Yediot Aharonot* of November 23, 2001, recognized this:

> In the fast widening "pockets of despair," to be found all over the [occupied] territories, there is an inexhaustible supply of potential suicide bombers. While in the past Israel's Military Intelligence tried to keep up a current numerical estimate of the arsenal of potential suiciders, nowadays the terrorist organizations have no problem to get as many as they want, and can even afford to pick and choose among the potential recruits.[3]

There are rejectionists in both the Israeli and Palestinian communities, people who want no part of a peace agreement with the other, who will do whatever they can to prevent one, who reject the other's legitimacy as a people or nation and wish only to destroy the other or reduce it to simple subjection. That is true of the religious fanatics, Hamas or Islamic Jihad, and of several of the small and relatively impotent secular organizations on the Palestinian side. It is not true of the Al-Aqsa Martyrs' Brigade, whose actions, even suicide bombings, are directed against occupation, and not against the existence of Israel. But all these organizations act as rebels even against the Palestinian Authority itself, which has little leverage to control them so long as its people are kept in such despair. It is a different matter if, on the Israeli side, the rejectionists are the government itself, as the narrative so widely believed among Palestinians would hold, using all its power to see that the conflict is kept stridently alive.

This suggests priorities for any Israelis who want to see the peace and security of their own country. They need to see to it that such rejectionism and sabotage is not in fact the policy of their government. And they need to address that despair among Palestinians, not by driving them still deeper into despair but by treating them with basic humanity. Only so will Israel itself find peace.

DESCENT INTO HELL

How has it got so far?

The new governments that replaced the Clinton and Barak administrations in early 2001 were a death-knell to the negotiations that had proceeded so far and come so close to resolution of the conflict by the time the Taba meetings ended. The new Bush administration in the United States ostentatiously washed its hands of the Middle East, disowning and denigrating anything that had been done by Clinton and declaring that it had no interest in nation building or in mediating such conflicts as this. The resulting blank in US policy was not, in fact, a blank at all, but a license to the new Sharon government to do anything it pleased. The mantra for President Bush, whatever Sharon's government did, was: "The Israelis have the right to defend themselves."

In Israel, Ariel Sharon, having promised Israelis their personal safety under his government, proceeded not to provide it. Whatever military restraints might have been exercised during Ehud Barak's heavy military crackdown on the Palestinians, hard as they might be to discern, were now rescinded by Sharon. He boasted that he had never shaken hands with Arafat, even on such occasions as the Wye conference of 1999. As prime minister, he would not deal with him at all, and George Bush tamely followed his lead by never inviting Arafat to the White House or dealing with him in any way. Sharon let it be known that no Palestinian state, if any such should come into being at all, would ever possess more than 42 percent of the West Bank. After his March 13 blockade of Ramallah, he quickly placed every village and town in the West Bank and Gaza under practical siege. As early as March 16, 2001, MK Naomi Chazan, Speaker of the Knesset, complained of these measures: "never before has their implementation been so cruel and senseless," a case of "collective punishment."[4]

As savagery spread, reporter Gideon Levy remarked how Israelis as diverse as Rehavam Ze'evi, Yossi Sarid, Shimon Peres, and Ariel Sharon were all singing the same chorus, that Israel had to "do something" about terrorism, meaning in all cases, bombing: "bombing population centers of helpless civilians." To call these "surgical strikes" to hit "point-specific targets" of "terrorist facilities" was simply false, Levy observed, when in fact "entire cities are plunged into terror and blackout, neighborhoods are emptied of their residents and dozens of innocent civilians are hurt."[5]

Large percentages of Israelis had come to accept such draconian response. According to a Peace Index survey of March 28–29, when asked "Do you support or oppose the policy of closure or encirclement of Palestinian cities and towns?" 71 percent of the Jewish respondents answered that they were very supportive (46 percent) or quite supportive (25 percent) of this policy, while only 16 percent were opposed and 13 percent were unsure.[6]

On April 6, Mohammed Dahlan, Palestinian security chief in the Gaza Strip, agreed, at the urging of the United States and on Arafat's orders, to meet with high-ranking Israeli commanders at the US Ambassador's residence in Herzlia for "security coordination." On his return, in company with his two top lieutenants in US embassy cars, he came to the Erez crossing point onto the Gaza Strip, where it was necessary to change cars, walking across the 100 yards between the Israeli and Palestinian checkpoints. Israelis in watchtowers all around the well-lit area opened fire with machine guns. The firefight lasted three full hours before Sharon, reacting very slowly to telephone calls from King Abdullah of Jordan, President Mubarak of Egypt, the European Union, and some very rough language from Secretary of State Colin Powell, called a ceasefire. The Israelis had a full repertoire of excuses for this episode, but for the Palestinians this was a benchmark of treachery.[7]

With the ever reliable Rabbi Ovadia Yosef, spiritual leader of Shas, declaring in a sermon ahead of the weekend Passover holiday that God must annihilate the Arabs and rain missiles down on them—"It is forbidden to be merciful to them, you must give them missiles, with relish—annihilate them. Evil ones, damnable ones!"[8]—the Israeli army began to face a crisis. Reserve officers, organized in a movement called *Yesh Gevul*, "There is a limit," announced their refusal to serve in the West Bank or Gaza. The number of declared refuseniks who had formed this organization was as yet only 100, but reporters estimated that 2,500 had actually refused to serve since the Palestinian uprising began in September.[9]

The Mitchell Commission brought in its long-awaited report early in May, recommending that Israel should freeze all settlement construction in the occupied territories and lift its economic blockade of Palestinian areas. It called on the Palestinians to take immediate steps to arrest and jail "terrorists" operating within its jurisdiction, and to take "concrete action" to make clear that it will make a "100 percent effort to prevent terrorist operations." It recommended further that Israel transfer to the Palestinian Authority all the tax revenues that it had been withholding since the beginning of the *intifada* as a way of starving out the Palestine Authority, and allow 140,000 Palestinians who were employed in Israel before the start of the *intifada* to return to their jobs. It criticized harshly the Israeli army's policy of demolishing homes in Palestinian areas. The Israeli government, it said, should "ensure that the security forces and settlers refrain from the destruction of homes and roads, as well as trees and other agricultural property in the Palestinian areas." It urged a "cooling-off period" to allow both sides to implement confidence-building measures, some of which had already been detailed in the Sharm el-Sheikh agreement of the previous October that had set up the committee.

But the report shied away from recommending an international force of observers or protectors, knowing that the Bush administration would veto any such proposal. And it escaped stating the obvious responsibility of Ariel Sharon for igniting the violence through his visit, with his huge and heavily armed escort, to the Temple Mount in September, saying that the killing had begun only the following day when Israeli troops shot dead seven Palestinians on the sacred plaza. It concluded only that Sharon's escapade was provocative and "poorly timed."[10]

The Mitchell Commission report made small progress. Foreign Minister Shimon Peres asserted that Israel backed the report even as he rejected out of hand the settlement freeze that was at its heart.[11] Back in Washington, government treated the report as a very hot potato, gingerly touching around its edges as the Bush administration tried to find ways of reacting to it, wondering whether to get involved or not.[12]

And then an event further transformed the situation. On May 18 a 21-year-old Palestinian stood in the large crowd waiting to pass through a security check at the entrance to a shopping mall in the Israeli coastal town of Netanya. At about 11.30 in the morning he detonated the explosive belt he was wearing, killing five Israelis and wounding more than 100 others, in the most horrifying suicide bombing Israel had witnessed yet during this *intifada*.

By evening, Israel had launched its F-16 fighter-bombers against targets all over the West Bank and Gaza, the first such full-scale aerial attack on the civilian population since 1967. Nine Palestinians were known at once to have been killed, one in Ramallah, and eight, all of them police officers, in a raid on the police station and adjacent prison in Nablus.[13]

Secretary of State Powell responded to this turn of events with urgent appeals for calm and an end to violence, but he was in such a policy straitjacket that he had to assert once again the Bush administration's non-policy, that a more active US role would be imprudent so long as violence raged.[14]

US Vice President Richard Cheney himself took umbrage at this use of US F-16s against civilian targets: "I think they should stop, both sides should stop, and think about where they are headed here, and recognize that down this road lies disaster." Just hours later Israeli tanks shelled the home of Palestinian security chief Jibril Rajoub, who had frequently taken part in peace negotiations with the Jewish state. Cheney's comments called into question Israel's strategy of combating Palestinian guns, bombs, and mortars with sophisticated and devastating weaponry, much of it supplied or paid for by the United States. But he declined to say what, if anything, Washington would do to force Israel to keep the aircraft grounded. "It's a very delicate situation," he said.[15]

EFFORTS TO MAKE CONTACT

I had made my own effort to contact the new Bush administration even before the January Inauguration Day. I had been accustomed to dealing with the Reagan administration, with the elder Bush and with Clinton through either their chiefs of staff or their national security advisers for many years, and so it was to Condoleezza Rice that I wrote on January 8, 2001, enclosing copies of the letters I had written to Arafat, Barak, and Clinton during December. A response came from an assistant saying no plans for the Middle East would be made until after the administration took office, and I have never heard further from her or her office since.

On the day, May 31, 2001, that Faisal Husseini died, unexpectedly, of a heart attack while in Kuwait, I wrote to Colin Powell of the importance of Orient House:

> The death this morning of Faisal Husseini entails not only great loss for the Palestinian people but a serious danger for the peace. This should concern our policy makers in the United States.
>
> Your predecessor, James Baker, so much appreciated the leadership of Mr Husseini for the peace, and the importance of Jerusalem in the relation between Israelis and Palestinians, that he enshrined the position of Orient House, as representation in Jerusalem of the PLO (never of the PA), in the agreement that created the Madrid Conference....
>
> Now, with Mr Husseini's death, the forces in Israeli society represented by Jerusalem Mayor Olmert, Prime Minister Sharon, Party Leader Ze'evi,[16] and government Minister Avigdor Lieberman[17] are likely to seize the occasion to shut down Orient House and reinforce Israeli claims to all of Jerusalem.

Orient House was not immediately seized, and I felt sure that US intervention had played a role in saving it.

THE PERIOD OF "CEASEFIRES"

Sharon, after the F-16 bombing raids of March 18, declared a unilateral ceasefire on May 22, saying Israeli forces would only shoot in self-defense and would no longer initiate operations.[18] The Palestinians at first dismissed Sharon's declaration as a media ploy, especially since he had simultaneously, in the same rare television address to his nation, rejected out of hand the Mitchell Commission's call for a freeze on settlements.[19] Following an Israeli disaster unrelated to the fighting, on

May 24, when an ill-constructed wedding hall in Jerusalem collapsed, killing 23 persons and injuring over 300 more, the Palestinian Authority communicated its "deep condolences to the state and the Israeli people" for the victims, and instructed its own department of civil defense to mount rescue parties and assist the Israelis in searching through the rubble for survivors and for more bodies.[20] But this did little to humanize relations as, on June 1, another monstrous suicide bombing traumatized the peoples of the region.

This was an attack particularly on youth, as teenagers, many of them the children of recent Russian immigrants, crowded a popular beachside club, the Dolphinarium, in Tel Aviv late on a Friday evening. Numbers of deaths, first reported as "at least 17," soon climbed to 20 besides the bomber himself. The injured numbered 120 more.

This constituted a test of Sharon's ceasefire declaration. Would he refrain from retaliating? Palestinians everywhere braced for an attack. Sharon, using the Shabbat rest to postpone the decision another 24 hours, summoned his senior cabinet members to convene on the Sunday morning, but they were expected to rescind the ceasefire.[21] The bombing was first attributed to Islamic Jihad, but they denied the charge and Sharon, of course, was anxious to blame it directly on Arafat, as usual. Israeli officials, pleading for Arafat somehow to take hold of the situation, recognized: "The problem is that the bombers want a massive Israeli retaliation. They want a war."[22]

Clearly they did. The rejectionists on both sides of this conflict know how to join in a common cause to prevent any flinching from the fight. Though they differ from one another on which of the two peoples they would like to destroy, they know how to play off one another's most savage instincts to provoke the cyclical retaliations that keep the violence in play.

Arafat now called, himself, for an immediate and unconditional ceasefire, deploring and condemning the Tel Aviv attack. Israel's government declared itself unready to accept words only, demanding deeds, and in fact one specific deed: the rearrest of all those Islamic militants who had been released the previous Fall.[23] But while Arafat urgently pressed his police to hold the line against violence,[24] the US administration shrank back from sending any high-level diplomatic mission.

The question of sending CIA Director George Tenet back to the area was in the air. Tenet had successfully fostered cooperation between Israeli and Palestinian security forces during the Clinton months earlier in the crisis. The Israeli government had told the Bush administration that it was not eager to see his intervention again.[25]

Akiva Eldar, in *Ha'aretz*, wrote of how this Palestinian child-killer had now placed the conflagration on the very doorsteps of European and US leaders at the very moment when all the world was expecting a new Israeli invasion of the Gaza Strip.[26] Danny Rubinstein recognized the obstacles facing Arafat in any attempt to stem the violence. Who would be responsive to his ceasefire commands? Suicide bombings and terrorist attacks on civilians in Israel came not from any agency under his command but from the extremists of Hamas and Islamic Jihad. The firing at Israeli military and the settlers in the West Bank and Gaza came mainly from the Tanzim youth movement within the ranks of Fatah, over which Arafat should have influence, but that influence was hard to wield because, in the eyes of nearly all Palestinians these attacks were legitimate struggle against an occupying power.[27]

Amid these extravagant pressures, the mutual ceasefires held. This constituted, for myself, perhaps the most telling evidence to date that Sharon should not be classified simply among the rejectionists, however many members of his following may be just that. The quiet was fragile, and broken by several hours of gunfire between Israeli forces and Palestinians in Gaza, as all roads were stopped and people prevented from moving in or out of Palestinian communities.[28] But the Bush administration relented, and announced on Tuesday, June 5, that George Tenet would indeed go to the Middle East in an effort to maintain calm.[29]

Europeans made their weight felt now, as Israel appeared unable to prevent some 24 security experts from the European Union from taking up their posts to monitor the ceasefire at two key Palestinian flashpoints, Beit Jala and Rafah. They were organized by Alistair Cooke, security adviser to EU special envoy Miguel Moratinos, with the encouragement of Arafat's close adviser Nabil Sha'ath.[30] Most observers feared that the lull in violence would not last, Nabil Sha'ath describing the situation as a "tinderbox," and Peres criticizing Sharon and Ben-Eliezer for their constant verbal attacks on Arafat. "I think," said Peres, "he represents 4 million Palestinians."[31]

Despite continued outbreaks of violence the security men from the two sides came to agreement on the Tenet proposals by late on Monday June 11. The proposed ceasefire would come into effect on June 13. It was greeted with skepticism,[32] but the uneasy truce so begun was the first serious effort to calm the situation since the violence had broken out.[33]

FATE OF THE TENET CEASEFIRE

Now began the argument over how much ceasefire quiet was quiet enough. Featured in the Tenet "workplan" was the idea of a timeline for the "cooling-off period" that, in turn, had featured in the Mitchell Commission's report. An initial week of no violence was prescribed, and a period of waiting thereafter before serious negotiation could begin. I wrote a memo on June 22, addressed to both Condoleezza Rice and Colin Powell, summarizing much of my own convictions on the Middle East, such things as have already appeared in these pages, but breaking no new ground. I had had no response as yet to anything I had written to this administration, so this memo was really just an attempt to open a dialogue.

As Sharon headed off to the United States, by way of Great Britain, on June 24, there was another assassination, the first since the ceasefire. Palestinian militant Osama Jawabri, 29, of the Al-Aqsa Martyrs' Brigade was killed when his cell phone exploded as he made a call. Arafat at this stage was busily arresting Palestinian militants, including members of his own Fatah movement.[34]

Accustomed as he was to praise in Washington for anything he might say or do, Sharon was disappointed to find less than complete agreement from Bush when he went to the White House. The President urged that Sharon be more receptive to political steps taken by the Palestinians, but Sharon insisted that the Palestinians had not done enough to stop the violence. He wanted to see a full ten days of total absence of violence before beginning any cooling-off period. The difference between the two leaders was put in terms of the United States wanting 100 percent effort, while Sharon demanded 100 percent results.[35]

Powell, traveling to the Middle East, declared on his way that it was entirely up to Sharon to decide when the level of violence was sufficiently low to progress beyond the current level of ceasefire.[36] But in Israel, officials expressed shock, surprise, and recrimination that Bush should have disagreed publicly with Sharon. What the United States had seen as a minor rift was described in Israel as a growing chasm, essentially weakening Israel's alliance with Washington.[37]

Powell, arrived in Jerusalem for his 36-hour visit, began laying out plans to monitor the truce. He set out a timetable: seven days, rather than Sharon's ten, of absolute quiet, followed by six weeks more of "cooling off"—seven long weeks in all—before the sides would engage each other in peace talks. How the reduction of violence would be measured, as quiet enough or not, was unclear.[38]

Arafat sat down with the international press during the Powell visit, refusing to be baited into any negative comment on Sharon or on the Bush team. Asked his reaction to a hint by Sharon that he might agree to the Palestinians getting 56 percent of the East Bank rather than the 42 percent that he had earlier suggested as a maximum,[39] Arafat widened his eyes in mock delight and whistled. "Fifty what?" he asked in English. "Fifty-six," the reporters replied. Grimacing, Arafat said: "Fifty-six? Whew. Too much!"[40]

Yet Powell left uncertainty behind him over the timeline of the ceasefire as he left.[41] Nabil Sha'ath doubted that the two sides would ever sit down together so long as it was entirely up to Sharon to decide. He told how he had challenged Powell: "Can you guarantee one day with zero violence in Washington, D.C.?"[42]

The Tenet ceasefire, begun June 13, fragile as it was, deserves our attention. While so much violence continued throughout this time that people questioned the reality of the ceasefire, they kept speaking of it as the status quo until the horrendous suicide bombing of the Sbarro pizzeria in Jerusalem on August 10. It was the best chance that has existed since the unleashing of the *intifada* in September 2000. The way its tenuous tenure was broken gives us some measure of who bore responsibility for the continuance and escalation of violence. It tests either of the two narratives: the Israeli account that Arafat is responsible for all violent actions of Palestinians, or the Palestinian narrative that the violence is the deliberate choice of Sharon, who stirs the pot every time there threatens to be some respite.

The assassination policy is one key. This is undeniably a government-initiated activity. Its purpose, in the Israeli account, is to preserve the safety of Israeli citizens—the central promise made by Sharon when he took office. To the Palestinian mind, Sharon seemed always to aim for the provocation of further violence rather than any purpose or possibility of restraining it.

That of course raised the further question, whether the Palestinians, for lack of any national discipline, allowed themselves to be led around on a string by cynical provocations from Sharon or any other Israeli provocateurs. There was a history to this, in Rafael Eitan's or Yitzhak Shamir's boasted views of Palestinians as cockroaches shut up in a bottle, which Israelis could shake up and drive them crazy.

On the Palestinian side, there were the shooting, or sometimes rock-throwing attacks on Jews living in the settlements on occupied land. This included the escalating attacks on Gilo. None of the Palestinian organizations possessed any of the heavy or high-tech weapons that the Israelis employed so casually, but they did have mortars, generally homemade and highly inaccurate, which they fired at settlements and often, in the case of some Palestinians in Khan Yunis, at the isolated village of Sderot which was in Green-Line Israel. When eventually these were used against Gilo they raised the level of alarm significantly.

There were further the attacks on Israeli soldiers or other security personnel, whether in occupied territory or in Israel itself. And of course the most flagrant and terrifying of all the violent Palestinian activities were the bombings, especially those that affected civilians, whether in the settlements or, as was most frequent, in Israel itself. Of those, the suicide bombings, increasingly the dominant type, most horrified the Israeli public and world opinion.

The question in all these cases was of who controlled these attacks, Arafat and the PA or others beyond their control, and whether Arafat took such steps as he could to stop them. Sharon kept up a constant drumbeat of accusations that everything came from Arafat, or was tacitly tolerated and condoned by him and his PA associates. Much of the Israeli public believed that, and US authority and public opinion generally echoed it. Short of some evidence, at least prima facie, that these actions came from or were condoned by the responsible Palestinian authority, all of that has to be suspect as mere propaganda and, if it proves so, questioned as to its motive.

Were Sharon and his associates trying to undermine and delegitimize Arafat and the PA? And if so, why? Clearly they went out of their way to demolish police stations and security capabilities anywhere under the PA, killing policemen as if they could all, by reason of their office, be classified as "terrorists," and disrupt the functioning and destroy the records of any other governing or civil institutions in the Palestinian areas. Did they prefer to destroy any legitimate authority and deal only with the rabidly rejectionist leadership among Palestinians? And again, if so, why? The tactic was more consistent with a plan to demolish Palestinian society altogether and even drive the Palestinian population out of the country, the familiar "transfer" proposal, killing as many as that intent required, than with anything else.

These are truly dreadful speculations, and should surely not be assumed without as much evidence as should be demanded about any hidden agendas on the Palestinian side. But when we recognize that these were the obvious inferences believed throughout the Palestinian population, it becomes clear where the Palestinian despair had its origin, and how problematic it was for anyone in authority among Palestinians to control the manifestations of that despair.

DETERIORATING SITUATION

Violence from both sides, always with multiple Palestinian deaths to every Israeli killed, continued through the summer. The definitive end of the ceasefire, languishing now since June 13, came on August 9 in the form of the shocking suicide bombing of a popular and crowded Sbarro pizzeria in Jerusalem, killing 16, including the bomber, 6 children among them, wounding another 132. The suicide attack was the worst since the one that had killed 21 people in the Tel Aviv disco in June.[43]

Israel responded with the most sweeping attack to date on the Palestinian Authority, both militarily and politically. F-16 fighter planes descended on Ramallah, firing missiles to destroy another police station. Tanks entered throughout the Palestinian-controlled areas of the Gaza Strip for what the Israelis described as "pinpoint actions." But more drastic still was it that Israeli officers occupied Orient House, the primary Palestinian institution in Jerusalem, lowering the Palestinian flag from its roof and raising an Israeli flag in its place, removing all its documents and taking in half a dozen Palestinian guards for questioning. The action had potentially far-reaching political significance.[44] Eight other Palestinian offices about the city were confiscated as well, including the building in Abu Dis, just over the municipal line, that housed the Palestinian intelligence services.

President Bush demanded of Arafat that he condemn the bombing. Colin Powell told the Israelis they needed to hold back, assuring them that the United States would continue to put pressure on Arafat.[45] Arafat himself, in fact, was occupied with arresting Palestinian militants at this time.[46]

For my own part, recognizing that the seizure of Orient House was an enormously drastic and destructive step, I wrote at once to Colin Powell that August 10, though I had not had any sort of response yet from anyone in the Bush administration:

> The seizure yesterday of Orient House may well have the most serious import of all the day's tragic events in the Middle East. It is a direct defiance of something that has been central to United States policy ever since 1991, when Secretary of State Baker made the establishment and guarantee of Orient House one of the principal underpinnings of his work to convene the Madrid Conference. I want to urge on you that it is important for the United States to challenge this action.

Reminding him of the identification of the house with Faisal Husseini's steadfast work for peace, I continued:

> Apart from the technicalities of its status, Orient House has represented, for Palestinian consciousness, not only their most

constructive efforts toward peace but a Jerusalem home for those efforts, something of deepest significance for them, as central a symbol, a secular symbol, of their aspirations for standing in Jerusalem as the religious sites themselves. To take that from them is likely to produce more deleterious effect, in creating despair and provoking further violence, than almost any other action that could be taken by the Israelis in revenge for yesterday's terrible bombing attack. Collective punishment is already familiar, but the closure of Orient House will still be able to shock.

COUNTDOWN TO FURTHER CATASTROPHES

After the Sbarro bombing the cabinet resolved that they would keep Orient House and the other offices they had seized. Both sides were now making targets of each other's symbols, in each case the very things that could most inflame the other party.

On the Sunday, August 12, another suicide bomber attacked a café in the outskirts of Haifa. About 15 people were wounded but none gravely. Islamic Jihad claimed the bombing. An eight-year-old Palestinian girl, Sabreen Abu Snaineh, was shot in the head during intense exchanges between soldiers and Palestinians in Hebron. Ahmed Qurei said that Palestinians would use "political and armed resistance" to oust Israeli forces from the Palestinian institutions they had occupied in the hours after the Sbarro bombing. Ridding Orient House of its Israeli occupiers was rapidly become the Palestinian rallying cry. Arafat was so concerned about his standing among Palestinians that he invited Hamas and Islamic Jihad to join him in a coalition, a "unity government" like that which united Israeli forces from the Labor Party across to the ethnic cleansing advocates of Moledet. Nevertheless, the PA arrested four Hamas members over the weekend, including one who was said to have sent the pizzeria bomber. The Israelis waved off these arrests as too little too late.[47] The following days and weeks witnessed Israeli re-occupation of Jenin and Bethlehem, with dire results for their inhabitants.

I had been in fairly frequent contact over the previous 15 years with every Israeli prime minister with the one exception of Binyamin Netanyahu, against whom I had held the judgment that there was no point in discussing anything with him. If one is concerned for non-violence in a conflict, I am convinced, there is no substitute for engaging with those most involved. And so I put some days, at this stage, into composing a letter to Prime Minister Sharon, which I finished and dispatched on August 20.

> Dear Prime Minister Sharon,
>   Shalom!
>   For many years now I have been in close communication both with your adversaries, including Mr Arafat, and many of your predecessors as prime minister, always seeking ways of reconciling the interests of your two peoples and finding peaceful ways for them to relate to one another. As Israel and the Palestinians sink deeper, these days, into violent hostility, I still believe your differences are reconcilable. The safety of Israel and the human rights of Palestinians are equally of concern to me.

And I summed up, at this point, the argument I had presented years ago to Yitzhak Shamir, on how exclusive reliance on military defense could only lead, in the long run, to the collapse of Israel and its society, adding:

> As the punitive raids on Palestinians and their territories increase, to the point where the Palestine Authority could actually collapse, regional war with the neighboring countries becomes a strong possibility. Only the prospect of their defeat by Israel would hold them back if the Palestinians were crushed, and it is doubtful if they could refrain in the face of an enraged public opinion. We all have to dread that, in that event, you would make use of Israel's nuclear arsenal, with devastating effect on the interests of the entire world.
>   It has been a presupposition of your government, from its beginning, that any action by any Palestinian is carried out under the direct responsibility of Mr. Arafat. Your responses have consequently been calculated to undercut Arafat's authority within his community at every point, and have made it constantly less possible for him to bring the anger among Palestinians under control so as to prevent violence.

Recognizing that Sharon's thesis had been to blame Arafat personally for every violent act by Palestinians, I went back over my own experience with him ever since 1985, and my conviction that his life's work had been to lead his people to accept the Israeli state and the right of the Jewish people to that state alongside a Palestinian state. That he should now be working to destroy that accomplishment was not credible, however little capacity he had shown to administer the Palestinian Authority.

> No one other than Arafat has the authority to quell the Palestinian uprising or direct it into fully non-violent ways. It has

appeared to many of us that, each time there is any threat of the outbreak of peace, your forces have undertaken some action—the killing of Palestinian leaders by helicopter gunship attacks or sabotaged telephones, the seizure of Palestinian territory or, recently, the highly symbolic Orient House office, the tank incursion into Jenin or many other actions—calculated to unleash further uncontrollable anger among the Palestinian public and make Arafat's task of curbing it impossible. The threat, terrible to all your Israeli citizens, of suicide bombings is increased rather than diminished with every such action on your part. For myself, I have genuinely suspected you, who promised Israel an end to this violence, of treating your own citizens, cynically, as mere bait for these bombers. I have wondered whether your intention is to prepare Israeli and world opinion to accept a cataclysmic campaign of ethnic cleansing on your part, the thing that Kach and others in Israel have tried to disguise over the years under the euphemism of "transfer."

That means there is an asymmetry between Palestinian and Israeli actions in this tragic slide into violence. It is not a simple tale of Palestinian provocation and Israeli response. Instead, Palestinian actions are fundamentally those of enraged individuals or rejectionist organizations, of which Mr Arafat's Palestine Authority, of its essence, is not one, whereas Israeli actions are uniformly the considered actions of government. The only exception to that is in the savage depredations of Israeli settlers against Palestinians, both in Gaza and in the West Bank, which you have controlled no better than Arafat has controlled the savageries of angry Palestinians.

I then went into the argument over whether the Palestinians had shown bad faith by their rejection of the "generous offer" at Camp David, in terms already familiar to readers here, and to my thesis about basing relations with the Palestinians on international law, as thoroughly as I had in writing to Arafat, Barak and Clinton before.

Because the relation, for so many years, has been based solely on superiority of military force, while law has been so utterly neglected, the Palestinians find themselves subjected to absolute Israeli control over their lives, and respond accordingly with desperate efforts to free themselves. Those actions of despair, what you define simply as terrorism, are bound to continue so long as the disparity deriving from that scornful dismissal of law continues.

I realize it must be a terrifying proposal that Israel should place itself on a level of equality with Palestinians. To put the resolution of the Israeli-Palestinian conflict on the grounds of law rather than superiority of military force would in fact overturn—not reverse—the fatal disparity of power that turns every Israeli action into a diktat. Your two sides would confront each other on a level field, the outcome to be determined by principles of justice, which are not against either the one or the other of you. Last year's negotiations, unsuccessful and inadequate though they were, should offer, in what they did accomplish, reassuring proof of this.

Commenting, then, on the way the Taba negotiations had shown progress beyond the "generous offer" of Camp David, disproving the thesis that the Palestinians were unresponsive, I took up the neuralgic issues of the West Bank settlements and the Right of Return.

On both these issues, the Palestinian negotiators have consistently made clear that their demand was that the basis of law be acknowledged and accepted, that historic Israeli responsibility for the damage done to Palestinians be admitted. If granted that, they remained ready to negotiate agreements on the basis of reality. For instance:

They have not ambitioned return of refugees in a way that would overturn the achieved demography of Green-Line Israel, however much they call for Israeli recognition of the damage done to Palestinians in 1948.

They recognize that the key phrase of Resolution 194's statement of a right of return is "*to live in peace*," a condition that could not be realized if the very demographic basis of Israeli society were challenged.

They have been ready to negotiate minor adjustments to the border and the presence of some Israelis within the bounds of a Palestinian state, under Palestinian law and protection, though not the territorial dismemberment of the Palestinian state into Bantustans.

Even the troubled question of Jerusalem, though not much addressed at Taba, has seen constructive proposals and negotiation and been shown as far from intractable.

With that, my letter went into a plea for Israel's acceptance of its actual obligations under international law as its basis for making peace both with the Palestinians and with the Arab societies around it.

I brought up the mechanisms by which each society, Israeli and Palestinian, had striven to delegitimize the other, Israelis by classifying all Palestinian society itself as terrorist, Palestinians, with the misguided backing of the UN, classifying Zionism as racism. Oslo had brought mutual acceptance of one another's legitimacy as peoples, but it was much endangered now, from both sides, by the current violence, the world repulsion from Israeli excesses manifested by the misuse of the Durban Conference on Human Rights as an anti-Israeli forum just that summer. I instanced the work of Israeli peace activists as showing the possibilities for peace within his own Israeli society.[48] In conclusion, I reminded him of my regular contact with Rabin:

> I look at your government, and your personal history, with more alarm than I did that of Yitzhak Rabin. But I hope you realize that I appeal to you in your humanity and in your full personal dignity and capacity for humane judgment, in which I do totally believe.

I had written this letter with a certain diffidence, which I tried to overcome, not quite believing that Sharon would take it seriously. It came therefore as a great surprise to me when I received, some time later, the following letter, dated September 24, 2001:

> Dear Professor Helmick,
> We thank you for your letter dated August 20, 2001, to Prime Minister Ariel Sharon, and appreciate your input.
> Your letter has been reviewed and the contents duly noted. It was a pleasure to read such an informed and in-depth analysis of the situation.
> Sincerely,
(Mrs.) Marit Danon
Personal Secretary to the Prime Minister

I surely have to acknowledge, in my own assessment of Ariel Sharon and his intentions, the generosity of that response to a letter that must have made very difficult reading for him.

Habitually, when I wrote any such letter as I had sent to Sharon, I sent copies to the others most directly concerned. In this case that meant Arafat, Colin Powell, and President Bush. To the President, I wrote not only a cover letter but also a more substantial appeal, dated, like the letter to Sharon itself, August 20, 2001.

Dear President Bush,
   Christ's Peace!

For many years now I have been communicating directly with a series of US administrations—President Reagan's, your father's, and the Clinton administration—as well as with Mr Arafat and other leading Palestinian figures and the series of Israeli Prime Ministers over that time, by visits and correspondence. The Middle East has become much a concern of mine, my sympathy with both sides and my effort to help both to find the peace.

The deteriorating situation there has become, despite your evident wish to stand back from it, a major conundrum facing your administration. I am very aware of the difficulties of it, and the powerful pressures to which your administration, like every other, is exposed. I have just written a lengthy letter to Prime Minister Sharon, the first time I have written to him. I enclose a copy here for your information.

Your desire, and Secretary of State Powell's, to act even-handedly, addressing your exhortations for good behavior equally to both sides, loses sight, I believe, of one very essential factor, which I point out in my letter to Prime Minister Sharon. It is really untrue to presuppose, as Israeli government statements and much of the American media consistently do, that every action of any Palestinian comes directly under the supervision and responsibility of Mr Arafat. He is dealing with an extremely agitated Palestinian public over which he does not have total control. Efforts, over all the years of Israeli occupation, by Israeli authority to curb terrorism from Palestinian dissidents have had no more success than Arafat's, despite the full control the Israeli Army had over Palestinian territory.

Arafat's PA presides over territory in which even he himself is unable to move or communicate freely. His authority with his own people is diminished by every action of Israeli government that demonstrates his tenuous control over the region he supposedly governs. He faces dissent from rigorously organized and heavily armed rejectionist groups, Hamas and Islamic Jihad and several secular organizations besides. Efforts on his part to control them, arrest their militant members or put them out of business, which he periodically makes, especially after each major atrocity, further erode such authority as he has with his own people. He cannot afford to let it fall apart altogether.

The people he attempts to govern have been exposed to unimaginable suffering and disillusionment. I spare you the details, because

I'm sure you've heard them all. In the terrorist actions that continue to multiply, it is their despair that is having voice. And that makes it all the more misguided that the Israeli government's policy is to hammer them harder and tighten the screws further, not only when there is some particular act of outrage by Palestinians against Israelis, but even more conspicuously whenever there is a threat of peace breaking out, i.e., when Arafat has expended some bit of his tenuous authority in an effort to curb Palestinian violence.

Every military action on the Israeli side, by contrast, does come from deliberate policy decision by Prime Minister Sharon or other main officials of Israeli government and military under his immediate direction. Deliberate provocation appears to be an essential ingredient of this policy, to ratchet up Palestinian anger every time anything happens that might contribute to control it.

In writing to Prime Minister Sharon, I was at pains to point out the disparities between Israelis and Palestinians. This, the disparity between the ability of Palestinian and Israeli authority to turn on or turn off violent action at command, is among the most important. I heard your impatient comment last week that "Chairman Arafat is not doing enough," recognized in it the pressures exerted on you to voice publicly disapproval of Palestinians but not of Israelis, whatever you may actually perceive, and felt that public account should truly be taken of this imbalance. That is not a matter of enmity to one side or the other. It is rather a recognition of the reasons things are deteriorating so drastically. I have even brought up to Mr Sharon, in my letter, the interpretation to which his actions are open, that in these calculated provocations he deliberately exposes his own Israeli citizens to the danger of these terrifying suicide bombers simply as bait, to justify still more drastic action he wishes to take against the Palestinians.

With that, I summed up the contact I had made years before with Yitzhak Shamir, who had subsequently come to work with the Madrid Conference despite his own hardline record, and expressed my readiness to give the same benefit of the doubt to Sharon. But I went through the many evidences in his career of the intention simply to destroy Palestinians. The measure of his commitment to any improvement in the situation should take all that into account.

No let-up in the violence followed, rather intensive fighting at Hebron, in the Gaza Strip, in Beit Jala, and Bethlehem. The assassinations became so frequent and flagrant that even President Bush and his spokespersons raised objections to the Israelis. It was in that context that Secretary of State Colin Powell wrote to me, in a letter dated August 29.

Dear Father Helmick:

Thank you for your thoughtful letter on Orient House and the current state of Israeli–Palestinian relations. Orient House has long symbolized the importance of political dialogue and reconciliation between Israelis and Palestinians. It is vital that both parties remain committed to these objectives and avoid actions which threaten the fundamental belief in a negotiated settlement and increase the risk of further deterioration. I have made these views very clear, both publicly and in our diplomatic discussions with the Israeli government.

Both sides should recognize that down the path of escalation and retaliation lies disaster. In this time of heightened tension, I continue to urge Israelis and Palestinians to refrain from incitement and provocation, and to take immediate steps to restore an atmosphere of restraint and calm. At the same time, the Palestinians must do more to stop the violence, preempt attacks by suicide bombers, and arrest those responsible for the violence.

We remain deeply engaged in this process, and are in close contact with both sides, trying to find ways to restore a sense of trust between them.

Thank you for sharing with me your thoughts on the situation. I appreciate your commitment to Israeli–Palestinian reconciliation.

Sincerely
Colin L. Powell

But the world would change, now, with the attacks on the United States of September 11, 2001. The troubles of the Middle East became a footnote to the main action.

9
America goes to war: September 11, 2001 to the indefinite future

9/11

When two passenger aircraft hurtled into the twin towers of the World Trade Center in New York, bringing those lofty icons of US capitalist power crashing to the ground, a third plane into the military sanctum of the Pentagon in Washington, a fourth falling from the sky over Pennsylvania, a new story began which we need not tell here.

I spent close to two hours of the evening, that September 11, 2001, sitting in a discussion panel at a local New England television station. Some ideas had already become clear to me. We could not tolerate such attacks, and must hold accountable those responsible for them. But when I spoke that evening of the sea of anger that existed in the world against the United States, among people who had flown no airplanes into our towers, another panelist answered: if anyone felt that way toward us, we must make them fear us. I responded that this was exactly what the suicidal hijackers had tried to accomplish with us. His response: "People have been telling us for years that we should do all these things only by diplomatic means, and look where it got us!" I could only answer: "Well, our diplomacy must not have been very good."

Soon however, I put together a paper titled "US policy options after the September 11 attacks," which I sent to Secretary of State Powell on September 21.

I asked first why the attack happened. It had been planned five to seven years, hence was not about the Palestinian *intifada*. The attackers made it clear that their complaint was about US military presence in Saudi Arabia. They were not the impoverished religious fanatics we expected as suicide bombers, but educated engineers, secular enough to be drinkers and womanizers. They employed the symbolism of the weak against the strong, turning our strength and technology against us by using just knives and their own bodies. Any further attack would likely have that same character, exploring all the weaknesses to which our high-tech way of life leaves us exposed.

Their objective, as they killed great numbers of people and destroyed iconic buildings, was to demoralize. I had already, in previous days, been warning that the liquid natural gas container ships that came, weekly, into Boston Harbor would make a likely target. Blowing one of those up would have an impact on the city like a nuclear bomb.

Osama bin Laden and his Al-Qaeda organization were already the suspects, with support from the Taliban government of Afghanistan at least to the extent of harboring him. The people of Afghanistan had already suffered plenty from that regime.

I identified, then, three geographical theaters that would be of concern. Afghanistan would be the first, and we should have some clear idea how far its government was responsible. That need not mean cruise missiles right away, for all the bloodthirsty talk going around the country. If we were to prove only that we could kill better than anyone else, we would receive cyclical retribution for every blow while losing the moral high ground and the cooperation even of our closest allies. I made a comparison here with Sharon's use of massive retaliation to every blow as a method that had done nothing to promote the safety of his own people in Israel, saying we could easily make life for citizens of the United States about as safe as it was now for citizens of Israel. Noting that the prelude, clearly connected, to the 9/11 attack in the United States had been the murder, two days before, of Ahmed Shah Massood in the Panjshir region of Afghanistan, a way of making the Taliban safer from retribution for the planned action, I recommended that the United States rely on the Northern Command in Afghanistan, even weakened as it was by the death of Massood, helping them, through Tajikistan, to rescue their own people, who had suffered more than us from the Taliban, from their oppressive situation. We ought not to be the danger, I argued, the enemy of the Afghani people, renewing the hold of the Taliban over them by making them rally around it, but rather the source of hope and help in their liberating themselves (*not* being "liberated" by us) from the Taliban.

Iraq was the second area of concern, for the reason that the continued presence of US forces in Saudi Arabia—the motive for the 9/11 attacks—had to do with Iraq. In 1991 the United States had known better than to invade deep into Iraq and occupy it, which would have been disaster for us and for the Iraqis. But when the Kurds in the north and the Shi'ites in the south of Iraq mounted the rebellions which could have toppled Saddam Hussein, we abandoned them, at the bidding of the Saudis, who preferred to keep a Sunni Muslim dictatorship in Iraq, and for fear of the destabilization of that fragile country. My own association with the Iraqi Kurds, ever since 1973, convinced me that there was a way of transforming Iraq through its own internal forces, not by invasion and occupation.

The Kurds, ever since 1987, had been faithful to a resolve not to seek separation from Iraq but the promotion of a democratic Iraq. They had created participatory institutions of government in their northern enclave and made Iraqis of the other ethnic and religious communities welcome to take part in those institutions, in that way training a central group from those communities in democratic interaction. They had been desperately impoverished, subject to a double economic blockade: first, the sanctions imposed from outside on all Iraqis, including themselves, and second, the internal isolation imposed on them by the Hussein regime. Their want had been such as to drive them, for a time, to civil conflict among themselves, which they had since contained. But if the United States were to assist them, a thing that could easily be done, to become a political, economic, and democratic success, their example would so illustrate what Iraqis could have without Hussein that he could not withstand their demands for his ouster.

Israel–Palestine was the third area of concern. Though that conundrum had not been the motive of the 9/11 attacks, it was still the source of a deep anger which our country was responsible to address. Denial over this complex of issues was as extreme as US denial over Vietnam. If we failed to address it, that way lay catastrophe, for ourselves as much as for anyone else.

Our resources for addressing these urgent concerns had never been greater than at that point, when practically all the nations of the world were so much with us. Because what we were fighting was basically not a war but a massive crime against humanity, our best resource was genuine enforcement of law, much more important than simple use of force. The UN, whose cooperation was promised by Secretary General Kofi Annan, was the instrument that would give our demands the requisite legitimacy. Other nations would agree with us on common policy and give, by their agreement, force of law, by their free and common decision within the UN, not by ukase from the United States. I concluded:

> Our nation prides itself, as we constantly affirm, on being governed by law, not by the arbitrary demands of men. For most of our history peoples of all nations have seen us as a great beacon of justice. Currently, the peoples of the Middle Eastern and Muslim world do not see us so, but as the perpetrators of grave injustices against themselves. We are required, in justice, to pursue and punish those who, in response to that perception, have committed monstrous crimes. We have need to hold accountable nations who have harbored such terrorists and fostered these actions – through the now readily available concurrence of the international community, acting in the UN

forum. But for those who simply harbor great anger against us for what they perceive as offenses against them, what we need is reconciliation. We pursue that by hearing their narratives, without any effort at denial on our part, and by truly demonstrating our justice, not ignoring their plea.

THE MIDDLE EAST IN ECLIPSE

The Israeli–Palestinian conflict went its way in the background of the American *Jihad* that developed after the 9/11 attack. The murder, on October 16, 2001, of Rehavam Ze'evi, tourism minister in the Sharon government and long-time advocate of "transfer," set off the Israeli government's fiercest hunt for perpetrators yet.[1]

The Ze'evi murder created such pressures that the Bush administration had to turn its gaze from Afghanistan long enough to dispatch the former chairman of the Joint Chiefs of Staff, General Anthony Zinni, to try to calm the situation. Colin Powell gave a significant speech calling for an end to the occupation.[2] I made an effort to win Arafat's cooperation with such efforts through a letter of October 24, following that up with letters to Powell and Condoleezza Rice on October 26, welcoming Powell's invocation, in the speech he had just given in Louisville, Kentucky, of an "end of occupation." If such promises were only smoke, and Arafat responded to them, he would be gone, and that would be bad news for the Israelis as well as for his own people. It was time the United States really committed itself to bring such things about. I took occasion to recommend both to Powell and Rice the things that had been the substance of my correspondence all through the last year.

Any hopes from the Zinni mission, however, were quickly dashed. A series of three suicide bombings over the next weekend killed 25 innocent Israelis. The Israelis responded this time not only with the missiles against police stations and Arafat's headquarters that were by now standard, but by destroying Yasser Arafat's three helicopters in Gaza City, grounding him and confining him to the West Bank town of Ramallah.[3]

Predictably, this did nothing to still the escalation of violence. By January 18, 2002, having refused Arafat permission to attend the Christmas celebrations in Bethlehem as he had been accustomed to do each year since 1994, the Israelis confined him strictly to the Muqada, his headquarters compound in Ramallah, where he has remained a prisoner ever since.[4] An extraordinary initiative (February 18, 2002)[5] by which the Saudis offered Israel full welcome into their Middle Eastern world and peace in exchange for their withdrawal to the territory they held before the 1967 war made no impression on the Sharon government.

THE IRAQ WAR LOOMS

Meanwhile the United States was turning its attention from Afghanistan to Iraq. This development so alarmed me that I wrote to Colin Powell again on March 1, 2002.

> Dear Secretary of State Powell,
>   Christ's Peace!
>   All the talk that circulates about Iraq leaves me apprehensive that some terrible mistake in policy may likely happen. I write to you as the one person among those who decide our national policy who best understands that wars are things to be prevented rather than sought.

With that, I detailed my own close association with the Iraqi Kurds ever since 1973. I believed firmly that they had so much reason to distrust the United States and its CIA, from their past experience, that they should not be used, as had the Northern Command in Afghanistan, as a military arm to defeat Saddam Hussein. But I advanced again my conviction that there was an alternative, non-military way to undo Hussein's grip on Iraq by making them the showcase of the life Iraqis could have without Saddam Hussein. The cost to the United States would be minimal by comparison with the cost of a war. What was needed was not handout aid, but the creation, by some targeted investment, of an international opening for Kurdish resources and the development of entrepreneurship among their people. This would show Saddam Hussein as the useless President, giving each of the constituencies under his domination knowledge of a leadership and compatriots who were living so much better.

His domination was built on fear, but a US attack, especially after all the time Iraqis had experienced out sanctions regime, could cause people instead to rally around him.

The problems to be faced would be, first, to bring about political change in Iraq without breaking up the state, and second, to keep the Turks happy. Neither of these was insuperable. Success of such a Kurdish-based effort would anchor the Kurds within the Iraqi society to which they would have brought such benefit, thus relieving the Turks of the danger of an Iraqi Kurdish separatism that could motivate their own Kurds to rebel.

I concluded my letter with my great apprehension that plans for a US military incursion into Iraq were imminent. It could produce a debacle, and alienate not only the Arab world but also even our European allies from us. I truly hoped that better reason would prevail.

CONTINUED TURMOIL

Looking for restraint or respect for law in the Israeli–Palestinian situation had by now become almost a joke. The Sharon government, having first had to fear that the Bush administration would cool toward the prime minister and his violent ways in order to cull favor with the Arab states after the 9/11 catastrophe, cottoned onto the strategy of identifying its crushing of the Palestinians with the Bush "war on terror" very quickly.

And the US government itself became increasingly lawless. The incarceration of its prisoners at Guantanamo Bay in a way designed to circumvent any legal process was hallmark to its mentality. One could expect no pressure on Israel to adhere to law of any sort to be exerted by the ideologues who had captured the making of US policy. Sharon would not be allowed by this US regime to initiate expulsion of the Palestinians from a cold start. That would embarrass the United States. But to the extent that Sharon's policies were geared to drive the Palestinians to ever-greater extremes of desperation and violent reaction, there were no brakes.

Thus in the month of March, 2002, the huge and destructive Israeli raids on the Balata refugee camp at Jenin,[6] with a death toll still uncounted, led directly to a suicide bombing in Jerusalem that snuffed out nine Israeli lives.[7]

By mid-month, with 20,000 troops in action, soldiers in full battledress ripping their way through large Palestinian refugee camps, tearing up roads and rounding up for questioning all males between 15 and 45 years of age, backed by the fire of Apache attack helicopters, which gutted homes and Palestinian Authority offices, Israel was engaged in the largest military offensive in the Palestinian territories since the 1967 war. In less than two weeks the Israeli army had killed more than 160 Palestinians. Defense Minister Ben-Eliezer himself threatened to resign because of the scale of the operation.[8]

Such tactics only stoked the rage that led to more suicide bombings, most of this happening out of sight, as the world's and especially the US media gave their attention to the more exciting scenes of the US war in Afghanistan.

The Arab League, meeting in Beirut, endorsed the proposal of Saudi Arabia's Crown Prince Abdullah, offering Israel full peace in return for their withdrawal from the territories they had conquered in the 1967 war.[9] The offer had been endorsed by the Palestinian Authority as well.[10]

Then on the evening of the Passover supper (March 27), a Hamas suicide bomber transformed the solemn Seder into a horrible bloodbath, blowing himself up just outside the dinner room at a hotel in Netanya.[11] Nineteen Jews were killed, bring the month's total to 136.[12]

Israel declared Arafat "an enemy." Troops and tanks smashed into the Mouqada compound, Arafat's headquarters in Ramallah, shelling his private offices and battling with his security guards. Israeli tanks, troops, and helicopters were reported to be in control of the city, the unofficial Palestinian capital, after room-to-room fighting inside Arafat's offices. Henceforth, the imprisonment of Arafat in his headquarters would take on a new and more menacing character.[13]

These tactics cured nothing in Israeli–Palestinian relations. Death tolls mounted, Palestinian and Israeli, the Palestinians three times as high as the Israelis. But on June 18 another monstrous suicide bomb galvanized Israeli response still further. The bomber blew himself up on a bus in Jerusalem carrying high school students and adult commuters, killing at least 19 and wounding another 52.[14] Since the end of March Israeli troops had ranged freely over any part of the Palestinian territories, but now they moved definitively into practically all the Palestinian towns and cities, with full backing and encouragement from President Bush.[15]

THE BUSH SPEECH OF JUNE 24, 2002

But President Bush was under pressure now from British Prime Minister Tony Blair, who had expended much of his own credit and standing in British public opinion, alienating especially his own party, by his support for the Bush war policies. Always concerned for the Palestinians, Blair now insisted on some new policy to defend their rights and promise them eventual fulfillment of their demand for a state as carrot to appease even his own people. A Bush speech on Middle East policy was due, but delayed after the June 18 bombing.[16] The speech, a major event in the developing course of the conflict, came on June 24 as the Israelis were again pouring over a hundred tanks and other armored vehicles into Ramallah and around Arafat's battered headquarters.[17] Bush promised the establishment of a Palestinian state within three years, spelling out a rather vague process through which that would be achieved and giving no indication of the size or character of the state, but then, in a last-minute textual change in the speech, demanded that the Palestinians must first oust Arafat from his position of leadership before any part of the process could begin. Bush had effectively endorsed the position of Prime Minister Ariel Sharon of Israel, which he had until now resisted: that no negotiations can take place until Mr. Arafat is replaced.

I had not attempted writing to President Bush himself for some time. His White House did not seem particularly responsive to outside opinion. But I wrote to him now, on August 6.

> Dear Mr President,
> Christ's Peace!
> Traveling with the Reverend Jesse Jackson in the Middle East last week, I got a close, sharp view of the current situation, updating what I have learned in dealing closely with Palestinian and Israeli leadership ever since 1985. All the parties we met— ... Foreign Minister Peres, ... Defense Minister Ben Eliezer, Religious Affairs Minister Rabbi Michael Melchior; MKs from Labor, Meretz and Shinui parties; religious leaders, Jewish ... Christian ... and Muslim; President Arafat ... and the entire Palestine Authority cabinet—agreed on the urgent need for a greater active US government involvement in mediating among the conflicting parties.
>
> The crux of what these parties saw as nearly total American disengagement is your excommunication of President Arafat, which means that so long as Arafat remains the elected President of the Palestinians the US has no role other than to give unlimited support to the policies of one element in the complex and fragile coalition that now governs Israel: its far Right wing, including Prime Minister Sharon.
>
> You have clearly decided not to deal with President Arafat, and have refused to meet or communicate with him ever since you became President. Your Secretary of State persisted in recognizing that Arafat was essential to any peace process until, good soldier that he is, he received his marching orders recently under the decree of excommunication you issued, apparently acceding to the wishes of your Vice President and his camp. Our European allies, whose leaders you met directly after that, agreeing with and praising the many constructive things you had said in that same speech, immediately dissociated themselves from the banning of Mr Arafat, as did the Russians, the Saudis, and other Arab states, and all our allies. They argued that the Palestinians have democratically elected Arafat and the choice is theirs. He may not be put aside by us foreigners without their electoral choice. Even those countries

that do not have elected governments themselves were appalled that the United States, with its democratic traditions, would ever seek to do such a thing.

Beyond the anti-democratic character of that action, it should be clear that you have thereby guaranteed the re-election of President Arafat. All the frustration and disappointment Palestinians have experienced with his administration of the Palestine Authority will count for nothing against their rejection of this outside diktat of their electoral choice.

Rejecting Arafat is further a reversion to the classical error of Israeli and American governments that kept this conflict in stalemate all through the 1970s and 1980s. Israeli governments consistently held, all that time, that they did not like the Palestinians put before them and would prefer to choose as leaders different, basically more compliant, Palestinians themselves. That is the very policy whose failure had to be recognized by the time of Madrid and Oslo.

With that, I summarized my own personal experience of Arafat since my early meetings in 1985, and my conviction that for him, at this point, to be an obstacle to peace would mean jettisoning his own whole life's work. The actual reason for disliking Arafat was that he did not knuckle under and become the instrument of Israeli policy with regard to questions of territory, freedom, and so on. That is the very reason why the Palestinians continued to choose him as leader, despite their problems with him as PA administrator.

I went through the limitations that the Israeli restrictions place on him, the wholesale assassination of his police forces and the reduction of his people to despair placed on Arafat's capacity to rein in the terrorists, as he was so often bidden. Concluding, I wrote:

> I hope I have not overburdened you, Mr President, with this letter. What you had to say in your Middle East policy address was most encouraging on a whole series of points. The long-term safety of Israel too depends on fulfilling the hopes you expressed. But your refusal to deal with the elected President Arafat, and consequently with any level of Palestinian leadership that would not define itself as quisling, extricated you from any real engagement with the Middle Eastern conflict, and left instead a total vacuum of American policy, a thing that cannot do otherwise than provoke the most intense and increasing violence.... I urgently ask that you reflect further on it.

AND THEN IRAQ

More than ever, from this time, the drive by the Bush administration for war with Iraq took precedence over everything else. By the beginning of the year the prospect was so daunting that I wrote once again to Secretary of State Colin Powell, on January 7, 2003. I reminded him first of my earlier letter of March 1, 2002, continuing:

> The problem that faces you and the country is whether we can in fact see Saddam Hussein replaced as leader of Iraq by a stable and, we would hope, democratic regime. Regime change is actually what we (I include myself) would like to see. Like many others, I have been arguing that regime change is not a cause that would justify a war in Iraq. Even the President, after intoning that regime-change theme for so long, has had to back off and say that the weapons of mass destruction are the issue. That issue would justify a war only if an imminent threat of their actual use by Saddam Hussein, or by terrorists in whose hands he might put them, could be shown. That becomes dubious enough that it appears possible enough that we may not have this war after all....
>
> I am of the opinion that it can best be done without a war, and that working toward it without a war would even obviate the clear obstacles that stand in its way, of which the first is the fear of a disintegration of Iraq into fragmentary states.
>
> To begin with, the Kurds have a solid commitment against separatism, to which they have been faithful ever since the late 1980s. I have my own role in that. Having been associated with Kurdish rights ever since 1973, when the elder Mustafa Barzani began to rely heavily on the advice of my close associate Richard Hauser in London, I argued the point strenuously to both Massoud Barzani and Jalal Talabani from 1987 on. The perspective I urged upon them was that the Kurds would never have any help from the international community if they threatened the stability of Iraq and the other countries within which their people lived, the international borders, but that they could expect such help if they set themselves three priorities, to the clear exclusion of separatism:
>
> 1) human rights protection against the genocidal attacks they suffered;
> 2) cultural rights in the face of the prohibition of their language and the teaching of their traditions and history in various of the countries; and

3) free communication among the Kurds in the various countries, but in such a way as not to threaten the stability of those nations and their borders.

Both Barzani and Talabani responded very positively to these ideas. They committed themselves to them and have remained faithful to them ever since, even through the Gulf War, their subsequent uprising, its brutal suppression (until they had some American assistance to bring their people back from their refuges in Turkey and Iran), and the contention between them during the 1990s. This is very little recognized....

In our current situation, we have to worry about two things with regard to Kurdish ambitions. If they were to separate from Iraq, the Iraqi Republic itself would fragment, and their independent status would attract Kurds in the other countries around, drastically destabilizing at least Turkey and Iran. The Turks fear this so much that they prepare themselves to pounce at the first sign of Kurdish separatism.

Danger of Iraqi fragmentation, however, comes primarily from the Shi'ites, the actual majority of Iraqis who have nevertheless been systematically excluded from a voice in government ever since the British pieced together an Iraq in the 1920s.

The Shi'ites have every reason to want out of the Iraqi polity, or to take it over in ways that would provoke violent resistance from the other elements in the population. In their leadership, they have little experience of anything like democracy, and their tradition inclines toward imposition on the others in Iraq. Hence their ascendancy would be something for the rest of Iraq to fear mightily and to resist. That is not at all to say, though, that the Shi'ite people are incapable of a democratic life or a pluralism, as the outstanding work of Professor Abdul Aziz Sachedina of the University of Virginia can show.[18] Required is a model of successful democracy within the country that is open to them and their participation. That can come from the Northern Kurds.

Here is the next extraordinary trait in the established behavior of the Iraqi Kurds. As they constructed their institutions after the election in Northern Iraq of 1992, they welcomed the participation of the other population groups in Iraq, granting generous place to the Iraqi National Congress. The Kurds, as we all saw, fell out among themselves in ways that altogether disrupted the effectiveness of the Iraqi National Congress. The reasons for that should be understood. The regionally based rivalry of KDP and PUK was a struggle over the radically restricted supplies available to them under the combined effect of the international sanctions against all Iraq and the further internal embargo against their region by the Iraqi government. The Kurds had maintained a remarkable unity throughout their earlier rebellion under Mustafa Barzani in the 1970s, a unity fractured after their 1975 defeat. But Talabani and the younger Barzani had achieved a new cooperation and community of purpose in their efforts from the late 1980s through the time of their 1992 election, perhaps the most democratic election ever seen in their part of the world, until that extreme want among their people drove them apart. Under the relatively more prosperous conditions they have achieved under the autonomy, they have basically regained that capacity to work with one another.

The exile leadership of the other Iraqis has been a disappointment, as Talabani has well recognized....

In my view, a democratic Iraq can better be achieved without a war. I would see that done by using what is really there, namely the experience of the Northern Kurds in running their autonomy. They have done this in a way that does not imply either exclusivism or their ascendancy over the rest of the Iraqis. They have managed it as a desperate enterprise under the most threatening circumstances of military danger and extremes of want. If made into a political, economic and democratic success, in ways the United States could easily achieve, they would be a magnet for the rest of Iraq....

This would constitute a slower way to eliminate the government of Saddam Hussein than a bullet or a fast military campaign, but not so slow as the eleven years of sanctions we have just witnessed. The Kurds, and those associated with them, have some real experience in democratic life behind them now, and would be acquiring more as this process developed. The other population groups within Iraq, who have less or no actual experience of democratic life but strong aspirations for it, would learn it in their association with the Northern Kurds. The democratic development would be indigenous, not something imposed from outside, enabled by Americans rather than imported, and growing in an atmosphere friendly to us rather than hostile and suspicious.

By contrast, a change of regime resulting from a war would mean high risk of the territorial fracturing of Iraq, a strong and most likely very violent effort by the Shi'ite majority to snatch up all the cards, and a move, most likely successful, by the Sunni Arab generals simply to replace Saddam with another of themselves. Anything that the US government described as democratization of Iraq, under its aegis, would be understood, not only by Iraqis but by everyone in the Middle East, as subservient government. If we had an American army of occupation in the country, we would face a situation more like that of the British in Aden than like that of MacArthur in Japan. And if we abstained from inserting an occupying force, we would only make it easy for the generals to impose another dictatorship like Saddam's....

I have tried to show, here, that a real alternative to war exists that would realize the American desire for a regime change in Iraq. I hear such gung-ho enthusiasm for a war coming from our Washington leadership that I suspect some of your colleagues would be very disappointed not to have a war. I should say in conclusion that I have great apprehension of what such a war would entail, and see much of the comment from many of our leaders simply in the category of denial.

Contrary to the sanguine expectations that our thus-far reluctant Middle Eastern friends would fall in line once we got the war going, I expect that several of the regional governments most closely associated with us would actually fall. That includes Saudi Arabia, Egypt and, very likely, Jordan. That prospect would explain their visible lack of enthusiasm for the war. Their replacements would not be to our liking, and we would very probably find ourselves not in one war but in a series of them, with the successor governments of each of these countries. Our very probable military occupation of Iraq would be a quagmire for us, and the kind of incident we suffered on September 11, 2001, would become our commonplace experience. This would be the result not of the wickedness of our foes but of our own lack of wisdom. The paradigm for this progression of failures can be seen in Thucydides. We could well bring down the entire American power position in the world.

Thucydides, of course, had described how the mighty Athenian Empire, supreme, untouchable arbiter of its world, had engaged in the succession of four Peloponnesian Wars many centuries ago, and seen its enormous power evaporate entirely.

A conference I attended between this time and the beginning of the war brought together many of the military figures responsible for advance planning, for psychological warfare and for the management of the prison camp in Guantanamo Bay, along with journalists and professors on both sides of the issue. The topics were mind-blowing: interrogation, on which we were told of practices already in common use that amounted to torture; "targeted killing" (the preferred Israeli phrase), with directors of the Israeli assassination program who defended it as a perfectly moral response and urged it upon their US counterparts; pacification, which its advocates interpreted to mean the imposition of an alternative political ideology on a reluctant population by terrorizing them into submission.

Shortly after that the war began, over the objections of our most important traditional allies, with a "coalition of the willing," most of these nations that had nothing to contribute to the war other than to stand in the cheering section, one that had been assembled simply by intimidation. I will not attempt here to detail this story here.

Sharon had meanwhile won, by a large margin, a general election on January 28, 2003, that gave him a clear right-wing majority in the Knesset and relieved him of need for the Labor Party in his coalition. The Labor candidate for prime minister, Amram Mitzna, had devoted practically all his campaign to the building of a separation wall between Israelis and Palestinians rather than advocating a genuine peace. The electorate judged he had nothing to offer. Sharon, at first reluctant to see a barrier raised that might be the defining of a border, eventually began building his own version of a "fence." The only good thing that can be said of it is that he has located it in so outrageously invasive a way that it has to come down. A wall is the last thing Israel needs. It was originally a bad idea of Shimon Peres. It can only exacerbate and make permanent the hostility between Israelis and Palestinians, who need a clearly recognized but open border that allows both peoples free access to the whole territory while knowing what is theirs and what is not.

The indeterminate proposals made by President Bush in his June 24, 2002, speech were picked up by other parties, Russia, the European Union, and the UN, and dressed up enough to stand as the "roadmap" to peace sponsored by "the quartet." It is without much content. Content is provided instead by civilian recommendations such as the Geneva Accord, which its proponents, veterans of the Taba negotiations of January, 2001, see as the completion of those negotiations, the Ayalon-Nusseibeh Statement of Principles, or the proposals of Gush Shalom. None of those have official standing, but they demonstrate the solubility of all the outstanding issues of the conflict and the genuine availability of negotiating partners for both sides. The roadmap's sole content, in effect, is to say, to the Sharon government and the neoconservative hawks of the US administration, that it would embarrass George Bush if nothing good happens. That is what Sharon and the US hawks are not supposed to do.

10
So what really happened at Camp David and Taba?

A near war among the interpreters broke out, in 2001 and 2002, as to what had actually happened at Camp David and Taba. That is really our theme in this book, and an important element in determining whether we can look for a genuine resolution of this conflict, or a transformation of it into a productive political dialogue.

The received version, as we may call it, is that negotiation failed because Arafat would not "make the painful compromises" which, Israel and the United States felt, Barak had made. Part of that narrative is that he and his team never even made an effort to respond to the US and Israeli proposals. Both Clinton and Barak made that the theme of personal denunciations of Arafat right after Camp David.

Clinton came around to believing the Gordian knot could be cut, and strove mightily to bring about the conclusion of a peace agreement before his own leaving office, or at least before Barak's, but later he reaffirmed his belief that the whole thing had failed because of Arafat. Barak's ambivalence about Arafat as a partner led him to the stop-start attitude toward subsequent negotiations, through Taba, that in fact had much to do with depriving the negotiators of the time they needed to reach a proper conclusion. Subsequent recriminations, especially from the Sharon camp, have brought it about that much of the Israeli and US publics believe not only that Arafat caused the failure of negotiations but also that he did it with malice, having already decided to launch a campaign of violence instead.

Clinton and Barak, of course, are the parties whose oxen were gored by the failure, Clinton robbed of what he had hoped would be a closing triumph of his presidency, Barak's political career brought down in total ruin. Their disenchantment has to be read, with however much sympathy, in terms of those brute facts.

When one hears any interpretation different from that "received version," described consequently as "revisionist history," one realizes that the purveyors of the received version are defending not only an interpretation but also a cause. If this is not what happened, then how can you justify the Israeli crackdown and reoccupation of all

290 Aftermath

Palestinian territory since? Not to challenge a narrative so destructive in its consequences, or not to permit examination of it, is to do a disservice to any prospects of peace.

I believe firmly, from my own readings of the situation, that the second part of the received version, namely that Arafat planned all along to launch a violent uprising as his alternative to a peace agreement with Israel, stands refuted by the history we have examined. Efforts on his part to bring the violence to an end were constantly frustrated by the extremes of despair to which his people were reduced by Israeli action, by the increasing destruction of any forces of police control available to him, and by Israeli government actions, each time any degree of calm seemed within reach, that seemed calculated to stir the pot. We need now, before concluding, to look at the arguments brought forward by those who had first-hand knowledge for and against the proposition that Arafat and his team failed to cooperate with the process of negotiation itself.

EARLY VIEWS

An early dissenting voice to that view appeared in the Winter 2000 Special Report from the Foundation for Middle East Peace, a Washington think tank and research organization. The report, titled *Crossroads of Conflict: Israeli–Palestinian Relations Face Uncertain Future*, questioned the premise that what the Israelis had offered was adequate to Palestinian needs.[1] Early in March Ian Lustick, Political Science Professor from the University of Pennsylvania, had given a quite luminous overall perspective on Israeli–Palestinian relations as one of the "Conversations with History" series conducted in the Institute of International Studies at the University of California Berkeley by Harry Kreisler. Lustick spoke his piece before the interpretation of Camp David became a crusading topic, and is the more valuable for that. He did get around, though, to citing tactical errors in the procedure, atypical of the master negotiator Clinton.[2]

Gilead Sher, who had been chief negotiator on the Israeli team, in total charge particularly at Taba, took a harder line when he addressed the Washington Institute for Near East Policy on April 16, 2001.[3] Sher, who had spent so much of the time at Taba outside the negotiation room, on the phone with Barak and absorbing all of Barak's gloom, was practically the only one, of either side, to come away from Taba without feeling the negotiators had been tantalizingly close to an agreement.

Gideon Levy weighed in with a column on June 17. Levy had earlier written of the anomaly that no written record existed of the Camp David negotiations, a damaging omission which, he thought, might be traced to "the trauma of the Shepherdstown document," that is, the way the leaking of President Clinton's bridging proposal the year before had buried the Israeli–Syrian negotiations over the Golan. But now, for lack of a record, every party had a different version of what it believed it had heard from the other parties. There was "no agreed numerical data on the size of the withdrawal from the territories ... no accepted proposal for a division of the Old City of Jerusalem and ... no acceptable formula for the refugee problem."[4]

Nabil Sha'ath, one of the principal Palestinian negotiators, gave his own assessment in an address to the Washington Institute for Near East Peace on July 3. He concentrated almost entirely on the Taba stage of the negotiations, of which, like almost all participants, Israeli and Palestinian alike, he gave a very hopeful account. Against the violence that had prevailed (since the date of Sharon's adventure on the Temple Mount) Sha'ath invoked a return to the principles of the Mitchell and Tenet reports.[5]

Comment on the positive outcome of the Taba sessions can be made more confidently now, because a careful record had been kept this time by the European Union's astute observer, Miguel Moratinos. Conscious of how great an obstruction it had been after Camp David that there was no official record and every party had drawn up its contending account of what it had heard from the others, Moratinos drew up what was called, because it was not official, a "Non-Paper," recording what he, as impartial observer, had heard at the meeting. The Non-Paper, dated January 2001, was eventually leaked early in 2002 and acknowledged by all the parties.[6] It gives a far more detailed account of the points of agreement and was, for that reason, of great use to the Israeli and Palestinian informal citizen negotiators, veterans of the Taba negotiations, who late in 2003 signed the Geneva Accord, a fully detailed model of a peace agreement that could fully resolve the Israeli–Palestinian conflict, demonstrating that all the issues were solvable and that both sides truly did have negotiating partners with whom to speak.[7]

ENTER ROBERT MALLEY

Robert Malley opened the really contentious part of the interpretation war with a *New York Times* op-ed on July 8, 2001. Malley, a member of the National Security Council staff at the Clinton White House since 1994, had been special assistant to the President for Arab–Israeli affairs and director for Near East and South Asian affairs in the NSC up to January 2001. At the end of the Clinton administration he became Middle East program director at the International Crisis Group and adjunct senior fellow at the Council on Foreign Relations. He was clearly an insider authority on what had occurred at Camp David and one not averse to critiquing his own team.[8]

In the *Times* op-ed, Malley's first contribution to the debate, he questioned what he already saw as:

> … an unusual harmony of opinion both here and in Israel: Camp David is said to have been a test that Mr. Barak passed and Mr. Arafat failed. Offered close to 99 percent of their dreams, the thinking goes, the Palestinians said no and chose to hold out for more. Worse, they did not present any concession of their own, adopting a no-compromise attitude that unmasked their unwillingness to live peacefully with a Jewish state by their side.

Against that consensus, Malley wrote that; "there is no purpose—and considerable harm—in adding to their real mistakes a list of fictional ones." And he proceeded to rebut what he called "dangerous myths" about the Camp David process.

"Myth 1: *Camp David was an ideal test of Mr. Arafat's intentions.*" But Arafat had made known his reluctance to go to Camp David on the grounds that gaps in the positions of the parties had not been sufficiently narrowed and that he felt both isolated from the Arab world and alienated by the close US–Israeli partnership. The summit came, too, at a low point in his relation with Barak, the man with whom he was supposed to strike this historic deal. Barak had shrunk from a number of Israeli commitments, including the long-postponed Israeli withdrawal from parts of the West Bank and the transfer to Palestinian control of villages abutting Jerusalem. It was a leap of faith for Clinton and Barak, both of whom had reason to wish it might be so, to believe that the core issues—territory, Jerusalem, refugees—could be resolved in a fortnight without having been discussed previously by the leaders.

"Myth 2: *Israel's offer met most if not all of the Palestinians' legitimate aspirations.*" But this was simply not so, wrote Malley. The Palestinians were actually offered 91 percent of the West Bank and Gaza, more than the United States and Israel had thought possible, but how was Arafat to explain the unfavorable 9:1 ratio in land swaps to his people? What was offered on Jerusalem, too, while "far more than had been thinkable only a few weeks earlier, and a very difficult proposition for the Israeli people to accept," was likewise not sufficient for basic Palestinian needs, and in need of further negotiation. And what was said of the future of refugees was too vague, leaving Arafat the impression that he "would be asked to swallow an unacceptable last-minute proposal."

"*Myth 3: The Palestinians made no concession of their own.*" Israeli and US officials were saying that Palestinian rejection of what had been on the table at Camp David meant an underlying rejection of Israel's right to exist. However, Malley pointed out, the Palestinians had already argued for the creation of a Palestinian state based on the June 4, 1967, borders, living alongside Israel. They had accepted the notion of Israeli annexation of West Bank territory to accommodate settlement blocs. They had accepted, too, the principle of Israeli sovereignty over the Jewish neighborhoods of East Jerusalem—neighborhoods that were not part of Israel before the Six-Day War in 1967. And, though they insisted on recognition of the refugees' right of return, they had quite explicitly agreed that it should be implemented in a manner that protected Israel's demographic and security interests by limiting the number of returnees. No other Arab party that had negotiated with Israel—not Anwar el-Sadat's Egypt, not King Hussein's Jordan, let alone Hafez al-Assad's Syria—had ever come close to even considering such compromises.

Thus Malley threw down the gauntlet over the interpretation of Camp David.[9]

THE DEBORAH SONTAG ARTICLE

Deborah Sontag, who had reported for the *New York Times* through the whole course of these events, published on July 26, 2001, her valedictory report, on completion of her Middle East assignment. Sontag interviewed just about every participant who would agree to talk about the Camp David/Taba series of negotiations, and did all the interviews herself. Her article stands as the second major blow to the "received version" of Camp David. She challenged the simplistic narrative that held that Barak had offered Arafat the moon, but that he had turned it down in favor of a violent campaign, a narrative that led to a conclusion that the conflict was insoluble.

Sontag outlined a picture of desperate striving by Barak and the Israelis to force a deal on Arafat before Barak, who had already lost his coalition, would himself be defeated. Barak himself would not agree to be interviewed for the Sontag article, though she was able to interview Arafat, and also many participants among both Israeli and Palestinian negotiators and the international observers. She related the intensive negotiation that had resumed after Camp David, the cordial dinner that Barak had shared with Arafat in late September, just a few days before Sharon's disruptive visit to the Temple Mount, and how even that had not stopped the progress of negotiation.

At the end of Camp David, Sontag wrote, all three parties had agreed that the chemistry had been bad, but agreed on little else. Clinton, dejected at that time, would later describe Camp David in more positive terms, as a "transformative event," because it forced the two sides to confront each other's core needs and allowed them to glimpse the potential contours of a final peace. Ben-Ami tried to convince the Israelis that Palestinians, from their vantage point, had indeed made real concessions. "They agreed to Israeli sovereignty over Jewish neighborhoods in East Jerusalem, eleven of them," he said. "They agreed to the idea that three blocs of the settlements they so oppose could remain in place and that the Western Wall and Jewish Quarter could be under Israeli sovereignty."

Taba, after that, came too late. People whom Sontag interviewed from both sides wondered why the Clinton proposals weren't made public earlier. Instead the negotiators met in Taba only much later that month, without Clinton or any US representatives. Most participants, Israeli or Palestinian, thought the session successful.

Contrary to the belief by many Israelis that the Palestinians had remained inflexible over the refugee right of return throughout the final status talks, a proposition that raises existential fears for Israel, Yossi Beilin reported that the two sides were constructing an "agreed narrative" to defuse the explosive character of this issue and protect the Jewish identity of Israel.[10]

REACTION TO THE SONTAG ARTICLE

The Sontag article detonated sharply among those for whom it was a matter of creed that Arafat alone was at fault. Ehud Barak himself raged, in a *New York Times* op-ed, not so much against Sontag as against his adversary, Arafat, and made a bid, cognate to what Sharon was asking at the time, for the exclusion of Arafat from the process.[11]

The principal characters were now upon the stage. Since an April 6, 2001, article in *Ma'ariv*, the excerpts from former foreign minister Shlomo Ben-Ami's detailed diaries of both Camp David and Taba had been circulating, from a variety of sources, and were widely used even in the Deborah Sontag special report. Ben-Ami had been trying to alert Israelis and the Israeli negotiating team of the realities of Palestinian effort in the Camp David process, which few were ready to recognize.

Ben-Ami was also convinced that the new American administration had failed disastrously in its responsibilities.[12]

THE DEBATE IN THE *NEW YORK REVIEW OF BOOKS*

The principal stage now became the weekly *New York Review of Books*.

Robert Malley had teamed up with Hussein Agha, a senior associate member of St. Anthony's College, Oxford, who had been involved in Israeli–Palestinian negotiations over many years, and from this time the two would sign a number of major articles together.

Essentially, Malley and Agha argued that the failure of the Camp David effort to produce the definitive end of the conflict rose from the different perspectives that the three parties (US as well as Israeli and Palestinian) brought to the table. Barak, as even the Ben-Ami diaries made clear, had been withholding fulfillment of prior agreements so that the Palestinians would be forced to negotiate them all over again and make new concessions. He wanted to leave Arafat no fallback options if the summit should fail, hence his insistence on holding this all-or-nothing summit.

Meeting Clinton one last time before the summit, on June 15, Arafat had set forth his case: Barak had not implemented prior agreements, there had been no progress in the negotiations, and the prime minister was holding all the cards. "The summit is our last card," Arafat said. "Do you really want to burn it?"

For the United States, then, the challenge was formidable. For the time, they believed this an historic opportunity. Neither Clinton nor his advisers were blind to the distrust between the two sides.

So was there a generous Israeli offer, and if so, was it peremptorily rejected by Arafat?

All Israelis agree, wrote Malley and Agha, that Barak broke every conceivable taboo and went as far as any Israeli prime minister had gone or could go. It was still hard to state confidently how far he was prepared to go. Barak wanted never to reveal his final positions, even to the United States. Members of the US team, if asked before, during, or even after Camp David to describe Barak's true positions, could not do so.

Hence each Israeli position was presented as immovable, a red-line approach at the uttermost limit of Israeli interests. Yet his red lines kept shifting, and he gave clear hints that Israel would show more flexibility if Arafat was prepared to "contemplate" the endgame. The bottom lines were false bottoms, tension and ambiguity was always there.

But strictly speaking, there never was an Israeli offer. Wanting to reserve Israel's position in the event of failure, the Israelis always stopped one or even more steps short of a proposal. Generally, ideas were presented as US concepts, not Israeli ones.

Malley and Agha ask why, since Camp David, the Palestinians have not been able to make their case. From their perspective, Oslo itself was the historic compromise, an agreement to concede 78 percent of mandatory Palestine to Israel.

And thus the path the United States had contemplated in the negotiations—getting a position close to the Israeli bottom line, putting it to the Palestinians and getting a counterproposal from them to bring back to the Israelis—took many wrong turns. It started without a real bottom line, continued without a counterproposal, and ended without a deal.

The Taba stage of the negotiations showed the distance traveled since Camp David by the end of the year. Clinton's December "parameters," like Camp David, did not present the terms of a final deal, but ways in which accelerated, final negotiations could take place. Yet in January, a final effort at Taba, without US officials, produced more progress and some hope. By then it was too late. Clinton was gone, and Sharon on the way.[13]

INTERVENTION BY DENNIS ROSS

The matter did not rest there. Dennis Ross wrote a reply in a letter to the editors published September 20, 2001, dismayed at what he had read. Conceding error and inadequacies on all sides, his main argument was to emphasize again Arafat's passivity at Camp David. And then Ross, like so many others, attributed the outbreak of the violence at the end of September to Arafat, saying he "allowed [it] to erupt and did nothing to prevent or contain it," This assumption that the violence sprang from Arafat's action or neglect is a position we have examined in detail in this book, and seen more occasion to raise such strictures about Sharon.

Ultimately, Ross's complaint against Arafat was that he showed no capacity to make a deal. That was exactly the question: whether any such thing had been offered him, or whether instead this was a negotiation process that needed to be carried further, as indeed it was.

The September 20 exchange concludes with a response from Robert Malley and Hussein Agha. They called Dennis Ross's letter "one of the more thoughtful and articulate presentations of the view that has been widely accepted since the failure of Camp David." But they challenge the central premise of his letter: that Arafat's faults were of a different nature than those of the others, or that they demonstrated an inherent incapacity in him of doing a permanent status deal. They paraphrased Ross's argument thus: Though conceding missteps on the Israeli and American sides, Ross had proceeded to deny any significant impact of their failures on the ultimate outcome of the effort. Yet if Arafat had been capable of reaching a deal, they would have had one; the fact that they had none was proof that he was incapable.

Former foreign minister Shlomo Ben-Ami, whose diaries on Camp David had been circulating for some time now, had by this time made himself heard again, in a long interview in the *Ha'aretz* magazine section by Ari Shavit, dated September 15. He described Barak as having fallen, after Camp David, into a depression that made it impossible for him to advance further with any sort of trust.

Asked why the summit had failed, Ben-Ami cited it as a common view that Camp David had failed because of wrongheaded negotiating tactics, because of the behavior of Ehud Barak, and because Barak had humiliated Arafat, showing him disrespect. But when all was said and done, Ben-Ami held, Camp David failed because of Arafat's refusal to put forward proposals of his own. Israelis felt the Palestinians were constantly trying to drag them into some sort of black hole of more and more concessions without knowing where the concessions were leading, or what was the finish line.

Shavit asked Ben-Ami about the personal relationship between Barak and Arafat, how Barak had comported himself, and whether he had in fact been too tough in his attitude toward Arafat. Ben-Ami responded: "Look, Ehud is not a very pleasant person. It's hard to like him." He described Barak as closed and introverted, allowing no emotional contact. All the Israeli team, he said, had experienced that. But ought anyone think that if Barak had been nicer to Arafat, that Arafat would have given up the right of return? Or the Haram al-Sharif?

But asked about the actual relations of the two at Camp David, Ben-Ami said that actually, they had never met at all. Once at a dinner that Madeleine Albright gave, while Clinton was in Japan, in order to break the ice, Barak had sat like a pillar of salt and said not a word for hours. Ben-Ami had been embarrassed, seeing that as a low point.

Did Ben-Ami therefore believe that the *intifada* was a calculated move by the Palestinians to extricate them from their political and diplomatic hardships? The question paralleled the Palestinian suspicion that Barak's and Ben-Ami's own consent to Sharon's provocative journey to the Temple Mount was their "exit strategy" from negotiation, as Saeb Erekat had been suggesting. Ben-Ami answered no. He was not attributing that sort of Machiavellian scheme to them.

Ben-Ami's account of Taba, detailed and nuanced, agreed basically with the reports of all others except Sher, in feeling that agreement had been so close they could touch it if they had only had more time.[14]

THE LEADERS ENTER THE CONTEST

In February of 2002, Arafat published an op-ed in the *New York Times* in his own name. "We wish to live as an equal neighbor," he wrote, speaking for all Palestinians, "alongside Israel." The Palestinians, he said, were ready to end the conflict. They were ready to sit down at once with any Israeli leader, regardless of his history, to negotiate freedom for the Palestinians, a complete end to the occupation, security for Israel and creative solutions to the plight of the refugees, while yet respecting Israel's demographic concerns. But they would only sit down, he asserted, as equals, not as supplicants; as partners, not as subjects; as seekers for a just and peaceful solution, not as a defeated nation grateful for whatever scraps were thrown their way. "For despite Israel's overwhelming military advantage, we possess something even greater: the power of justice."[15]

In a far more extensive article, Ehud Barak himself now entered the lists against Malley and Agha in the *New York Review of Books*. The June 13, 2002 issue carried two major contributions, one an interview with Barak by Benny Morris, the historian who had explored the Palestinian *naqba* experience of 1948 but since the new *intifada*, had been outspokenly angry with the Palestinians, and a reply by Agha and Malley.

The Barak interview had taken place in several sessions in late March and early April. It is all presented in the voice of Morris. It begins dramatically as Barak recalls a phone call from Bill Clinton just hours after the publication in the *New York Times* of what he describes as Deborah Sontag's "revisionist" article. Clinton said (according to Barak):

> What the hell is this? Why is she turning the mistakes we made into the essence? The true story of Camp David was that for the first time in the history of the conflict the American President put on the table a proposal, based on UN Security Council resolutions 242 and 338, very close to the Palestinian demands, and Arafat refused even to accept it as a basis for negotiations, walked out of the room, and deliberately turned to terrorism. That's the real story—all the rest is gossip.

Sontag and Malley, in Barak's view, were "naive journalists." Arafat and his colleagues, Barak believed, wanted a Palestinian state in the whole of Palestine.

Having thus converted the Palestinians into the relentless enemy, who could only be crushed, Barak read Arafat's mind as believing that Israel had no right to exist, and that he intended its demise. The Arabs were products of a culture in which to tell a lie created no problem, as it would in a Judeo-Christian culture. Truth for them was an irrelevant category. For them, there was no such thing as "the truth."

Barak dismissed summarily the thesis of the "revisionists" that Ariel Sharon's visit to the Temple Mount had anything to do with the *intifada*.

For the argument that the Israeli–US proposals offered the Palestinians not a contiguous state but a collection of "bantustans" Barak had no patience. How could the offer of 92 percent of the West Bank lead to anything other than contiguity? And that he had presented his (and Clinton's) proposals as a diktat, he responded that it was a lie, that everything proposed had been open to continued negotiations.

For all that, he held out no real hope for negotiation, and speculated that it would be 80 years after 1948 before Palestinians would be ready for a compromise with Israel. He pointed to the model of the Soviet Union, which had collapsed after something like 80 years, when the generation that had lived through the revolution had died.

Barak had invested some worry, too, about the Israeli Palestinians. He thought the time might come, in the fashioning of an eventual Palestine, when some areas with large Arab concentrations might be transferred, with their inhabitants, to the Palestinian state.[16]

Hussein Agha and Robert Malley were accorded right of reply to this interview with Barak, and their article followed immediately after in the June 13, 2002, issue of the *New York Review of Books*.

It was Barak's claim that the current Palestinian leadership wanted "a Palestinian state in all of Palestine," rejecting the two-state solution as they rejected the legitimacy of Israel's existence entirely. That being the core charge, central to his whole argument, it should be taken up, wrote Malley and Agha, issue by issue. They proceeded to do that in the rest of their article.

The Palestinians had formally adopted their position on the boundaries of their future state as early as 1988, when they publicly accepted the state of Israel and sought a Palestinian state based on the June 4, 1967, borders, to live at peace alongside Israel. At Camp David, Arafat's negotiators had accepted the proposal that Israel annex some West Bank territory to accommodate settlements. They did so with insistence on a one-for-one swap of land "of equal size and value," arguing that the annexed territory should neither affect the contiguity of their own land nor lead to the incorporation of Palestinians into Israel.

The ideas put forth by President Clinton at Camp David fell short of those demands. He had proposed, as a way to accommodate Israeli settlements, a deal by which Israel would annex 9 percent of the West Bank in exchange for turning over only a part of pre-1967 Israel that equated to

1 percent of the West Bank. That would entail the incorporation of tens of thousands of additional Palestinians into Israeli territory near the annexed settlements, and would also have meant that annexed territory encroached deep inside the Palestinian state. But in his December "parameters" Clinton suggested an Israeli annexation of between 4 and 6 percent of the West Bank in exchange for a land swap of between 1 and 3 percent. At Taba—is this a counterproposal or not?—the Palestinians presented their own map showing roughly 3.1 percent of the West Bank under Israeli sovereignty, with an equivalent land swap in areas abutting the West Bank and Gaza.

On Jerusalem, the Palestinians had accepted at Camp David the principle of Israeli sovereignty over the Western Wall, the Jewish Quarter of the Old City, and the Jewish neighborhoods of East Jerusalem, though those neighborhoods had not been part of Israel before the 1967 war. This was a negotiated offer though the Palestinians clung to the view that all of East Jerusalem should be Palestinian.

On refugees, in contrast to the issues of territory and Jerusalem, the Palestinians offered no position on how it should be dealt with as a practical matter, but instead they had offered a set of working principles. First, they insisted on the need to recognize the refugees' right of return as a matter of law, lest with the jettisoning of law the agreement lose all legitimacy with the vast refugee constituency, which was roughly half the Palestinian population. Second, they acknowledged that Israel's demographic interests had to be recognized and taken into account.

It was inaccurate, therefore, to say the Palestinians had taken no constructive positions. Though their proposals were not detailed, they were plentiful. Barak, of course, had broken serious taboos in his own proposals at Camp David, but the Palestinians believed they had made their own historic concession at Oslo, when they had agreed to cede 78 percent of what had been mandatory Palestine to Israel. Just as the Israelis rejected the idea that the Palestinians should take every concession as a starting point to ask for more, the Palestinians saw no justice in the Israelis' further whittling down what they saw as already a compromise position.

Having thus disposed of Barak's charge that the Palestinians sought to destroy the Israeli state, Malley and Agha went on to Barak's ignoring of his own deficiencies. On taking office, he had chosen to renegotiate the agreement Netanyahu had made on withdrawal of Israeli forces from the West Bank rather than implement it. He had continued and intensified settlement construction. He had delayed the Palestinian track while he concentrated on Syria, and failed to release Palestinian prisoners detained for acts prior to the Oslo agreement, as agreed. He failed also to carry out signed agreements to implement the third redeployment of Israeli troops and the transfer of the three Jerusalem villages. And his description of Arabs as people who "don't suffer from the problem of telling lies" revealed his penchant for disparaging judgment on an entire people.[17]

CONCLUSIONS

There is more in the Barak and Malley/Agha articles, but with that we have seen the main arguments raised by either side to determine whether Camp David, with its Taba appendage, was Palestinian perfidy, aptly punished by the subsequent Sharon warfare on the Palestinians, or a tragedy of lost opportunities for both peoples from which they should now be seriously seeking a healing exit. The exchanges of opinion would go on further, both Barak and the Malley–Agha team retaining the hospitality of the *New York Review of Books* for some time to come, and Israeli writers, peace activists, and angry rejectionists alike publishing their opinions in the Israeli press with a freedom US readers never see in their own popular media.

More and heavier attacks have been made, on Arafat's headquarters in Ramallah, on cities all over the West Bank and Gaza Strip. Suicide bombs have multiplied, deaths accumulated, all against a background of the US "war on terrorism" which tends to justify any action by those on whom the favor of the Bush administration shines.

Israelis and Palestinians, meanwhile, have produced a variety of joint model peace agreements, none sanctioned by the current Israeli government but with the clear blessings of the Palestinian Authority and Arafat. Most conspicuous is the Geneva Accord, centrally the work of Yossi Beilin, architect of each of the major Israeli advances toward peace in the last 15 years, currently out of office and the Knesset, and Yasser Abed Rabbo, long one of Arafat's most trusted allies and negotiators. The Accord was reached through three years of sedulous negotiation with the assistance of the Swiss Foreign Ministry. It is a detailed and thorough treatment of every outstanding issue of the conflict, signed with great solemnity in the presence of a multitude of international well-wishers, given cordial welcome by other foreign ministries throughout Europe and the Middle East, even in the United States, where the secretary of state received the principal signers. Ariel Sharon and his spokespeople could hardly contain their fury at the thought that anyone should dare conceive or sign such a thing. Strong peace-minded American Jewish groups, such as the Tikkun Community and Brit Tzedek, also lent their full support and hosted US lecture tours by the principal signers.

From their tiny corner of the world these two peoples could easily call down massive destruction on themselves and many other peoples around the globe. For their own sake and the sake of others they need to marshal their best forces, as they did in Oslo in 1993, at a time when little outside diplomatic help was available to them. The Israeli people can in fact be relied upon to choose the way of peace when they see a real opening for it. Palestinians have already made their difficult decision before, to live alongside Israel at peace, in a state of their own, and they have known well that only by doing so will they have a future of peace themselves.

Notes

INTRODUCTION

1. Simha Flapan, *Zionism and the Palestinians* (London, New York, Croom Helm, Barnes & Noble Books, 1979).
2. Simha Flapan, *The Birth of Israel: Myths and Realities* (New York, Pantheon, 1987).
3. The first quote is a commonplace of early Zionism, from Herzl through Ben-Gurion, originally the most quoted line of Theodor Herzl's *Judenstaat*. The second is Golda Meir's mantra, the reference to a widely publicized statement of June 1969. Ariel Sharon is widely cited, throughout the period in which he advocated and fostered the settlement of Jewish colonies in the occupied territories, as saying that the Palestinian state was Jordan.
4. Information on the Committee, now with a membership of some 2,600 American Jews, Christians and Muslims, can be found on its website <http://www.usicpme.org/>. Over the two-year interval between our 1985 visit to the Middle East and the public announcement of this new organization, we had kept calling meetings of American Jews, Christians, and Muslims. Each time we would look around the room, tell ourselves that these were the "usual suspects," the people who would be expected to take up a soft peacenik position on the conflict, and decide that we must convene a more mainstream group. We finally held a press conference in Washington to announce the formation of the Interreligious Committee in June 1987.
5. Now Palestinian ambassador both to the United Kingdom and to the Holy See.
6. The Holy See did have long-range plans at this time, of course, with regard to the Soviet empire.

PART I: CHAPTER 1

1. General information on this earlier history can be had from many sources. A useful one is Mark Tessler, *A History of the Israeli–Palestinian Conflict* (Indiana University Press, 1994). Tessler deals with the Rabat summit of the Arab League in 1994 that recognized the PLO as sole legitimate representative of the Palestinian people on p. 484, Arafat's 1994 address to the UN on p. 484, the 1982 Fez Plan on pp. 607–9, 613–14, and in many further references.
2. Security Council Resolution 242, of 1967, passed several months after the Six-Day War that gave Israel total control of all Palestine, plus the Sinai peninsula and the Golan Heights, has ranked ever since as the touchstone of any peace resolution of the Middle Eastern conflict. It is described, by a stretch of simplification, as an exchange of land for peace. Resolution 338, one of a sequence of ceasefire demands made during the October War of 1973, is usually cited alongside 242. What it does is simply to refer back to the

requirements of 242, still not implemented after, by that time, six years, and demand that the parties meet those requirements.
3. Alain Gresh, *The PLO: The Struggle Within: Towards an Independent Palestinian State* (London, Zed Books, 1985; first published in French, Paris, Papyrus, 1983).
4. The 1917 statement by the British government that it favored the establishment of a Jewish homeland in Palestine.
5. The UN General Assembly decision (Resolution 181 of November, 1947) to partition Palestine into two independent states, one Jewish, one Arab.
6. The Labor and Likud parties had won nearly equal numbers of seats in the 1984 Knesset election, and this device was the only way either could lead a Grand Coalition government. Shamir was due to replace Peres as prime minister on October 14.
7. Member of the Knesset.
8. Patriarch of Antioch for the Greek Catholic Church, resident, like the Patriarch of Antioch for the Greek Orthodox Church, in Damascus. The Greek Catholics are an important denomination in Lebanon and among Palestinians.
9. Mapam, from the beginning of the State of Israel, had been the sister socialist party to Mapai, Ben-Gurion's party that stands at the origin of the Labor Party. Mapam has always been a bit further to the left. The clearest presentation I know of the relation between Mapai and Mapam from that early time is in Benny Morris, *1948 and After: Israel and the Palestinians* (Oxford, Clarendon Press, 1994, pp. 49 ff).
10. This visit became famous later, as many suspected that the Vice President had used his time in Jerusalem to advance the arms deals with Iran that became a major feature of the Iran–Contra scandal.
11. Khalidi, scholarly head of a leading Jerusalem family, had founded the Institute for Palestine Studies in Beirut some year earlier, and for many years edited the *Journal of Palestine Studies*. He has been a fellow at Harvard University since 1982. At a 1983 conference on the Middle East at Emory University in Atlanta, I had heard former President Jimmy Carter recognize Khalidi as the most reasonable Palestinian voice he knew. Khalidi would help me considerably with my own endeavors over the next two years.
12. The Geneva Conference, called for in UN Security Council Resolution 338 as the opportunity for the international community, including the Soviet Union and Europe, to address the entire complex of the Middle East conflict, opened for just a single day, December 21, 1973, and closed the same afternoon after only seven hours, leaving the United States as effectively the only mediator in the conflict to the exclusion of all others. A useful account can be found in Fred J. Khouri, *The Arab-Israeli Dilemma*, 3rd ed. (Syracuse University Press, 1985, pp. 371–6).
13. An apostolic delegate is the Vatican representative to the bishops of a country or region with which the Holy See has no formal diplomatic relations. Where there are diplomatic relations—between the Vatican State and the country, not between the Church and the country—the Vatican diplomat will have the rank of nuncio (equivalent to ambassador). It was a matter of considerable resentment to Israelis, mentioned with much distaste by Mrs. Vered, the counselor on religious affairs at the Israeli Foreign Ministry, that the apostolic delegate was described as missioned to Jerusalem, to Jordan *and to Palestine*.
14. My account of the Vance–Dayan meeting draws simply on Arafat's.

15. These two episodes were both the work of Abu Nidal's breakaway Fatah Revolutionary Council. The Karachi hijacking had occurred just a few days before on September 5, 1986, the very day of Arafat's Harare speech. Four guerrillas, disguised as maintenance men, seized a Pan-Am 747 during a fueling stop. Things got out of control when the pilot escaped by leaping from the cockpit, immobilizing the plane on the ground. As Pakistani police stormed the plane, passengers tried to escape by an emergency exit. Twenty died before the hijackers surrendered. The following day, September 6, two of Abu Nidal's men, posing as photographers, entered the Neve Shalom Synagogue, Istanbul's largest, locked the door from inside with an iron bar, opened fire on the worshippers with a machine gun and then blew themselves up, killing 21 of the congregation and wounding four. The two spectacular terrorist attacks so dominated the international press that they distracted media attention from Arafat's Harare speech, and may well have been timed for that purpose.
16. Both had refused to lay siege to cities that had refused to admit them, but instead, appealing to common Islamic values between them and the citizens, persuaded them to act as friends.
17. At the request of the Reagan administration, he had visited President Khadafy in Libya. Members of Congress reacted with fury when they heard this, another instance of rejection of any form of communication with adversaries other than by violence. Wilson had to leave his Vatican post, though without attributing it directly to this incident.
18. Moshe Amirav, minister in Yitzhak Shamir's Likud cabinet, instituted covert conversations with Sari Nusseibeh, then a professor at Bir Zeit University, about the future of Israel and Palestine in the course of 1987. Amirav, long a supporter of the right-wing positions of Menachem Begin and Shamir, had been a participant in four wars when, during the Lebanon War of 1982, he decided that Israelis and Palestinians had somehow to do better. He introduced himself to Nusseibeh as the right wing, with whom the Palestinians had to do business if they were to come to a peaceful agreement with Israel. Nusseibeh introduced him to Faisal Husseini, my friend since 1981 and the leading Palestinian in Jerusalem. Together, in secret meetings in one another's homes, they hammered out an understanding of what conditions would be required if the two sides were to agree, an understanding that still stands as the template for an ultimate resolution of the conflict. Shamir, when Amirav told him of these conversations, expelled him from cabinet and party, and put him on trial for the offense of speaking to the PLO. Amirav had to retreat from politics and confine himself to an academic position as professor in Tel Aviv after this. His accomplishment, as he recognized, was prophetic rather than practical, but in more recent years he has emerged again as consultant to prime ministers seeking to make the peace. Amirav published an important article in the *Jerusalem Post* (international edition, week ending October 24, 1987), "How Likud could achieve peace," and has written and lectured on his experience frequently since. My own acquaintance with him and his story is from two videotaped interviews made by my own associates from Boston College, one in June 2000, the other in January 2002.
19. Videotaped interview with Husseini, taken in June 2000. Abu Jihad was soon assassinated, in front of his wife and daughter, at his villa in Tunis by an Israeli commando unit because of this activity.
20. The PNC was held in September. I had been invited to attend, and wrote back

that I thought I would squander my access to Israelis and Americans if I did so.
21. UN General Assembly Resolution 3379, November 10, 1975.
22. There were two such meetings in Stockholm, one with a Palestinian delegation led by Arafat's close lieutenant, Bassam Abu Sharif, the second with Arafat himself. Bassam Abu Sharif had published an important op-ed article in the *New York Times* on June 22, 1988 explaining the Palestinian acceptance of 242/338 as a part of international legality while also calling for recognition of the rest of the UN's resolutions as equally part of international legality. 242, he said, made no mention of the national rights of the Palestinian people or their right to self-determination. For this reason alone they accepted 242 and 338 but in the context of the other resolutions which do recognize the national rights of the Palestinian people. Here was the source of much of the confusion over whether Arafat's recognition of 242/338 was conditional or not, and the reason for the State Department's desire for the "two-paragraph" statement.
23. The entire transaction is fascinating to follow, from the convening of the Palestine National Council in Algiers on 12 November 1988, which made its declaration of Palestinian independence and implied its acceptance of the State of Israel, through the cold and dismissive reception of its declarations by both US and Israeli governments; on to Arafat's application for a US visa to come to New York and address his acceptance of the three preconditions to the United Nations; the US rejection of the visa application; the UN General Assembly's vote to transport the entire Assembly to Geneva in order to hear Arafat, despite its reluctance to offend the United States as host country; Arafat's speech to the General Assembly in Geneva, which was rejected by the United States as not fully meeting its conditions, by Israel's Prime Minister Shamir as merely "double talk"; the emergency press conference the following morning at which Arafat would make the statement that finally satisfied the United States (but not Israel) and consequently the initiation of a US/PLO dialogue, for which US ambassador to Tunisia Robert Pelletreau would be the "only authorized channel." The whole dramatic sequence can be followed in the daily issues of the *New York Times*, and doubtless elsewhere, from November 13 through December 15, 1988. The specific information about all the phone communication of the night of December 13, Robert Murphy at the State Department to Ulf Hjertonsson at the Swedish Embassy in Washington to Swedish Foreign Minister Sten Andersen in Stockholm to Bassam Abu Sharif in Genera, who briefed Arafat on exactly what words he must use to satisfy US requirements, and especially Reagan's communication to Secretary of State Shultz is partly from private sources but was extensively written up in the *New York Times* on December 16, 1988.
24. A good account of the development can be found in Donald Neff, *Fallen Pillars: US Policy towards Palestine and Israel since 1945* (Washington D.C., Institute for Palestine Studies, 1995, pp. 166ff).
25. Andrew Young had had to resign his position as US ambassador to the UN simply for having been at a cocktail party where two PLO representatives were also present.
26. Only many years later, when on February 11, 1999 the Israeli newspaper *Ha'aretz* reported it, did I find that Yitzhak Rabin and Shimon Peres had looked into these matters. The *Ha'aretz* report was picked up by the *New York Times* that same day. Rabin was then defense minister, Peres foreign minister in the unity government of Yitzhak Shamir, his turn as prime

minister under the rotation. According to an unattributed account, apparently leaked by a participant in the talks, Rabin and Peres sent Labor MK Ephraim Sneh to Paris as their representative. Confronted with this report, Sneh told *Ha'aretz* he had heard from Rabin that Shamir had approved the talks. Peres maintained that Shamir was content with reports that the talks were about missing Israeli soldiers and took no further interest. Shamir contended that the talks had been held without his knowledge or approval.

PART I: CHAPTER 2

1. Cf. Introduction, Note 4.
2. As reported to me privately by friends in the PLO.
3. Hussein visited these "guests" at the Baghdad hotel where they were held, ostentatiously taking in his arms a seven-year-old British boy, Stuart Lockwood, to demonstrate his fondness for children. A famous photo circulated through all the Western press, showing the boy looking with horror at the dictator who held him. It is reproduced in Lawrence Freedman and Efraim Karsh, *The Gulf Conflict, 1990–1991: Diplomacy and War in the New World Order* (Princeton University Press, 1992), opposite p. 218.
4. Private communications.
5. Patrick Seale, English journalist and author, gives a full account of this killing, confirmatory of information I received, in his book, *Abu Nidal: A Gun for Hire* (New York, Random House, 1992, pp. 32–9).
6. Letter of September 1, 1991.
7. Patrick Seale drew the same conclusion, and it is in fact the main thesis of his 1992 book on Abu Nidal, which he wrote following an assertion of Abu Nidal's betrayal by Abu Iyad himself shortly before his death (ibid., pp. 39–53).
8. This sacred site is of immense religious importance both to Jews and Muslims. The platform—a large plaza—was built up by Herod the Great, who buttressed it with huge retaining walls around the hilltop of the Second Temple, which he also enlarged and embellished. Centuries after the Roman destruction of the Temple, the platform became the site of the Al-Aqsa Mosque (built by the Caliph Walid between 705 and 715) and the Dome of the Rock (built by the Caliph Abd al-Malik in 691–2), associated both with Muslim reverence for all the Jewish prophets and with the night-time journey of Mohammed (Sura 17 in the Koran) to the "distant mosque" (masjid al-Aqsa) from which he was taken up in a vision to heaven. The sole remnant of the temple to which Jews had access was the Western retaining wall, long known as the "Wailing Wall" where Jews mourned the destruction of the temple. Praying at the wall has become Jewish tradition. Orthodox Jews will not ascend to the platform itself, lest they tread on the site of the Holy of Holies, the inner sanctum of the temple, whose exact location is uncertain. Their adopted place of prayer, at the wall, is therefore vulnerable to missiles thrown from the platform above them.
9. Cf. Introduction (section: "States of mind").
10. The Geneva Conventions of 1949 continued a tradition begun in 1864 to regulate the laws of war. The Fourth Convention, of August 12, 1949, concerned itself with the protection of civilian persons in times of war, and contains extensive materials on the duties of occupying powers. Requirements for the protection of civilian persons under occupation are the burden of Part

II, "General protection of populations against certain consequences of war," Articles 13–26.
11. This is the meaning of Article 2 of the UN Charter, which defines the basic purpose of the organization. Every member nation, by virtue of signing the Charter, renounces, by solemn treaty obligation, any acquisition of territory by force.
12. Sununu, with his Lebanese heritage, had shown much interest in a long correspondence I held between 1988 and 1990 with Raymond Eddé, who would likely have been elected president of Lebanon but for a veto by Syria. That correspondence had, at Eddé's request, been published in book form under my name earlier that year, *La Question Libanaise selon Raymond Eddé* (Paris, Cariscript, 1990).
13. The conference would take its name from Madrid, where its first formal sessions were held, 30 October to 1 November 1991. Subsequent sessions would take place in Washington at intervals over the next year.
14. The structure of the Madrid Conference negotiations, in all their complexity, are laid out on the website of the Israeli Foreign Ministry, http://www.us-israel.org/jsource/Peace/madrid1.html.
15. That would change after the 1995 mid-term election when, after being stymied on his domestic policies, especially his comprehensive medical plan, he lost both houses of Congress to the Republican opposition. For the remaining six years of his presidency, his hands were so tied in domestic policy that he necessarily turned his attention to foreign affairs, and proved astonishingly adept at it. In those first two years I had once, in a television interview, picked up the famous canard about President Ford, and said Clinton would have to learn to walk and chew gum at the same time.
16. Now US ambassador to Israel after many years at the State Department's Middle East desk.
17. A distinguished cardiac surgeon, of Kashmiri origin, and president of the most prominent Islamic center in the Boston area.
18. Pelletreau had been the one and only US official permitted, during the period of the US/PLO dialogue, to speak to an officer of the PLO, though only at the level of Yasser Abed Rabbo, an Arafat confidant in Tunis at the same level as Pelletreau, then US ambassador to Tunisia.
19. Details of this process were spelled out in a *New York Times* article by Clyde Haberman on Sunday September 5, 1993, shortly after the news broke but several days before the actual signing on September 13.

PART I: CHAPTER 3

1. Currently prime minister of Israel, Sharon has a long military record, from his command of an infantry company in Israel's 1948 Independence War through his command of the Paratroop Corps in the 1956 Sinai Campaign and his prominent role in command of an armored division in the Sinai desert in the 1967 war. In the Yom Kippur War of 1973 he led the crossing of the Suez Canal, which brought about victory in the war. His violent clashes with Palestinians start with 1953, when he founded and led the "101" special commando unit to carry out retaliatory operations. As minister of agriculture in Menachem Begin's government, from 1977, he fostered the large-scale settlement of Israelis in the occupied territories, and as defense minister in 1981 was a principal force in the Israeli invasion of Lebanon. That war left him with a conviction, by an Israeli

investigative commission, of "indirect responsibility" for the massacre of Palestinian civilians in the Sabra and Shatila refugee camps in Beirut. Dismissed then from the defense ministry but retaining his cabinet position as minister without portfolio, Sharon made his way back through further cabinet posts which enabled him to keep promoting Israeli settlements on occupied land, eventually becoming foreign minister in Binyamin Netanyahu's government in 1998, where he was able to create delays in the final status negotiations mandated under the Oslo accords with the Palestinians. Made interim Likud party leader after Netanyahu's defeat in 1999, he managed to inflame Palestinian passions through his demarche, accompanied by 1,000 armed men and making a claim of exclusive possession, onto the platform known to Jews as the Temple Mount and to Muslims as the Noble Sanctuary on September 28, 2000, an incident seen by many as the start of the renewed violence of recent years. With the promise that he could suppress that violence, he won election as prime minister of Israel in a special election of February 6, 2001, and has governed the country since.
2. Eitan, with a long military record in all Israel's wars since 1948, was chief of staff for the Lebanon War of 1982, and like Sharon was convicted of "indirect responsibility" for the Sabra and Shatila refugee camp massacres that climaxed that war. Dismissed from the military at that point, he founded, in 1983, the Tzomet party (Movement for Renewed Zionism), which demands the full retention by Israel of the occupied Palestinian territories. Eitan had the habit of expressing his hostility to Palestinians often and in the crudest manner, never more obviously than at his testimony before the Knesset's Foreign Affairs and Defense Committee at the time of his forced retirement from the army, in April 1983. He told the legislators: "When we have settled the land, all the Arabs will be able to do about it will be to scurry around like drugged roaches in a bottle." (David K. Shipler, *Arab and Jew: Wounded Spirits in a Promised Land*, Penguin Books, 1987, pp. 234f).
3. Operations Officer in the war of 1967, Ze'evi advanced the idea of "transfer" of the whole Palestinian population, their forced evacuation from all West Bank and Gaza territory, from 1987, and in 1988 founded the Moledet ("Homeland") party to propound such expulsion, becoming in that way successor to the Kach party of Rabbi Meir Kahane, which had been excluded from Israeli elections because of its racism. On that platform, he served as minister without portfolio in Yitzhak Shamir's government from February 1991 to January 1992, and was welcomed into Ariel Sharon's government as minister of tourism in March 2001. He was assassinated by Palestinians in a Jerusalem hotel on October 17, 2001.
4. Gene Sharp's books, fundamental to the study of non-violent protest, include the three-volume *The Politics of Nonviolent Action* (Boston, Extending Horizon Books, Porter Sargent, 1973), *Gandhi as a Political Strategist* (Boston, Extending Horizon Books, 1979) and *Social Power and Political Freedom* (Boston, Extending Horizon Books, 1980).
5. Amal, whose acronym names means "hope," was the brainchild of Musa al-Sadr, the Gandhi-like figure who had led Lebanon's deprived Shi'ites to a sense of their own worth and power, and identified their quest for self-realization with a more general movement for "the dispossessed" of all confessional groups. It had continued to flourish even after the 1978 disappearance of Musa al-Sadr, who is thought to have been murdered at the instigation of Libya's Colonel Khadafy. Best information on Musa al-Sadr can be had from Fouad Ajami, *The Vanished Imam* (Cornell University Press, 1988).
6. The UN Security Council had in fact demanded Israeli withdrawal from this

occupation of southern Lebanon from its beginning in the invasion of 1978. SC Resolution 425, passed unanimously with the concurrence even of the United States, had been left unimplemented since that time.
7. Dated December 22, 1993.
8. The *New York Times* carried an Associated Press bulletin of this incident as its lead story on February 25. On the following day they gave it full coverage, Clyde Habermann writing of the shooting incident itself, Joel Greenberg giving background on the animosities that surrounded the site, Alison Mitchell information on Goldstein himself.
9. Dated May 10, 1994.
10. A great deal of literature accumulated on the economic effects of closures, which prevented Palestinians from getting to jobs in Israel, and the village-by-village isolation that hindered the marketing of their products. The best study, though dealing only with Gaza and not with the West Bank, is Sara Roy, *The Gaza Strip: The Political Economy of De-development* (Washington, D.C., Institute for Palestine Studies, 1995).
11. *New York Times*, Serge Schmemann, September 24, 1995.
12. These figures come from the Oslo 2 Map, with text, published by the Begin-Sadat Center for Strategic Studies, Bar-Ilan University,<http://www.biu.ac.il/SOC/besa/publications/maps/oslo2map.htm>.
13. A document of 1964, revised 1968. A text, provided by the Israeli Ministry of Foreign Affairs, but based on the English rendition published in *Basic Political Documents of the Armed Palestinian Resistance Movement;* Leila S. Kadi (ed.) (Palestine Research Centre, Beirut, December 1969) pp.137–41 that indicates all articles that the Palestinians agreed to revoke according to the Oslo 2 Agreement can be found at <http://www.mfa.gov.il/mfa/go.asp?MFAH00pv0>.
14. The electoral reform was of course the subject of vast debate in Israel. The decision to go to direct election of the prime minister, in a vote separate from that for the 120 members of the Knesset, was taken March 18, 1992, the day before the Knesset's dissolution for that year's election, in *Basic Law: The Government* (1992), <http://www.oefre.unibe.ch/law/icl/is00000_.html>, Section 3b, but was not implemented until the 1996 election. Of the great amount of literature, the most helpful are Daniel J. Elazar and Shmuel Sandle (eds.), *Israel at the Polls,* 1992 (Lanham, MD, Rowman & Littlefield, 1995), especially ch. 3, "Fragmentation and realignment: Israel's nationalist parties in the 1992 elections," by Etta Blick, pp. 67–102, which shows the dissatisfaction out of which the new law emerged; and Asher Arian and Michal Shamir, (eds.), *The Election in Israel, 1992* (State University of New York Press, 1995), especially ch. 3, "Penetrating the system: the politics of collective identities," by Hanna Herzog, pp. 81–102; ch. 13, "The rise of instrumental voting: the campaign for political reform," by Tomar Hermann, pp. 275–98; and ch. 14, "Reforming Israel's voting schemes," by Gideon Doron and Barry Kay. After the 1996 elections comparable books were published: Elazar and Sandler (eds.), *Israel at the Polls, 1996* (this time London, Portland OR, Frank Cass, 1998), especially the chapters "Religion, ethnicity and electoral reform: the religious parties and the 1996 elections," by Eliezer Dan-Yehiya, pp. 73–102; "The direct election of the prime minister: a balance sheet," by Bernard Gusser, who believes the two-way race for prime minister actually caused the smaller parties to group around their platforms, pp. 237–57; and "Elections 1996: the candidates and the 'new politics,'" by

Michael Keren, who believes the direct PM election allowed the small parties to fracture Israeli politics still further, pp. 258–72; and Arian and Shamir, *The Elections in Israel, 1996* (State University of New York Press, in conjunction with the Israel Democracy Institute, Jerusalem, 1999), especially ch. 7, "The electoral consequences of political reform: in search of the center of the Israeli party system," by Reuven Y. Hazon; and ch. 11, "The bias of pluralism: the redistributive effects of the new electoral law," by David Nachmias and Itai Sened. The decision to elect the prime minister directly was subsequently reversed, by a Knesset vote of March 7, 2001, in *Basic Law: The Government* (2001), <http://www.us-israel.org/jsource/Politics/Basic_Law_Government01.html>, section 3b.

15. The best account of this episode and its effect is in Khalid Hroub, *Hamas: Political Thought and Practice* (Washington, D.C., Institute for Palestine Studies, 2000, pp. 142, 244–6). For contemporary accounts, *New York Times*, January 6, 1996, where Serge Schmemann, describing the general satisfaction of Israeli government figures with this killing, writes "If Mr. Ayyash's killing was an Israeli hit, there was little doubt that it was approved by Prime Minister Shimon Peres, since the secret service would not conduct so sensitive a mission on its own." For the role of the Shin Bet leader, identified only as "K," *New York Times*, January 9, 1996, p. 4, where Joel Greenberg, giving an account of his resignation after many other dismissals from Shin Bet before the retirement of the chief and the recriminations for their having failed to shield Rabin from attack, writes, "The timing of the resignation today seemed linked to the killing on Friday of Yahya Ayyash.... Although Israel has not taken responsibility for Mr. Ayyash's death, it is widely believed to be the work of Shin Bet, which saw him as its primary target. With that task accomplished and the Shin Bet's tarnished reputation at least partly restored, the time was apparently right for the resignation announcement. In his letter, 'K' called the Shin Bet 'the spearhead in the uncompromising fight against terrorism' 'I believe that I can now finish my task with a feeling of complete assurance that the service has recovered and can fulfill its mission,' he wrote." For a bit of insight into how the press assesses the importance of what it reports, it is worth noting that this nodal event, from which so much proceeded, never made the front page of the *New York Times*, the "newspaper of record" in the United States.

16. *New York Times*, November 3, 1995, gives an account of the wave of vengeance attacks mounted by Islamic Jihad in the wake of Shikaki's killing on October 26.

17. Hamas campaigns against Israeli civilians have regularly been direct retaliation following attacks on themselves. Their first major outburst had come after the killing of Palestinians on the plaza of the Al-Aqsa Mosque in November 1990, after the Palestinians had been hurling rocks down from the plaza onto Jews worshipping at the Western Wall (Hroub, *Hamas*, p. 249). The organized military wing of Hamas, the Izziddin al-Qassem Brigade, came into being early in 1992, initiating a series of attacks on Israeli military, culminating in the kidnap/killing of Israeli border guard Nassim Toledano in December, 1992 (ibid., p. 244). Prior to the Baruch Goldstein massacre at Hebron, Hamas felt it had "managed... to embarrass Israel militarily, politically, and in front of public opinion ... by restricting its struggle to the occupied land and by targeting only the military." The suicide bombings it carried out after Hebron were understood, within its own ranks, as "violating its own policy

312 Notes to Chapter 3

of not targeting civilians." (ibid., p. 246). But the killing of Ayyash led, though only after much deliberation, to the revenge attacks of February and March, 1996 (ibid., pp. 106, 142, 157, 244–6).
18. *New York Times*, February 25 and 26, 1996. A first count of 25 was soon raised to 27.
19. These were the first suicide bombing attacks since August 21, 1995, in which four had died. There had previously been seven such attacks. The largest deaths tolls before this had been 22 on a Tel Aviv bus in October 1994, and 21 at a bus stop near Netanya, January 1995 (*New York Times*, Serge Schmemann, February 25, 1996).
20. *New York Times*, February 26, 1996.
21. *New York Times*, Joel Greenberg, February 27, 1996.
22. *New York Times*, Serge Schmemann, February 25, 1996.
23. *New York Times*, Serge Schmemann, February 28, 1996.
24. *New York Times*, Joel Greenberg, March 1, 1996.
25. *New York Times*, Associated Press report, March 3, 1996; *New York Times*, Schmemann, March 4, 1996.
26. *New York Times*, March 5, 1996.
27. *New York Times*, Serge Schmemann, April 12, 1996.
28. *New York Times*, Serge Schmemann, April 13, 1996.
29. *New York Times* articles, April 13, 14, 15, 1996.
30. *New York Times*, April 16, 1996.
31. Hala Jaber, *Hezbollah: Born with a Vengeance* (Columbia University Press, 1997), pp. 169–70. *New York Times*, Douglas Jehl, April 19, 1996. The *Times*' Serge Schmemann reported the Israeli regret, and a call by Peres for a ceasefire.
32. A letter to the editor, May 30, questioned the "without a tear," citing the protest demonstrators that Israeli peace activists had held in Tel Aviv against the Qana killings.
33. *New York Times*, May 30 and 31, 1996.
34. A complex dynamic was at work here. Levy, the first Sephardic Jew to rise in Israeli politics to the point where he seemed eligible for major office, had been dissuaded by Sharon from running as Likud candidate for prime minister against Netanyahu, with the promise that he would then receive a high position. Israel's Sephardim, the Jewish immigrants from Arab countries, had been relegated to the ranks of proletarians and felt neglected by the more socially oriented Labor Party. For that reason they had tended to vote predominantly Likud, even though they had little of the extremism, either religious or secular, of the country's Ashkenazi population and believed that they, having lived with Arabs, would know better than their Ashkenazi compatriots how to make peace with the Palestinians. Levy had to be given a major post in the government to satisfy Likud's Sephardic constituency, but felt indebted to Sharon. Netanyahu would then infuriate Levy by leaving him out of major decisions that fell within the mandate of the Foreign Office, running his foreign policy from the prime minister's office and not even bringing Levy on his visits overseas.
35. *New York Times*, Serge Schmemann, June 19, 1996. The *Times* ran an editorial on June 20 urging the need to restrain Sharon and Rafael Eitan, the hard-line rightist, once chief of staff for the invasion of Lebanon but excluded from the army after his role in the Sabra-Shatila massacre, who had first been ruled out of any cabinet position because of some financial scandals, but had now been made one of the three deputy prime ministers.

Notes to Chapter 3   313

36. *New York Times* editorial Sunday, July 14, 1996, after the visit's conclusion, described Clinton as muting everything because of the upcoming presidential election.
37. *New York Times*, June 26, 1996.
38. *New York Times*, July 5, 1996.
39. *New York Times*, July 9, 1996.
40. *New York Times*, Steven Erlanger, July 10, 1996.
41. *New York Times*, July 11, 1996.
42. *New York Times*, Douglas Jehl, Jerusalem, July 12, 1996.
43. *New York Times*, July 17, 1996.
44. *New York Times*, Douglas Jehl, July 22, 1996.
45. *New York Times*, July 24, 1996.
46. *New York Times*, July 30, 1996.
47. *Ha'aretz* article cited in *New York Times*, Douglas Jehl, August 2, 1996.
48. *New York Times*, Neil Farquhar, August 3, 1996.
49. *New York Times*, Neil Farquhar, August 6, 1996.
50. *New York Times*, Reuters report, August 7, 1996.
51. *New York Times*, Reuters report, August 7, 1996.
52. *New York Times*, Douglas Jehl from Cairo, August 8, 1996.
53. A comprehensive and useful discussion of this entire sequence can be found in Helena Cobban, *The Israeli-Syrian Peace Talks, 1991–96 and Beyond* (Washington, D.C., United States Institute of Peace Press, 1999), especially, for this sequence, ch. 7, "Disintegration," pp. 151–73.
54. *New York Times*, Steven Erlanger, October 16, 1998. His articles would accompany the conference throughout.
55. Netanyahu, in these latter days of his administration, seemed more and more in thrall to Sharon. An op-ed column by William Safire, *New York Times*, October 19, 1998, took it as a sign of Netanyahu's seriousness that he turned at this point to Sharon "whose eyes light up at the sight of a map."
56. *New York Times*, October 19, 1998.
57. *New York Times*, Steven Erlanger, October 20, 1998.
58. *New York Times*, Deborah Sontag, October 20, 1998.
59. *New York Times*, Sege Schmemann, October 20, 1998.
60. *New York Times*, Deborah Sontag, October 21, 1998.
61. *New York Times*, Steven Erlanger, October 22, 1998.
62. *New York Times*, Steven Erlanger, October 23, 1998.
63. *New York Times*, October 24, 1998.
64. *New York Times*, Serge Schmemann and Steven Erlanger, October 25, 1998.
65. Established in 1996, Gesher (bridge) was formed as a breakaway from the Likud party. David Levy, the much-insulted and neglected foreign minister at the start of Netanyahu's administration, by founding Gesher, was protesting Netanyahu's refusal to integrate Sephardim into the upper echelons of the Likud party. Source: Israeli Foreign Ministry, 2003, American-Israeli Cooperative Enterprise, <http://www.us-israel.org/jsource/Politics/gesher.html>.
66. Established in 1988 as a religious Zionist alternative to the National Religious Party (NRP), Meimad (Dimensions–Movements of the Religious Center) was discouraged by the NRP's increasingly right-wing positions on the peace process and security matters. Meimad hoped to incorporate Orthodox religious practice into Israeli public life, but did not want to do so by restrictive legislation. In 1999, Meimad joined Barak's One Israel party. Israeli Foreign Ministry, <http://www.us-israel.org/jsource/Politics/Meimad.html>.
67. Election results, *New York Times*, Deborah Sontag, May 18 and 19, 1999.

PART II: CHAPTER 4

1. *New York Times*, May 18, 2003.
2. The Meretz party, <http://www.meretz.org.il/English/HomePage.htm>, is to the left of Labor. It was formed in 1973 as a merger of David Ben-Gurion's old Mapam party, the more radical labor group Ratz, a party emphasizing civil rights, and the then centrist Shinui party, which subsequently took up its own separate status.
3. Shinui, <http://www.shinui.org.il/elections/eng/>, whose Hebrew name translates as "change" or "reform," is a centrist secular party, committed to the separation of religion and state in Israel and therefore refusing to take part in any coalition with an ultra-Orthodox religious party. Barak could not afford to include any such party in his coalition without risking the loss of Shinui and its six seats as members of the government coalition, yet even if he did take in the religious parties he could nonetheless depend on Shinui's votes for any peace proposals.
4. Shas, <http://www.us-israel.org/jsource/Politics/shas.html>, is the Orthodox religious party of Sephardic Jews, keenly conscious of ethnic difference from the Ashkenazi (western European) Jews who had long formed the religious establishment in Israel. The party looks first for ever ampler state subsidies to its network of religious schools, and will join in coalition with either right or left on condition that they promise to maintain or increase that subsidy. The party's religious leader, Rabbi Ovadiah Yosef, is able to set party policy decisions rather much on his own initiative. The Israeli government's refusal to extend Rabbi Yosef's term as Sephardic Chief Rabbi (Rishon Letzion) had been one of the main reasons for the Shas party's establishment.
5. UN General Assembly Resolution 3379 of November 10, 1975.
6. A poignant testimony to this was the article by Fouad Moughrabi, "A year of discovery," in the *Journal of Palestine Studies*, Vol. 26, No. 2, Winter, 1997, pp. 5–15. Moughrabi, ardent Palestinian-American peace advocate of many years standing, returned to live for the academic year 1995–96 as a Fulbright Scholar at Birzeit University, conducting research on Palestinian society. In America he had mixed in the most friendly and open way with Jewish colleagues for many years, many of them his close companions in peace efforts. He was shocked to find how, at every level of Israeli society, he was treated as some sort of marginal adjunct to humanity, not really worth Israelis' attention or concern.
7. The raid, for the assassination of PLO spokesperson Kamal Nasser and Fatah operations officers Youssef Najjar and Kamal Radwan, resulted also in the killing of a number of Lebanese bystanders and two police officers, and the blowing up of a Beirut office building. It is described in P. Edward Haley and Lewis W. Snider (eds.), *Lebanon in Crisis: Participants and Issues* (Syracuse University Press, 1979, pp. 31, 163f). Barak's own role in this, secret at the time, had become part of his *resumé* by the time he was elected prime minister, mentioned, for example, in Boston's *Jewish Advocate*, May 21–27, 1999.
8. Source, Israel Foreign Ministry, American-Israeli Cooperative Enterprise, 2003, <http://www.us-israel.org/jsource/biography/barak.html>.
9. *New York Times*, Associated Press report, June 24, 1999. Of Netanyahu, Assad had said: "Working with that man was useless."
10. The SLA (South Lebanon Army), under the leadership of General Emile Lahoud, which assisted Israel in controlling the occupied south of Lebanon.

11. *New York Times*, Associated Press report, June 24, 1999.
12. *New York Times*, Deborah Sontag, Saturday, June 26, 1999.
13. *New York Times*, Deborah Sontag, June 25, 1999.
14. Patrick Seale, "Window of opportunity for Syria and Israel," *Middle East International* (henceforth *MEI*), No. 603, July 2, 1999.
15. *New York Times*, July 1, 1999.
16. *New York Times*, Deborah Sontag, July 3, 1999
17. *New York Times*, July 5, 1999.
18. *New York Times*, Deborah Sontag, July 7, 1999.
19. *New York Times*, Douglas Jehl, July 8, 1999.
20. *New York Times*, Douglas Jehl, July 10, 1999; and Deborah Sontag, July 11, 1999.
21. *New York Times*, July 12, 1999.
22. *New York Times*, op-ed, Milton Viorst, July 13, 1999.
23. *New York Times*, Deborah Sontag, July 14, 1999,
24. *New York Times*, William A. Orme, Jr., July 14, 1999.
25. The image I had been using regularly in my correspondence with Yitzhak Rabin and Assad about the "security zone" in Lebanon.
26. *New York Times*, John Broder, July 15, 1999.
27. *New York Times*, John Broder, July 17, 1999.
28. *New York Times*, *Agence France-Presse* report, July 18, 1999.
29. *New York Times*, Jane Perlez, July 19 and 20, 1999. There was only a year and a half left for Clinton to work on the Middle East problem, as Donald Neff commented: "Nothing could help refurbish, if not redeem, Clinton's flawed presidency more than going down in history as the man who brought peace to the Middle East" (*MEI* No. 605, July 30, 1999, p. 9).
30. An especially large Israeli settlement just west of Jerusalem, hemming in the Arab quarters of East Jerusalem, its lands extending down the Judean hills almost to Jericho, very nearly severing the West Bank Palestinian territories into two segments, north and south.
31. *New York Times*, Jane Perlez, July 21, 1999.
32. *New York Times*, Joel Greenberg, July 23, 1999.
33. *New York Times*, Joel Greenberg, July 26, 1999.
34. *MEI*, No. 605, July 30, 1999, pp. 6–7.
35. *New York Times*, Deborah Sontag, July 27, 1999.
36. Khalid Amayreh in *MEI*, No. 605, July 30, 1999, pp. 12–13; No. 606, August 20, 1999, p. 6.
37. *New York Times*, July 28, 1999.
38. *MEI,* No. 606, August 20, 1999, pp. 4–5
39. *New York Times*, Ethan Bronner, August 1, 1999.
40. *New York Times*, Douglas Jehl, August 3, 1999.
41. *New York Times*, Douglas Jehl from Damascus, August 2, 1999. Arafat had been to Cairo to consult with Mubarak. On the Sunday he was in Damascus courting representatives of George Habash's Popular Front for the Liberation of Palestine (PFLP), always the first resort of rejectionists who wanted no part of Fatah's peace efforts. Arafat would continue these visits to his own internal opposition for the next month.
42. *New York Times*, Philip Shenon in Washington, August 10, 1999.
43. *New York Times*, Ethan Bronner, August 16, 1999.
44. *New York Times*, Ethan Bronner, August 11, 1999.
45. *New York Times*, Ethan Bronner, August 18, 1999.

46. *MEI*, No. 607, Khaled Amayreh, September 3, 1999, pp. 7–9.
47. *New York Times*, Deborah Sontag, September 2, 1999.
48. *New York Times*, Jane Perlez, September 3, 1999.
49. *New York Times*, Deborah Sontag, September 3, 1999.
50. *New York Times*, Jane Perlez, September 4, 1999.
51. *MEI*, No. 608, September 17, 1999, Michael Jansen, pp. 9–10.
52. *New York Times*, Jane Perlez, September 5, 1999.
53. *New York Times*, Deborah Sontag, September 5, 1999.
54. *New York Times*, September 10, 1999.
55. *New York Times*, Deborah Sontag, September 11, 1999.
56. *New York Times*, September 14, 1999.
57. *New York Times*, Deborah Sontag, September 15, 1999.
58. *New York Times*, Deborah Sontag, September 18, 1999; *MEI*, Graham Usher, No. 609, October 1, 1999.
59. *New York Times*, September 21 and 22, 1999.
60. *New York Times*, Jane Perlez, September 24, 1999.
61. *New York Times*, Deborah Sontag, September 28, 1999; *MEI* No. 609, October 1, 1999, Graham Usher, pp. 14–15.
62. *New York Times*, October 13, 1999; *MEI* No. 611, Graham Usher, October 29, 1999.
63. *MEI*, No. 610, Khalid Amayreh, October 15, 1999.
64. *New York Times*, Joel Greenberg, October 14, 1999.
65. *New York Times*, Douglas Jehl, October 14, 1999.
66. *MEI*, No. 610, October 15, 1999, Editorial, p. 3, Graham Usher, "Behind the News," pp. 18–20.
67. *New York Times*, Deborah Sontag, from Oslo, November 2, 1999.
68. *New York Times*, Jane Perlez from Oslo, November 3, 1999.
69. *New York Times*, Deborah Sontag, November 5, 1999.
70. *New York Times*, William A. Orme, Jr., November 5, 1999.
71. *New York Times*, *Reuters* report, November 13, 1999.
72. *New York Times*, Alessandra Stanley, November 18, 1999.
73. *New York Times*, November 24, 1999.
74. *New York Times*, November 20, 1999.
75. *New York Times*, November 29 and 30, 1999.
76. *New York Times* editorial, December 1, 1999. *MEI* No. 614, December 10, 1999, gives a text of the statement, an editorial on the tarnishing of Arafat's place in history, and an extensive analysis of the damage done (written by Graham Usher, pp. 3–6).
77. *New York Times*, Reuters report, December 4, 1999.
78. *New York Times*, Tom Friedman op-ed, December 5, 1999.
79. *New York Times*, December 6, 1999.
80. *New York Times*, December 8, 1999.
81. *New York Times*, December 9, 1999.
82. *New York Times*, Deborah Sontag, December 10, 1999
83. *New York Times*, William A. Orme, Jr., December 10, 1999.
84. *New York Times*, William A. Orme, Jr., December 14, 1999.
85. *New York Times*, Douglas Jehl, December 14, 1999.
86. *New York Times* editorial, December 15, 1999. *MEI*, No. 615, pp. 3-8, editorial and articles by Donald Neff from Washington, Michael Jansen from Damascus, and Patrick Seale.
87. Charles Enderlin, *Shattered Dreams: The Failure of the Peace Process in the*

Middle East, 1995–2002 (New York, The Other Press, 2003, pp. 128f). Enderlin quotes from a videotaped interview with Martin Indyk in Washington, February 19, 2002. The "Houston" sentence is a reference to the radio call made by the astronauts of the ill-fated *Apollo 13* mission when multiple operating systems of their craft broke down simultaneously in outer space.
88. Ibid., p. 132.
89. *New York Times*, Douglas Jehl from Damascus, December 16, 1999.
90. *New York Times*, William A. Orme, Jr., December 16, 1999.
91. *New York Times*, John M. Broder, December 17, 1999.
92. *New York Times*, Joel Greenberg, December 17, 1999.
93. *MEI*, No. 616, January 14, 2000, Haim Baram, p. 5.
94. *New York Times*, Deborah Sontag, December 23, 1999.
95. *New York Times*, December 25, 1999.
96. *New York Times*, Reuters report, December 27, 1999.
97. *New York Times*, Deborah Sontag, December 28, 1999.
98. *New York Times*, December 28, 1999.
99. *New York Times*, Deborah Sontag, December 29, 1999.
100. *New York Times*, Deborah Sontag, December 31, 1999.
101. *New York Times*, Deborah Sontag in Jerusalem, David Sanger in Washington, January 3, 2000; John Broder in Shepherdstown, January 4, 2000.
102. *New York Times*, David Sanger, January 5, 2000.
103. Enderlin, *Shattered Dreams*, p. 133.
104. *New York Times*, Associated Press, January 5, 2000.
105. *New York Times*, Deborah Sontag, January 5, 2000.
106. *New York Times*, Deborah Sontag, January 9, 2000.
107. *New York Times*, David Sanger, January 10, 2000.
108. *New York Times*, Deborah Sontag, January 11, 2000.
109. It was only after this text was leaked that Assad, in Syria, decided he would not send his team back. Shara, writing in the Beirut daily *Al-Safir* at this time, characterized Barak's maneuvering as "false promises and ongoing attempts to postpone the meeting of the border committee." *MEI*, No. 617, January 28, 2000, Michael Jensen, p. 6.
110. *Ha'aretz*, January 13, 2000.
111. *New York Times*, Barbara Crossette, in Washington, January 18, 2000.
112. *New York Times*, Susan Sachs, in Damascus, January 18, 2000.
113. *New York Times*, Deborah Sontag, January 26, 2000.
114. *MEI*, No. 618, February 11, 2000, p. 4.
115. *New York Times*, William A. Orme, Jr., February 23, 2000.
116. *MEI*, No. 619, February 25, 2000, Peretz Kidron, p. 8.
117. *New York Times*, John F. Burns, Beirut, February 14, 2000.
118. *New York Times*, Deborah Sontag, March 1, 2000.
119. *New York Times*, Deborah Sontag, March 2, 2000.
120. *New York Times*, Jane Perlez in Dhaka, Bangladesh, March 21, 2000.
121. A full discussion of this in *MEI*, No. 622, April 7, 2000, from Michael Jansen, p. 4, and from Lamis Andoni, p. 7.
122. *New York Times*, Jane Perlez, Geneva, March 27 and 28, 2000.
123. <http://www.israel.org/mfa/go.asp?MFAH00rs0>.
124. *New York Times*, Alessandra Stanley in Rome, February 16, 2000. Trevor Mostyn, in *MEI*, No. 619, February 25, 2000, pp. 10–11, recounts the work of the Palestinian ambassador to the Holy See, my old friend Afif Safieh, in negotiating this statement, its consistency with the Vatican–Israeli

agreement of 1994, and its congruence with the position of the Lambeth Conference of the Church of England, which had visited this subject in 1996.
125. *New York Times*, Alessandra Stanley in Rome, March 2, 2000.
126. *New York Times*, Gustav Niebuhr, March 12, 2000. Alessandra Stanley, March 13, 2000.
127. *New York Times*, Joel Greenberg, March 14, 2000.
128. *New York Times*, Deborah Sontag, March 19 and 20, 2000. In *MEI*, No. 622, 2000, p. 9, Haim Baram wrote of a curious Gallup poll, first published in *Ma'ariv*, comparing the Pope's popularity in Israeli society with that of Rabbi Ovadia Yosef, the Pope coming out marginally more respected as religious leader (41 percent to 37 percent).
129. *New York Times*, Alessandra Stanley, March 22, 2000. All the Pope's speeches throughout the visit appear on the Vatican website, <http://www.vatican.va/holy_father/john_paul_ii/travels/sub_index/trav_holy land-2000.htm>, under the title "Jubilee pilgrimage to the Holy Land (March 20–26, 2000)."
130. *New York Times*, Alessandra Stanley, March 23, 2000; *MEI*, No. 621, March 24, 2000, Khaled Amayreh, p. 11. For the violence after the Pope's speech at Dheisheh, *MEI*, p. 12, Muna Hamza-Muhaisen.
131. *New York Times*, Alessandra Stanley, March 24, 2000.
132. *New York Times*, articles by Alessandra Stanley and Deborah Sontag, March 25, 2000.
133. *New York Times*, William A. Orme, Jr., March 26, 2003.
134. *New York Times*, Alessandra Stanley and Deborah Sontag, March 27, 2000.
135. *MEI*, No.21, p. 3, has an editorial praising the Pope's visit. "With the peace process at a standstill it was a relief to see Pope John Paul, ailing and exhausted, taking centre stage in a Middle East still torn by hatred and suspicion. Astonishingly, where so many pitfalls surrounded him, the Pope trod securely among them and left behind an impression of sincere and even-handed sympathy for all victims of prejudice and intolerance."
136. *New York Times*, Deborah Sontag, March 28, 2000.
137. *New York Times*, Deborah Sontag, March 29, 2000.
138. *New York Times*, Joel Greenberg, March 28, 2000.
139. *New York Times*, William Burns, from Adasiye, Lebanon, March 30, 2000.
140. *New York Times*, Deborah Sontag, April 4, 2000.
141. *New York Times*, Susan Sachs in Beirut, April 8, 2000.
142. *New York Times*, April 18, 2000.
143. *New York Times*, Deborah Sontag, April 19 and 20, 2000. Arad had been captured as far back as the Israeli invasion of Lebanon in 1982 and not heard of since.
144. *New York Times*, Deborah Sontag, April 28, 2000.
145. *New York Times*, Associated Press report, April 29, 2000.
146. *New York Times*, Reuters report, May 3, 2000.
147. *New York Times*, Associated Press report, May 4, 2000.
148. *New York Times*, Deborah Sontag, May 5, 2000. *MEI*, No. 625, May 19, 2000, gave extensive coverage of these raids, by Michael Jansen and Jim Quilty, pp. 8–10.
149. *New York Times*, Deborah Sontag, May 6, 2000.
150. *New York Times*, Deborah Sontag, May 9, 2000.
151. *New York Times*, Deborah Sontag, May 11, 2000.

152. *New York Times*, Joel Greenberg, May 18, 2000.
153. *New York Times*, Reuters report, May 19, 2000.
154. *New York Times*, Deborah Sontag, May 20, 2000.
155. *New York Times*, William A. Orme, Jr., May 23, 2000.
156. *New York Times*, Deborah Sontag, May 24, 2000.
157. *New York Times*, Joel Greenberg, May 24, 2000. As usual, the coverage in *MEI*, No. 626, June 2, 2000, of this debacle in southern Lebanon, is among the most useful: an editorial drawing the lessons from the episode, including a clear recognition that this was not a defeat for the Israeli Army, much as it was a humiliation (p.3); Michael Jansen on its political effects in Lebanon (high prestige for Hezbollah, especially for the mature restraint it showed in its march into the new territory, pp. 4–6); Jim Quilty on the atmosphere in towns and villages liberated from the Israeli occupation and the mild treatment of captured collaborators (pp. 6–8); Ian Williams, from New York, on the role of the UN's Terje Roed-Larsen as honest broker in the midst of these tumultuous times (pp. 8–9); Lamis Andoni (from Boston) on Washington efforts at spin control (pp. 9–10); and Khalid Amayreh on the rivalry between Hezbollah and Arafat, portrayed in the Arab public as winner and loser, Hezbollah encouraging resistance to Israeli occupation while Arafat was "locking up Palestinian freedom fighters to please Israel (p. 9)." Haim Baram wrote of the defeat syndrome among Israelis (p. 11).
158. *New York Times*, Deborah Sontag, William A. Orme, Jr., Joel Greenberg, May 25, 2000.
159. *New York Times*, Deborah Sontag, May 1, 2000. Graham Usher, in *MEI*, No. 624, May 5, 2000, saw the new round of negotiations as nothing more than the opening of a new crisis. He quotes Saeb Erekat, saying that the third redeployment was supposed to return to the Palestinians 90 percent of the West Bank, whereas Abu Dis, Azariya, and Sawahara al-Shaqiya together amounted to only 0.3 percent. He speaks of Palestinian expectation that Dennis Ross, on his arrival, would represent a US effort to "practice its role and oblige the Israeli government to honor its commitments," while Ross himself described his role only as a "listening mode," trying to "assess" whether a Framework Agreement was at all attainable. Arafat, thought to be conceding too much to the Israelis, could muster at this point only 40 percent approval from Palestinians in the West Bank and Gaza, his lowest rating since he returned to Palestine in 1994. The Fatah candidates for student council at Bir Zeit University lost the student council elections to Hamas for the second successive year (pp. 9–11).
160. *New York Times*, Deborah Sontag, May 2, 2000. Lamis Andoni, seeing the limitations Clinton was placing at this time to a Palestinian state, wrote of "the false prize of statehood," Washington endorsing a Palestine that would be "redefined and dwarfed by Israel into a fragmented entity stripped of East Jerusalem and the prerequisites for sovereignty or independence" (*MEI*, No. 624, May 5, 2000, p. 10).
161. *New York Times*, Deborah Sontag, May 4, 2000.
162. *New York Times*, Reuters report, May 8, 2000. *MEI*, No 625, May 19, 2000, Graham Usher, pp. 5–6.
163. *New York Times*, Deborah Sontag, May 9, 2000.
164. Khaled Amayreh gives a full account of this frightening escalation of violence in *MEI*, No. 625, May 19, 2000, pp. 4–5.
165. *New York Times*, Deborah Sontag, May 15, 2000. In *MEI*, No. 625, May 19,

2000, Peretz Kidron gives a lengthy analysis of the struggle Barak had to wage, with "combat tactics," to keep his coalition from dissolving just a week before he was to visit Washington again (pp. 6–8).
166. *New York Times*, Deborah Sontag, May 16, 2000. A William A. Orme, Jr., article this day described the events simply as "games" that had got out of hand.
167. *New York Times*, op-ed, Milton Viorst, May 24, 2000.
168. *New York Times*, Deborah Sontag and William A. Orme, Jr., May 17, 2000.
169. *MEI*, No. 626, June 2, 2000, pp. 12–15, Khalid Amayreh.
170. *New York Times*, Deborah Sontag, May 20, 2000.
171. *New York Times*, Deborah Sontag, May 21, 2000.
172. *New York Times*, Deborah Sontag, May 22, 2000.
173. *New York Times*, William A. Orme, Jr., May 26, 2000.
174. *New York Times*, Joel Greenberg, May 26, 2000.
175. *New York Times*, William A. Orme, Jr., June 1, 2000.
176. *New York Times*, op-ed, William Safire, June 1, 2000. For the Allon Plan, proposed to the Labor government in 1967, which envisioned Israeli annexation of the whole Jordan valley and "Back of the Mountain," that is, the extensive but largely desert areas of the West Bank running down to the Jordan and the Dead Sea, see MidEast Web, <http://www.mideastweb.org/alonplan.htm>.
177. *New York Times*, Elaine Sciolini, Lisbon, June 2, 2000.
178. *New York Times*, Deborah Sontag, June 5, 2000.
179. *New York Times*, Deborah Sontag, June 6, 2000.
180. *New York Times*, Deborah Sontag, June 7, 2000.
181. *New York Times*, Deborah Sontag, June 8, 2000; *MEI*, No. 627, June 16, 2000, Peretz Kidron, pp.11–12.
182. *New York Times*, William A. Orme, Jr., June 8, 2000.
183. *New York Times*, Associated Press report, June 9, 2000.
184. *New York Times*, Deborah Sontag, June 11, 2000.
185. *New York Times*, Elaine Sciolini, Washington, June 11, 2000. *MEI*, No. 627, June 16, 2000. Editorial on Assad's legacy, p. 3, reckoning that Assad "would be judged in the longer term not so much by his contribution to the Arab cause or Syria's regional role, as by the state in which he is perceived to have left Syria in terms of the wellbeing of his people," which it saw as "utter failure." An article by Najm Jarrah (pp. 4–7) described the chaotic conditions of government that Bashar al-Assad encountered on succeeding his father.
186. On the way to Washington, Arafat made his first visit to Damascus in six years, his people hoping that the death of Hafez al-Assad might bring a turning from the cold and bloody relationship that had existed between the Damascus government and the Palestinian leadership for near 25 years. 360,000 Palestinian refugees live in Syria, and their future depends on whatever consensus can be won between Syria and the PLO. Graham Usher commented perceptively on both this mission and Arafat's Washington visit, in *MEI*, No. 627, June 16, 2000, pp. 7–8. Lamis Andoni (essay, p. 20) thought it unlikely that Bashar al-Assad, whose only strength and legitimacy stemmed from his father's legacy, would hasten to embrace the foe his father had loathed with such utter disdain.
187. *New York Times*, Jane Perlez in Washington, June 16, 2000.
188. *New York Times*, William A. Orme, Jr., June 20, 2000.
189. *New York Times*, Deborah Sontag, June 20, 2000.

190. *New York Times*, Deborah Sontag, June 21, 2000. As Peretz Kidron pointed out, *MEI*, No. 628, June 30, 2000, pp. 5–7, the parties now disrupting Barak's coalition had all been part of the Netanyahu government up to 1999. He called this unstable situation "enemies as allies."
191. *New York Times*, Deborah Sontag, June 22, 2000.
192. *New York Times*, Deborah Sontag, June 23, 2000.
193. *New York Times*, Deborah Sontag, June 24, 2000.
194. *New York Times*, Jane Perlez in Jerusalem, June 29, 2000.
195. *New York Times*, Associated Press report, June 30, 2000.
196. *New York Times*, June 26, 2000.
197. *New York Times*, Deborah Sontag, July 1, 2000.
198. *New York Times*, Deborah Sontag, July 4, 2000.
199. *New York Times*, Deborah Sontag, July 5, 2000.
200. *New York Times*, July 6, 2000.

PART II: CHAPTER 5

1. *MEI*, No. 629, July 14, 2000, Editorial, p. 3.
2. *MEI*, No. 629, July 14, 2000, "The battering of Barak," Haim Baram, pp. 6–.
3. The Hanieh account was later published serially in seven parts, in Arabic, in *Al-Ayyam*, July 29 to August 10, 2000. For non-Arabic-readers those are available in English translation at <http://www.nad-plo.org/eye/cd papers.pdf>. Since all parts of the translation are paginated consecutively, references here will cite the number in the seven-part series and the page number, Akram Hanieh #1, p.3. The series is not in quite the same genre as the Ben-Ami diary, to which reference will soon be made, which also constitutes a major source, but which is more the day-by-day recording of Ben-Ami's impressions. What Hanieh gives is a subsequent account.
4. Passed December 11, 1948, in anticipation of the end of the war, specifying conditions for the termination of the conflict.
5. The "Land for Peace" resolution of November, 1967, for resolving the aftermath of the Six-Day War of the previous June and the Israeli capture of the West Bank and Gaza Strip, the Sinai desert and the Golan Heights.
6. This was the first of four ceasefire demands in the 1973 war. It called on the parties to implement the demands already made six years before in Resolution 242.
7. At the time, as I wrote the series of papers that follow, I had been following events closely in the Israeli press and in daily meetings with Israelis and Palestinians over the six weeks I spent in Jerusalem up to early July. Reconstructing it now, I am indebted for this starting analysis to Deborah Sontag, *New York Times*, July 7, 2000; to Graham Usher's writing on the "Make or Break" summit in *MEI*, No. 629, July 14, 2000, pp. 4–5; and to Charles Enderlin's book, *Shattered Dreams*, pp. 158–76.
8. *New York Times*, Deborah Sontag, July 10, 2000.
9. *New York Times*, William A. Orme, Jr., July 11, 2000.
10. *New York Times*, Jane Perlez in Washington, July 11, 2000.
11. A US millionaire who kept buying up any Palestinian property he could acquire, in order to place Israeli settlements where they would most obstruct any possibility of a Palestinian state.
12. On all this turbulence, see Khalid Amayreh in *MEI*, No. 629, July 14, 2000, pp. 9–10.
13. Readers will recognize here that I use some of the language of John Paul

322 Notes to Chapter 5

Lederach's methodology of conflict transformation. I drew here from his *Building Peace: Sustainable Reconciliation in Divided Societies*, Washington, US Institute of Peace, 1997, particularly Chapter 7, "Resources: making peace possible," pp. 87–97.

14. *Los Angeles Times*, Faisal Husseini, op-ed, July 9, 2000.
15. *New York Times*, Deborah Sontag, Thurmont, MD, July 12, 2000.
16. *New York Times*, John Kifner in Lebanon, July 12, 2000.
17. *New York Times*, Joel Greenberg, Jerusalem, July 12, 2000.
18. *New York Times* op-ed, Limor Livnat, July 12, 2000.
19. The charitable association that governed it on behalf of the faithful.
20. *Ha'aretz*, Amir Oren, article "Chief rabbis prepared to forgo control of certain 'holy places,' but Old City sites will need tripartite religious agreement," July 12, 2000.
21. *New York Times*, Deborah Sontag, July 13, 2000.
22. Hanieh, #2, "Rules of the game in the Catoctin Hills," pp. 6–8.
23. Hanieh, #3, "The search for an honest broker," pp. 11–12.
24. Ben-Ami's diaries appear at the website of the American–Israel Cooperative Enterprise with the very lengthy web reference: <http://search.netscape.com/ns/boomframe.jsp?query=Shlomo+Ben-Ami+diaries&page=1&offset=0&result_url=redir%3Fsrc%3Dwebsearch%26amp%3BrequestId%3Dfb56fd68dc7bfeba%26amp%3BclickedItemRank%3D5%26amp%3BuserQuery%3DShlomo%2BBen-Ami%2Bdiaries%26amp%3BclickedItemURN%3Dhttp%253A%252F%252Fwww.ourjerusalem.com%252Fhistory%252Fstory%252Fhistory20010422.html%26amp%3BinvocationType%3Dprevious%26amp%3BfromPage%3DNSCPNextPrev&remove_url=http%3A%2F%2Fwww.ourjerusalem.com%2Fhistory%2Fstory%2Fhistory20010422.html>.
25. *New York Times*, Jane Perlez, Thurmont, MD, July 14, 2000.
26. *MEI*, No. 630, July 28, 2000, Khalid Amayreh in Hebron, "Clashes on the ground," p. 7.
27. Hanieh #4, "Peace according to the criteria of the Gallup Institute," pp. 13–14.
28. Ibid., pp. 14–16.
29. *New York Times*, July 17, 2000, reporting what Clinton had told the *New York Daily News*; Jane Perlez on expectations from the talks; William A. Orme, Jr., on the Tel Aviv protests.
30. *New York Times*, July 18, 2000, Deborah Sontag, from Thurmont, MD.
31. *New York Times*, Jane Perlez, July 19, 2000.
32. *New York Times*, Jane Perlez and Deborah Sontag, July 20, 2000.
33. *New York Times*, Deborah Sontag, July 20, 2000.
34. *New York Times*, Deborah Sontag, July 21, 2000.
35. *New York Times*, William A. Orme, Jr., July 21, 2000.
36. *New York Times*, Deborah Sontag and William A. Orme, Jr., from Thurmont, MD, July 22, 2000.
37. *New York Times*, Marc Lacey in Nagi, Japan, July 23, 2000.
38. *New York Times*, Deborah Sontag, Thurmont, MD, July 23, 2000.
39. *New York Times*, John Kifner, July 23, 2000.
40. *New York Times*, Jane Perlez, Monday, July 24, 2000.
41. *New York Times*, Deborah Sontag, July 25, 2000.
42. Text in *New York Times*, July 26, 2000.
43. Ben-Ami diary, entry for July 24–25.

44. The Hanieh account describes this episode extensively, Hanieh #5, p. 20.
45. The Ben-Ami diaries, in the only form in which I have found them available (note 24 above), are excerpts only, quite possibly chosen according to someone else's agenda. There is a gap between the three entries for July 13, 14, and 15, and these two excerpts from the night of July 24–25.
46. This entire account of the gloomy day of failure at Camp David is based on *New York Times*, Jane Perlez, July 26, 2000.
47. The Kurdish hero warrior who, in 1187, defeated the Crusader army at the Horns of Hattin in Galilee and went on to recapture Jerusalem.
48. For the return of both leaders, *New York Times*, John Kifner, Jerusalem, July 27, 2000.
49. *New York Times*, Marc Lacey, Washington, July 27, 2000.
50. *New York Times*, James A Baker II, op-ed, "Peace, one step at a time," July 27, 2000.
51. *MEI*, No. 630, July 28, 2000, Graham Usher, "Camp David: the American bridge," pp. 4–6
52. *New York Times*, John F. Burns, Jerusalem, July 28, 2000.
53. *New York Times*, Amos Oz, op-ed, "The specter of Saladin," July 28, 2000. Peretz Kidron had recognized clearly how much middle ground, acceptable to both sides, had actually been achieved on the question of refugee return, citing such authorities as Meron Benvenisti, the former deputy mayor of Jerusalem who had long believed that the Israeli practice of setting out "facts on the ground" (preemptive establishment of settlements and expulsion of Palestinian residents) had made the resolution of these questions or the establishment of a Palestinian state impossible, but who now saw extraordinary progress on these issues. *MEI*, No. 630, July 28, 2000, article "A learning experience," pp. 7–9.
54. *MEI*, No. 630, July 28, 2000, Haim Baram, "The real debate," p. 8.
55. *New York Times*, John Kifner, Jerusalem, July 29, 2000.
56. *New York Times*, John F. Burns, Jerusalem, July 30, 2000.
57. *New York Times*, John F. Burns, July 31, 2000.
58. *New York Times*, John F. Burns, July 31, 2000.

PART II: CHAPTER 6

1. *Ha'aretz* columnist Yoel Marcus was especially offended by what he saw as hypocrisy in the Knesset's humiliating Peres as a way of pummeling Barak. "The present Knesset, given its irresponsible behavior, has lost any moral or political right to continue even to exist." *Ha'aretz*, "Days that make you want to vomit," August 4, 2003.
2. *New York Times,* John F. Burns, August 1, 2000.
3. *New York Times,* John Kifner, August 2, 2000.
4. *New York Times*, John Kifner, August 3, 2000.
5. *New York Times*, Susan Sachs in Cairo, August 5, 2000.
6. *New York Times*, John Kifner, Beirut, August 6, 2000.
7. *New York Times*, John Kifner, Merj'uyun, Lebanon, August 10, 2000.
8. *New York Times*, op-ed by Jimmy Carter, July 6, 2000.
9. *International Herald Tribune*, August 7, 2003, reprinted from the *Los Angeles Times*.
10. *New York Times*, op-ed, Tom Friedman, August 11, 2000.
11. *New York Times*, from Agence France-Presse, August 8, 2000.

12. *Ha'aretz*, editorial, August 9, 2000.
13. *Ha'aretz*, Amos Harel, August 10, 2000.
14. *Ha'aretz*, editorial, August 11, 2000.
15. *New York Times*, Jane Perlez in Washington, August 14, 2000.
16. *New York Times*, John F. Burns, August 16, 2000.
17. *The Jerusalem Post*, citing the *Al-Hayat* interview, August 13, 2000.
18. *Ha'aretz*, Baruch Kra, "Police reopen Temple Mount," August 14, 2000.
19. *New York Times*, Jane Perlez, August 14, 2000.
20. *Jerusalem Post*, Lamia Lahoud, August 13, 2000.
21. *New York Times*, John F. Burns, August 17, 2000. European opposition to a September 13 UDI had also figured heavily in Arafat's reflections. Particularly German Foreign Minister Joschka Fischer and Spanish Foreign Minister Josep Pique had argued against it, both on the urging of Israel's Shlomo Ben-Ami. *Ha'aretz*, Amnon Barzilai, August 13, 2000.
22. *Ha'aretz*, Mazal Mualem, August 16, 2000.
23. *MEI*, No. 632, September 1, 2000, Graham Usher, in East Jerusalem, "Running out of options?" pp. 4–5.
24. *New York Times*, John F. Burns, August 19, 2000.
25. Ibid.
26. *New York Times*, John F. Burns, August 22, 2000.
27. *New York Times*, John F. Burns, August 25, 2000.
28. *New York Times*, John F. Burns, August 26, 2000.
29. *New York Times*, John F. Burns, August 27, 2000.
30. *New York Times*, William A. Orme, Jr., August 28, 2000.
31. *New York Times*, Deborah Sontag, September 1, 2000.
32. *New York Times*, David Sanger, New York, September 5, 2000.
33. *New York Times*, Deborah Sontag, Jerusalem, September 6, 2000.
34. *New York Times*, David Sanger, UN, September 7, 2000.
35. *New York Times*, Jane Perlez, September 7, 2000. For a sampler of what the two leaders said, see *Ha'aretz*, Aluf Benn, September 7, 2000.
36. *Ha'aretz*, Aluf Benn, "Turning up the heat on Arafat," September 6, 2000; Yoel Marcus, "Nip it in the bud," on the Barak--Likud connection, September 8, 2000.
37. *New York Times*, Jane Perlez, September 8, 2000.
38. *New York Times*, Jane Perlez, September 9, 2000.
39. *MEI*, No. 633, September 15, 2000, Haim Baram, "Barak's narrow horizons," pp. 8–9.
40. *New York Times*, Deborah Sontag, September 7, 2000.
41. *New York Times*, Deborah Sontag, September 11, 2000. Graham Usher, in *MEI*, No. 633. September 15, 2000, saw this decision as an inglorious climbdown: "The second time as farce," pp. 6–7.
42. *Ha'aretz*, Amira Hass, September 11, 2000.
43. *Ha'aretz*, Baruch Kra, August 22, 2000.
44. *Ha'aretz*, Gideon Levy, "Not the best way to end the conflict," September 17, 2000.
45. *New York Times*, William A. Orme, Jr., September 15, 2000.
46. *Ha'aretz*, Nitzan Horowitz and Daniel Sobelman, "*Newsweek* publishes Beilin-Abu Mazen deal," September 18, 2000.
47. *Ha'aretz*, Akiva Eldar, September 21, 2000. A full text of this October 31, 1995 document is published in *Ha'aretz* as a feature, September 21, 2000.
48. Ibid.

49. *New York Times*, Christopher S. Wren at the UN, September 15, 2000.
50. *New York Times*, Deborah Sontag, September 21, 2000.
51. *New York Times*, Deborah Sontag, September 23, 2000. On the expropriations for the purposes of the ring road, see also *Ha'aretz*, Baruch Kra, "Arab land expropriated for new road," September 21, 2000.
52. *New York Times*, Deborah Sontag, September 23, 2000. On Indyk's career, cf. *MEI*, No. 634, September 29, 2000, Donald Neff, "Indyk's indiscretion," p. 13.
53. *Ha'aretz*, Danny Rubinstein, September 25, 2000.
54. *New York Times*, Deborah Sontag, September 26, 2000. See also *Ha'aretz*, Aluf Benn, Daniel Sobelman, and Amira Hass, September 26, 2000.
55. Ibid.
56. *Ha'aretz*, Gideon Alon, "Knesset panel okays law to 'secure' J'lem," September 26, 2000.
57. Just on September 26, Foreign Minister Ben-Ami and the Israeli delegation in Washington had pressed the Clinton administration once again to open final status negotiations with the Palestinians based on the proposals that had surfaced at Camp David and ideas raised afterward concerning sovereignty over the Temple Mount. *Ha'aretz*, Aluf Benn and Amira Hass, "Israel wants to begin talks on final status," September 27, 2000. And Barak announced his acceptance of the idea that Jerusalem would be the capital of two states on the very morning that Sharon produced the massive religious crisis by his adventure on the Temple Mount. *Jerusalem Post*, Herb Keinon and Jeff Barak, "Barak to *Post*: Jerusalem and Al-Quds will be side by side," September 28, 2000; *BBC*, "Barak agrees to twin Jerusalem capitals," September 28, 2000.
58. *Ha'aretz*, Yoel Marcus, "The year of the agreement," September 29, 2000.
59. The *New York Times* carried an Associated Press story of the Sharon visit on September 28, 2000. Its own much fuller account, by Joel Greenberg, including the attack in the Gaza Strip, appeared on September 29, 2000.
60. *New York Times*, Deborah Sontag, September 30, 2000.

PART II: CHAPTER 7

1. *New York Times* accounts: William A. Orme, Jr., September 1, 2000; separate articles by Deborah Sontag and William A. Orme, Jr., September 2, 2000.
2. *Ha'aretz*, Amos Harel, October 2, 2000.
3. *Ha'aretz*, Sharon Gal, Amit Benaroya, David Ratner, October 2, 2000.
4. *Ha'aretz*, October 4, 2000.
5. This became a frequent reference point in newspaper articles over these days. *Ha'aretz*, Tuesday, October 3, 2000, Amos Harel, Aluf Benn, Ori Nir, and Sharon Gal, "Intense clashes persist in Israel, territories." And cf. *MEI*, No. 635, October 13, 2000, Graham Usher, from Um al-Fahm, "Erasing the Green Line," pp. 6–8.
6. *New York Times*, Joel Greenberg, "Old anger of Israeli Arabs finds vent, October 3, 2000;" *Ha'aretz*, Amos Harel, October 4, 2000.
7. *Ha'aretz*, Joseph Algazy, "Gov't panel to probe events in Arab towns," October 4, 2000.
8. *Ha'aretz*, Dan Margalit, "A democracy on the defensive," October 5, 2000.
9. *Ha'aretz*, Nehemia Strasler, "Without live bullets, without dead bodies," October 6, 2000.
10. *New York Times*, Deborah Sontag, "A biblical patriarch's tomb becomes a battleground," October 4, 2000.

11. *New York Times*, Reuters report appended to a Deborah Sontag article, "A day of relatively calm chaos in Jerusalem," October 7, 2000.
12. *New York Times*, Joel Greenberg, October 8, 2000.
13. *New York Times*, Deborah Sontag, October 8, 2000.
14. Communication by Jeff Halper, Coordinator of ICAHD, the Israel Committee Against House Demolitions and editor of the critical magazine *News from Within*, October 9, 2000.
15. *Jerusalem Post*, October 9, 2000.
16. *Ha'aretz*, Jala Bana, October 10, 2000.
17. *New York Times*, Deborah Sontag, October 8, 2000.
18. For example, *New York Times*, William A. Orme, Jr., October 4, 2000.
19. Title of his op-ed in *Ha'aretz*, October 3, 2000.
20. Text, *MEI*, No. 635, October 13, 2000, p. 12.
21. *New York Times*, Associated Press report, October 8, 2003. And cf. *MEI*, No. 635, October 13, 2000, Ian Williams, New York, "The veto that wasn't," pp. 11–12.
22. *New York Times*, Joel Greenberg, "Sharon touches a nerve, and Jerusalem explodes," September 29, 2000.
23. *BBC*, "Violence engulfs West Bank and Gaza," September 30, 2000.
24. *Ha'aretz*, Baruch Kra, Amira Hass, and Yossi Verter, "Sharon on Temple Mount sparks riots," September 29, 2000.
25. *Ha'aretz*, citing Reuters, "US says Sharon Temple Mount visit caused tensions," September 30, 2000.
26. *Ha'aretz*, Amos Harel, Nitzan Horowitz, Baruch Kra, and Amira Hass, "No end in sight, as violence spreads also to Israel," October 2, 2000.
27. *Ha'aretz*, Akiva Eldar, "How Sharon made a volcano out of the Temple Mount," October 2, 2000.
28. *Ha'aretz*, Ze'ef Schiff, "Both sides are losing control," October 2, 2000.
29. Ibid.
30. *Ha'aretz*, Danny Rubinstein, "Kindling a religious war," October 2, 2000.
31. *Ha'aretz*, Amos Harel, Aluf Benn, Ori Nir, and Sharon Gal, "Intense clashes persist in Israel, territories," October 3, 2000.
32. *Ha'aretz*, Amir Oren, "The tide is at its lowest," October 3, 2003.
33. *Ha'aretz*, Akiva Eldar, "How Sharon made a volcano out of the Temple Mount," October 2, 2000.
34. *MEI*, No. 635, October 13, 2000, Peretz Kidron, West Jerusalem, "Blame game."
35. *Ha'aretz*, Aviv Lavie, "Our victims are stories, theirs are mere numbers," October 3, 2000.
36. *Boston Globe*, Charles Sennott, "Blame, bullets fly in Mideast," October 4, 2000.
37. *New York Times*, Jane Perlez, October 5, 2000.
38. *New York Times*, Joel Greenberg, October 5, 2000.
39. *New York Times*, William A. Orme, Jr., October 9, 2000.
40. *Ha'aretz* editorial, October 10, 2000.
41. *New York Times*, Chris Hedges, Nazareth, October 10, 2000.
42. *New York Times*, Deborah Sontag, October 12, 2000.
43. *Ha'aretz*, Danny Rubinstein, October 10, 2000.
44. The same day as the attack, in Yemen harbor, on the US destroyer *Cole*. *New York Times*, October 12, 2000.
45. *New York Times*, Deborah Sontag, "Peace hopes fade. Brink of open war,"

October 13, 2000. And cf. *MEI*, No 636, October 27, 2000, Graham Usher, Ramallah, "Days of fear, days of rage," p. 7.
46. *New York Times*, Eric Lipton, New York, October 13, 2000.
47. *New York Times*, Deborah Sontag, October 14, 2000.
48. *New York Times*, William A. Orme, Jr., October 14, 2000.
49. *New York Times*, Deborah Sontag, October 15, 2000.
50. *New York Times*, David Shipler, op-ed, October 15, 2000.
51. Table assembled by William A. Orme, Jr., *New York Times*, October 16, 2000.
52. *New York Times*, Jane Perlez, October 16, 2000.
53. *New York Times*, Susan Sachs, Cairo, October 16, 2000.
54. *New York Times*, Chris Hedges, Gaza, October 16, 2000.
55. *New York Times*, Deborah Sontag, October 18, 2000.
56. *New York Times*, William A. Orme, Jr., and Joel Greenberg, October 18, 2000.
57. *Ha'aretz*, Akiva Eldar, "Goodbye to Rabin's legacy," October 19, 2000.
58. *Ha'aretz*, Aluf Benn and Amos Harel, October 19, 2000.
59. *New York Times*, Deborah Sontag and William A. Orme, Jr., October 21, 2000.
60. *New York Times*, Christopher S. Wren, October 21, 2000.
61. *MEI*, No. 636, October 27, 2000, Ian Williams, New York, "The US reverts to type," pp. 13–14.
62. *New York Times*, Deborah Sontag, October 22, 2000.
63. *Ha'aretz*, Aluf Benn, "US opposes plan for 'unilateral separation'," October 23, 2000.
64. *New York Times*, Deborah Sontag, October 23, 2000.
65. *New York Times*, Joel Greenberg, October 23, 2000.
66. *MEI*, No. 136, October 27, 2000, Khalid Amayreh, Hebron, "Murderous repression," pp. 6–8
67. *Ha'aretz*, Aluf Benn and Yossi Verter, "Barak working to avoid another summit," October 22, 2000.
68. *Ha'aretz*, Yossi Verter, "'Concerned citizen' Netanyahu is back," October 25, 2000.
69. *New York Times*, John Kifner, Jerusalem, October 26, 2000.
70. *New York Times*, David Sanger, Washington, October 26, 2000. See also *Ha'aretz*, Breaking news, "Clinton intends inviting Arafat, Barak for separate talks," October 25, 2000. The president had asked first, in telephone calls to both, that they come to Washington for a three-way summit, but agreed to separate talks at Arafat's request. Barak held out for the proposition that any contacts toward resumption of the peace process should begin only after the cessation of violence in the territories.
71. *New York Times*, John Kifner, Ramallah, October 28, 2000.
72. *New York Times*, John Kifner, October 29, 2000.
73. *Ha'aretz*, Amira Hass, "Millennial Bethlehem finds a new defiance," October 24, 2000.
74. The Fourth Geneva Convention (text at <http://www.unhchr.ch/html/menu3/b/92.htm>), adopted August 12, 1949, in Geneva, by the Diplomatic Conference for the Establishment of International Conventions for the Protection of Victims of War, pertains particularly to the behavior of occupying powers in occupied territories. Its Article 49 lays down unequivocally the regulation that: "The Occupying Power shall not deport or transfer parts of its own civilian population into the territory it occupies."

75. *New York Times*, John Kifner, October 29, 2000.
76. *New York Times*, Chris Hedges, Gaza, October 29, 2000.
77. *Ha'aretz*, Yossi Verter, "Sharon's demand for veto power snags unity government talks," October 24, 2000.
78. *New York Times*, John F. Burns, October 30, 2000.
79. *New York Times*, Deborah Sontag, October 31, 2000.
80. *New York Times*, John Kifner, November 1, 2000.
81. *Ha'aretz*, Ha'aretz staff, November 2, 2000.
82. *Ha'aretz*, breaking news, 17:55, November 2, 2000.
83. *New York Times*, Deborah Sontag and Joel Greenberg, November 2, 2000.
84. *Ha'aretz*, successive Breaking news reports, November 2, 2000.
85. *New York Times*, *Associated Press* report, November 3, 2000.
86. *New York Times*, Jane Perlez, November 6, 2000.
87. *New York Times*, Barbara Crossette, UN, November 9, 2000.
88. *New York Times*, Deborah Sontag, November 10, 2000.
89. *New York Times*, Jane Perlez, Washington, November 10, 2000.
90. *New York Times*, Neil MacFarquhar, UN, November 11, 2000.
91. *New York Times*, Susan Sachs, November 13, 2000.
92. *New York Times*, Jane Perlez, November 13, 2000.
93. *Ha'aretz*, Aluf Benn, November 14, 2000.
94. *Ha'aretz*, Amos Harel, Amira Hass, Aluf Benn, and Nadav Shragai, November 14, 2000.
95. *New York Times*, November 14, 2000.
96. E-mail communication, November 13, 2000.
97. *New York Times*, Deborah Sontag, November 15, 2000.
98. Separate article, *New York Times*, Deborah Sontag, November 15, 2000.
99. *Ha'aretz*, Amira Hass, "A different definition of 'restraint,'" November 15, 2000.
100. As the intifada proceeded, LAW produced, and continues to produce, daily reports on killings, assaults, and other human rights abuses, all of them carefully archived and available on their excellent website, <http://www.law-society.org>. For the International Commission of Jurists' website on Israel–Palestine, see <http://www.icj.org/world_pays.php3?id_mot=24&lang=en>.
101. *New York Times*, William A. Orme, Jr., November 17, 2000.
102. *Ha'aretz*, Ha'aretz staff, "Israel targets Palestinian economy," November 17, 2000.
103. *Ha'aretz* analysis, Danny Rubinstein, "Arafat seems serious," November 19, 2000. Also Amira Hass, Amnon Barzilai, and Amos Harel, "Arafat orders ceasefire in PA areas," November 19, 2000.
104. *Ha'aretz* editorial, "Time for gestures of conciliation," November 20, 2000.
105. *New York Times*, Deborah Sontag, November 18, 2000.
106. *New York Times*, Deborah Sontag, November 21, 2000.
107. *New York Times*, Jane Perlez, Washington, November 21, 2000.
108. *New York Times*, Susan Sachs, Riyadh, Saudi Arabia, November 22, 2000.
109. *New York Times*, William A. Orme, Jr., Gaza, November 22, 2000.
110. *New York Times*, various reporters, November 23, 2000.
111. *The Washington Post*, Jimmy Carter op-ed, "For Israel, land or peace," November 26, 2000.
112. *New York Times*, Deborah Sontag, November 29, 2000.
113. *New York Times*, Jane Perlez, Washington, November 29, 2000.
114. *New York Times* editorial, November 29, 2000.

115. *New York Times*, Deborah Sontag, November 30, 2000.
116. *New York Times*, William A. Orme, Jr., December 1, 2000.
117. *New York Times*, Joel Greenberg, December 2, 2000.
118. *New York Times*, William A. Orme, Jr., December 5, 2000.
119. *New York Times*, Laurie Goodstein, New York, December 7, 2000.
120. *New York Times*, Deborah Sontag, December 8, 2000.
121. *New York Times*, Joel Greenberg, December 9, 2000.
122. *New York Times*, Deborah Sontag, separate article, December 10, 2000.
123. *New York Times*, editorial, December 11, 2000.
124. *New York Times*, William A. Orme, Jr., December 12, 2000.
125. *New York Times*, Deborah Sontag, December 15, 2000.
126. *New York Times*, Joel Greenberg, December 16, 2000.
127. *New York Times*, Deborah Sontag, December 18, 2000.
128. *New York Times*, Deborah Sontag, December 19, 2000.
129. *New York Times*, Jane Perlez, Washington, December 21, 2000.
130. *New York Times*, Deborah Sontag, December 22, 2000.
131. *New York Times*, December 23, 2000.
132. *New York Times*, Jane Perlez, December 24, 2000.
133. *New York Times*, John Kifner, Bethlehem, December 25, 2000.
134. *New York Times*, Jane Perlez, Washington, December 26, 2000.
135. *New York Times*, Jane Perlez, Washington, December 27, 2000.
136. *New York Times*, Jane Perlez, December 28, 2000.
137. *New York Times*, John Kifner, December 28, 2000.
138. *New York Times*, Jane Perlez, Washington, December 29, 2000.
139. *New York Times*, John Kifner, December 30, 2000.
140. *New York Times*, John Kifner, December 31, 2000.
141. *New York Times*, Deborah Sontag, January 2, 2001; Joel Greenberg, Ramallah, January 2, 2001.
142. *Al-Ayyam* (PA), January 2, 2001.
143. *New York Times*, Jane Perlez, Washington, January 3, 2001.
144. *New York Times*, Jane Perlez, January 4, 2001.
145. *New York Times*, Deborah Sontag, January 5, 2001.
146. *New York Times*, Joel Greenberg, January 5, 2001.
147. *New York Times*, Jane Perlez, Washington, January 6, 2001.
148. *New York Times*, Deborah Sontag, Jerusalem, January 6, 2001.
149. *New York Times*, Jane Perlez, New York, January 8, 2001.
150. *New York Times*, Deborah Sontag, January 9, 2001.
151. *New York Times*, Joel Greenberg, January 10, 2001.
152. *New York Times*, Deborah Sontag, January 12, 2001.
153. *New York Times*, Deborah Sontag, January 13, 2001.
154. *New York Times*, David Sanger and Frank Bruni, January 14, 2001.
155. *New York Times*, Associated Press report, January 14, 2001.
156. *New York Times*, Joel Greenberg, January 16, 2001.
157. *New York Times*, Deborah Sontag, January 17, 2001.
158. *New York Times*, Joel Greenberg, January 18, 2001.
159. *New York Times*, Deborah Sontag, January 19, 2001.
160. *New York Times*, Deborah Sontag, January 20, 2001.
161. *New York Times*, Deborah Sontag, January 21, 2001.
162. *New York Times*, Elie Wiesel, op-ed, January 24, 2001.
163. *New York Times*, William A. Orme, Jr., January 25, 2001.
164. *New York Times*, Jane Perlez, Washington, January 25, 2001.

165. *New York Times*, William A. Orme, Jr., January 26, 2001.
166. *New York Times*, Deborah Sontag, January 27, 2001.
167. *New York Times*, Deborah Sontag and William A. Orme, Jr., January 28, 2001.
168. *New York Times*, Jane Perlez, January 29, 2001.
169. *New York Times*, Deborah Sontag, January 29, 2001.
170. *New York Times*, Deborah Sontag, February 2, 2001.
171. *New York Times*, Deborah Sontag, February 7, 2001.
172. *New York Times*, Joel Greenberg, February 9, 2001.
173. *New York Times*, William A. Orme, Jr., February 8, 2001.
174. *New York Times*, various reporters, February 10, 2001.
175. *New York Times*, Deborah Sontag, February 12, 2001.
176. *New York Times*, Deborah Sontag, February 21, 2001.
177. *New York Times*, Susan Sachs, February 27, 2001.
178. *New York Times*, Deborah Sontag, March 8, 2001.
179. *New York Times*, William A. Orme, Jr., February 24, 2001.
180. *New York Times*, Joel Greenberg, March 13, 2001.

PART III: CHAPTER 8

1. *Yediot Aharonot*, Alex Fishman, "A dangerous liquidation," November 25, 2001. Translated by Gush Shalom.
2. *New York Times*, James Bennet, "A Hamas chieftain dies when Israelis attack his home," July 23, 2002. *Gush Shalom*, press release, "Sharon answers ceasefire offer with carnage; Rabin-Pelosof resigns from the government," July 23, 2002. *New York Times*, David Stout, Washington, "White House rebukes Israel for attack, calls it 'heavy-handed,'" July 23, 2002. *Boston Globe*, Dan Ephron, "Israel blasts residence of Hamas chief," July 23, 2002; *Boston Globe* editorial, "Saving Israel from itself," July 24, 2002. *New York Times*, David R. Sanger, "Bush denounces Israeli air strike as "heavy handed,"' July 24, 2002. *Boston Globe*, Dan Ephron and Charles A. Radin, "Deadly raid condemned; Palestinians demonstrate; US speaks out," July 24, 2002. *Shalom Center*, Rabbi Arthur Wexler, "The meaning of the Gaza bombing," July 24, 2002.
3. *Yediot Aharonot*, Alex Fishman, "A dangerous liquidation," November 25, 2001.
4. *Jerusalem Post*, Naomi Chazan, March 16, 2001.
5. *Ha'aretz*, Gideon Levy, "Quiet, please, we're bombing," April 1, 2001.
6. *Ha'aretz*, Ephraim Yaar and Tamar Hermann, April 4, 2001.
7. *Ma'ariv*, Uri Avnery, "Ambush at Erez checkpoint," April 7, 2001.
8. *Ha'aretz*, Ha'aretz Service, April 9, 2001.
9. *Guardian*, Ewen MacAskil in Jerusalem, "Israel's reservists 'refusing to serve in West Bank,'" April 10, 2001.
10. *Independent*, May 5, 2001. The United States had urged both Israelis and Palestinians to keep the report secret for two weeks while they prepared their comments, but the *Independent* had the report at once, and *Ha'aretz* printed a full text of the 32-page document on May 6, 2001.
11. *New York Times*, William A. Orme, Jr., May 17, 2001.
12. *New York Times*, Jane Perlez in Washington, May 17, 2001.
13. *New York Times*, Deborah Sontag, May 19, 2001.
14. *New York Times*, Jane Perlez in Washington, May 19, 2001.

15. *Guardian*, Suzanne Goldenberg and Brian Whitaker, "Heading for disaster. Cheney warns Israel. Sharon threatens all-out force. Tanks continue firing." May 21, 2001.
16. Leader of the Moledet party and a life-long advocate of Palestinian "transfer," the euphemism for ethnic cleansing (or worse). His murder by Palestinians the following year would be one of the major crises of the *intifada*.
17. Lieberman had already hit his stride, even as Sharon was still assembling his Cabinet, asserting that, should the Egyptians get too excited about what Israel did to Palestinians, Israel had nuclear missiles that could reach Cairo.
18. *New York Times*, Deborah Sontag, May 23, 2001.
19. *Guardian*, Suzanne Goldenberg, May 23, 2001.
20. *Ha'aretz*, Ha'aretz Service, May 25, 2001.
21. *Ha'aretz*, Amos Harel, Aluf Benn, and Daniel Sobelman, "Israel holds back after 18 die in TA bombing," June 3, 2001.
22. *New York Times*, Deborah Sontag, June 2, 2001.
23. *New York Times*, Deborah Sontag, June 3, 2001. *Ha'aretz*, Amos Harel, Aluf Benn, and Daniel Sobelman, "Arafat orders his security chiefs to stop all attacks. Skepticism rampant that cease-fire cosmetic." June 4, 2001.
24. *New York Times*, Deborah Sontag, June 4, 2001
25. *New York Times*, Jane Perlez, Washington, June 4, 2001.
26. *Ha'aretz*, Akiva Eldar, "Choose your own partner," June 4, 2001.
27. Jessica Montell, head of the Israeli human rights organization B'Tselem, would tell me the following January that her organization differed from the several Palestinian human rights organizations in including the Jewish settlers in occupied territory among the civilians who should never be attacked.
28. *New York Times*, William A. Orme, Jr., June 5, 2001.
29. *New York Times*, Jane Perlez, Washington, June 6, 2001.
30. *New York Times*, Douglas Frantz, June 8, 2001.
31. *New York Times*, Deborah Sontag, June 9, 2001.
32. *New York Times*, Deborah Sontag, June 13, 2001.
33. *New York Times*, Douglas Frantz, June 14, 2001.
34. *New York Times*, Associated Press report, June 25, 2001.
35. *New York Times*, Jane Perlez, Washington, June 27, 2001.
36. *New York Times*, Jane Perlez, Washington, June 28, 2001.
37. *New York Times*, William A. Orme, Jr., Jerusalem, June 28, 2001.
38. *New York Times*, Jane Perlez in Jerusalem, June 29, 2001.
39. A story to this effect, telling that Sharon had offered such a map to Bush during his Washington visit, had appeared in *Ha'aretz*: Aluf Benn, Daniel Sobelman, Natan Guttman, and Associated Press correspondents, "Sharon maps out a deal with PA; Powell: Prime Minister must decide when cooling-off period begins," June 28, 2001.
40. *New York Times*, Deborah Sontag, June 29, 2001.
41. The episode in question was described by Palestinians as a rampage by the Jewish settlers from Maale Levona, northeast of Ramallah, who stoned houses and burned fields in the Palestinian villages around them. The settlers, however, claimed that these were enemy villages, and that they were entitled to storm them. The story is told in *Ha'aretz*, Ada Ushpiz, "Revenge on the rampage," June 29, 2001.
42. *New York Times*, Deborah Sontag, June 30, 2001.
43. *Ha'aretz*, "Suicide bomber kills 14, wounds 132," August 10, 2001.

44. *New York Times*, Clyde Haberman, August 10, 2001.
45. *New York Times*, Jane Perlez, Washington, August 10, 2001.
46. *Ha'aretz*, "Palestinian Authority arrests two terrorist cells in West Bank," August 10, 2001.
47. *New York Times*, Clyde Haberman, August 13, 2001.
48. Gush Shalom is perhaps the most outspoken of the Israeli peace activist groups, under the leadership of its octogenarian founder Uri Avnery, bravely supported by the younger Adam Keller and a highly committed membership. When the larger mass-movement peace organization Shalom Ashav (Peace Now) largely collapsed with the beginning of the new *intifada*, Gush Shalom kept the banner high, providing a center for the many other Israeli movements for peace or for human rights, and setting the theme week by week for Israeli peace activism through paid ads in the Israeli press and a weekly column written by Uri Avnery himself. The *80 Theses Draft for a New Peace Camp: Where did we go wrong?*, first published on April 13, 2001, a basic document of the movement, is available, in English and a variety of other languages, on the movement's website, <http://www.gush-shalom.org/english/index.html>, along with much more. In more recent times, Gush Shalom has published its own draft formula for a peace settlement between Israelis and Palestinians, and comparative analyses of its proposal and the other outstanding and similar proposals, the Geneva Accord and the Statement of Principles submitted by Ami Ayalon and Sari Nusseibeh and signed by large numbers of Israelis and Palestinians.

PART III: CHAPTER 9

1. *Ha'aretz*, Bradley Burston, "Killing of icon of Israeli far-right puts pressure on Sharon and Arafat to take new action," October 17, 2001; Aluf Benn, Gidon Alon, Amos Harel, and Nadav Shagrai, "Ultimatum to Arafat: Turn over PFLP leaders and Ze'evi murderers," October 17, 2001. *New York Times*, James Bennet, "Right-wing Israeli minister is killed," October 17, 2001.
2. *Ha'aretz*, Ha'aretz Staff and Associates, "Powell: End *intifada*—and occupation," November 20, 2001. Aluf Benn, "Analysis / For the Americans, the ball is in Arafat's court," November 20, 2001.
3. *New York Times*, "Chain of events in the Middle East conflict, a chronology," August 21, 2003. *New York Times*, Anthony Lewis, op-ed, "Hope against hope," December 8, 2001.
4. *New York Times*, chronology, August 21, 2003.
5. *Ibid.*
6. *New York Times*, James Bennet, March 1, 2002; *Boston Globe*, Charles A. Radin and Said Ghazali, March 1, 2002.
7. *The Other Israel*, Adam Keller and Beate Zilversmidt, March 2, 2002.
8. This entire description drawn from the *New York Times*, editorial, March 14, 2002.
9. *Boston Globe*, Susan Sevareid of Associated Press, March 26, 2002; The full formal endorsement: *New York Times*, Neil MacFarquhar, March 28, 2002.
10. *New York Times*, Reuters report, March 24, 2002.
11. *New York Times*, Todd Purdum, "Bush diplomacy yields few positive signs," March 28, 2002; Serge Schmemann, "News analysis: after a dire day, trying to see beyond revenge," March 28, 2002.
12. *New York Times*, chronology, August 21, 2003.
13. *New York Times*, Joel Brinkley and Serge Schmemann, March 29, 2002.

14. *New York Times*, James Bennet and John Kifner, June 19, 2002.
15. *New York Times*, Reuters report, June 19, 2002.
16. *Boston Globe*, Anthony Shadid, Washington, June 20, 2002.
17. *New York Times*, John Kifner and David E. Sanger, June 24, 2002.
18. Sachedina's book, *The Islamic Roots of Democratic Pluralism*, was published by Oxford University Press in 2001.

PART III: CHAPTER 10

1. *The Foundation for Middle East Peace*, Winter 2000 edition.
2. Conversations with History, video series produced by the Institute of International Studies, UC Berkeley, "Coming to terms with Israel," Harry Kreisler in conversation with Ian Lustick, March 4, 2001. Transcript available at <http://globetrotter.berkeley.edu/conversations/>.
3. Peacewatch, Special policy Forum Report, Gilead Sher, "The brink of peace? An inside look from Camp David to Taba," April 18, 2001.
4. *Ha'aretz*, Gideon Levy, "On the basis of the nonexistent Camp David understandings," November 16, 2000.
5. *Peacewatch*, Special Policy Forum Report, Washington Institute for Near East Policy, Nabil Shaath, "Challenges facing the Palestinian Authority and the peace process," July 3, 2001.
6. *MidEastWeb*, "Taba negotiations: the Moratinos Non-Paper," January 2001, at <http://www.mideastweb.org/moratinos.htm>.
7. Text: *Ha'aretz*, October 21, 2003. An op-ed on the formal signing in Geneva, *New York Times*, Yossi Beilin and Yasser Abed-Rabbo, "An Accord to remember," December 1, 2003.
8. A short bio is available at <http://www.wolfmanproductions.com/malley.htm>.
9. *New York Times*, Robert Malley, op-ed, "Fictions about the failure at Camp David," July 8, 2001.
10. *New York Times*, Deborah Sontag, Special report, "Quest for Mideast peace: how and why it failed," July 26, 2001.
11. *New York Times*, Ehud Barak, op-ed, "Israel needs a true partner for peace." July 30, 2001.
12. *Ma'ariv*, Interview with Ben-Ami and excerpts from his diaries, April 6, 2001.
13. *New York Review of Books*, Hussein Agha, Robert Malley, feature, "Camp David: the tragedy of errors," August 9, 2001.
14. *Ha'aretz* magazine section, Ari Shavit, "End of a journey," interview with Shlomo Ben-Ami, September 15, 2001.
15. *New York Times*, Yasser Arafat, op-ed, "The Palestinian vision of peace," February 3, 2002.
16. *New York Review of Books*, Benny Morris, "Camp David and after: an exchange: (1. An interview with Ehud Barak,)" June 13, 2002. Interestingly, Malley and Agha had taken up this suggestion of transferring some territory inhabited mainly by Israeli Arabs to the Palestinian state as part of the swap in an article in *Foreign Affairs*, "The last negotiation," May/June 2002.
17. *New York Review of Books*, Hussein Agha, Robert Malley, "Camp David and after: an exchange (2. a reply to Ehud Barak)," June 13, 2002.

Index

A

Abbas, Abul 16, 38
Abdel-Meguid, Ahmed 48
Abderrahman, President of Indonesia 186
Abdullah, King of Jordan 258
Abu Ala (Ahmed Qurei) 49, 68, 89, 115, 119, 130, 149, 204, 241–4, 267
Abu-A'ram, Khalil 135
Abu Dis 113, 115, 157, 266
Abu Hanoud, Mahmoud 193, 255
Abu Iyad (Salah Khalaf) 39–40
Abu Jaber, Kamal 178
Abu Jihad, (Khalil al-Wazir) 5, 32
Abu Mazen 94, 101, 115, 131, 160–3, 169, 196–7
Abu Musamih, Sayid 63
Abu Nidal 2, 39–40
Abu Rdaineh, Nabil 195
Abu Sharif, Bassam 34
Abu Snaineh, Sabreen 267
Abu Tariq 28–30
Abu Zaid, Hazma 39
Achille Lauro 6, 12, 16, 38
Afghanistan 2, 276–80
Agha, Hussein 295–301
Ahmed, Abdel Rahin 13, 15, 48
Albright, Madeleine 75, 97–9, 116, 120, 165, 197
    meetings 92–3, 98, 104, 117–18, 147, 194, 207
Algiers, PNC congress in 32, 195
Allon Plan 116
Amal movement 55, 109
Amirav, Moshe 31
Amman 5, 18, 20–2, 25, 28
Annan, Kofi 95, 207, 210, 277
anti-Semitism 4, 152, 170
Al-Aqsa Martyrs' Brigade 254–6, 263
Al-Aqsa Mosque 41, 64, 115, 153–5, 185, 201, 206, 210, 226
Arad, Ron 109
Arafat, Yasser 186, 261–5, 289–90, 293–8
    at Camp David Summit 128–31, 147–50, 160–5, 167–71
    author's correspondence 6–7, 32–3, 39–40, 51–4, 57–61, 74–5, 90–2, 119–27, 131, 186–9, 207–8, 221–6, 232, 235–6, 278
    author's meetings 5–7, 11–16, 22–6, 27–30, 251–2
    Cairo Declaration 13, 26
    dealings with Hamas 246
    General Assembly address 34
    Harare Conf. address 23–4, 28–9
    Israeli actions against 278–9, 281
    meeting with Pope 105–6
    various dealings *see* Barak, Ben-Ami, Clinton, Peres, Hussein, Saddam;, Sharon
    White House lawn meeting 48–59
    Wye River Plantation meeting 75–7
Armistice Line 32, 93, 100
Asfur, Hasan 115
Ashraf, Mian 47
Ashrawi, Hanan 45, 52, 146, 170, 181
al-Assad, Bashar 109, 117, 121
al-Assad, Hafez 56, 70, 84, 93, 97–8, 104, 108–9, 117, 121, 293
Awad, Moubarac 53–4
Ayyad, Ibrahim 22
Ayyash, Yahya 63

B

Baghdad 21, 39, 56

Index

Baker, James 17, 40, 44–5, 168, 260, 266
Balfour Declaration 14
Baltiansky, Gadi 98, 198
Barak, Enud 98–103, 108–11, 115–16, 119, 178, 289–90, 293–301
   at Camp David Summit 128–33, 141–2, 147–51, 159–65, 167–71
   author's correspondence with 82–3, 180–3, 190–3, 227–9
   background 83–4
   coalitions 85–6, 97–8, 101, 114, 117–19, 171, 172, 190, 194–5, 209, 211, 214
   dealings with Arafat 85, 87, 89, 94–6, 101, 113–14, 198, 207, 214, 233
   dealings with Clinton *see* Clinton
   election 77, 81
   forcing of election 227, 232
   and Taba negotiations 242–5
   Temple Mount crisis 204–6, 209–12
Baram, Haim 89, 195
Barghouti, Marwan 114, 225
Barzani, Mustafa 284–6
Bashir, Tahseen 5
Beerman, Leonard 251
Begin, Menachem 132, 134, 147, 175, 220, 223
Beilin, Yossi 47–9, 119, 169, 196–8, 242, 246, 294, 301
Beirut
   attacks on 65–6, 83, 85, 103
   meetings in 93, 205, 280
   PLO withdrawal 5–6, 13, 27, 35
Ben-Ami, Shlomo 130, 193, 203, 206, 233
   Camp David Summit diary 147–52, 164, 294–5, 297
   dealings with Arafat 241
   and Taba negotiations 242–5
Ben-Eliezer, Benyamin 253, 262, 280
Ben-Gurion, David 54, 190

Benvenisti, Meron 187
Berger, Sandy 100, 116, 129, 149, 163, 165, 194, 197
Bethlehem 61–2, 106, 213–14, 226–7, 234, 252, 267, 273, 278
Bin Laden, Osama 276
Blair, Tony 281
Boucher, Richard 160, 205
Brinker, Menachem 170
B'Tselem group 135
Buber, Martin 2
Burg, Avraham 89, 146, 246
Bush, President George H. W.
   administration 255–64, 266, 273–4, 278, 280, 284
   author's dealings 17, 271–3, 282–3
   election 232, 235
   and Taba negotiations 244
   speeches 281–2, 288

C
Camp David Summit 1–2, 253–4, 289–302
   author's papers 135–40, 142–5, 154–9, 166–7
   Declaration of Principles 161–2
   see also Arafat; Barak; Ben-Ami; Clinton; Erekat
Carter, President Jimmy 22, 147, 179, 220, 232
Ceaucescu, Nicolae 24–5, 28–9
Center Party 85, 195
Charny, Israel 3
Chazan, Naomi 3, 257
Chirac, President Jacques 170, 207, 240
Christopher, Warren 47, 67, 96
Clinton, President Bill 89, 93, 98–100, 102, 104, 108, 185, 289–90, 298–9
   at Camp David Summit 128–30, 133, 141, 147–54, 159–65, 167–71
   author's correspondence 46–8, 68, 70–4, 173–8, 229–32
   dealings with Arafat 95–6, 117,

Index 337

119, 189, 194, 210, 216–17, 238–40, 295
  dealings with Barak 85–6, 88, 96, 116, 119, 189, 194, 210, 212, 216–17, 219
  dealings with Netanyahu 67–9
  knowledge of Middle East 112
  proposals for peace accord 234–41
  at UN General Assembly 193–4, 197
  White House lawn meeting 48–59
  Wye River Plantation meeting 75–7
Clinton, Hillary 152, 170
Cluverius, Wat 20, 24
Cohen, Ran 132
Cohen, Stephen 107
Cohen, William 220
Cooke, Alistair 262

D
Dahlan, Mohammed 131, 133, 148, 220, 225, 257
Damascus 26, 56, 69, 70, 93, 97, 99, 101, 103
Daniel, Roni 202
Dayan, Moshe 22–3, 142, 225
Deeb, Ali Hassan 90
Dekel, Yaron 172
Demirel, Suleiman 216
Democratic State 14–5, 35
Deri, Aryeh 203
Dinitz, Simha 5, 41
Dome of the Rock 115, 201
Duberstein, Ken 33–4
al-Durrah, Muhammad 202
Dusahi, Maher 96

E
ed-Din Ibrahim, Sa'ad 5
Egeland, Jan 49
Ehrenkranz, Joseph 48
Eilad, Giora 103
Eitan, Rafael 51, 72, 264
Eldar, Akiva 205, 211, 262
el-Solh, Kamil 195

Enderlin, Charles 99
Erekat, Saeb 210
  as PLO delegation member 45, 52, 89, 221, 241–3
  at Camp David Summit 130–1, 162–4, 168–9
Erlanger, Steven 76–7

F
Fahd, King of Saudi Arabia 11
Fatah 14, 35, 39, 114, 204, 214–18, 237, 262–3
Fez plan 11
Fishman, Alex 254, 256
Flapan, Simha 2
Ford, President Gerald 101
Four Mothers movement 168, 218

G
Galilee 55, 65, 99, 107, 203
  Sea of 93, 100
Gandhi, Mohandas 53
Gantz, Benyamin 218
Geneva Accord 288, 291, 301
Geneva Conference 20, 22
Geneva Convention 42, 73, 87, 213, 223, 228, 230
Geneva, meetings in 34, 104, 108, 225
Gesher party 77
Gittlesohn, Roland 41, 43
Golan, Galia 3
Golan Heights, negotiations over 97–105
Goldstein, Baruch 57, 63, 181, 184, 209, 241
Gorbachev, President Mikhail 24
Gore, Albert 167
Granot, Elazar 18–9
Greenberg, Joel 103, 205
Green Line 96, 140, 158, 176, 264, 270
Gresh, Alain 14
Gromyko, Andrei 22

H
Haber, Eitan 46, 56

Habib, Philip 5, 12, 35
Haetzni, Elyakim 113
Haifa 42, 139, 158, 267
Hakim, Maximos 18
Hallal, Abbas 109
Hamas
　actions 63–5, 76, 243, 281
　dealings with PLO 57, 60
　Israeli actions against 63–5, 255
　various dealings *see* Arafat,
　　Peres, Rabin
al-Hamid, Hayil Abd 39
Hammami, Said 2
Hanieh, Akram 128–9, 146–7, 150
Haram al-Sharif 142, 164, 194, 199,
　221, 231, 237, 239–40, 297
　see also Temple Mount
Harare Conference 22–9
Harel, Aharon 18–20, 28
Hartmann, David 144–5
Hass, Amira 218
al-Hassan, Hani 5, 12, 27, 29, 30
Hassan, Heba 195
Hassbacker, Ayalet 215
Hauser, Richard 2–3, 284
Heiberg, Marianne 49
Helmick, Raymond
　correspondence *see* Arafat,
　　Barak, Bush, Clinton, Hussein
　　of Jordan, Peres, Powell,
　　Rabin, Rice, Shamir, Sharon
　first visit to Middle East 3
　meetings *see* Arafat, Bush,
　　Hussein, Peres
　paper on Camp David Summit
　　135–40, 142–5, 154–9, 166–7
　paper on Resolution 242, 142–5
Hezbollah 55–6
　actions by 65–6, 85, 90, 97,
　　104, 109–11
　Israeli actions against 65–6, 84,
　　88, 110
Hirschfeld, Yair 49
Holbrooke, Richard, US Ambassador
　212, 216
Holocaust 2–4, 106
Holst, Johan Jorgen 49

Holy Sepulchre 107, 153–5
al-Hoss, Selim 93, 109
Hrawi, Elias 70
Hussein of Jordan, King 6, 11–12,
　17–20, 28, 39–40, 69–70, 293
　author's meeting with 21–2, 25
　dealings with Netanyahu 69–70
　Wye River Plantation meeting
　　75–7
Hussein, Saddam 38–40, 276–9,
　284, 286
　dealings with Arafat 39
Husseini, Faisal
　articles in *LA Times* 140,
　　179–80
　death 260
　director of Orient House 119,
　　127, 141, 154
　PLO delegation member 45, 52

I
Ibrahimi Mosque 57
Indyk, Martin 99, 197
Interreligious Committee for Peace in
　the Middle East 4–5, 37, 47–9,
　67
Iran 23, 69, 285
Iraq 2, 21, 38–9, 43–4, 174, 230,
　276–80, 284–7
Islamic Jihad 51, 55–6, 60, 63–4,
　195, 209, 215, 254–6, 261–2,
　267, 272
Istanbul 26
Itzik, Dalia 159
Izzidin al-Qassem Brigade 65

J
Jackson, Rev. Jesse 251–4, 282
Jacobs, Steven 251
Jaffa 42, 64, 139, 158, 203, 240,
　251
Jagland, Thorbjorn 216
Jansen, Michael 103
Japan Conference 148, 153, 160,
　162–3, 173, 297
Jawabri, Osama 263
Jericho 53, 56, 61, 84, 116, 21

Jordan, River 14, 100
Judea 42, 73, 82, 175–6, 184, 191

K
Kaddumi, Faruk 12, 15, 23
Karachi hijacking 26
Kashriel, Benny 113
Kassissieh, Issa 119, 131, 217, 221
Katsav, Moshe 172
Kennedy, President John F. 131, 174
Khadafy, President Moammar 24, 28
Khaddam, Abdulharim 69
Khaja, Nazir 251
Khalidi, Walid 19, 45
Khatib, Ghassan 194
Kidron, Peretz 103
al-Kidwa, Nasser 31, 47, 126
Kiryat Arba settlement 42, 57–9, 184
Kissinger, Henry 35, 146
Klinghofer, Leon 6
Kollek, Teddy 3
Kolvenbach, Peter Hans 21
Kreisler, Harry 290
Kurtzer, Dan 47
Kuwait
  invasion 38, 40, 43, 143, 174, 230
  meeting in 27–8, 188

L
Labor Party 18
Laghi, Pio 7, 16, 21, 25
Lahad, Antoine 108–9
Lancry, Yehuda 216
Lavie, Aviv 205–6
Law, Bernard 7, 17, 24, 30
Levy, David 67–8, 86, 94, 130, 132, 171–2, 183
Levy, Gideon 196, 257, 290
Levy, Yitzhak 99, 130, 215
Libya 23, 28
Lieberman, Avigdor 260
Likud 171, 198
Lipkin-Shahak, Amnon 148, 161, 233, 241–2

Livnat, Limor 141, 173
Lockhart, Joe 153, 194
Lustick, Ian 290

M
Maale Adumim settlement 88, 94, 113
Madrid Conference 44–6, 50, 122, 273
Malley, Robert 291–301
Mapam party 18
Marcus, Yoel 199
Margalit, Avishai 170
Massood, Ahmed Shah 276
McLarty, Thomas 47
Meimad party 77
Meir, Yitzhak 183
Mejia, Jorge 30
Melchior, Michael 253, 282
Menuhin, Hephzibah 2
Menuhin, Yehudi 2
Meretz party 3, 47, 81, 85, 106, 118, 132, 172, 195, 205, 282
Meridor, Dan 147, 195
Mikki, Hisham 241
Milo, Roni 195
Mitchell, George 216
Mitchell Commission 216, 232, 258–60, 263, 291
Mitterrand, Francois 24
Mitzna, Amram 288
Mofaz, Shaul 166, 184
Moledet party 66, 267
Moratinos, Miguel 244–5, 262, 291
Mordechai, Yitzhak 195
Morris, Benny 298
Moskovitz, Irving 134
Mossad 40
Mubarak, Hosni 5, 48, 70, 87–8, 92, 117, 160, 186, 207, 220, 258
Murphy, Peter 25
Murphy, Richard 20, 34
Musallam, Sami 12, 15

N
Nablus 61–2, 94, 113, 115, 203, 215, 232, 252, 259

naqba 115, 230, 298
Nashashibi, Rashid 3
Nasrallah, Hassan 103
National Religious Party (NRP) 85, 99, 104, 130–1, 183, 215
Ne'eman, Zvi 17
Negev 234, 237
Netanyahu, Binyamin 119
    as prime minister 67–77
    charges against 108
    dealings with Clinton *see* Clinton
    dealings with Sharon 67
    dealings with King Hussein 69–70
    election stand 62, 66
    Wye River Plantation meeting 75–7
Northern Ireland 1, 3, 83, 173, 187, 216
Nusseibeh, Sari 32, 288

O
Obaijat, Hussein 216
Ocalan, Abdullah 125
Olmert, Ehud 92, 260
One Israel party 77, 81, 195
Oran, Oded 102, 113, 161
Orient House 45, 260
    Israeli occupation of 266–7, 269
    see also Husseini
Oslo Declaration of Principles 49–50
    responses to 51–60
Oslo 2 agreement 61–2, 70
Oz, Amos 169–70

P
Palestine National Council (PNC) 15, 33, 188
Parsi-Tzadok, Marav 85
Peace Now movement 3, 95, 102, 170
Pelletreau, Robert 38, 48, 57–8
Peres, Shimon 214–5, 259
    author's dealings with 62, 253
    dealings with Arafat 241
    dealings with Hamas 63–5
    election stand 62–6
Pollard, Jonathan 76–7
Pope John Paul II 6–7, 30, 97, 105–8, 160, 253
    meeting with Arafat 105–6
Powell, Colin 33–4, 244, 247, 258–60
    author's correspondence 260, 263, 266–7, 274, 275–8, 279, 284–7
Pundak, Ron 49

Q
Al Qaeda 276
Al Quds 157, 169
Qurei, Ahmed *see* Abu Ala

R
Rabbo, Yasser Abed 38, 130, 241–2, 301
Rabin, Yitzhak 31, 47
    author's correspondence with 46, 54–7, 59
    dealings with Hamas 46
    reaction to assassination 62–3
    White House lawn meeting 48–59
Rabinovich, Itamar 93
Rabin-Pelosof, Dalia 255
Rachid, Mohammed 131
Rahim, Tayib Abdel 169
Rahum, Ofir 242
Rajoub, Jibril 120, 193, 259
Reagan, President Ronald 1, 27, 31, 33–4, 73, 224, 260, 272
Regan, Donald 17
Rice, Condoleezza
    author's correspondence with 260, 263, 278
Roed-Larsen, Terje 49, 95, 109, 148
Rosen, David 145
Rosen, Michael 253
Ross, Dennis 94, 99, 104, 114–15, 120, 165, 189, 194, 216, 240
Rubinstein, Danny 209, 262
Rubinstein, Elyakim 130, 133–4, 161, 198
Rudman, Warren 216

S

Sachedina, Abdul Aziz 285
Sadat, Anwar 2, 5, 141, 147, 179, 293
Saffin, Said Muhammed 195
Safieh, Afif 7
Said, Abdel Moneim 178
Samaria 42, 73, 82, 138, 175–6, 184, 191
  see also Juadea
Sarid, Yossi 106, 108, 118, 172, 205, 243, 257
Saudi Arabia 39, 109, 160, 275–6, 280, 287
Savir, Uri 17, 19–20, 22, 36, 41, 49, 62, 233
Schiff, Ze'ev 205
Schmemann, Serge 65, 76–7
Schulz, George 34
Schwarz, Richard 43–4
Seale, Patrick 84–5, 98
Sha'ath, Nabil 5, 45, 93, 160, 168, 236, 262, 264, 291
Shafi, Haidar Abdel 45, 52
Shalom, Silvan 104
Shamir, Yitzhak 17–19, 27, 30, 37, 41–8, 179, 264, 268, 273
  author's correspondence with 41–4
Shapiro, Sam 49
al-Shara, Farouq 69, 98
Sharansky, Natan 66, 76, 85, 98–9, 108, 117–19, 130–1, 167
Sharm el-Sheikh 93, 211, 215, 258
Sharon, Ariel 104–5, 254, 257, 296–7
  administration 260–5, 280
  as leader of Likud 92, 190
  author's correspondence with 267–71
  dealings with Arafat 246
  dealings with Netanyahu 67
  elections 245–7, 288
  and Temple Mount crisis 199–201, 205–7, 245, 259
  opposition to Barak 101, 111, 159, 172, 185

Wye River Plantation meeting 75–7
Sharp, Gene 54
Shas party 81–2, 85, 97–8, 101, 104, 106, 114, 117–18, 130–2, 203, 214, 258
Shavit, Ari 66, 145, 297
Sheetrit, Meir 194
Shehadeh, Salah 255
Sheinbaum, Stanley 33–4, 126
Sher, Gilead 169, 233, 240–2, 244, 290, 297
Shikaki, Fatih 63
Shiloh, Michael 7, 17, 45
Shin Bet 63
Shinui party 19, 81, 85, 132, 195, 282
Shipler, David 210
Sinai 35, 93, 102, 175
Siniora, Hanna 17, 19–20, 24, 27–8, 35
Sneh, Ephraim 169, 212, 233, 243
Solano, Javier 216
Sontag, Deborah 108, 115, 146, 293–4, 298
South Lebanon Army (SLA) 97, 104, 108–11
Suderi, Yitzhak 101
Sununu, John 40, 43–4, 47

T

Taba negotiations 1–2, 242–5, 289–302
Talabani, Jalal 284–6
Taliban 276
Tanzim 204, 211, 262
Tauran, Jean-Louis 25
Temple Mount 183–5, 199–201, 227, 237, 240, 243
  see also Barak, Haram al-Sharif, Sharon
Tenet, George 164, 194, 261–2, 264, 291
Third Way party 66
Tomb of Abraham and the Patriarchs 57, 62
Tomb of Joseph 62, 115, 203–4

Tomb of Rachel 62
Tripoli (Lebanon) 12
Tulkarm 94
Tunis 7, 12, 18, 21–3, 25, 28, 32, 39, 45, 120, 125, 188
Tzemel, Leah 3

U

Unilateral Declaration of Independence (UDI) 76, 119, 129, 163, 177–8, 182, 184, 186–7, 194–5, 212
United Nations Charter (Article 2) 137, 142, 220, 230
United Nations General Assembly
    Resolution 181, 24, 156, 223, 228, 230
    Resolution 194, 129, 137, 140, 143, 176, 181, 187, 190–1, 223, 228, 230, 236, 270
United Nations Security Council
    Resolution 242: author's and Arafat's discussion 22–6, 27–30; author's correspondence regarding 173–8, 180–2, 186–9, 190–3, 221–6, 227–9, 229–32; author's papers 133–4, 142–5
    Resolution 338, 12–13, 15, 20, 23–31, 129, 146, 150, 223, 228, 230, 239, 298
    Resolution 425, 108, 111, 143, 174, 230
    Resolution 448, 161
    Resolution 1322, 205, 224, 228, 230, 235
United Torah Judaism party 85, 132
Usher, Graham 89, 169

V

Vance, Cyrus 22–3, 225
Vatican 7–8, 16, 20–1, 25, 27, 30, 34, 91, 97, 105–6, 134, 156, 160, 253
Vered, Yael 17
Viorst, Milton 115
Virshubski, Mordechai 19

W

wars
    Gulf War (1990–1) 38, 40, 44, 285
    October War (1973) 2, 83
    Six-Day War (1967) 184, 293
    World War II (1939–45) 4, 105, 107, 144
Weiner, Justus 43–4
Weizman, Ezer 101, 106
Weizmann, Chaim 54
Western Wall 41, 107, 185, 200, 237, 239, 294, 300
Wilson, William 16, 27, 31, 33–4, 126
Wye River Plantation Memorandum 75–7, 87–90
Wye 2 agreement 92–4

Y

Yaacobi, Gad 48
Yahalom, Shaul 198
Yaron, Amos 109
Yassin, Ahmed 165, 193, 255
Yishai, Eli 130, 132
Yisrael B'-Aliya party 66, 85, 98–9, 102, 104
Yitzhaki, Yair 185
Yosef, Ovadia 85, 106, 108, 132, 258
Young, Ronald 4–5, 47

Z

Ze'evi, Rehavam 51, 72, 257, 260, 278
Zinni, Anthony 278
Zionism 32, 91, 271
Zureik, Elia 191